NATURE TOURISM, CONSERVATION, AND DEVELOPMENT IN KWAZULU-NATAL, SOUTH AFRICA

BRUCE AYLWARD

and

ERNST LUTZ

Editors

CONTENTS

Conclusions   351
Appendix 9-A. The Social Accounting Matrix
Framework   353
References   367

10 Creating a Nature Tourism Economy: A Multicriteria Analysis of
    Options for Policy, Institutions, and Management
    Bruce Aylward   369

    Conceptual and Analytical Framework for an Integrated Multimarket
    Model   371
    Methodology   374
    Analysis of Options   388
    Examining the Trade-offs and Potential Synergies:
    Multicriteria Analysis of Policy Options   419
    Conclusions and Recommendations   426
    Appendix 10-A. Scenario Results   429
    References   433

    Annex: A Multimarket Model for Nature Tourism
    Bruce Aylward   435

    Objectives and Approach   435
    Analytical Framework   436
    Notes   447
    References   447

    Maps   449

    Index   455

List of Boxes

List of Figures

List of Tables

ACKNOWLEDGMENTS

We are very grateful to the World Bank's Research Committee, which supported this work with a research preparation grant in 1996, funding for a more complete development of the research proposal in 1998, and full funding of the proposed work in 1999.

Initially, the main partner institution in South Africa was the KwaZulu-Natal Nature Conservation Service (now called Ezemvelo KwaZulu-Natal Wildlife); toward the latter part of the project the Development Bank of Southern Africa (DBSA) became more prominent. The partnership of both of these institutions is gratefully acknowledged.

Survey work in developing countries is challenging, and the project faced innumerable technical, administrative, and budget issues. A successful completion in terms of conducting the work, analyzing the survey data, and writing up the results is largely due to the outstanding professional qualities of Bruce Aylward and Kreg Lindberg, including their personal commitment to sustainable tourism beyond what a contract or terms of reference might have specified. Biodiversity expert Peter Goodman from KwaZulu-Natal Wildlife also made a valuable contribution and interacted ably with the economists on the core team to broaden their perspective on the multiple goals and impact of nature tourism.

Hans Binswanger, as director of the Environmentally and Socially Sustainable Department (ESSD), Africa Region, at the World Bank, provided essential support and strategic advice. The support of the new ESSD director, James Bond, and the manager for the Environmental and Social Unit for Africa, Rick Scobey, is also gratefully acknowledged.

Many local consultants contributed to the project during various phases including (in alphabetical order) Geert Creemers, Theuns Eloff,

Stuart Ferrer, Barry James, Lindi Mulder, David Mullins, Shandir Ram-lagan, Lisa Scriven, and Aki Stavrou. We are most grateful for their work.

Sarah Porter worked with Bruce Aylward and Erica Wilson worked with Kreg Lindberg to analyze and write up two of the surveys.

A "kick-off" workshop was held in the Mkhuze Game Reserve in June 1999, and the preliminary results were also presented and discussed at Mkhuze in June 2001. Both of these events were cosponsored by KwaZulu-Natal Wildlife and the World Bank, and involved local researchers and stakeholders.

The DBSA organized a policy workshop in May 2002 and subsequently a side event at the World Summit on Sustainable Development in September 2002. At the side event, the research outcome of the project was presented and an invited panel of experts explored how best to put these ideas into practice. The summary report is a joint publication of the DBSA and the Bank. (Copies of the PDF file are available on request from Elsa Kruger-Cloete at elsak@dbsa.org).

We are grateful to the Trust Fund for ESSD funded by Norway and Finland for cofinancing the publication of this book.

Copyediting was done by Alfred Imhoff and Nancy Berg.

Ernst Lutz   **Elsa Kruger-Cloete**
World Bank   *Development Bank of Southern Africa*

FOREWORD

This book is a coproduction of the World Bank and the Development Bank of Southern Africa and is a summary of a World Bank research project. It provides a multifaceted lens through which to take a new look at sustainable nature tourism development and conservation. The summary report, also copublished by the World Bank and the Development Bank of Southern Africa, was prepared for and presented to a Side Event of the World Summit on Sustainable Development in Johannesburg in September 2002.

The World Bank's interest in the project came from a need to deliver effective policy advice to clients on the key environmental, social, and economic issues associated with the development of nature tourism. The Development Bank of Southern Africa's interest lies in the knowledge we can leverage and replicate elsewhere: building a nature tourism economy that can take activities in the region to a new level, while making headway toward social and economic development.

The object of the research was to assess how various institutional, policy, and managerial options can enhance nature tourism's contribution to the "triple bottom line." There are win–win outcomes but also trade-offs among various policy objectives, including economic growth, poverty reduction, and conservation finance and biodiversity conservation. This collaborative report highlights the complementarities and the trade-offs in promoting and managing sustainable nature tourism development and conservation.

Nature tourism is important for many developing countries, including South Africa. If wisely managed, nature tourism offers valuable opportunities for generating revenues for development and for conservation.

The Bank developed its approach and methods through a case study of a well-known area, KwaZulu-Natal, where 21 percent of the gross domestic product originates from nature tourism, and the local economic impact of expenditures by tourists is substantial. Ezemvelo KwaZulu Natal Wildlife (formerly KwaZulu-Natal Nature Conservation Service) was selected as a collaborating institution for its reputation for biodiversity conservation.

This work draws on a range of analytical and research "building blocks" and culminated in a framework for a multimarket model developed by the lead researcher, Bruce Aylward. With respect to the policy options, a number of key findings emerged from the analysis:

- Efforts to improve conservation of biodiversity go beyond a wildlife industry to build the foundations of a nature tourism economy.

- Providing concessions to the private sector in public protected areas contributes to equitable development and job creation, while generating conservation finance.

- Foreign tourism demand for wildlife viewing is not responsive to price, making a case for price differentiation between foreigners and residents to augment conservation finance.

The recommendations are fairly specific to the Ezemvelo KwaZulu-Natal Wildlife area. By combining various options into an integrated package to achieve economic development, equity, and conservation, such a balanced approach provides pro-poor tourism opportunities for local communities by reinvesting the proceeds in on-the-ground work in the reserves and in the community. It requires collaboration with private game reserves to drop fences and could contribute to a successful transformation of wildlife management into a nature tourism economy.

When possible, our respective institutions will support countries, institutions, and communities seeking to implement such balanced approaches toward the achievement of the multiple objectives of sustainable nature tourism development.

James Bond   **Mandla Gantsho**
Director, ESSD Department   *Managing Director and Chief Executive*
Africa Region, World Bank   *Development Bank of Southern Africa*

PART I

OVERVIEW AND SUMMARY

CHAPTER 1

THE ACTUAL AND POTENTIAL CONTRIBUTION OF NATURE TOURISM IN ZULULAND

Considerations for Development, Equity, and Conservation

Bruce Aylward

Through overuse or inappropriate use, nature tourism can lead to degradation or destruction of the environmental assets on which it is based and thereby go through a boom-and-bust cycle. But if managed wisely, it offers potentially valuable opportunities for generating revenues not only for development but also for conservation. From 1999 through 2002, the World Bank Research Committee and the Bank's Africa Region provided support for a research project entitled Nature Tourism and Conservation. The Bank's interest in the project reflected its felt need to enhance its capacity to deliver effective policy advice to clients with respect to key environmental, social, and economic issues associated with the development of nature tourism. The Bank chose to develop the approach and methods through a case study in the KwaZulu-Natal Province of South Africa (KZN), in conjunction with its local technical partner organization in the case study, KZN Wildlife.

The objective of the research effort was to assess how various policy, institutional, and managerial alternatives can enhance nature tourism's contribution to biodiversity conservation, economic development, and social equity, with a particular focus on the intermediary role played by alternatives for increasing money flows from conservation activities. In other words, the research explored the trade-offs and complementarities involved in promoting, expanding, and managing nature tourism, given a number of different criteria for evaluating success. The most important questions that were examined include

- What are the net local economic benefits from nature tourism? Do expenditures by nature tourists stay within the local economy, and to what extent do they boost the local economy by providing additional rounds of local expenditures?

- Do lower socioeconomic groups in the local communities adjacent to parks benefit from nature tourism? Are there ways to increase those benefits?

- Is there potential for local tourism by previously disadvantaged groups, and if so, how can it be encouraged?

- Is nature tourism leading to the degradation of the natural resource base? What are the main managerial options for improving the resource base or minimizing degradation?

- How should park entrance fees be structured? Should differential pricing be used? In particular, should foreign visitors be charged more?

- Is it better to raise conservation funds through changes in destination pricing or through taxes on the tourism trade?

- How do increases in fees lead to improvements in conservation, and what are the trade-offs or complementarities with development and equity objectives.

Many of these policy questions can be examined in light of the "market" for nature tourism, which can be divided into demand and supply components. As a result, the data and analyses necessary for answering these and other relevant questions were examined in a series of demand and supply studies, which were followed by synthesis work drawing together an economic model of nature tourism in the study area and an assessment of the policy alternatives. The separate studies on these topics that were commissioned as part of the project make up the remainder of this volume. Box 1.1 summarizes the studies and their location in the current volume.

BOX 1.1 STUDY COMPONENTS AND THE STRUCTURE OF THE VOLUME

Demand Studies

Household Survey (chapters 2 and 5). This survey targets the South African population at large, although a stratified sample is used. The aim is to assess current levels of participation in various nature tourism activities, to investigate which factors influence the decision to participate and the intensity of that participation, and to assess how these factors can be influenced through policy.

Visitor Survey (chapter 3). This survey targets foreign and domestic visitors in public and private conservation areas and accommodation facilities in the study area and in Mpumalanga (at Kruger National Park). The study explores which factors and policy decisions influence the selection of particular itineraries within South (and Southern) Africa. The study also records tourist expenditure patterns.

Source Market Survey (chapter 4). This survey targets potential visitors to South Africa by applying questionnaires in a source market—in this case, the Netherlands. The study examines which factors and policy decisions influence the selection of South Africa as a destination over competing destinations.

Focus Group Survey of Africans and Asians (chapter 5). This survey assesses whether there is latent demand for nature tourism among previously disadvantaged groups in South Africa. Focus group techniques are used to explore both preferences before and after a visit to KZN Wildlife reserves and the factors that influence decisions to engage in nature tourism.

Supply Studies

Census–Geographic Information System Inventory (incorporated into chapter 1). This study provides an overview of nature tourism operations in the study area by collecting existing data on public and private conservation areas and accommodation facilities from the KZN Wildlife and KZN Tourism Authority databases and supplementing this information with a direct telephone survey of these facilities.

(continued)

BOX 1.1 (Continued)

Ecological Survey (chapter 6). This study explores the relationship between nature tourism and biodiversity conservation in terms of the impact of current and anticipated levels of tourism in the region on the physical and biological resources of both private and public conservation areas in the study area.

Game Sales Study (chapter 7). This study seeks to examine the size and relative importance of the sale of live game to private and public reserves in the study area, and to contrast observed patterns with those found in the South African game sales market as a whole.

Producer Survey (chapter 8). This survey examines the costs, benefits, and returns of a sample of the public and private game reserves in the study area.

Policy Analysis

Regional Economic Model: A Social Accounting Matrix, or SAM (chapter 9). The SAM model enables an assessment of the impact of nature tourism on employment and household income in the study area and the province, as well as the potential impact of changes in tourism expenditures and demand.

Policy Analysis (chapter 10). The study components detailed in chapters 1 through 9 inform the understanding of the contribution of nature tourism to conservation finance, biodiversity conservation, development, and social equity. Either directly or indirectly, the study components also form the basis for the analysis of policy options and recommendations presented in this chapter.

Before assessing the potential for improving outcomes through alternative scenarios of policy, managerial, and institutional change, it is useful to ground the analysis in the current status of nature tourism in the study area and the degree to which nature tourism already contributes to conservation, development, and equity. Nature tourism's current contribution, then, forms the baseline against which alternative scenarios can be compared. Following an introduction to the study area, the rest of the chapter provides a snapshot of the current contribution made by nature tourism in the area.

OVERVIEW OF NATURE TOURISM IN ZULULAND

KwaZulu-Natal and the Study Area

KwaZulu-Natal is one of 10 provinces that make up the Republic of South Africa (map 1.1; see page 449). The province—which was constituted in 1994 from the union of the former KwaZulu homelands and Natal—contains a diverse range of cultures and natural ecosystems, all of which have contributed to a rich history that is currently being exploited to encourage domestic and international tourism. KZN Wildlife manages a large number of protected areas in the province that cover 675,000 hectares (map 1.2; see page 450). The Drakensberg Park, the escarpment of which forms a natural border with Lesotho to the south of the province, is the largest of these areas and one of the principal tourist attractions in the country. Otherwise, most of the larger protected areas lie in the northeastern region of the province, which is the object of study in this project.

The northeastern corner of the province incorporates much of what is commonly referred to as Zululand, the ancestral homelands of the Zulu people. These lands are bordered to the north by the province of Mpumalanga and the countries of Mozambique and Swaziland. To the south and west lie the remainder of KwaZulu-Natal and Durban, the provincial capital and vibrant hub of industrial and tourist activity in the province. To the east are the warm waters of the Indian Ocean, bordered by long stretches of sandy beach and the Saint Lucia wetlands complex, a World Heritage site.

Due to the range of studies undertaken in the context of this project, the "study area" is more a set of thematic overlays than a fixed geographic region. What forms an appropriate region for the purposes of an economic model will not necessarily be the most useful region from the perspective of assessing biodiversity. Thus, the maps employed in the different assessments differ slightly. The assessment of public protected areas and private game reserves as well as the assessment of land uses and inventory of accommodation facilities target most of Zululand (the pink area in map 1.2).[1] The SAM is confined to a set of magisterial districts (five in all) that occupy the northeastern half of Zululand (map 1.3; see page 451).[2]

For simplicity's sake, the larger area will be referred to as "Zululand," whereas the more limited area examined in the social accounting matrix (SAM) will be called "northeastern (NE) Zululand." Meanwhile, many of the other studies—in particular the ecological, producer, and demand surveys—have as their focus the heart of tourism in Zululand, formed by the nucleus of three large public protected areas—Hluhluwe-Umfolozi Park (HUP), the Ithala Game Reserve, and the Mkhuze Game Reserve—along with a large number of smaller private game reserves and accommodation facilities that line the corridor formed by the N2 highway as it bisects Zululand on its way from Richards Bay to Saint Lucia and on up to the Pongolapoort Dam and the southern tip of Swaziland.

Nature Tourism Assets: Protected Areas and Game

The province of KwaZulu-Natal has a vibrant and diverse tourism industry. Zululand offers a tourism product that focuses primarily on nature. In part, this is a result of the natural endowment of the area and its relative remoteness from the industrial centers of Durban and Gauteng. But it is also a reflection of the strong land management and conservation ethos that characterized the Natal Parks Board, a provincial parastatal that was formed in 1947 to manage the protected area system (Hughes 2001). At present, about 8.4 percent (6,752 square kilometers) of the province is under protection, compared with 5.4 percent for the country as a whole (World Bank 2001; Hughes 2001). The board's successor—currently named "KZN Wildlife" but previously known as the KZN Nature Conservation Service—has continued to demonstrate a strong commitment to conservation while trying to fulfill its regulatory role and develop its own nature tourism business.

Of the larger Zululand study area shown in map 1.4 (see page 452), fully one-half (52 percent) is made up of communal land, with another 25 percent of the area under private ownership and dedicated to commercial uses. The term "commercial farms" refers to land that was previously exclusively owned by white farmers, and the term "communal lands" refers to land previously part of the KwaZulu "homeland" in the apartheid system. The remainder of Zululand is "under conservation." KZN Wildlife manages 415,000 hectares (17 percent) of conserved land in the study area. The largest individual protected areas in the area are Hluhluwe-Umfolozi Park (96,500 hectares), Mkhuze Game Reserve (38,000 hectares), and the Ithala Game Reserve (29,500 hectares). The Greater Saint Lucia

Wetland Park includes a large number of terrestrial, wetland, and coastal reserves (including Mkhuze), encompassing a total of 250,000 hectares.

Private game ranches and reserves (PGRs) add another 167,000 hectares (7 percent of the total), thus forming a potentially important component in land conservation in the area. Map 1.4 provides a visual presentation of land use data illustrating that the PGRs cluster in a "Z" shape stretching from the Ithala Game Reserve east to the Pongolapoort Dam and then running south along the N2 corridor between HUP and the Mkhuze Game Reserve before curling under the Mkhuze Game Reserve to the east (and above the bulk of the Greater Saint Lucia Wetland Park). Data on the growth in land area being conserved by private landowners during the past decade show that these areas have grown by 55 percent during the period, effectively adding 5,000 hectares to the area under conservation management in Zululand each year (figure 1.1).

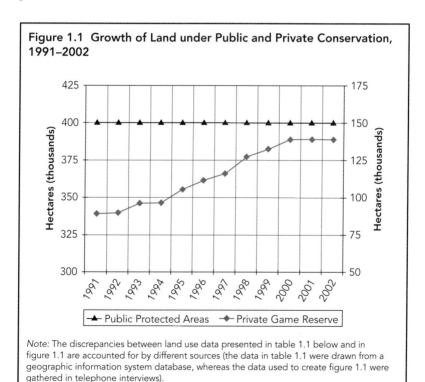

Figure 1.1 Growth of Land under Public and Private Conservation, 1991–2002

Note: The discrepancies between land use data presented in table 1.1 below and in figure 1.1 are accounted for by different sources (the data in table 1.1 were drawn from a geographic information system database, whereas the data used to create figure 1.1 were gathered in telephone interviews).

Source: James and Creemers (2000) and author's estimates for 2001 and 2002.

Table 1.1 Land Use and Tourist Accommodation in Zululand

Land Type	Area (hectares)	Percent	Structured Beds	Camping Beds	Total Beds	Total Beds (adjusted)	Percent	Beds per 1,000 Hectares
KZN wildlife reserves	415,000	16.6	1,602	4,265	5,867	3,023	23.7	7.5
Game ranches	167,396	6.7	2,148	390	2,538	2,277	17.9	16.4
Total "conserved" land	582,396	23.3	3,750	4,655	8,405	5,300	41.6	9.8
Commercial and other land	607,604	24.3	6,239	2,173	8,412	6,963	54.7	n.a.
Communal land	1,306,000	52.3	478	0	478	478	3.8	n.a.
Total for the study area	2,496,000	100.0	10,467	6,828	17,295	12,741	100.0	5.1

Note: "n.a." means not available. Camping beds are separated from structured beds because they do not represent physical beds. For the purpose of comparison, camping bed numbers are normalized to bed numbers by dividing by three.

Source: James and Creemers (2000).

Accommodation and Tourism Services

Private accommodation facilities outside public protected areas or private game reserves include hotels, bed and breakfasts (B&Bs), campsites, holiday flats, and guesthouses. Map 1.5 (see page 453) shows that many of these operations are clustered in the same areas as the private game reserves: along the N2 and in the area bounded by Ithala, HUP, Mkhuze, and Saint Lucia. Table 1.1 provides details on the types of accommodation offered by all the sectors of the Zululand tourist industry. The total number of beds exceeds 10,000, with 40 percent located in protected areas and game reserves. The density of beds is greater on the private game reserves (16 per hectare) than in the KZN Wildlife–managed reserves (7.5 per hectare).

There has been a significant increase in the overall number of beds available in the study area during the past decade (figure 1.2). The growth is almost exclusively in structured beds as opposed to camping beds.

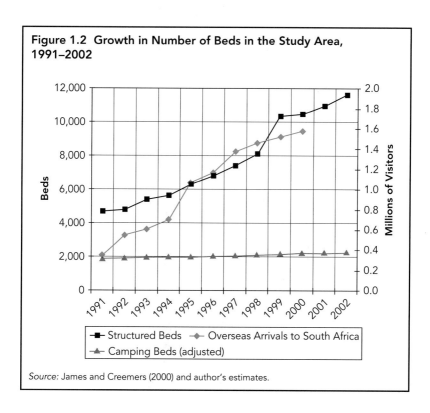

Figure 1.2 Growth in Number of Beds in the Study Area, 1991–2002

Source: James and Creemers (2000) and author's estimates.

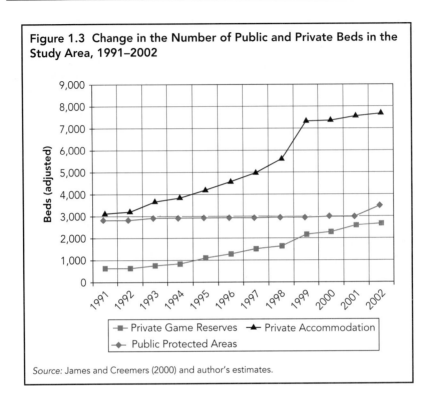

Figure 1.3 Change in the Number of Public and Private Beds in the Study Area, 1991–2002

Source: James and Creemers (2000) and author's estimates.

The camping market is primarily made up of local visitors and, indeed, figure 1.2 shows that the growth in structured beds largely has accompanied the growth in overseas visitors to the country. The bulk of this growth in capacity has been in the private sector, with the KZN reserves holding steady at just over 2,000 beds during the past 10 years (figure 1.3). During the period, there has also been a proliferation in beds at accommodation facilities that are "without land" (within towns or not on farms or reserves).

Therefore, while the KZN Wildlife reserves and the private game reserves currently each have a capacity of approximately 3,000 beds, the accommodation market that is "without land" totals almost 8,000. Though a good number of these will be hotels, B&Bs, and other types of lodging found in towns, such as in Saint Lucia, they are all likely to be related to nature tourism—given that even where visitors are not engaging in game viewing in the large terrestrial parks, they are often

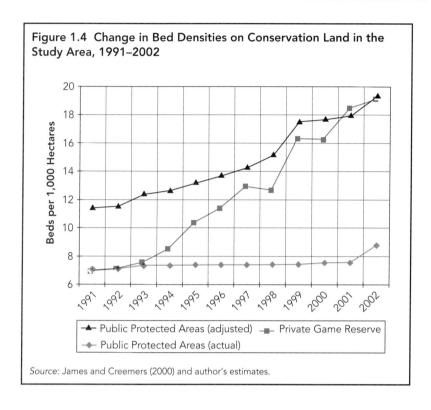

Figure 1.4 Change in Bed Densities on Conservation Land in the Study Area, 1991–2002

Source: James and Creemers (2000) and author's estimates.

enjoying the beach, the lagoon, and the coastal waters that are also largely protected within the Greater Saint Lucia Wetland Park.

The increase in bed numbers on the private game reserves exceeds the growth in land area, leading to a rise in the density of beds during the period (figure 1.4). Bed densities have more than doubled on these reserves, to just under 20 beds per 1,000 hectares. Bed densities on the KZN Wildlife reserves have, strictly speaking, remained constant during these periods. However, given that many visitors to these areas spend the night outside the KZN reserves, it is likely that a certain amount of the large increase in beds on private properties with no land represents an "effective" increase in the bed density of these areas.

To assess this "effective increase," a share of the accommodation "without land" can be considered as part of the "accommodation" in the KZN Wildlife area. If it is assumed that over half (55 percent) of the beds on these properties are used by visitors to the KZN Wildlife reserves, then the "effective" bed density in public areas in 2002 would equal that of the private game reserves. Of course, if this is true, then this accommodation represents beds displaced from the public sector to the private sector by virtue of the seeming "no-growth" policy of KZN Wildlife during this period.

NATURE TOURISM AND ECONOMIC DEVELOPMENT

As was explained above, nature tourism is one of the dominant land uses in Zululand. How that translates into nature tourism's contribution to economic development was investigated by conducting a more in-depth survey of nature tourism producers—that is, of public protected areas and private game reserves (see chapter 8, this volume)—and by employing the SAM developed for NE Zululand (see chapter 9). The principal findings of these studies are presented below.

Economic Development Indicators for NE Zululand and KZN

The SAM serves not only as a useful model for assessing changes in policy (as is discussed in chapter 10); it also provides a snapshot of the regional economy. The innovative part of the SAM as developed was to include explicit accounts for nature tourism and, thus, also provide a clear picture of the contribution of nature tourism to the regional and provincial economies. It is helpful to simply list here the key messages emerging from the SAM with respect to nature tourism, along with the supporting indicators:

1. Nature tourism plays a major role in the economy of NE Zululand and, indeed, KZN as a whole:
   - Nature tourism accounts for 21 percent (R415 million) of the gross geographical product (GGP) of the NE Zululand economy.
   - Nature tourism supplies 30 percent of total employment (7,000 jobs) in the study area.
   - The share of nature tourism in the total gross domestic product of KZN Province is 6 percent (R5.4 billion), and this sector supports 80,000 jobs.

2. Nature tourism's impact on unrelated tourism sectors is marginal:

- Nature tourism's production impact on unrelated tourism sectors is just 3.1 percent, due to the relatively small secondary sectors in the study area.

- Of the employment generated by nature tourism, only 8 percent is indirect (that is, in other than jobs related to the nature tourism sector).

3. A significant portion of nature tourism spending in NE Zululand leads to economic output in the rest of the province, although these effects are marginal relative to the size of the KZN economy (R92 billion) and total spending on nature tourism in KZN (R5.4 billion):

- Nature tourism's total contribution to provincial GGP is R545 million; in other words, nature tourism in NE Zululand generates R129 million (or 25 percent of the total) toward non–NE Zululand provincial GGP (beyond the R415 million generated in NE Zululand).

- Nature tourism spending in NE Zululand leads to the creation of 2,500 jobs in the rest of the province.

- However, nature tourism in NE Zululand contributes only 0.1 percent and 0.2 percent, respectively, to KZN GGP and employment.

- Still, the NE Zululand share of total spending and employment in the nature tourism sector in the province is significant at 10 percent and 12 percent, respectively.

4. Foreign tourists play a very important role in the economic impact of nature tourism in the study area. Foreign tourists generate 57 percent of the nature tourism production impact, compared with 26 percent from the rest of South Africa and 14 percent from the rest of KZN.

5. The public sector's role in the overall nature tourism industry is limited. The private sector's share of the nature tourism production impact is 88 percent, compared with the public sector's share of 11 percent.

Private Game Reserves and Public Protected Areas

As was noted above, the past decade has seen a significant realignment in land use in the tourism center of Zululand along the axis of the three dominant terrestrial protected areas: Hluhluwe-Umfolozi Park, Mkhuze Game Reserve, and Ithala Game Reserve. This conversion—as well as the increase in tourism to South Africa and to KZN Wildlife areas, and to HUP in particular—has led to many of the economic development benefits listed above. However, the sustainability of this "development," particularly for the private reserves, may ultimately rest with nature tourism's degree of profitability.

The specific role of different sources of revenues, or conservation finance, is presented later in this chapter. Here, the results of a survey of producers are summarized (see chapter 8, this volume). The survey drew on a sample of game reserves in the study area stratified for property size, from which 27 (of 59) were selected, along with the three major public protected areas (HUP, Ithala, and Mkhuze). The survey attempted to document the inputs, outputs, and assets of the operations and the resulting expenditures, assets, and revenue information in financial terms. It is helpful to list here the key findings emerging from the survey; the overall profitability of these nature tourism enterprises is presented in table 1.2:[3]

1. The overriding finding is that the private game reserve business is a difficult one, in which many operations are still struggling to turn an operating profit:

   • Occupancies are extremely variable (from less than 5 percent to 70 percent) but average 20 percent.

   • Only 3 of the 12 properties for which the full set of data on costs and revenues were available had positive annual net cash incomes.

   • The profitable reserves were all more than 1,000 hectares in size, and annual gross incomes ranged from R200 to R450 per hectare.

2. The tourism accounts of the three KZN Wildlife areas are performing well in terms of operating profits, but large centrally managed on-reserve and headquarters expenditures erode this profitability:

   • Ithala's low occupancy rate led it to run a slight operating loss, which declines to −R340 per hectare per year once centrally provided costs of land management, administration, and other costs are included.

- HUP's tourism operating surplus and game sales operations provide a cash influx of R10 million and R20 million, respectively, but the inclusion of central costs implies that it still does not cover its full annual costs at −R31 per hectare.
- Mkhuze turns a small operating profit on tourism and in the year surveyed it had unusually large game sales revenues (enough to cover central costs), giving it a positive (R143 per hectare per year) net cash income.

3. Consistent with other niche tourism market segments, indications are that property owners are not exclusively focused on the bottom line:

- Of 23 private game reserve owners responding, only 40 percent said that running a game reserve was "more a business than a way of life," with the largest portion (48 percent) of the remainder suggesting that it was "equally a way of life and a business."
- The vast majority of reserve owners (23 of 27) included in their reasons for going into the nature tourism business their personal interest in or love for wildlife (James and Goodman 2001).

Tourist Itineraries and Expenditures in KwaZulu-Natal

A survey of foreign and resident tourists conducted in the study area provides information on the extent and pattern of tourist itineraries and expenditures in the study area (table 1.3). Foreign visitors typically spend 2 weeks or more in the country, of which 3.5 nights on average are spent in NE Zululand. Day visitors typically take one day trip to HUP, while overnight visitors typically spend 2 nights in the park. As far as residents are concerned, itineraries in NE Zululand are fairly similar, with the exception that day visitors spend less time in the study area as a whole. Residents typically visit the study area as a destination, as reflected by the negligible amount of time on their itineraries outside the study area.

Within NE Zululand, the principal difference between foreigners and residents is that foreigners spend more than twice as much per night (R450) on average than do residents (R200). The difference is moderated when expenditures in the rest of the country are considered; however, this is largely an artifact of the sample, and the brief travel time outside the

Table 1.2 Profitability Trends for Private Game Reserves and Public Protected Areas

Measure	Private Game Reserves				KZN Wildlife Reserves
	Bed and Breakfast	Small	Medium-Size	Large	
Number of properties	1	5	5	1	3
Average size (hectares)	120	735	1,646	5,413	55,000
Capital invested (millions of rand)	2.42	10.82	8.67	33.24	203.51
Per-reserve annual average (millions of rand)					
Gross income	1.66	0.48	0.60	3.52	23.04
Variable expenditures	1.66	0.56	0.60	0.97	25.56
Net cash income	−0.002	−0.07	−0.009	2.55	−2.52
Per-reserve averages (rand per hectare)					
Capital invested	20,167	14,289	5,854	6,141	3,502
Annual gross income	13,889	624	379	651	386
Annual expenditures	13,905	725	362	179	461
Annual net cash income	−16	−100	18	471	−75

Source: Chapter 8, this volume.

Table 1.3 Visitor Numbers, Length of Stay, and Expenditures by Type of Visitor to Hluhluwe-Umfolozi Park

Visitors to HUP	Length of Stay			Expenditures	
	At HUP (days and nights)	Inside NE Zululand (nights)	Outside NE Zululand (nights)	In NE Zululand (rand per capita per night)	In Rest of South Africa (rand per capita per night)
Foreigners					
Day visitors	1.0	3.4	13.8	432	606
Overnight visitors	2.0	3.5	12.4	467	682
Residents					
Day visitors	1.0	1.7	0.4	208	551
Overnight visitors	2.0	3.2	0.7	206	629

HUP = Hluhluwe-Umfolozi Park.

Source: Chapters 4 and 9, this volume.

study area (so that those in the sample who do stay overnight skew upward the per capita expenditure per night). In comparison, a study of the KwaZulu-Natal domestic tourism market, Seymour (1998) found that the average spent in KZN (including travel to KZN) per overnight visitor ranged from R383 (September) to R728 (January). The results from the study area are limited to NE KZN and exclude travel expenditures to KZN, but they are still roughly consistent with Seymour's results.

The distribution of expenditures differs somewhat across the studies, with shopping expenditures making up between 20 and 37 percent of total costs in Seymour's study (travel costs to KZN excluded), and only 4 percent in the present survey. Compared with other costs, shopping expenditures seem unreasonably high in the Seymour study. For example, in the January survey, shopping expenditures were twice as high as those on accommodation.

The figures can also be compared with other international visitor surveys. Tourism South Africa, known as SATOUR (1998), reported average expenditures of R17,500 for foreign visitors to South Africa. This is about R7,500 more than the figures from the current study. However, SATOUR's numbers included all prepaid expenditures (including airfares), and no correction was made for the portion of air and package expenditure retained in source market countries, nor for travel to multiple countries. Comparing expenditures while in South Africa, the two surveys produce fairly similar results. SATOUR reported average expenditures of R5,900 while inside South Africa, whereas the survey done for the present study respectively indicates R5,000 and R5,100 for day visitors and overnight visitors.

NATURE TOURISM AND SOCIAL EQUITY

Like any economic activity, nature tourism will have an impact on social equity, regardless of whether the impact is explicitly intended. This impact can be assessed in many ways, two of which are employed here. The first is whether the activity can be judged progressive against current norms. In other words, does nature tourism (or the alternative policies that will be evaluated below) improve the situation of those who are worse off, relative to those who are better off? The second way is simply to assess what the level of impact is for specific target groups; that is, does the activity improve the lot of landless workers, poor people, or disadvantaged minorities? In the South African context, it is crucial to assess the effects on previously disadvantaged groups and rural poor people. Income level and employment skill level serve as a proxy for these groups.

The SAM's findings on the economic effects of nature tourism show the sector to be a progressive one, for it provides improved opportunities for the less well off in terms of employment and capital and leads to effects that are neutral to progressive for enterprises and households (figure 1.5):

- Nature tourism's effects on labor go proportionately more to unskilled (46 percent for nature tourism vs. 32 percent for the economy as a whole) and semiskilled (24 percent vs. 15 percent) workers as compared with the figures for skilled workers (30 percent vs. 53 percent).

- Nature tourism's effects in returns on capital go proportionately more to local communities (12.7 percent for nature tourism vs. 9.7 percent for the economy as a whole) and small commercial entities (25 percent vs. 15 percent) as compared with large commercial entities (27.8 percent vs. 66 percent).[4]

- Nature tourism's effects on small commercial enterprises are significantly higher than those of overall spending (26 percent vs. 15 percent).

- Nature tourism's effects on rural and low-income households are in proportion to the larger economy, with 40 percent (R114 million) going to low-income households and 79 percent (R224 million) to rural households.

In the study area, there are many types of properties involved in nature tourism: public- and private-sector operations, small and large operations. The extent to which these various operations favor social equity can be assessed through an examination of employment effects at accommodation facilities. For the case of private game reserves, the number of lesser-skilled (that is, nonmanagement) jobs per bed or per tourist rises with the price of accommodation on the reserve (table 1.4).

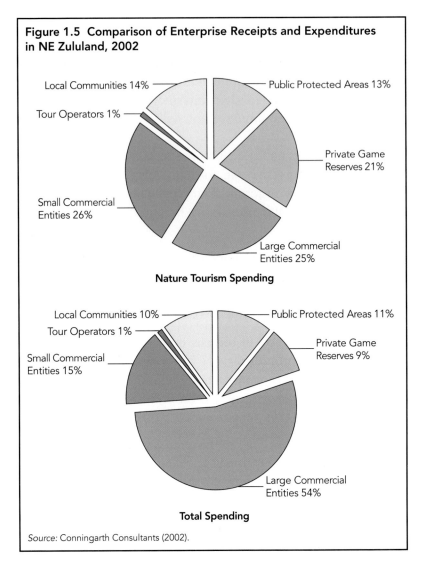

Figure 1.5 Comparison of Enterprise Receipts and Expenditures in NE Zululand, 2002

Local Communities 14%

Tour Operators 1%

Small Commercial Entities 26%

Public Protected Areas 13%

Private Game Reserves 21%

Large Commercial Entities 25%

Nature Tourism Spending

Local Communities 10%

Tour Operators 1%

Small Commercial Entities 15%

Public Protected Areas 11%

Private Game Reserves 9%

Large Commercial Entities 54%

Total Spending

Source: Conningarth Consultants (2002).

When adjusted for the actual level of expenditures required to fill one bed at the highest price level, however, the lower price ranges generate more nonmanagement employment per rand spent, with accommodation prices of R50 and below providing twice the employment generated by higher priced reserves of R150 and above. It is also important to note that these figures merely reflect the employment effects of tourism services on the property. It is quite likely that visitors staying

Table 1.4 Bed Price as a Determinant of Nonmanagement Employment on Private Game Reserves

Bed Price (Rand per person)	Sample Size (N)	Nonmanagement Tourism Employment per Bed		Average Bed Price (Rand per person)	Jobs per Unit of Expenditure (jobs per R1,388 spent per night)
		Average Jobs	Standard Deviation		
More than 750	5	1.28	0.65	1,388	1.28
401–750	12	0.57	0.42	687	1.14
251–400	10	0.39	0.33	360	1.51
151–250	26	0.31	0.25	238	1.84
51–150	85	0.28	0.19	142	2.70
50 or less	52	0.15	0.12	50	4.03

Source: James and Creemers (2000).

at higher priced lodging generate substantially more employment through their spending on other tourist services than do those on low-budget back-packing or camping trips. This is reflected in the overall multiplier effects of spending by different tourist categories (see chapter 9, this volume).

Comparative figures on employment are not available from KZN Wildlife. Anecdotal observation suggests, however, that staffing per vis-itor at KZN parks is relatively low. Furthermore, it is reported that the wages earned by those working in the public-sector reserves are sub-stantially higher than those in the private sector, reflecting the policies of KZN Wildlife as a parastatal body and the employment rules and wage schemes it must follow.

If this were the case, it would appear that the private game reserves provide more socially equitable employment in that wages may be lower, but they reflect market prices for labor and permit the employment of a larger workforce. A system that pays semiskilled and unskilled employees higher wages but as a result hires fewer people would appear to be regressive. Moreover, such a system may have a negative feedback effect on community development because, instead of having jobs at the market rate, a share of the workforce remains unemployed and must vie for a share of the income brought home by those who are employed and are earning more than the market rate. This, of course, begs the question of whether the market rate is itself socially equitable.

NATURE TOURISM AND BIODIVERSITY CONSERVATION

The achievements of KZN Wildlife (and its predecessor organizations) with respect to the conservation of biodiversity in the study area are well known and publicized (de la Harpe and Charlton-Perkins, no date; Dennis, de la Harpe, and Barker 1999; Hughes 2001). Hluhluwe and Umfolozi were first set aside as game reserves in 1895, and beginning in the 1920s the Natal Parks Board led efforts to restore white (and black) rhinoceros populations. In the late 1800s and early 1900s, the only surviving breeding herd of white rhinos inhabited the Umfolozi area, with total numbers falling as low as 30 by the 1920s. However, a successful decades-long effort to protect and restore the population eventually lead to Operation Rhino, in which the Natal Parks Board worked to capture and move rhinos to other reserves to reestablish breeding herds. Currently, about 2,000 white rhinos roam the Hluhluwe-Umfolozi Park, 4,000 have been translocated from the park, and their worldwide population exceeds 7,000.

As has been documented by Hughes (2001), the Parks Board had other conservation success stories in its early years, including the leatherback sea turtle protection program and the establishment of the conservancy movement (private game reserves) and extension programs. In the past two decades, the board has shifted gears toward integrating conservation and development with a strategy aimed at the sustainable development of the wildlife industry in Natal, which included four components: the sale of wildlife, ecotourism in the board-run parks, the emergence of private game reserves, and the growth of local economic benefits from the parks system.

The sale of live game is a rousing success. In the past two decades, more than 1,000 animals have been sold at auction. Tourism to the parks has also increased dramatically, leading to increased revenues for the board (and its successors). In addition, the number of hectares under private management as game reserves in Zululand increased by roughly 5,000 hectares a year in the 1990s. And as discussed above, not only has nature tourism provided a significant economic base for the development of Zululand, but it appears to be on balance a progressive industry, with substantial benefits accruing to the less well off.

In the ensuing discussion of conservation finance, a number of these achievements are explored in a more deliberative fashion, with a specific focus on the role and policies of KZN Wildlife. Regardless of the extent to which nature tourism is judged to be self-sufficient in the financial terms of such an analysis, it is clear that the effort to develop a wildlife or nature tourism industry has succeeded in the study area, with positive outcomes for conservation of biodiversity. Typically, the effects of nature tourism on the environment are interpreted by recreation ecology in terms of their negative impact on ecosystems because inevitably the consumptive and nonconsumptive uses of reserves encroach on nature in its "pristine" state.

However, in the study area, this type of negative impact appears of limited significance in the public reserves, which have a long history of effective land management for conservation. Rather, the phenomenon cof rapid growth in the amount of land managed for conservation by the private sector suggests that the most important outcome, in terms of biodiversity conservation—resulting from the growth of nature tourism in the study area—is the encouragement and incentive given to the private sector to invest in conservation. Beyond the returns from game sales and nature tourism receipts that flow to KZN Wildlife for reinvestment in conservation or to local businesses and households to support their livelihoods, it is important to assess the positive impact that the development of the private reserves has had on biodiversity conservation.

To answer this question, an ecological survey was undertaken to examine a range of ecological and management variables across the same stratified, random sample of 27 private game reserves employed in the producer survey. Three public protected areas (PPAs)—HUP, Ithala, and Mkhuze—were included, as well as controls. Data were gathered by means of interviews with landowners, a physical assessment, and a geographic information system query of landscape, ecosystem, community, and species coverage. It is helpful here to summarize the key messages and indicators regarding the ways in which and the extent to which the PGRs have had an impact on biodiversity conservation (above and beyond those already realized in the KZN Wildlife reserves), beginning with the achievements and then turning to the challenges:[5]

1. PGRs make a substantial contribution to each of the priority landscape classes present in the study region; in priority class 2, shown in table 1.5, those reserves involved in tourism contribute twice as much as the public protected areas.

2. PGRs have enhanced landscape connectivity by providing natural areas located between the large public protected areas.

3. PGRs contribute to the representation of important vegetation communities, including two (of 23) communities that are not included in public protected areas, making their contribution particularly significant.

4. PGRs help restore historical herbivory and predation processes and contribute to the maintenance of individual species populations, though this effect varies with the size of the property, which is positively correlated to the number of species present.

Table 1.5 Contribution of Public Areas, Game Ranches, and Tourism Ranches to the Representation of Priority Landscapes

Priority Class	Study Region Total by Class (hectares)	Public Protected Areas		Private Game Reserves			
				Total Sample of 27		22 PGRs in Tourism	
		Area (hectares)	Percentage of Regional Total	Area (hectares)	Percentage of Regional Total	Area (hectares)	Percentage of Regional Total
1	151,554	25,096	16.6	3,743	2.5	3,743	2.5
2	356,546	13,556	3.8	26,164	7.3	26,164	7.3
3	910,348	128,927	14.2	99,910	11.0	97,572	10.7
4	1,062,301	241,232	22.7	64,315	6.1	55,855	5.3
Total	2,480,749	408,811	16.5	194,132	7.8	183,333	7.4

PGR = Private game reserve.

Source: Chapter 6, this volume.

5. The ecological footprint of PGRs is modest, with most of the properties being less than 3 percent transformed, this being an improvement due to the cleaning up and restoration of properties that occurs as landowners shift from cattle to game, but still substantially more (about 10 times more) in per-hectare terms than that of public protected areas.

6. PGRs' contribution to connectivity, to the maintenance of representative species populations, and to the maintenance of genetic vigor is limited by the size of private game properties and the fences that encircle them.

In other words, the contribution made to date by PGRs to biodiversity conservation is significant, but much of the potential remains to be captured—improved cooperation among private operators and between private operators and KZN Wildlife, with the objective of "dropping" fences and integrating land and wildlife management regimes being required to fully capitalize on this potential.

THE ROLE AND EXTENT OF CONSERVATION FINANCE

"Conservation finance" is a relatively new and trendy term. As such, it is prone to misunderstanding, confusion, or at best a lack of clear understanding of to what precisely it refers. Money flows that are intended for use in conservation can come from a multitude of sources and can be destined for a number of uses—therein lies the confusion. Typically, such flows stem from one of two sources: either those individuals who actually "use" the areas conserved or those who simply care about conservation. The former type of flow typically accrues in the form of revenues, drawn from fees, charges, licenses, and the like. The latter type of flow is effectively made up of donations—whether sourced from direct-mail campaigns, taxes, debt swaps, or the like. Thus, conservation finance can be divided into two components: conservation "revenues" and conservation fundraising.

"Finance" and "financing," of course, traditionally refer to money flows required for investing in capital accumulation. In the case of conservation finance, this distinction between capital and recurrent costs is largely lost. The immediate unmet needs of most public protected areas imply a need for recurrent as much as capital funds. In fact, conservation revenues are not really financing but rather income from a capital asset. Fund-raising efforts, however, might be viewed as financing, in the sense that giving is predicated on the concept of eventually obtaining a return—that of biodiversity conservation. The difficulty with this type of financing is that it is rarely provided upfront in large amounts and therefore is not secure over time. On balance, then, it would seem prudent to first maximize conservation revenues and then meet conservation shortfalls through fund-raising efforts.

Conservation finance can be an important instrument for achieving economic development, social equity, and biodiversity conservation. Given the vibrant wildlife industry in the study area, the "revenues" aspect of conservation finance is the appropriate focus here. In the following sections, a brief introduction and overview is provided of the different revenue streams that are generated by the multiple uses of biodiversity in the study area, all of which can be loosely grouped (directly or indirectly) under the nature tourism trade. The objective is to summarize available information on the current status of these financial flows to the KZN Wildlife reserves and to the private game reserves. In the process, the current policies that determine the role and extent of the contribution that nature tourism makes to conservation finance are presented, to set the stage for the ensuing analysis of policy alternatives. The presentation begins with the direct revenues generated by live game sales, hunting, and game viewing.

Game Sales

To examine the importance of live game sales, a game sales study was undertaken to characterize the market, report on market trends in quantities and prices, and examine the factors that determine these trends (chapter 7, this volume). The analysis is multiscale in that it examines the game sales market for South Africa as a whole and for the province of KZN, and then it zooms in on game sales in the core of the study area using the data collected from the sample of KZN Wildlife reserves and private game reserves in the Ecological Survey and Producer Survey. The main results from this study as they pertain to Zululand are presented below, although because the vast majority of the KZN market activity occurs in the study area the references to KZN serve as a proxy for Zululand.

As was mentioned above, KwaZulu-Natal (and specifically the Natal Parks Board and its successor KZN Wildlife) has played a unique role in the game sales industry in South Africa. Given this historical position, the province is well placed to benefit from this growing industry. Moreover, the Zululand area is the center of not only KZN's but also South Africa's active live game sales market. The reputation of KwaZulu-Natal's auctions (both for game quality and variety available), especially those held by KZN Wildlife, attracts a large audience of buyers from around Southern Africa as well as overseas. This favorable reputation contributes to the fact that current game auctions in the province account for a significant proportion—28 percent in 2001—of South Africa's total annual game sales turnover (R87 million, or US$10 million).

Market turnover (gross revenue in nominal terms) and volumes of game sold in KZN's public and private auctions have risen since the mid-1990s (figure 1.6). In real terms, turnover increased by 64 percent from 1995 to 2001. In 2001, the total value accounted for about R24 million, and more than 3,500 animals were sold. More than 80 percent of this revenue came from the sale of three species: nyalas and black and white rhinoceroses.

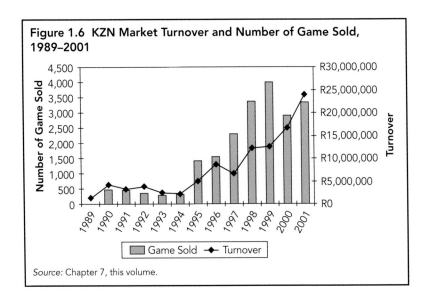

Figure 1.6 KZN Market Turnover and Number of Game Sold, 1989–2001

Source: Chapter 7, this volume.

The latter two species fetch a huge premium on the market, with prices averaging R550,000 for a black rhino and R260,000 for white one.

Both the private sector (through the Natal Game Ranchers Association) and KZN Wildlife conduct their own auctions in the province. But the vast majority of species sold and turnover generated takes place at the annual KZN Wildlife auction (figure 1.7). The

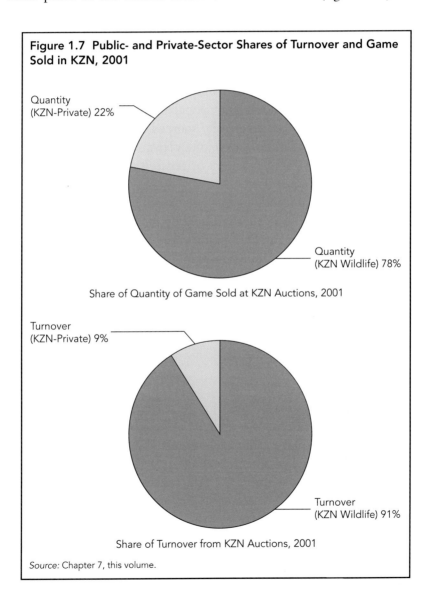

Figure 1.7 Public- and Private-Sector Shares of Turnover and Game Sold in KZN, 2001

Quantity (KZN-Private) 22%

Quantity (KZN Wildlife) 78%

Share of Quantity of Game Sold at KZN Auctions, 2001

Turnover (KZN-Private) 9%

Turnover (KZN Wildlife) 91%

Share of Turnover from KZN Auctions, 2001

Source: Chapter 7, this volume.

Ranchers Association's auctions, however, have been running only since 1999 and could increase their share of game sold and turnover generated as their auction builds its own reputation. The contribution to total revenue from the sale of live game varies widely across 17 properties of different sizes included in the Producer Survey (Chapter 7, this volume).

Although medium-size private game reserves relied on live game sales for 20 percent of their revenues, small reserves derived only 10 percent of revenues from such sales, and for the four large private reserves surveyed live game sales were a negligible proportion of total revenue. The Ecological Survey found that to date most animals purchased by the private game reserves in the study area come from local (that is, KZN) sources. Although some game populations tend to be lower in this province and, hence, are more easily sourced elsewhere (for example, cheetahs, giraffes, and waterbucks), often fewer than 15 percent of the game sold to these game ranchers originated from other provinces (James and Goodman 2001).

In sum, the contribution of game sales to public-sector conservation finance is significant. The auctions held by KZN Wildlife in 2001 set a new turnover record for the organization, surpassing 2000's record of R15 million by more than R7 million. According to KZN Wildlife, these auctions generated enough revenue in 2001 for the organization to offset management costs by as much as 15 percent (the latest results for KZN Wildlife auctions can be found at http://www.kznwildlife.org/auction02_results.htm).

Hunting

Hunting in the study area is largely for the purpose of meat and trophies. Foreigners are the chief source of demand for trophy hunting, and residents dominate the market for meat hunting. Hunting in the public protected areas included in the core study area is limited. There is no hunting in Hluhluwe-Umfolozi Park, reflecting its historic role in species protection and the economic importance of the game viewing that takes place in the area. Conversely, at the Mkhuze Game Reserve hunting is undertaken in a controlled area at the southern end during the winter months. The modest Mkumbi hunting lodge serves hunters in season and is used as a bush camp out of season.

Table 1.6 Share of Hunting in Private Game Reserve Total Revenues

Property Size	Sample Size	Hunting as a Percentage of Revenue	Stated Purpose	Sample Size	Hunting as a Percentage of Revenue
Small	5	34.3	Strictly game viewing	4	0.3
Medium-size	7	49.5	Strictly hunting	1	93.0
Large	4	48.2	Both	11	51.4
			Total	16	42.0

Source: Chapter 7, this volume.

Although hunting is of only marginal importance as a source of revenues for the public areas, it makes up much of the revenues of private game reserves. Of 16 reserves providing data, the average share of total revenue generated by hunting was 42 percent, reflecting a heavy reliance on hunting by a good number of the properties (table 1.6). This is indicative of the area, in which the pattern is often for farmers to convert 500 to 4,000 hectares of cattle land to game land and begin by marketing themselves as hunting operations. Properties that establish substantial wildlife populations with a representative number of species will then often move into the game viewing market. In contrast, a few properties moved directly to game viewing.

An alternative way to view the revenue shares is to consider the type of operation the property runs: strictly game viewing, a mix of game viewing and hunting, or strictly hunting. On properties where hunting and game viewing are offered, about half of total revenue comes from hunting. One element to consider in hunting revenue is that the income often depends on the value of the animal shot. Higher-value trophy species may bring in disproportionately more income from hunting even with lower client numbers than game viewing or lower-value trophy species.

A final observation on the private game reserve data set is that there appears to be a relationship between the degree to which revenue from hunting shares significantly in total revenues of a property and the degree to which it is profitable. Though the sample is small, this provides some evidence of the benefits of devoting properties to multiple uses.

Game Viewing

Revenues at KZN Wildlife Areas

Game viewing produces a number of sources of revenue for KZN Wildlife, which can be grouped as

- entrance fees paid by day and overnight visitors on arrival,

- accommodation charges paid by overnight visitors,

- trading revenues from sales in restaurants and shops,

- trails, rides, and tours income, and

- other revenue collected at camps in the reserves (including permits and fines).

Figures for the 2000–01 financial year show that KZN Wildlife garnered more than R94 million in total revenue from game viewing, of which 41 percent (R39 million) came from the HUP, Ithala, and Mkhuze combined (table 1.7). HUP on its own provided 32 percent of total KZN

Table 1.7 Revenues and Expenditures for Game Viewing at KZN Wildlife Reserves, 2000–01

Category of Revenue, Expenditure, or Resource	HUP	Ithala	Mkhuze	Other KZN Wildlife Reserves	KZN Wildlife Reserves Grand Total
Land area (hectares)	96,000	29,654	37,985	511,561	675,200
Revenue source (millions of rand)	29.8	5.7	2.9	55.6	94.0
Accommodation	14.5	3.4	1.9	30.3	50.1
Trading sales	8.3	0.8	0.6	11.8	21.5
Income from trails, rides, and tours	3.4	0.4	0.2	1.3	5.3
Entrance fees	2.3	0.2	0.2	5.3	7.9
Other income collected at camps	1.3	0.9	0.0	7.0	9.2
Expenditures	16.8	5.4	2.7	46.7	71.5
Personnel	7.5	3.7	1.7	28.5	41.4
Other	9.3	1.7	0.9	18.2	30.1
Net game viewing profit	13.0	0.3	0.2	9.0	22.4
Community levy	1.8	0.5	0.3	2.6	8.6

HUP = Hluhluwe-Umfolozi Park; KZN = KwaZulu-Natal.

Source: KZN Wildlife data.

game viewing revenue. Accommodation makes up about half of total revenues for each of the three reserves, and trading and trails revenue make up from 20 percent to 40 percent of revenues. Entrance fees provide 8 percent of revenues (R2.34 million) for HUP, 3 percent (R0.9 million) for Ithala, and 6 percent (R170,000) for Mkhuze.

Conservation revenues are, therefore, substantial at these KZN reserves. It is also worth emphasizing that, in addition to the entrance fees, KZN Wildlife charges visitors a modest community levy (currently R10 per night per overnight visitor) as part of the accommodation charges. This money goes into a fund for projects in outlying community areas. The revenue from this charge is relatively small, totaling R2.6 million in 2000–01 from the three reserves in the core study area.

Expenditure figures for services directly related to these accommodation and gate profit centers show that all three game viewing operations turn a profit on these accounts. Gross operating margins calculated on this basis are very high for HUP at 78 percent, but a modest 5 percent and 7 percent, respectively, for Ithala and Mkhuze. HUP alone generates 58 percent (R13 million) of its total operating profit on these accounts. The majority of this stems from a single camp, Hilltop Camp, which generated a R8.2 million operating profit in 2000–01.

Clearly, HUP and Hilltop are the outstanding performers and play a dominant role in the game viewing economy of the KZN Wildlife reserves. Still, as was indicated above, it is important to stress that large costs associated with operating these reserves and all central administrative costs—including running the large reservation department that serves the camps—are not included in these operating profit figures, and that when these costs are included all three of the reserves do not cover their full costs.

Pricing at KZN Wildlife Areas

Entrance fees to KZN parks and reserves have traditionally been kept low, and efforts to reap revenues have centered on the pricing of accommodation (George Hughes, personal communication, 1998). During the period in which the fieldwork for the demand studies was undertaken (in 2000), entrance fees were R9 per person plus R1 for the community levy and a R30 fee per vehicle. For foreigners, this represented US$1 to US$2 per person depending on group size. In 1999, the entrance fee was R7 per person. An additional R10 per night went to the community fund for those staying in structured accommodation and R5 per night for those camping.

In the annual pricing policy effective November 1, 2001, KZN Wildlife altered these policies. The community levy (and rescue levy) are now subsumed within the entrance fee, and only day visitors will pay the entrance fee at the gate. For overnight visitors, the entrance fees are included in the accommodation charges. Entrance fees for the three reserves in the core study area have risen to R30, which (given the rapid devaluation of the rand) now converts into about US$2.50. Foreigners are still subject to the same fees and charges as residents.

Accommodation charges have varied widely over time in rand terms. From 1991 to 2000, the weighted average price for comparably structured accommodation at Hluhluwe, Umfolozi, and Mkhuze increased from R42 to R187 per person, quadrupling the price in nominal terms (table 1.8). Relative to the South African urban consumer price index—that is, for the urban South African nature tourist—the price went up in real terms by 120 percent, or approximately 9 percent a year in real compounded terms. For the relatively well-off American tourist paying in dollars, however, the price went up by only 27 percent in real terms, or just 3 percent a year in real terms.

To put the latter cost in perspective, this average price rose from US$21 to US$27 per person per night. However, the majority of this price rise took place in Hluhluwe (that is, in Hilltop Camp), where occupancies have run quite high historically (occupancy was 90 percent in 2000, according to the data gathered for the Ecological Survey). It is interesting, however, that the price rises at Hilltop have been more severe in real dollar terms in the low-end accommodation, while the price of lodge accommodation has actually fallen in real dollar terms. In short, prices of accommodation have risen over time, often significantly so for the average South African, but only modestly for the foreign visitor paying in dollars.

Revenues at Private Game Reserves
Private game reserves in the area not only offer their own wildlife experience but will also typically offer their guests a guided tour of the KZN Wildlife reserves. The larger the reserve, the more diversity of species

Table 1.8 Comparison of Accommodation Prices in Hluhluwe-Umfolozi Park and Mkhuze, 1991 and 2000

Bed Category	Price per Person per Night, 1991			Price per Person per Night, 2000		Annual Growth Rate in Price	
	Rand	Constant 2000 Rand	Constant 2000 US Dollars	Rand	US Dollars	For Constant 2000 Rand (percent)	For Constant 2000 US Dollars (percent)
A. Mkhuze Game Reserve							
1. Cottage	55	112	28	163	23	4	–2
2. Chalet	44	90	22	163	23	7	1
3. Rest hut	29	58	15	110	16	7	1
4. Bush camp	50	101	25	200	29	8	1
5. Weighted average	43	88	22	154	22	6	0
B. Umfolozi Game Reserve							
1. Cottage	55	112	28	180	26	5	–1
2. Rest hut	29	58	15	95	14	6	–1
3. Chalet	44	90	22	145	21	5	–1
4. Bush camp	50	101	25	180	26	7	0
5. Bush lodge	99	202	50	275	40	3	–3
6. Weighted average	41	84	21	164	24	8	1
C. Hluhluwe Park							
1. Lodge	132	269	67	250	36	–1	–7
2. Cottage	39	79	20	250	36	14	7
3. Rest hut	26	54	13	130	19	10	4
4. Weighted average	41	83	21	218	31	11	5
Weighted average	42	85	21	187	27	9	3

Source: KZN Wildlife data; Geert Creemers personal communication, 2001; Statistics South Africa; data from Federal Reserve Board of Minneapolis and the International Monetary Fund.

and landscapes it can offer the tourist. The Phinda Game Reserve is one of the larger private game reserves in the core study area (14,000 hectares). Phinda, which is owned by Conservation Corporation Africa, has stocked the Big Five species (lion, leopard, elephant, rhinoceros, and buffalo) on the reserve and is dedicated exclusively to upmarket game viewing. Charges per person at Phinda vary significantly with the season, and discounts are offered to South Africans during low periods. Standard published (rack) rates at Phinda can reach or exceed US$400 per person per night.

The nature of the attraction and the quality of the service at Phinda make such pricing levels feasible. More generally, the survey of accommodation suggests that in Zululand there is a series of pricing levels in the game reserves (and other accommodation areas) starting at R50 per night and moving in steps to R150, R250, R400, R750, and R1,500 per night.

Private game reserves' responses to the Producer Survey suggest that on average about 30 percent of revenues come from game viewing (table 1.9). Trading and other services are not included in private game reserves' game viewing revenues because the share attributable to hunters as opposed to those on photographic safaris is not clear. However, such averages mask enormous variability from property to property.

Examining the share of revenue attributable to game viewing on the basis of whether properties engage in hunting or game viewing or both provides a more accurate picture. Game reserves undertaking both hunting and viewing have a relatively low average (on the order of 20 percent)

Table 1.9 Share of Game Viewing in Private Game Reserve Total Revenues

Property Size	Sample Size	Game Viewing as a Percentage of Revenue	Stated Purpose	Sample Size	Game Viewing as a Percentage of Revenue
Bed and breakfast	1	72			
Small	5	28	Strictly game viewing	5	73
Medium-size	7	21	Strictly hunting	1	0
Large	4	35	Both	12	17
Total	17		Total	18	29

Source: Chapter 8, this volume.

for the revenues from game viewing. Those properties that engage strictly in game viewing (and game sales) generate more than 73 percent of their revenues from game viewing. For this group, game sales account for 10 percent of revenues; when trading and other services are included, the share of revenues from game viewing rises to 80 percent.

Thus, the extent of revenue generation from game viewing in the private sector varies dramatically from one property to the next. It is clear, however, that occupancies among the surveyed properties are low and that many operators are having difficulty making the pure game viewing experience pay.

In sum, it appears that live game sales, hunting, and game viewing are all generating significant revenues in the core study area. The KZN Wildlife areas play a dominant role in revenues generated from game sales, and the private game reserves provide the bulk of the hunting revenues. A direct comparison of market share in game viewing is difficult. But even given the limited number of responses from the sample of private game reserves represented in the Producer Survey—and not considering the large number of accommodation facilities that have no land—the gross revenues of the private properties exceed the total of the three KZN Wildlife reserves (including game sales).

Still, despite the multiple uses of biodiversity resources, many private operations are struggling to break even, and the public reserves themselves—often touted as one of the best examples of making wildlife conservation pay—are far from covering their full costs. Though it certainly is the case that the sources of finance summarized above and detailed in later chapters are helping to pay for conservation, it is hard to make the case that sufficient monies are being generated for additional conservation improvements.

NOTES

1. Specifically, the assessment of public protected areas and private game reserves covers four magisterial districts under the Uthungulu Regional Council: Hlabisa, Ingwavuma, Lower Umfolozi, and Ubombo; and five magisterial districts under the Zululand Regional Council: Mhlabatini, Mtonjaneni, Ngotshe, Nongoma, and Simdlangentsha. Note that references to Zululand do not refer to the area covered by the Zululand Regional Council but to the larger area including Uthungulu (the northern part of which is also known as Maputaland).

2. The districts are Hlabisa, Ingwavuma, Ubombo, Ngotshe, and Enseleni.

3. The survey collected a full set of data on costs and benefits for 12 of 27 PGRs. Useful data were collected for all three of the KZN Wildlife areas, with the exception of nonland fixed asset figures for buildings and other installations for Mkhuze.

4. The share of private game reserves (21 percent vs. 6 percent) may lessen these effects to the extent that these are large commercial operations.

5. The messages and indicators are drawn from the original Ecological Survey by James and Goodman (2001) and the subsequent article by Lindberg, James, and Goodman (chapter 6, this volume).

REFERENCES

Conningarth Consultants. 2002. *Social Accounting Matrix for North Eastern KwaZulu-Natal (RSA). A Report to the World Bank.* Johannesburg, South Africa: Conningarth Consultants.

de la Harpe, R., and W. Charlton-Perkins. No date. *Hluhluwe Umfolozi Park, Great Game Parks of Africa.* South Africa: Struik.

Dennis, N., R. de la Harpe, and B. J. Barker. 1999. *The National Parks and Other Wild Places of Southern Africa.* London: New Holland.

Hughes, G. R. 2001. "The Natal Parks Board Experience in Southern Africa." In T. L. Anderson and A. James, eds., *The Politics and Economics of Park Management.* Lanham, Md.: Rowman & Littlefield.

James, B. M., and G. Creemers. 2000. *Technical Report on Accommodation Database.* Report to the World Bank Research Project on Nature Tourism and Conservation. Cascades, KwaZulu-Natal: Brousse-James & Associates and KZN Wildlife.

James, B. M., and P. S. Goodman. 2001. *Ecological Study.* Report to the World Bank Research Project on Nature Tourism and Conservation. Cascades, KwaZulu-Natal: Brousse-James & Associates and KZN Wildlife.

SATOUR (Tourism South Africa). 1998. *A Survey of South Africa's Foreign Visitor Market.* Pretoria: SATOUR.

Seymour, James. 1998. *KwaZulu-Natal's Domestic Tourism Market: June '98–September '98.* Durban, South Africa: KwaZulu-Natal Tourism Authority.

World Bank. 2001. *The Little Green Data Book 2001.* Washington, D.C.

PART II

MARKETS FOR NATURE TOURISM: DEMAND STUDIES

INTRODUCTION TO PART 2: DEMAND ANALYSES

Kreg Lindberg

An important component of this research project was to understand current demand for nature tourism in the study region, including the characteristics of visitors and the factors that affect their trip decisionmaking. Related goals were to understand what might be done to increase domestic, especially non-White, nature tourism demand, as well as how both domestic and international demand would be affected by policy and managerial changes (particularly changes involving visitor fees). The chapters contained in part 2 all focus on explaining nature tourism demand. Because of the overlap in issues and methods across chapters, background information is presented here.

There is a substantial literature on evaluating demand for outdoor recreation and nature tourism.[1] Many studies focus on estimating consumer surplus (CS), the economic welfare gain that visitors receive from their visit. For example, if a visitor were willing to pay $20 to visit a park but had to pay only $5, then she received a welfare gain of $15. Such evaluations are useful for cost–benefit analyses of a park's contribution to societal welfare. However, this project focused on price-responsiveness—that is, what effect fee increases will have on the number of visitors.

Similar methodologies are utilized, regardless of purpose. In addition, similar predictors are used as independent variables in the models, including: entrance fees, other financial and opportunity costs associated with visitation (such as accommodation and transport), the price of substitutes, site quality (for example, level of congestion), and visitor demographic characteristics. The following sections describe the various methodologies that have been used to estimate demand. Loomis and Walsh (1997) is a good introduction to these methods, which are also discussed in Bockstael, McConnell, and Strand (1991), Freeman (1993), Herriges and Kling (1999), and Shah (1995). Illustrative studies and results from developing countries are also presented, with an additional listing of such studies available in Lindberg and Aylward (1999).

ACTUAL PRICE AND VISITATION (TIME SERIES)

Ideally, demand curves will be estimated by varying the price of the good (in this case a park visit) and observing how many people visit at each price. However, many sites do not charge fees, and those that do rarely adjust their fees sufficiently to estimate a demand curve. Costa Rica has both changed fees and systematically gathered visitation data over several years, and Lindberg and Aylward (1999) illustrated time-series analysis of these data.

An alternative to the time-series approach is a cross-sectional approach that evaluates visitation at a set of parks as a function of price and other causal variables. However, in addition to the problem of limited price variability, it is difficult to measure and control for the numerous variables, such as site quality and proximity to markets, that affect visitation levels across individual sites.

TRAVEL COST METHOD

Because most sites do not price in a market situation, various nonmarket valuation methods have been utilized to evaluate demand. Perhaps the most popular method has been the travel cost method (TCM), which uses expenditure on various trip costs, such as transportation, to trace out a demand curve, from which the value (CS) visitors receive from the destination visit itself can be inferred. Because visitors to a given site may come from a range of origins, their travel distance and travel cost vary, and this variability is used to estimate a demand curve. TCM can be extended to include valuation of quality attributes when data are available on sufficient sites with variability in the attributes of interest.

Many economists prefer revealed preference (RP) approaches like TCM over stated preference (SP) approaches like contingent valuation

(CV), because RP is based on actual behavior. However, though TCM has been applied in the international nature tourism context, the model is not well suited to this context. Individual-level TCM assumes that visitors make several trips to a site in a given period (usually a year). In international nature tourism, it is more likely that visitors will make one trip per lifetime.

In principle, zonal TCM models can be used to overcome this limitation because the dependent variable changes from trips per person per period to trips per population per period, where population is for each of the defined zones (for example, a country or region). However, there is often a problem in defining sufficient relevant zones. Using South Africa as an example, most international nature tourism visitors will come from Europe or North America. Within each of these regions, there is little variability across countries in terms of distance to South Africa. There is greater variability across the two regions, but this only provides two points for estimating the demand curve—in other words, (1) low participation rates and distances between potential origin zones that are much less than distances to the destination limit; and (2) TCM's applicability in international, and especially intercontinental, nature tourism.

These concerns are complemented by a range of additional assumptions, and violation of these assumptions may significantly affect estimates. First, TCM assumes that travel costs are accurately identified. Some costs are relatively easy to estimate, but others are much more difficult. The opportunity cost of time has been a particularly problematic issue for TCM. Second, TCM is easiest to apply when there is a single destination. In cases with multiple destinations, which are common in international tourism, demand must be allocated across the destinations. Third, the demand curve must be accurately estimated, and this includes measuring and including the cost of substitutes. Fourth, TCM assumes that visitors will react to all prices in the same manner, and this is unlikely in the international tourism context. For example, because of past experience about what is "normal" or "reasonable," visitors may react quite differently to an entrance fee increase of $200 than to an airfare increase of $200. Though the data needed for TCM analyses were collected as part of the expenditure survey noted in chapter 9, such analyses are not presented in this volume.

CONTINGENT VALUATION

The contingent valuation method uses responses to hypothetical fee scenarios to determine maximum visitor willingness-to-pay (WTP) for a visit. For example, a dichotomous choice CV question would ask visitors whether they would have come to the site if the entry fee had been $X, with X being varied across respondents. An equivalent open-ended CV question would be, "What is the maximum amount you would be willing to pay to visit this site?" Because of its hypothetical nature, CV is quite flexible and can be used to value site attributes. However, the hypothetical nature also makes it susceptible to criticism. Many early criticisms (such as starting point bias for iterative bidding formats) have been overcome by refining CV methods. Nonetheless, several concerns exist in both theory and practice.

First, above all there is the concern that respondents will not take the task seriously and will not reply in a manner consistent with their actual behavior (hypothetical bias). For example, respondents may pay less attention to budget constraints in the context of a CV question than in the context of an actual purchase. Second, respondents may perceive an incentive to report lower WTP or more price-responsiveness than would actually be the case in an effort to avoid having to pay higher fees (strategic bias). Strategic bias may occur less in international nature tourism than in domestic recreation because visitors are less likely to return to the same destination and thus to have an incentive to understate WTP. Moreover, strategic and hypothetical bias may work in opposite directions, possibly offsetting each other. However, the net effect is uncertain. Third, in practice the CV scenario may present an unclear or inaccurate market. For example, the scenario may elicit views on "appropriate" fees rather than on whether the respondent would cancel a visit if a specific higher fee were charged. In addition, the scenario may state or infer that the site may no longer exist if the fee is not paid, thereby eliciting WTP for non—use values (that is, existence value) as well as use value (Echeverría, Hanrahan, and Solórzano 1995). This provides an inaccurate measure of visitor response to price changes; that is, the appropriate market is the right to visit the park, not the existence of the park. Because responses will depend on the information provided, this information must be as realistic as possible.

Nonetheless, CV also offers benefits relative to TCM in the present context. For instance, the explicit focus on price in its likely format (for example, increase in entrance fee or tour cost) allows CV to overcome some of the weaknesses of TCM, and in those respects may give more valid estimates of price-responsiveness. For example, specification of a high entrance fee in a CV scenario may lead respondents to consider whether substitutes are available or whether the fee is "fair."

SITE SELECTION AND PARTICIPATION

Like TCM, site selection (SS) models are based on actual trip behavior, with travel costs being an important independent variable. However, TCM focuses on demand over a period of time (such as trips per year), whereas SS and other approaches based on the random utility model (RUM) focus on individual choice occasions—the probability that a site is chosen for a given trip is modeled as a function of variables such as the price and quality of that site, the price and quality of competing sites, and demographic variables such as income. This trip-level SS model is typically analyzed using multinomial logit (MNL) or nested logit analysis, and is complemented by a participation (Par) model of number of trips taken per period, analyzed using count data models (for example, Poisson or its negative binomial extension). As with other methods, variations exist. Thus Font (2000) used repeated site selection as an alternative to linked site selection and participation models.

No applications of SS and participation models in the developing-country context were found in the literature, but recent examples from North America include Hausman, Leonard, and McFadden (1995), Kerkvliet and Nowell (2000), and Siderelis and Moore (1998); see Parsons, Jakus, and Tomasi (1999) for a review of four commonly used models.

CHOICE MODELING

Choice modeling (CM) has grown out of conjoint analysis within the transport and marketing fields and can be viewed as a general form of CV.[2] Like the SS approach, CM focuses on individual choices, but in this case using hypothetical sites characterized by specified attributes and levels (specific entrance fee levels, natural qualities, and so forth).

Because it is a stated preference technique, CM suffers from some of the same criticisms that CV does (for example, hypothetical bias). However, it provides richer information than does CV because of the ability to model relationships between several attributes at a time. Relative to CV scenarios, CM scenarios also involve less focus on the price attribute; depending on one's view of actual and ideal consumer behavior, this may be a benefit or a drawback of CM. Further comparison of these two approaches is presented in Boxall and others (1996). As in CV, CM allows evaluation of attributes that are difficult or impossible to measure in RP studies, as well as levels of attributes that fall outside actual ranges and thus cannot be measured in RP (for example, prices higher than those actually charged).

CM is used to estimate the probability that consumers will choose a particular product (for example, will visit a particular park) based on the attributes of that product relative to those of others in the market. Because price can be one of the attributes, these techniques can be used to estimate the responsiveness of visitation levels to price changes.

CM is relatively new, and no applications to developing-country natural area visitation were found in the literature, though Mercer, Zinkhan, and Holmes (1995) used the related conjoint analysis in surveys of domestic and international visitors at Iguassu Falls in Brazil. Boxall and others (1996) have used CM in various North American recreation and tourism settings, such as to estimate the effect of environmental quality changes on recreation moose hunting (see, for example, Huybers and Bennett 2000). CM also can be used to model national-level visitation and its responsiveness to price and quality attributes. For example, Haider and Ewing (1990) used CM to estimate the effect of accommodation size and service level, location (town/rural and proximity to beach), price of trip, and other attributes on market share for Barbados, Cuba, Jamaica, Martinique, and Saint Vincent and the Grenadines.

CONTINGENT BEHAVIOR

The terminology is not fully standardized, so it is worth noting that, as used here, contingent behavior (CB) is defined in contrast to CV. In CV, respondents are asked their maximum WTP for the visit or whether they would make the visit at a stated price. In CB, the response is richer and more nuanced, with respondents being given the option to change the number of trips or the number of days on a given trip. For example, in their "trip response method," Teasley, Bergstrom, and Cordell (1994) asked respondents how many trips they would take to a site at a given price. In their "hypothetical travel cost" analysis, Layman, Boyce, and Criddle (1996) asked respondents how the number of fishing trips would change under alternative fishery management practices (see, for example, Eiswerth and others 2000). In the only developing-country example found in the literature, Chase and others (1998) asked visitors to three national parks in Costa Rica how their itinerary would change (in terms of days spent in each park) in response to entrance fee changes.

Analysis of CB is based on trips being a function of price, other site characteristics, and demographic characteristics. Because CB typically includes both RP data (such as current number of trips or days at each site) and SP data (such as number given a hypothetical scenario), it combines some of the desirable features of both approaches. In addition, it may be easier for visitors to report their intended changes in behavior than to identify their WTP for a site. Loomis (1993) found that responses to intended behavior questions were both valid and reliable.

METHODS USED IN THE SOUTH AFRICA PROJECT

The following table illustrates the approaches used in the analyses presented in the chapters in part 2. Note that the site selection model in chapter 2 provides data utilized in the participation model in chapter 5.

Chapter	Methods Used			
	CV	CB	CM	SS and Par
2. Household survey			✓	SS
3. Visitor survey	✓	✓		
4. Origin market survey			✓	SS
5. Latent market				Par

PRICE-RESPONSIVENESS RESULTS FROM OTHER STUDIES

It should be stressed that price responsiveness can be highly variable, depending on the characteristics of the site and the visitors who travel to it. However, research suggests that visitation to natural areas generally is price inelastic—that is, the number of visits will decrease by less, in percentage terms, than the price increase. Nonetheless it is recognized that even modest responses may be important, especially where tourism is seen as a local economic development option.

In the United States, research (summarized by Loomis and Walsh 1997) and anecdotal evaluation of the U.S. Department of the Interior and U.S. Department of Agriculture Recreation Fee Demonstration Program (2001) indicate that nature tourism visitors in that country are not highly price responsive. In Australia, Knapman and Stoeckl (1995) used travel cost analysis to estimate elasticities for Kakadu National Park and Hinchinbrook Island National Park, with an elasticity of –0.014 being illustrative for the former and –0.0015 for the latter. They noted that Australian empirical studies typically generate elasticity estimates of –0.033 to –0.40.

There are relatively few estimates of price-responsiveness for developing country natural areas. In a study of wildlife viewing demand at Lake Nakuru National Park, Kenya, Navrud and Mungatana (1994) estimated price elasticities of –0.17 to –0.84 for foreigners and –1.77 to –2.99 for residents. The greater price responsiveness for residents is likely caused by their lower income levels, which make them more sensitive to price changes.

Chase and others (1998) used contingent behavior models to estimate price elasticities for international tourism at three national parks in Costa Rica. These estimates were –2.87 for Volcán Poás, –1.05 for Volcán Irazú, and –0.96 for Manuel Antonio. Note that one of these indicates significant price-responsiveness and the other two indicate roughly unitary elasticity (neither elastic nor inelastic). However, in an analysis using actual price and visitation data for the same parks, Lindberg and Aylward (1999) found elasticity values of –0.0513, –0.296, and –0.238, respectively. There may be several explanations for the difference, with perhaps the most likely being that visitors had full information on fees at the decision point (time of survey) in the contingent behavior study, although in reality most of the visitors apparently did not know the actual entrance fee at the point of their decision to visit the parks. Chase (1995) found that almost three-quarters of visitors did not know the fee at the time of arrival at the respective park. By this point, visitors had made a psychological, financial, and time commitment to their visits— these were sunk costs in reality, but variable costs in the survey by Chase and others (1998). Moreover, substitutes were clear to respondents in the survey by Chase and others, but presumably were less apparent or available to visitors faced with a higher-than-expected fee on arrival.

Especially in the international context, the choices of other actors, and particularly of tour operators, can play an important role. To some degree, operators probably behave like individual visitors. For instance, they may be unlikely to shift away from unique sites in the face of a price rise. However, the decisionmaking process of operators may diverge from that of visitors, in part because of greater information about substitutes. For example, in response to a contingent valuation survey a visitor may report a willingness to pay an additional $20 in tour costs to visit the site in question. However, if the tour operator believes that a different site is a good substitute and will not be raising fees, the operator may shift the tours to that site.

NOTES

1. As used here, nature tourism refers to all park visitation, including visitation that is elsewhere referred to as outdoor recreation.
2. Choice modeling can refer to analysis of actual or hypothetical (scenario-based) choices. As used here, choice modeling refers to analysis of hypothetical choices. Other terms have also been used to refer to this type of analysis, including conjoint, stated choice, choice experiment, or experimental choice modeling.

REFERENCES

Bockstael, N. E., K. E. McConnell, and I. E. Strand. 1991. "Recreation." In J. B. Braden and C. D. Kolstad, eds., *Measuring the Demand for Environmental Quality.* Amsterdam: North Holland.

Boxall, P. C., W. L. Adamowicz, J. Swait, M. Williams, and J. Louviere 1996. "A Comparison of Stated Preference Methods for Environmental Valuation." *Ecological Economics* 18:243–53.

Chase, L. 1995. Cuotas de Entrada a los Parques Nacionales en Costa Rica. Unpublished manuscript.

Chase, L. C., D. R. Lee, W. D. Schulze, and D. J. Anderson. 1998. "Ecotourism Demand and Differential Pricing of National Park Access in Costa Rica." *Land Economics* 74:466–82.

Echeverría, J., M. Hanrahan, and R. Solórzano. 1995. "Valuation of Non-priced Amenities Provided by the Biological Resources within the Monteverde Cloud Forest Preserve, Costa Rica. *Ecological Economics* 13:43–52.

Eiswerth, M. E., J. Englin, E. Fadali, and W. D. Shaw. 2000. "The Value of Water Levels in Water-based Recreation: A Pooled Revealed Preference/Contingent Behavior Model." *Water Resources Research* 36(4):1079–86.

Font, A. R. 2000. "Mass Tourism and the Demand for Protected Natural Areas: A Travel Cost Approach." *Journal of Environmental Economics and Management* 39:97–116.

Freeman, A. M. 1993. *The Measurement of Environmental and Resource Values: Theory and Methods.* Washington, D.C.: Resources for the Future.

Haider, W., and G. O. Ewing. 1990. "A Model of Tourist Choices of Hypothetical Caribbean Destinations." *Leisure Sciences* 12:33–47.

Hausman, J. A., G. K. Leonard, and D. McFadden. 1995. "A Utility-Consistent, Combined Discrete Choice and Count Data Model: Assessing Recreational Use Losses Due to Natural Resource Damage." *Journal of Public Economics* 56:1–30.

Herriges, J. A., and C. L. Kling, eds. 1999. *Valuing the Environment Using Recreation Demand Models.* Aldershot, U.K.: Edward Elgar.

Huybers, T., and J. Bennett. 2000. "Impact of the Environment on Holiday Destination Choices of Prospective UK Tourists: Implications for Tropical North Queensland." *Tourism Economics* 6(1):21–46.

Kerkvliet, J., and C. Nowell. 2000. "Tools for Recreation Management in Parks: The Case of the Greater Yellowstone's Blue-Ribbon Fishery." *Ecological Economics* 34:89–100.

Knapman, B., and N. Stoeckl. 1995. "Recreation User Fees: An Australian Empirical Investigation." *Tourism Economics* 1(1):5–15.

Layman, R. C., J. R. Boyce, and K. R. Criddle. 1996. "Economics Valuation of the Chinook Salmon Sport Fishery of the Gulkana River, Alaska, under Current and Alternate Management Plans." *Land Economics* 72(1):113–28.

Lindberg, K., and B. Aylward. 1999. "Price Responsiveness in the Developing Country Nature Tourism Context: Review and Costa Rican Case Study." *Journal of Leisure Research* 31(3):281–99.

Loomis, J. 1993. "An Investigation into the Reliability of Intended Visitation Behavior." *Environmental and Resource Economics* 3:183–91.

Loomis, J. B., and R. G. Walsh. 1997. *Recreation Economic Decisions: Comparing Benefits and Costs,* 2nd ed. State College, Pa.: Venture.

Mercer, D. E., F. C. Zinkhan, and T. P. Holmes. 1995. "Assessing Forests for Their Ecotourism Potential: A Case Study of the Atlantic Coastal Rain Forests in

Southeastern Brazil." SCFER Working Paper 77. Research Triangle Park, N.C.: Southeastern Center for Forest Economics Research.

Navrud, S., and E. D. Mungatana. 1994. "Environmental Valuation in Developing Countries: The Recreational Value of Wildlife Viewing." *Ecological Economics* 11:135–51.

Parsons, G. R., P. M. Jakus, and T. Tomasi. 1999. "A Comparison of Welfare Estimates from Four Models for Linking Seasonal Recreational Trips to Multinomial Models of Site Choice." *Journal of Environmental Economics and Management* 38:143–57.

Shah, A. 1995. *The Economics of Third World National Parks: Issues of Tourism and Environmental Management.* Aldershot, U.K.: Edward Edgar.

Siderelis, C., and R. L. Moore. 1998. "Recreation Demand and the Influence of Site Preference Variables." *Journal of Leisure Research* 30(3):301–18.

Teasley, R. J., J. C. Bergstrom, and H. K. Cordell. 1994. "Estimating Revenue-Capture Potential Associated with Public Area Recreation." *Journal of Agricultural and Resource Economics* 19(1):89–101.

U.S. Department of the Interior and U.S. Department of Agriculture. 2001. *Recreation Fee Demonstration Program: Progress Report to Congress Fiscal Year 2000.* Washington, D.C.

CHAPTER 2

THE INTERNAL MARKET FOR NATURE TOURISM IN SOUTH AFRICA

A Household Survey

Kreg Lindberg

M any countries and subnational regions conduct analyses of their domestic or inbound international tourism markets. For example, Seymour (1998) provided an overview of the characteristics and extent of the KwaZulu-Natal (KZN) domestic tourism market. In addition, analyses of the nature or ecotourism market segment increasingly are being conducted, although largely with a focus on outbound markets in the United States and Europe (for example, World Tourism Organization 2002). Less common are analyses of the domestic nature tourism market, a market that in many countries is critical to the financial and political success of protected areas.

This chapter provides an analysis of the South African domestic nature tourism market, based on a survey of households in KwaZulu-Natal and Gauteng. It provides data on market and trip characteristics and how demand would be affected by policy changes such as a fee increase. It should be read in conjunction with the domestic visitor component of chapter 3 and with chapter 5. These provide, respectively, additional detail on those traveling to nature reserves in the study region (as well as to Kruger National Park) and richer information on why some residents do not travel to nature reserves.

After a brief description of the survey versions used, the chapter discusses recent and ideal trips for respondents who have not traveled to nature reserves in the past three years, followed by ratings of characteristics in reserve choice for past and likely future reserve visitors. This is followed by an analysis of recent trips to nature reserves, including associated expenditures. These descriptive sections are followed by demand analyses using site selection and choice modeling methodologies. Information on sampling, survey administration, respondent demographic characteristics, and additional results are presented in appendixes to this chapter.[1]

SURVEY VERSIONS

Because some residents visit reserves and others do not, three versions of the survey questionnaire were developed to cater to differences in past and intended future visitation behavior. The version completed by each resident was determined by responses to initial "screener" questions. Respondents (residents completing the questionnaire) were asked whether they "have made any trips to game or nature reserves in South Africa or neighboring countries during the past three years." Game or nature reserves were defined as follows:

> By trips to game or nature reserves we mean travel to public or private natural areas involving at least one overnight stay and a primary motivation being to view wildlife, enjoy scenic landscapes, or hunt. This does not include visits to municipal parks or going to dams for boating, swimming, or other water sports, nor does it include day visits to reserves.

If the response was "yes," respondents completed the questionnaire for Past visitors. If the response was "no," respondents were asked: "Would you say it is likely or unlikely that you will make such a trip in the next three years?" If the response to this was "yes," respondents completed the Likely future visitor questionnaire. If the response was "no," respondents completed the Unlikely future trip questionnaire. The average completion time, in minutes, for each version was 26 (Past), 18 (Likely), and 12 (Unlikely). The logic of the screener survey and version completed is shown graphically in figure 2.1. For the remainder of the chapter, "nature reserves" (or simply "reserves") includes game reserves, and travel to reserves is referred to as nature tourism.

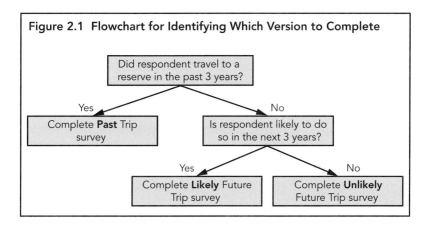

Figure 2.1 Flowchart for Identifying Which Version to Complete

CHARACTERISTICS OF THE INTERNAL DEMAND FOR NATURE TOURISM

This section presents descriptive statistics that characterize the past or intended behavior of the respondents in the survey with respect to nature tourism activities.

Recent and Ideal Trips: Likely and Unlikely Future Survey

In order to better understand the travel behavior of residents who have not recently visited reserves, respondents were asked about ideal trips and recent nonbusiness travel. Respondents in the Likely and Unlikely groups were posed this hypothetical question: "If you had unlimited time and money to do whatever you wanted on your next holiday, (1) what would you do? (2) where would you do it? and (3) with whom?" The purpose of this question was to see if people were even considering nature-oriented destinations. Table 2.1 gives the percentages in each group who would engage in nature tourism activities in South Africa or elsewhere (all tables in this chapter are based on data from the household survey).

The results indicate that many respondents are thinking of nature tourism trips, even if they are not taking them. Almost a quarter (22 percent) of those who have not recently gone or intend to go to reserves in the near future report that such travel would nonetheless be part of their "dream trip." This may be an underestimate because dream

Table 2.1 Ideal Trips—Nature Tourism in South Africa and Elsewhere (percent)

Group	In South Africa	Elsewhere in Africa	Elsewhere in the world	Total
Unlikely	16	3	3	22
Likely	23	3	1	27

Source: Data from the Household Survey.

trips were classified as oriented toward nature tourism only when the response specifically indicated this.

These trips would involve the following travel partners (largest three categories, multiple responses allowed, in percent):

Unlikely future visitor
Wife/husband	45
Children	32
Immediate family	22

Likely future visitor
Wife/husband	48
Children	31
Immediate family	24

Such travel clearly would be strongly family oriented.

When asked, "What trips have you undertaken for recreation (non-business trips) in the year 2000?" the reported destinations are as follows:

Unlikely future visitor (in percent; 46 percent took trips in 2000):
Northeastern KZN	7
Natal Midlands and Drakensberg	14
Natal North Coast	9
Natal South Coast	28
Gauteng	14
Mpumalanga / Northern Province	7
Western Cape	14
Eastern Cape	7

Likely future visitor (in percent; 67 percent took trips in 2000):
Northeastern KZN	10
Natal Midlands and Drakensberg	17
Natal North Coast	7
Natal South Coast	20
Gauteng	10
Mpumalanga / Northern Province	9
Western Cape	17
Rest of South Africa	6

In terms of duration, the majority in both surveys reported one to five days. In terms of motivation, the two most frequent categories were (in percent):

Unlikely future visitor
Visit family or friends 62
Holiday, relaxation 57

Likely future visitor
Visit family or friends 52
Holiday, relaxation 62

Travel to Nature Reserves

Most Unlikely and Likely future visitors have been to a nature reserve, though not in the past three years. First visits to reserves, for those who have been, are shown in table 2.2. These results suggest that experience at reserves at an early age helps lead to reserve visitation as adults. Respondents were asked additional questions to better understand non-visitation.

Unlikely Future Visitors

Those who had been to a reserve were asked: "Is there a reason why you have not gone to a reserve in the past three years and do not plan to go in the future?" Responses with at least 10 percent are (in percent, with multiple responses allowed):

Financial constraints 35
Time constraint 19
Parks too expensive / geared for foreigners 11

Table 2.2 First Visits to Nature Reserves, by Survey Version (percent)

Age of visitor (years)	Unlikely (59% have been)	Likely (78% have been)	Past (100% have been)
1–10	26	45	46
11–17	26	23	18
18 or older	48	33	35

Those who had not been to a reserve were asked: "Have you ever considered going to game or nature reserves, but decided against it or have you never considered such a trip?" Responses were (in percent):

Decided against it	14
Never considered it	86

Those deciding against were asked why. Of the 24 respondents in this category, 9 reported financial constraints, 5 reported family responsibilities, and 3 reported that the parks are too expensive. Those who never considered it were asked why. Responses were (in percent, with multiple responses allowed):

Financial constraints	39
Not interested in the parks / afraid of animals	24
Never thought about it	20
Lack of advertising	17
Time constraints	7

When asked, "What can the managers of South Africa's game and nature reserves do to make them more attractive to you as a place to visit?" responses with at least 10 percent were as follows (in percent, with multiple responses allowed):

Reduce cost / provide discounted rates	31
Advertise more / inform us about reserves more	21
Nothing	20

These results indicate that financial constraints are the major consideration for nonvisitation. Though one aspect is transport availability and cost, on-site costs (entrance fees and accommodation) also play a role.

To provide an indication of the general level of awareness of nature reserves, respondents in the Unlikely category were asked to name two reserves in KZN and elsewhere in South Africa. In the case of KZN reserves, 263 people (63 percent) named at least one and 121 people (29 percent) named two. The most commonly reported reserves were (in percent):

Hluhluwe-Umfolozi Park	51
Mkhuzi Game Reserve	11
Ithala Game Reserve	8
Saint Lucia Wetlands	7

When asked to name two reserves in the rest of South Africa, 322 people (77 percent) could name at least one and 122 (29 percent) could name two. The most commonly reported reserves were (in percent):

Kruger National Park	94
Pilanesberg National Park	8
Addo Elephant Park	6
Kalahari Gemsbok National Park	5

Given that more than half of the nonvisitors (Unlikely respondents) have been to a reserve at least once, 63 percent could name at least one reserve in KZN (the figure was 70 percent for those living in KZN), and even more could name at least one reserve nationally, lack of awareness about the existence of reserves does not seem to be a constraint on participation among this segment of society. However, as noted in chapter 5, there may be a lack of the more detailed information necessary to facilitate visitation, and awareness can vary across race.

Likely Future Visitors

Respondents in the Likely category were asked: "I'd like to learn more about why you've not traveled to game or nature reserves in the past three years but plan to go in the future. Can you tell me what has changed such that you now consider going to such a reserve?" Replies with at least 10 percent were (in percent, with multiple responses allowed):

Financial constraints	31
Time constraints	29
Business time constraints	10

Again, financial constraints are clear, with time constraints also playing a major role.

Respondents were then asked if they had any specific reserves in mind for their future trip; 77 percent did and 23 percent did not. Of those who did, the following reserves were considered (in percent, with multiple responses allowed):

Kruger National Park	54
Hluhluwe-Umfolozi Reserve	15
Natal-Drakensberg Park	10
Pilanesberg National Park	7

Respondents were asked why they consider this or these specific reserves(s) and not others. Replies with at least 10 percent were (in percent, with multiple responses allowed):

Well-known reserve / was recommended	22
New experience / never been there before	16
Close to home, local, and convenient	16
Wide range of animals	13
Enjoy animals	12
Beautiful scenery and nature	10

Rating of Characteristics in Reserve Choice: Likely Future and Past Visitors

Respondents were asked to rate the importance of the following 14 characteristics in the context of deciding (1) "which reserves to visit on a future trip" for Likely respondents, and (2) "which reserves they actually visited" for Past respondents. A scale of 1 (not at all important) to 5 (very important) was used:

1. Likelihood of seeing the Big Five

2. Likelihood of seeing a wide range of birdlife

3. Likelihood of seeing a wide range of animal species

4. Likelihood of seeing beautiful scenery

5. How positive your past visits to the reserve have been

6. How positive recommendations have been from other sources, including friends, family, travel agents, and guidebooks

7. The quality of tourism facilities and services at the reserve, including accommodation, guides, and roads

8. The number of other people you are likely to encounter in the reserve (crowdedness)

9. The small number of other people you are likely to encounter in the reserve (lack of other people)

[*Note:* The intended edits to the wording of items 8 and 9 were not made prior to final survey administration, with the result that the items probably do not capture well the intended meaning, and should be interpreted with caution.]

10. Travel time to the reserve

11. The cost of travel to the reserve

12. The cost of entrance fees charged at the reserve

13. The cost of accommodation at the reserve

14. The likelihood of contracting malaria or other diseases while at the reserve.

The mean (average) ratings for each item are shown in figures 2.2 and 2.3. For Likely future visitors, past visits was the least important item,

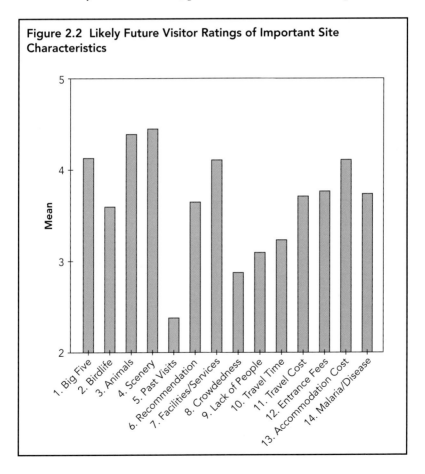

Figure 2.2 Likely Future Visitor Ratings of Important Site Characteristics

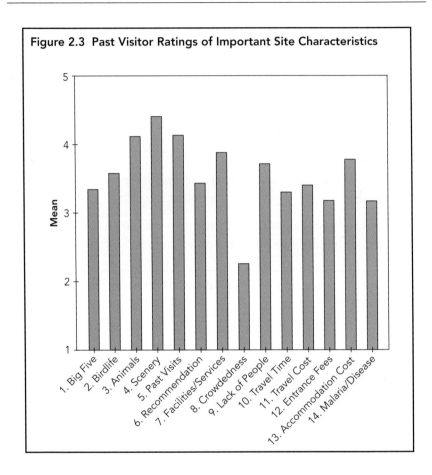

Figure 2.3 Past Visitor Ratings of Important Site Characteristics

while beautiful scenery, a wide range of animals, seeing the Big Five species, quality of facilities, and accommodation cost were the most important. For Past visitors, the importance of past visits is clearly much higher, while the importance of seeing the Big Five is lower, and crowdedness is much lower (keeping in mind that this item may not have been clear). Beautiful scenery, a wide range of animals, and accommodation cost remain important.

However, these averages can hide important variability across individuals. For example, for some people the Big Five may have been the most important characteristic, while for others it may not be at all important. Full distributions for the combined "importance data" are given in appendix 2-C.

When asked if there were "other considerations that would be important in your decision about which reserves to visit," 61 Likely future visitors noted one or more of the following (in percent):

Safety and security in park (for example, crime)	23
Good service / hospitality and maintenance of park	13
Good clean camping facilities	10
Security from wild animals	7
Good information facilities / promote the reserves	7
Transport should be provided for viewing animals	7

Past visitors noted one or more of the following:

Close to home, local, and convenient	21
Been before / traditional holiday venue	13
Best/favorite reserve	9
Well-known reserve / was recommended	9
Was invited / organized by someone else	8

Travel to Nature Reserves: Past Visitors

During the past three years, respondents in the Past category took the following number of trips that included visits to at least one nature reserve (all trips involved at least one overnight away from home; in percent):

1 trip	54
2 trips	14
3 trips	6
4 trips	4
5 trips	3
6 trips	5
7 or more trips	14

In the next section of the survey, detailed information was gathered regarding the respondent's most recent trip. For those who took more than one trip during the past three years, details were also collected on the second most recent trip. The combined information is used in the site selection evaluation discussed below, but selected results are presented here—the following represent combined responses to the first and second trip (if applicable).

Respondents were asked why they made the trip, in an open-ended format, and responses fell into the following categories (in percent):

Peace and quiet, relaxation, escape city	21
Holiday or vacation	20
Went to see friends or family / was invited	16
Love nature and the scenery	14
To see animals and the Big Five	14
To visit a specific park	9
Work-related activities	9
Fishing, hunting, diving	6
Been before, favorite place, was recommended	6
Hiking trails, night drives, 4×4 driving	5
Was in the area, touring the area	5
Have timeshare or own accommodation there	5

When asked which of the following categories was the prime motivation for the trip, responses were (in percent):

Visiting specific game or nature reserve	71
Visiting friends or relatives	11
Leisure, holiday	9
Business	9

Of those who were motivated to visit a specific reserve, the following were identified as the particular reserves that motivated the respondent (in percent):

Kruger National Park	28
Natal-Drakensberg Park	13
Hluhluwe-Umfolozi Reserve	12
Greater Saint Lucia Wetlands Park	10
Pilanesberg National Park	6

The distribution of trip length was (in percent):

2 days	13
3 days	24
4 days	17
5 days	9
6 days	2
7 days	13
8 or more days	21

The distribution of numbers of people in the party was (in percent):

1 person	2
2 people	23
3 people	7
4 people	27
5 people	10
6 people	8
More than 6 people	23

The distribution of total trip costs was (in percent):

Less than R1,000	19
R1,000–1,999	17
R2,000–4,999	26
R5,000–9,999	13
R10,000 or more	11

The distribution of transport costs was (in percent):

Less than R250	26
R250–499	21
R500–999	22
R1,000 or more	15

Sixty-four percent of respondents chose which reserves to visit themselves, whereas 36 percent reported that the reserves were chosen by someone else. When asked why they selected the reserves they visited, rather than others, replies were (in percent):

Close to home, local, and convenient	21
Been before / traditional holiday venue	13
Best/favorite reserve	9
Well-known reserve / was recommended	9
Was invited / organized by someone else	8
Have timeshare or own accommodation there	7
Beautiful scenery and nature	7
Peaceful, tranquil, uncrowded	7
Good hiking trails, night drives, and so on	6
New experience / never been there before	6
Working in the reserve/area	6
Fishing, hunting, diving	5
Was touring the area	5

Trip, Accommodation, and Entrance Fee Costs: Past Visitors

This section presents information on the costs associated with visiting reserves, based on responses in the Past trip survey. The first part of the section describes the data and how they were treated, whereas table 2.3 shows average costs across reserves based on analysis of this data.

A total of 426 reserve visits, made in the course of 374 trips, was recorded for the 258 respondents in the Past trip survey. Approximately 140 reserves are represented in the sample. However, these visits were not evenly spread; 384 (90 percent) of the 426 were made to the 39 reserves that were visited at least twice. These 39 are shown in table 2.3. The remaining reserves were excluded from this analysis. In the case of neighboring countries and "all other private reserves in NE KZN," specific reserves were not recorded, so an indicative reserve, such as Hwange in the case of Zimbabwe, was used for the site selection analysis in the next section. Likewise, for large parks such as Kruger, a specific location was used to calculate distances in the next section. These locations are shown in parentheses in table 2.3.

Of the original 426 trips, 42 (10 percent) involved multiple destinations—the respondent visited at least two reserves during the trip. Six reserve combinations occurred at least twice (in some cases representing only one respondent who visited the same combination twice), and data for these are presented in table 2.3.

Table 2.3 lists visit frequency, entrance fees, accommodation costs, and average total trip cost (including travel, accommodation, and food). Respondents who had a park pass recorded an entrance fee paid of 0 because the individual visit did not cost anything. Accommodation cost is presented for lodging inside the reserve, outside the reserve, and combined (average of the two, computed for each observation). If there was no charge (for example, timeshare or stayed with friends), a value of 0 was recorded. If accommodation was part of a package, a missing value was recorded, which does not affect the averages.

Entrance fee and accommodation cost were collected at the reserve level, so their values for multiple destination trips are simply averages across reserves, weighted by number of days (these values are not presented in table 2.3 but are utilized in the analysis below). Total trip cost was collected only at the trip level. Its values for individual reserves are based on trips involving only those reserves, and values for multiple destination trips are only for those trips.

Table 2.3 Visit Frequency and Average Costs per Person per Day across Reserves

Park	Visit frequency (percent)	Entrance fees (rand)	Accommodation (rand)			Trip total (rand)
			Inside	Outside	Combined	
All parks	100	24	135	119	129	185
Kruger National Park (Skukuza)	27.1	43	143	163	148	243
Ukhahlamba-Drakensberg Park (Giants Castle)	14.6	9	102	35	81	107
Hluhluwe-Umfolozi Park	10.8	28	188	123	176	205
Pilanesberg National Park	5.8	26	108	135	116	210
Greater Saint Lucia Wetlands Park (Saint Lucia Estuary)	7.8	10	64	136	84	116
Mabula Lodge	2.4	29	242		242	321
Mbalingwe	2.4	18	79		79	100
Pongola Game Reserve (Biosphere)	2.0	11	119		119	215
Hluhluwe + Greater Saint Lucia	2.0					207
Ithala Game Reserve	1.7	24	143		168	94
Marloth Park	1.7	0	38	0	15	106
Sabi Sabi Game Reserve	1.4	46	55	55	55	100
Zwartkloof	1.4	5	0		0	40
Bonamanzi Game Park	1.0	0	259		259	171
Kruger + Blydepoort	1.0					195
Kruger + Sabi Sabi	1.0					
Mkhuze Game Reserve	1.0	14	135		101	
Ndumo Game Reserve	1.0	8	145		145	257
Ntuli Nature Reserve	1.0	10	25		25	26

(continued)

Table 2.3 (Continued)

Park	Visit frequency (percent)	Entrance fees (rand)	Accommodation (rand)			Trip total (rand)
			Inside	Outside	Combined	
Other private nature reserve in NE KZN (Iqina)	1.0					
Sondela Nature Reserve (Warmbaths)	1.0	25	40		40	68
Shongweni Resource Reserve	1.0	10			13	44
Augrabies National Park	0.7	20	150		150	150
Blydepoort Nature Reserve	0.7	0	88		88	30
Coleford Nature Reserve	0.7	10	50		50	
Golden Gate National Park	0.7	25				226
Greater Saint Lucia + Ndumo + Tembe	0.7					31
Hluhluwe + Mkhuze	0.7					165
Kalahari Gemsbok National Park (Kgalagadi Transfrontier Park)	0.7	13			155	112
Madikwe	0.7	18	300		300	783
Milemare Nature Reserve	0.7					15
Swaziland Nature Reserves (Hlane)	0.7	20	163		163	85
Tala Game Ranch	0.7	28	108		108	
Zimbabwe Game Reserves (Hwange)	0.3		20		20	48
Tsitsikama Forest National Park	0.3	30				
Phinda Game Reserve	0.3	0	233		233	
Mpenjati Nature Reserve	0.3	28		175	408	
Botswana Game Reserves (Chobe)	0.3		120		120	
Bhakabung Nature Reserve (Pilanesberg)	0.3	0	400		400	

Mkhuze Falls	0.3			
Addo Elephant Park		18	415	8
Tembe Elephant Park		0	0	0
Oribi Gorge		8		175	0
Namibian Reserves (Etosha)		10	137	175	123
Oribi + Mapenyati				74	100

Note: All figures are per person per day and are based on the recollection of respondents. Therefore, it is to be expected that some error is contained in the figures, as well as variability due to differences in party size, type of accommodation, and other factors. Nonetheless, the figures provide an indication of amounts spent in general, as well as across reserves. The figures are also used in the analysis presented in the next section of the text.

The number of observations that led to these averages varied widely across parks, with Kruger generating by far the most observations and with several parks generating only one or two observations. Results are presented only for those parks with at least two observations for the variable, and blank cells indicate a reserve with only one or no observations. (In some cases, there was only one value for "inside" or "outside" accommodation, but two or more values for "combined." This can lead to a value not being shown in the former two columns, but having a substantial effect on the latter column. For example, in the case of Mpenjati, there was one observation, with a value of R875 per person per night, for "inside," and this substantially affected the "combined" value.) The "All parks" average is based on all data for the 39 parks (including those with only one observation), but it does not include data from other parks. All figures are in rand; using the exchange rate for February 20, 2001 (during the middle of the survey period), the figures can be converted to U.S. dollars by dividing by 7.7640.

Source: Data from the Household Survey.

Approximately 6 percent of the trips involved total trip lengths that were more than three days greater than the sum of the days spent in individual reserves (three days were treated as travel to and from the reserve). This is one possible cause for total trip costs being less than accommodation costs in some cases. For example, if a respondent spent R100 per night on accommodation while visiting a reserve but did not pay for accommodation while visiting family during additional days, the accommodation cost for the whole trip (and possibly total trip cost) will be less than the accommodation cost in the reserve on a per-person, per-day basis (table 2.3).

Keeping in mind the data limitations, the results shown in table 2.3 indicate that entrance fees average R24 per person per day, with Kruger being above average and parks in the project's study region (Hluhluwe-Umfolozi Park, or HUP; Ithala; Saint Lucia; and Mkhuze) being approximately average or below average. Accommodation inside parks tends to be more expensive than accommodation outside parks.

DEMAND ANALYSIS

This second half of the chapter presents the two models used in demand analysis for the household survey: site selection and choice modeling. Additional information on these methods is presented in the introduction to part 2.

Site Selection Model for Past Visitors

As noted by Loomis (1995), there are four steps in the recreation choice process: (1) whether to participate in an activity, (2) which site to visit if one chooses to participate, (3) how many trips to take to the site, and (4) how long to stay at the site. This section describes a site selection analysis of step 2: which site to visit on a given trip. The related participation analysis from this survey is presented in chapter 5.

Methods and Data

In site selection models, the probability of choosing a particular site from a set of possible sites is modeled as a function of the travel cost and the quality attributes of the various sites. Travel cost is typically based on travel distance between a respondent's home and the reserve, multiplied by cost per mile or kilometer with the assumption that the respondents drive to the sites; in some studies, however, other travel modes are included (for example, Hausman, Leonard, and McFadden 1995 allowed for travel by car, train, commercial plane, float plane, ferry, and boat in their study of the effect of the Exxon Valdez oil spill on recreation in Alaska).

Several aspects of the current data analysis are worth noting. First, the data pertain to trips involving an overnight stay. An overnight stay specifically in a reserve is not required (that is, one could stay at a nearby bed and breakfast), but day trips from home are excluded. Second, 54 percent of the sample took one trip and 14 percent took two in the past three years—these are included here. For the 32 percent of the sample that took three or more trips, only the most recent two are included in the data and analysis.

Third, trips involving travel unrelated to the reserve are included in the original data. For example, if a person visited a reserve as part of a visit to relatives, the trip is in the original data set. However, these trips are not appropriate to include in the site selection model because the trip purpose, and thus cost, is not solely attributable to the reserve visit. Therefore, allowing three days total for travel to and from reserves, the 6 percent of observations in which trip length was greater than sum of days in reserve plus three were deleted from the data (they are included in the figures shown in table 2.3 but are excluded from the site selection analysis).

Fourth, if the trip involved travel to a reserve other than those listed in table 2.3, it was deleted. Multiple destination trips shown in table 2.3 are included, but other multiple destination trips are excluded because of the difficulty of allocating costs across reserves in such trips (Mendelsohn, Peterson, and Johnson 1992). In the case of visits to multiple reserves in the country groupings (for example, to several reserves in Zimbabwe), they are treated as a visit to a single reserve and are included.

Of the original 374 trips, 23 (6 percent) were deleted on the basis of trip length exceeding time in reserves by more than three days, 39 (10 percent of the original) were deleted on the basis of visiting a reserve other than those in table 2.3, 14 (4 percent) were deleted on the basis of being multiple destination trips other than the six in table 2.3, and

3 (1 percent) were deleted because they traveled by plane rather than car. Sixteen respondents traveled primarily by bus. These observations were retained in the data set because their reported travel costs did not differ systematically from those calculated for cars. The remaining 295 observations (79 percent) were used for the site selection analysis. As a result of the multiple destination grouping and the above deletions, some parks and park combinations in the full data set were not visited in the modified data set, as indicated in the visit frequency column of table 2.3. This left a total of 40 park choice alternatives, including 5 multiple destination sets.

Road distances between each of the enumerator areas (EAs) and each of the reserves were calculated. These were converted into costs based on rates from the Automobile Association of South Africa. The rate used is R0.772 per kilometer, based on running costs only (fuel, service and repair, and tire costs) and a gasoline engine of 2.0 liters, as of May 2, 2001. Distances were multiplied by two to account for round-trip travel. In the case of multiple destination trips, the cost for the most distant destination was used.

Two sets of variables were created. The first was the set of "calculated" variables comprising (1) total transport cost, based on the conversion above; (2) transport per person per day, which is total transport cost divided by the number of person-days (that is, a family of four traveling for seven days = 28 person-days); (3) fee per person per day, using the average for the site visited; and (4) accommodation per person per day, using the combined average for the site visited.[2]

The second set was the "reported" variables. The variable types were the same as for "calculated," but reported data were used, when available, for the reserve actually visited. Such data were available in 74 percent, 74 percent, and 75 percent of the sample for transport, fee, and accommodation costs, respectively. For multiple destination sites, the fee and accommodation values were a weighted average across reserves based on number of days spent in each.

Results

Initial models were estimated using both sets of variables. The reported variables generated a better model fit, so they were used for further analysis. Likewise, the variable for transport cost per person per day generated a better model fit than did total transport cost, so it was used for further analysis.[3] The coefficients for both accommodation and entrance fee costs were nonsignificant, even after including interaction terms to allow responsiveness to vary across selected reserves (for example, Kruger and HUP). Therefore, they were removed.

A model with a bus transport cost interaction term was estimated to allow for differing sensitivity to distance for those traveling by car versus bus. The variable was marginally significant ($p = 0.099$) and positive, indicating less sensitivity to distance for bus passengers than for the overall data set. This is consistent with bus travel being less expensive than car travel, but there was negligible change to the transport cost coefficient. Therefore, the interaction variable was not included in the model results shown below.

The final model contains transport cost and a set of dummy variables for the reserves. The model had an adjusted pseudo-R^2 of 0.12 (relative to constants only) and was significant at 0.00000. The results are shown in table 2.4.

Of the three cost variables, only transport cost was significant, which suggests that neither accommodation cost nor entrance fee levels affected the probability of respondents visiting a given reserve. This may be a result of greater variability in transport costs than in accommodation costs and, especially, entrance fee costs. As noted below in the context of the choice model, accommodation price may also act as a signal of quality. Thus, price increases in the low range may lead to greater probability of selection (positive sign), assuming that the quality increase is commensurate with the price increase, whereas price increases in the mid to high range may lead to reduced probability (negative sign). The net effect may be nonsignificance for the variable.

All model results, but especially this conclusion, should be interpreted with caution given that the values for accommodation and fee costs are based on reports from respondents. These reports are susceptible to recall difficulties, as well as to being affected by the characteristics of individual trips (for example, number of persons traveling and type of accommodation utilized). In a very large data set, such characteristics might be expected to "even out" across observations, but this sample is small enough to be affected by potentially idiosyncratic observations.

The transport cost coefficient has a negative coefficient, as expected, and is highly significant. This indicates that the further away a reserve

Table 2.4 Site Selection Model Results

Variable	Coefficient	Significance
Transport cost per person per day (distance)	−0.040	0.000
Reserve variables		
Kruger National Park (Skukuza)	3.765	0.000
Pilanesberg National Park	1.334	0.081
Hluhluwe-Umfolozi Park	2.145	0.003
Ithala Game Reserve	0.593	0.479
Phinda Game Reserve	−1.124	0.359
Ukhahlamba-Drakensberg Park (Giants Castle)	2.039	0.005
Greater Saint Lucia Wetlands Park (Saint Lucia Estuary)	1.909	0.010
Kalahari Gemsbok National Park (Kgalagadi Transfrontier Park)	1.624	0.107
Mkhuze Game Reserve	−0.054	0.953
Blydepoort Nature Reserve	0.248	0.805
Sabi Sabi Game Reserve	0.749	0.388
Zimbabwe Game Reserves (Hwange)	0.995	0.419
Golden Gate National Park	−0.564	0.573
Swaziland Nature Reserves (Hlane)	−0.056	0.955
Tsitsikama Forest National Park	0.680	0.580
Tala Game Ranch	−1.710	0.095
Pongola Game Reserve (Biosphere)	0.717	0.381
Bonamanzi Game Park	−0.119	0.897
Marloth Park	1.018	0.225
Augrabies National Park	1.111	0.273
Mpenjati Nature Reserve	−1.592	0.196
Ndumo Game Reserve	0.322	0.725
Botswana Game Reserves (Chobe)	0.886	0.471
Ntuli Nature Reserve	−1.173	0.211
Sondela Nature Reserve (Warmbaths)	−0.440	0.635
Shongweni Resource Reserve	−1.421	0.133
Coleford Nature Reserve	−0.689	0.493
Milemare Nature Reserve	−0.355	0.723
Bhakabung Nature Reserve (Pilanseberg)	−1.476	0.232
Mabula Lodge	0.773	0.341
Mbalingwe	0.463	0.571
Madikwe	0.070	0.944
Zwartkloof	−0.102	0.908
Other private nature reserve in NE KZN (Iqina)	−0.062	0.946
Mkuze Falls	−1.136	0.354
Kruger + Blydepoort	0.660	0.471
Kruger + Sabi Sabi	0.557	0.543
Hluhluwe + Greater Saint Lucia	0.578	0.480
Hluhluwe + Mkhuze	−0.365	0.715
Greater Saint Lucia + Ndumo + Tembe	Base—no coefficient	

Source: Data from the Household Survey.

is, the more expensive the transport cost, and thus the less likely it will be visited, all else being equal. Of course, "all else" is not equal, because parks vary in the attractiveness of their natural attributes, facilities, and other factors. It was not possible to measure such attributes across parks as part of this project, but the set of dummy variables accounts for unmeasured attributes, as well as the "brand effect." For example, even if Kruger and HUP had exactly the same features, Kruger might be visited more often simply by virtue of its reputation.

The coefficients for each park give an indication of the combined effect of brand and unmeasured attributes. The "base" for the set of parks is the last one—the multiple destination of Greater Saint Lucia, Ndumo, and Tembe. The signs on the coefficients indicate whether a person is more or less likely to visit each of the other 39 parks than to visit the base, holding transport costs constant. Most parks have non-significant (at $p = 0.10$) coefficients, which indicates that they are no more or less attractive than the base park. The following six parks have coefficients that are significantly different from zero: Kruger, Pilanesberg, HUP, Ukhahlamba-Drakensberg, Greater Saint Lucia, and Tala. Of these, only Tala is negative, which indicates that it is less likely to be visited than the base. Kruger has the most positive sign, indicating the strongest combination of features and brand. HUP has the next most positive sign.

The following examples illustrate estimated market share and price responsiveness given the results shown in table 2.4. Enumerator area 16 is Newcastle in KZN. In the data set, 2 (18 percent) of the 11 trips taken by respondents in that EA were to HUP. The average number of person-days for trips from Newcastle was 25. Given this average, travel costs to each of the 40 reserves, and the reserve effects, the estimated HUP market share for Newcastle residents is 7 percent.

EA 23 (Waverley) is in Gauteng, and respondents in this area spent an average of 43 person-days on their trips. Actual visitation to HUP from this EA was 2 (5 percent) of the 37 trips, whereas estimated visitation from the model is 6 percent. As these examples illustrate, model predictions are based on coefficients estimated from the whole sample. Therefore, for individual EAs the model will generate estimates that closely match actual market share in some cases, but less closely match it in others.

Price responsiveness can be estimated by changing the cost value for HUP. Model results indicate that respondents are not responsive to entrance fee levels. However, one might make the assumption that this is because of limitations of the data set (which is possible), and that visitors respond to changes in fee costs in the same way they do to changes in transport costs (a common assumption in economics, though it may not be accurate).

In that case, responsiveness to entrance fees is estimated from modeled responsiveness to transport costs. As is shown in table 2.3, the average reported entrance fee for HUP was R28 per person per day, such that a 50 percent increase would be R14, for a total of R42.[4] Increasing transport costs by this amount in the case of Newcastle led to a 2.0 percent decline in market share (from 7.06 percent to 6.92 percent).

The effect of price changes on participation rates, and thus market size, is presented in chapter 5. Assuming that market size is not substantially affected by a price increase of this magnitude, the percentage change in number of visitors will equal the change in market share. This leads to a price elasticity of $-2/50 = -0.04$. This is quite close to the elasticity value of -0.036 calculated from the contingent behavior model in chapter 3. However, price elasticity for a given park will vary across EAs because of differences in distances to the various reserves; for example, the value for Waverley is $-1.2/50 = -0.024$.

Choice Modeling Evaluation: Likely Future and Past Visitors

As noted in the introduction to part 2, choice modeling (CM) is similar to the site selection approach in that it focuses on site choices, but in this case using hypothetical sites characterized by specified attributes and levels (for example, specific entrance fee levels or natural qualities).

Methods and Data

In the questionnaires given to the Likely future and Past visitors, respondents were presented with choice modeling scenarios. In these scenarios, respondents were asked to choose which of two reserves they would travel to on their next trip—or whether they would choose neither. These scenarios do not reflect specific existing reserves, but rather are hypothetical reserves with specified levels of four attributes: the likelihood of seeing the Big Five, Scenic Beauty, Travel Time, and Daily Accommodation and Fee Cost.

Although the fourth variable combines both accommodation and fee costs, accommodation normally will represent the majority of this cost attribute. A sample scenario and instructions are provided in appendix 2-D. Each respondent was presented four scenarios, and thus made four choices.

Three different levels were used for Big Five and Scenic Beauty: below average, average, and above average. Four different levels were used for travel time and daily cost: 3, 5, 7, and 13 hours, and R50, R150, R250, and R750. By systematically varying these levels across scenarios and observing respondent choices, one can evaluate the effect of each of the attributes using multinomial logit (MNL) analysis.

Results

The resulting model fit the data well, with an adjusted pseudo-R^2 of 0.30 (relative to constants only), which is quite good for such models. In addition, each of the attributes was highly significant, as were some demographic characteristics. Table 2.5 presents variables, coefficients, and significance levels. All variables with a significance level of 0.10 or better were retained. Almost all of the retained variables had levels below 0.05, which is the common standard for significance, and most had levels below 0.01. The variables that were tested in the model, but were not statistically significant, were education, income, gender, number of adults in household, whether African, whether Coloured, whether ever

Table 2.5 Choice Model

Variable	Coefficient	Significance
Constant	−0.40	0.075
Likelihood of seeing Big Five is average	0.76	0.000
Likelihood of seeing Big Five is above average	1.66	0.000
Scenic beauty is average	1.35	0.000
Scenic beauty is above average	2.08	0.000
Travel time of 5 hours	−0.49	0.011
Travel time of 7 hours	−0.93	0.000
Travel time of 13 hours	−1.96	0.000
Daily cost is R150	0.28	0.071
Daily cost is R250	−0.46	0.000
Daily cost is R750	−2.52	0.000
Respondent is Asian	−0.90	0.000
Number of children	0.23	0.000
Age of respondent	0.098	0.051

Source: Data from the Household Survey.

visited a reserve, when first visited a reserve, and how many reserves were visited in the past three years.

The results given in table 2.5 are interpreted as follows (in each case, the interpretation is ceteris paribus—that is, controlling for other variables). For each attribute, the lowest level served as the base, and coefficients show preferences relative to that base. As expected, respondents were more likely to select a reserve where there was an "average" likelihood of seeing the Big Five, relative to one where there was a "below average" likelihood (indicated by the positive sign on the "average" coefficient). Likewise, they were even more likely to choose a reserve with "above average" likelihood. There is a similar effect for scenic beauty. However, the magnitude of the effect is greater, which is consistent with the importance ratings noted above. Increases in travel time lead to decreases in probability of choosing the reserve, as one would expect. For reference, for residents in the surveyed areas driving to a reserve in the vicinity would typically take 2 hours, and it would be common to drive 4 to 5 hours to reserves.

Cost is often modeled as a continuous variable, and a separate model with such a specification led to the expected negative sign on cost. However, specifying cost as a set of dummy variables, with the lowest cost as the base, allows one to identify nonlinearities. In this case, the positive sign for cost = 150 indicates that the jump from R50 to R150 actually leads to an increased probability of the reserve being selected. This coefficient is less significant than others, so it should be interpreted with some caution. Nonetheless, it suggests a signaling effect in which respondents prefer a nonbudget accommodation in order to obtain a desired level of quality (there was no explicit statement in the survey about how quality might vary across price levels, but this presumably was implicit). This interpretation is supported by feedback from interviewers, who received comments from respondents to this effect. It is also consistent with the average accommodation prices shown in table 2.3, especially the value of R135 inside reserves. This positive jump from R50 to R150 is outweighed by cost considerations at higher levels—the R250 accommodation was less preferred than the R50 base option, and there was an even more substantial effect at R750.

The dummy variable for race was relative to a base of Whites, the group with greatest participation. Thus, the negative sign on the Asian variable indicates that Asians are less likely to choose one of the offered reserves than are Whites. Scenarios were only presented to respondents who had gone to a reserve in the past three years or intended to go in the future, so the broader effects of race on participation are not reflected in the model.

The only other significant demographic variables were children and age, with the former indicating that the more children the household has, the greater the chance of going to a reserve. Likewise, the older one is, the greater the chance of going to a reserve.

CM results can be used to estimate the participation probability or "market share" of reserves given a specified set of attribute levels. For example, using the results shown above, as well as the mean values for Asian (mean = 0.0714), children (1.00), and age (2.56 on a category scale), the estimated market share of two generic reserves and the "neither" option (do not go to a reserve) are as shown in table 2.6.

In the base case, reserve features are equal, so market share is equal, and most respondents would go to one of the reserves. Increasing the cost at Reserve 1 actually increases the market share there (holding the features of Reserve 2 constant at base levels) because of the possible "price signaling" effect noted above. It takes market share from both Reserve 2 and the "neither" option.

However, a further increase to R250, and especially to R750, greatly decreases its market share. If Reserve 1 were to charge R750, but have above average levels of Big Five and scenery, its market share would increase, but only marginally to 0.071. In other words, the jump to R750 has a dominant negative effect on quantity demanded, as is also seen in table 2.5.

Table 2.6 Choice Modeling Estimates of Market Share

	Market share across options		
Scenario	Reserve 1	Reserve 2	Neither
Base: both reserves having the same levels as follows: "average" for Big Five and scenery variables, travel time is 7 hours, and daily cost is R50	0.434	0.434	0.131
Daily cost rises to R150 at Reserve 1	0.504	0.381	0.115
Daily cost rises to R250 at Reserve 1	0.326	0.517	0.156
Daily cost rises to R750 at Reserve 1	0.058	0.723	0.219

Source: Data from the Household Survey.

It should be kept in mind that these scenarios were presented only to those who have been to reserves in the past three years or who plan to go in the next three years. As such, it says nothing about those who fall outside these categories. In addition, the reserves were presented in a hypothetical context and with only four attributes to keep respondent burden within reasonable limits. In practice, many other factors may affect reserve choice. Nonetheless, as these figures illustrate, CM can be a useful tool for explaining reserve choice, the factors that affect it, and the relative importance of these factors and their levels.

DISCUSSION

Chapter 5 discusses variation in nature tourism participation across races. The results presented here suggest that most respondents in the sample have at least a superficial awareness of nature reserves, and many have engaged, or would like to engage, in nature tourism.

Once a decision is made regarding whether to participate, the issue becomes one of what considerations affect the choice of which reserve to visit. The combined importance ratings in appendix 2-C indicate that general reserve features, particularly scenery and a wide range of wildlife, are very important. Additional considerations are quality of facilities, accommodation cost, and several characteristics of medium importance, led by the Big Five.

This information is complemented by open-ended replies to questions about why specific reserves have been considered or visited. Responses indicate the importance of recommendations and reputation, novelty, convenience to home, and past visits, with features of the reserves themselves (such as a wide range of animals) coming next in importance.

Of the three cost items evaluated in the importance ratings (travel cost, entrance fees, and accommodation cost), accommodation was rated as most important. However, only travel cost was statistically significant in the site selection model. The CM model may help explain this result. One would normally expect an increase in cost to lead to a decrease in quantity demanded. However, for some products price can be a signal of quality, and this appears to be the case for accommodation. Therefore, quantity demanded may actually increase with price up to a point, after which it decreases.[5]

Entrance fee cost was included in accommodation cost in the CM model, so the effect of that cost item in particular was not evaluated in the model. It was included in the site selection (SS) model, but was nonsignificant. This could be due to data quality or, perhaps more likely, to one or both of the following: (1) that entrance fees remain a minor share of total trip cost and (2) that Kruger, which has above average fee levels, was also the most visited, for reasons unassociated with entry fees.

This leaves travel cost, which was significant and of negative sign in the SS model. It should be noted that the effect of travel cost may be confounded with that of travel time—they typically are highly correlated and, as shown in the CM model, travel time coefficients also have negative signs. Despite this qualification, results from the SS model are broadly consistent with those from the On-Site Survey contingent behavior (CB) model (chapter 3) insofar as higher cost does negatively affect visitation, but only modestly.

Price elasticity with respect to entrance fees in the CB model was −0.036 in the case of HUP. Price elasticity for travel costs in the SS model was −0.040 in the case of the HUP–Newcastle combination. The CB value varies across the two parks modeled (it was −0.126 for Kruger), and the SS values vary across park–EA combinations (for example, it was −0.024 for HUP–Waverley). Nonetheless, the general relationship is consistent—for current reserve visitors, demand for reserve visitation is not very price responsive at or close to current cost levels.

Insofar as price is a barrier to increased visitation among South Africans not currently coming to reserves, higher prices will hinder efforts to achieve such increases. Thus, programs to reduce barriers, such as through subsidized transport and accommodation for school groups, may be necessary if overall price levels rise.

APPENDIX 2-A. SAMPLING, SURVEY ADMINISTRATION

Following a pilot (pre-test) administration, the household surveys were conducted in February and March 2001 by trained interviewers from DRA Development in the provinces of KwaZuluNatal and Gauteng, in each case based on a sample of enumerator areas, which are the basis for the South Africa census. In KZN, there are 15,466 EAs, but 1,352 contain no households and 1,784 contain fewer than 50 households. These were removed from the list of EAs, leaving 12,330.

Of these, 11,234 EAs had less than 50 percent of households with an annual household income of R42,000 or more. The remaining 1,096 EAs (those with 50 percent or more of households with this income level) were ordered by EA number and weighted by the number of households in each; then a systematic sample, with random start, of 16 EAs was taken. A similar process was followed in Gauteng.

In most EAs, a census of all households was taken. That is, each household was approached for participation in the survey (as noted below, in some cases the EA was split in half, and a census of only one-half of the EA was taken). If there was no response, interviewers returned to the household for a total of up to three visits. If contact was unsuccessful after those visits, the household was classified as a noncontact. Of the 3,737 households approached, 1,611 (43 percent) were not able to be contacted successfully, 1,285 (34 percent) refused to participate in the survey, and 841 (22 percent) completed the survey (details by EA are provided below). Of these completed surveys, 613 (73 percent) were in KZN and 228 (27 percent) in Gauteng.

Nonresponse is always an issue in survey research, but it appears to be exacerbated in the present case by the crime situation in South Africa. It was often difficult to establish contact with households (many had high walls and attack dogs, and some of those had no intercom that could be used to contact residents). In addition, there was a general hesitance to let strangers in. Moreover, sales marketing efforts, such as of time-shares, have led to resistance to anyone approaching homes.

Given the intentional selection of relatively high-income EAs and the high level of nonresponse, generalizations of the results to the broader regional population should be treated with caution. It is even more difficult to extrapolate to the national population because only two provinces were sampled. Nonetheless, survey results provide some important insights into the visitation of reserves.

The survey was conducted in person, and the questionnaire was in English. However, interviewers were able to conduct the interview in the main languages of the region, including Afrikaans, Zulu, and Sotho. In about 95 percent of the cases, respondents were able to participate in their mother tongue, whereas the remainder generally were happy to respond in a second language. In the rare case where language was a problem, an alternate interviewer was sent to conduct the interview. Brief descriptions of each enumerator area, as well as interviewer notes, are available from the author of this chapter. Table 2-A.1 provides response rate information.

Table 2-A.1 Response by Enumerator Area

| Enumerator area | Nonresponse | | | Completed | | |
	No contact (for example, not at home)	Refusals	Total	Past trip	Likely trip	Unlikely trip
Morningside	69	95	26	9	4	13
Lincoln Meade	88	45	80	27	28	25
Shortlands	53	21	24	2	5	17
Newlands East	42	39	90	2	17	71
Chatsworth	73	97	28	2	8	18
Pietermaritzburg	60	22	39	8	4	27
Umgeni Park	55	111	33	10	9	14
Musgrave	62	61	37	23	1	13
Umhlanga	58	26	29	8	3	18
Montclair	27	85	28	4	6	19
New Germany[a]	61	78	19	6	5	8
Newcastle	1	5	41	7	0	34
Umbilo	56	27	43	18	5	20
Queensburgh	70	100	18	3	6	9
Waterfall[a]	94	11	14	6	0	11
Pongola	86	41	60	24	5	31
Subtotal KZN	956	879	613	159	106	348
Kempton Park[a]	37	16	21	5	7	9
Athol	130	20	11	6	2	3
Waverley	56	113	61	32	11	18
Parkhurst	77	54	24	18	2	4
Alberton South[a]	75	20	20	4	8	8
General Kempheuwel[a, b]	60	15	15	3	5	7
Wingate Park[a]	54	64	21	16	3	2
Brakendowns[a]	36	25	13	3	7	3
Van der Bijl Park[a]	44	32	14	4	4	6
Gezina[a]	37	33	14	4	4	6
Roodepoort[a, b]	49	14	14	4	5	5
Subtotal Gauteng	655	406	228	99	58	71
Study total	1,611	1,285	841	258	164	419

[a]Only half that enumerator area was surveyed.
[b]The numbers of not-at-homes and refusals are estimated.

Source: DRA Development.

APPENDIX 2-B. DEMOGRAPHIC CHARACTERISTICS

The sample's demographic characteristics, by version, are shown in table 2-B.1. All figures are percentages for that survey version.

These results indicate a clear relationship between income and education and participation in nature tourism, with Past respondents having higher levels of both, Unlikely lower levels, and Likely in between. There is also a clear relationship with race; in particular, Whites make up a much higher percentage of Past respondents than Unlikely, whereas the reverse is true for Africans. The relationship between age and participation is less clear, as is the role of household composition. Moreover, because the latter may be related to income, race, and education, any effect may be caused by those more fundamental factors.

Table 2-B.2 illustrates type of participation by race. Roughly two-thirds of Africans and Coloureds surveyed have not gone to a reserve in the past three years and do not intend to go in the next three years. Conversely, only 12 percent of Africans and 17 percent of Coloureds surveyed have gone to reserves in the past three years, compared with 19 percent of Asians and 39 percent of Whites. Further analysis of participation by race is presented in chapter 5.

APPENDIX 2-C. IMPORTANCE RATINGS FOR LIKELY AND PAST VISITORS COMBINED

Table 2-C.1 and figure 2-C.1 show the distribution (in percentages) and mean of importance ratings by characteristic for the combined Likely future and Past trip data sets, with the latter including ratings for each trip if respondent took more than one.

APPENDIX 2-D. SAMPLE CHOICE MODELING SCENARIO

I'd like to find out more about the kind of reserve you would prefer for your *next* trip. In each of the following scenarios, two hypothetical reserves are described in terms of various characteristics. Please consider

Table 2-B.1 Demographic Characteristics, by Survey Version

Demographic characteristics	Unlikely future	Likely future	Past
Gender			
Male	44	52	47
Female	56	48	53
Age (years)			
18–30	20	34	23
31–40	23	26	26
41–50	24	17	20
51–65	23	18	18
Older than 65	10	5	13
Race			
African	31	24	9
White	59	63	86
Asian	8	11	5
Coloured	3	2	1
Highest level of education completed			
Some high school or less	22	9	7
High school graduate or equivalent	34	37	24
Some years at university, college, or technical school	8	12	14
Diploma from university, college, or technical school	22	23	28
Technical certificate from university, college, or technical school	7	6	6
Postgraduate diploma/degree studies	7	13	21
Number of adults in household			
1	13	12	13
2	52	49	60
3	20	26	17
4	9	10	7
5+	6	3	3
Number of children (under 18 years) in household			
0	46	43	55
1	18	20	15
2	18	20	21
3	12	12	5
4+	6	6	3
Gross annual household income in 2000 (excluding those who refused to answer) (thousands of rand)			
Less than 50	37	13	12
51–100	34	34	21
101–150	16	30	24
151–250	10	18	25
More than 250	2	5	18

Source: Data from the Household Survey.

Table 2-B.2 Participation in Nature Tourism and Race

	Race							
	African		White		Asian		Coloured	
Participation	Number	Percent	Number	Percent	Number	Percent	Number	Percent
Unlikely	128	68	245	43	34	53	12	67
Likely	39	21	104	18	18	28	3	17
Past	22	12	221	39	12	19	3	17
Total	189	100	570	100	64	100	18	100

Source: Data from the Household Survey.

Table 2-C.1 Distributions of Importance Ratings, Combined Data

Characteristic	Not at all important				Very important
	1	2	3	4	5
Big Five	16	10	14	21	38
Wide range birdlife	6	13	26	27	28
Wide range animals	2	4	18	30	46
Beautiful scenery	1	4	12	22	61
Past visits	3	3	14	32	40
Recommendations	10	13	17	30	30
Quality of facilities	2	8	18	31	40
Crowdedness	37	16	25	11	12
Lack of other people	9	12	31	18	30
Travel time	13	15	24	28	19
Travel cost	10	16	19	30	24
Entrance fee cost	13	14	22	28	23
Accommodation cost	6	6	20	29	37
Malaria/disease	20	14	13	13	41

Source: Data from the Household Survey.

each reserve, and then tell me which you would choose for your next game or nature reserve trip.

Assume for this question that these are the only reserves that are available for you to visit—for example, you can't choose an actual reserve such as Kruger instead of one of these. If neither of these reserves is attractive enough for you to travel to it, please select "neither of these reserves." (See table 2-D.1.)

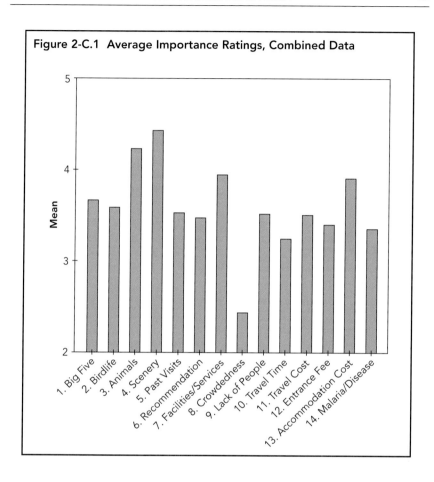

Figure 2-C.1 Average Importance Ratings, Combined Data

Table 2-D.1 Sample Choice Modeling Task

Characteristic	Reserves to choose from…		
	Reserve 1	Reserve 2	Neither Reserve
Likelihood of seeing the Big Five	Above average	Average	
Scenic beauty	Average	Above average	
Travel time from home (hours)	5	5	
Daily cost for accommodation and fees (average rand per person per day)	50	250	

NOTES

1. In reporting results, percentages are rounded to the nearest whole number, so totals do not always equal 100.

2. Travel costs could include both out-of-pocket expenses for gasoline and related expenditures and the opportunity cost of travel time. The former is represented by transport costs. The latter is typically calculated as a fraction of the wage rate. However, the appropriate fraction is not clear, especially in the relatively novel context of South Africa. Moreover, as Hausman, Leonard, and McFadden (1995) noted, it is not clear that recreational travel time is related to labor supply decisions. Therefore, the opportunity cost of travel time is not included in this analysis.

3. Because transport costs are the same regardless of the length of stay, one would expect total transport cost to generate a better model fit than does transport cost per person per day. However, that was not the case for this data. Because of the better fit, as well as comparability with other per-person, per-day cost variables, the latter is used in this analysis.

4. The actual fees charged at HUP from November 1, 1999, through October 31, 2000, were R8 per person for entry, R30 per vehicle, and R1 per person for the community levy. The reported average of R28 per person per day presumably reflects small groups (for example, the vehicle charge was spread across few people) and/or recall error.

5. The price elasticity for the increase from R150 to R250 is −0.53 (a 67 percent increase in price leads to a 35 percent decrease in quantity).

REFERENCES

Hausman, J. A., G. K. Leonard, and D. McFadden. 1995. "A Utility-consistent, Combined Discrete Choice and Count Data Model: Assessing Recreational Use Losses Due to Natural Resource Damage." *Journal of Public Economics* 56:1–30.

Loomis, J. B. 1995. "Four Models for Determining Environmental Quality Effects on Recreation Demand and Regional Economics." *Ecological Economics* 12:55–65.

Mendelsohn, R., J. Hof, G. Peterson, and R. Johnson. 1992. "Measuring Recreation Values with Multiple Destination Trips." *American Journal of Agricultural Economics*, pp. 926–33.

Seymour, J. 1998. *KwaZulu-Natal's Domestic Tourism Market: June '98-September '98.* Durban: KwaZulu-Natal Tourism Authority.

World Tourism Organization. 2002. The U.S. *Ecotourism Market.* Madrid.

CHAPTER 3

MARKET BEHAVIOR OF NATURE TOURISTS IN SOUTH AFRICA

A Visitor Survey in KwaZulu-Natal and Kruger National Park

Kreg Lindberg

M any countries and subnational regions conduct analyses of their domestic or inbound international tourism markets. However, few of these surveys evaluate detailed itineraries and how these itineraries would change in response to new or increased park fees—that is, the price-responsiveness of nature tourists.

This chapter provides an analysis of domestic and international visitors at two parks in KwaZulu-Natal, or KZN (Hluhluwe-Umfolozi, or HUP and Ithala), and at Kruger National Park (KNP). On the basis of survey responses, it provides data on trip characteristics and price responsiveness. It should be read in conjunction with chapters 2, 4, and 5, which also address market and demand issues.

After a brief description of sampling and survey versions, the chapter begins with a discussion of demographic and trip characteristics, followed by travel motivations and ratings of factors affecting destination choice. This is followed by a summary of park name recognition, past travel to South African parks, and opinions regarding appropriate entrance fees. The remaining sections analyze visitor demand, using contingent valuation and contingent behavior models. Additional demographic information is presented in appendix 3-A.[1]

SAMPLING AND SURVEY ADMINISTRATION

The data analyzed in this chapter were obtained through visitor surveys conducted on-site by trained interviewers from the company DRA Development. Following a pilot (pre-test), there were three phases in survey administration (all in 2000). In phase 1, visitors were surveyed at HUP and Ithala in March. In phase 2, visitors were surveyed at Kruger in August. In phase 3, visitors were surveyed at HUP during November.

There were eight versions of the survey questionnaire, with one expenditure version and one site choice version for each of the following categories of respondents: resident day visitors, resident overnight visitors, foreign day visitors, and foreign overnight visitors. In each category, visitors were administered either the site choice version or the expenditure version, on an alternating basis. Expenditure results are reported in chapter 9. The site choice data presented in this chapter are based on the following number of observations by park, as is shown in table 3.1 (all tables in this chapter are based on responses to the On-Site Visitor Survey).

For the resident and foreign day visitor questionnaires, respondents were asked a "minor scenario" involving response to hypothetical crowding in the parks, and an extra fee that visitors could pay to retain the same level of crowding (through access to a specified zone). For the resident and foreign overnight visitor questionnaires, respondents were asked a "major scenario" involving response, in terms of days spent in various parks, to a hypothetical change in fees at KwaZulu-Natal parks, KNP, and crowding at the site of administration (for example, at KNP when surveys were administered there).

In addition, foreign overnight visitors were presented a contingent valuation scenario involving an increase in departure taxes and/or ticket

Table 3.1 Observations by Park and Type of Visitor (percent in parentheses)

Park	Resident Day	Resident Overnight	Foreign Day	Foreign Overnight
Ithala Game Reserve	5 (4)	24 (7)	5 (5)	22 (7)
Hluhluwe-Umfolozi Park	64 (53)	134 (41)	58 (59)	194 (57)
Kruger National Park	53 (43)	169 (52)	36 (36)	124 (37)
Total	122	327	99	340

Source: On-Site Visitor Survey.

prices. In all cases, the scenarios were presented on an alternating basis, such that the scenario features varied from person to person. In the case of the major scenarios, the levels of the features were determined by a fractional factorial design.

In all versions, charts were used to present material visually to assist respondents in their task. In addition, the major scenarios were presented visually. Both the charts and the scenarios were available in English, French, and German.

CHARACTERISTICS OF DEMAND: OVERSEAS TOURISTS

This section presents descriptive statistics that characterize nature tourists visiting the sites and their behavior and choices.

Demographic Characteristics of the Sample

Detailed demographic characteristics are presented in appendix 3-A, with summary results as follows. A consistent feature across versions is the high proportion of males, which may reflect the screening of respondents— only those who had "significant" or "sole" input in the decision to come to South Africa (for residents, to the area) were surveyed.

Foreigners tended to have higher educational levels, though this may reflect national differences rather than visitor-specific differences. Foreigners in general, but especially day visitors, tended to be younger than residents. As expected, foreigners tend to have higher income levels, and overnight visitors tend to be wealthier than day visitors, a difference that is more pronounced among foreigners than among residents. There was greater refusal on the income question among foreigners, though this may be caused by the fact that categories were used for the resident surveys but not the surveys of foreign visitors.

Household size differed considerably between residents and foreigners, with the latter much more likely to be in households of one or two people. There were also differences between day and overnight visitors, though this effect is less pronounced. With respect to residence, there appeared to be little difference between overnight and day visitors for the two main source markets: Gauteng and KZN. Of the foreigners, the

Table 3.2 Party Composition and Past Experience by Type of Visitor

Composition and Experience	Resident Day	Resident Overnight	Foreign Day	Foreign Overnight
Party composition (average number)				
Adults	3.5	3.2	5.2	4.3
Children	1.6	0.48	0.14	0.13
People paying	3.2	2.6	1.8	3.1
Percentage of foreigners (for residents) or residents (for foreigners) in party	14	13	18	18
Past international nature tourism trips				
Africa, including South Africa	n.a.	n.a.	0.64	0.82
Africa, excluding South Africa	n.a.	n.a.	0.49	0.49
Africa	4.3	3.0	n.a.	n.a.
Asia, Latin America, Australia, and New Zealand	0.16	0.24	0.90	0.84

n.a. Not applicable.

Source: On-Site Visitor Survey.

German market clearly dominates the sample of visitors, with the Benelux countries and the United Kingdom being second and third largest. The United States is the largest non-European market.

Trip Characteristics

Party composition and past international nature tourism trip experience are shown in table 3.2. For resident day visitors, the most common party composition was two adults (50 percent) and no children (66 percent), with means of 3.5 and 1.6, respectively. The most frequent response for number of people paying is 2 (36 percent), with a variable average of 3.2. It was uncommon to have foreigners in the party, with only 14 percent reporting this. With respect to past international wildlife or nature-oriented trips during the past five years, the average for trips in Africa was 4.3 (43 percent reported none), whereas the average for Asia, Latin America, or Australia and New Zealand was 0.16 (89 percent reported none).

For resident overnight visitors, less than one-quarter (23 percent) reported being accompanied by children, and most of these had only one or two children traveling with them (8 percent and 10 percent, respectively).

Only 13 percent of respondents indicated that nonresidents accompanied them.

For foreign day visitors, the most common party composition was two adults (44 percent) and no children (93 percent), with means of 5.2 and 0.14, respectively. The most frequent response for number of people paying for is 2 (55 percent), with a variable average of 1.8. It was uncommon to have South African residents in the party, with only 18 percent reporting this. With respect to international wildlife or nature-oriented trips during the past five years, the average for those to Africa, including South Africa, was 0.64 (70 percent reported none), whereas the averages for other in Africa was 0.49 (76 percent none) and Asia, Latin America, or Australia and New Zealand was 0.90 (56 percent none).

For foreign overnight visitors, the most common party composition was two adults (59 percent) and no children (94 percent), with means of 4.3 and 0.13, respectively. The most frequent response for number of people paying for is 2 (65 percent), with a variable average of 3.1. It was uncommon to have South African residents in the party, with only 18 percent reporting this. With respect to international wildlife or nature-oriented trips during the past five years, the average for those to Africa, including South Africa, was 0.82 (67 percent reported none), while the average for other in Africa was 0.49 (70 percent none) and Asia, Latin America, or Australia and New Zealand was 0.84 (59 percent none).

Overall, foreigners traveled together with more adults and fewer children than was the case for residents. There is some mixture of parties in terms of foreigners traveling with South Africans and vice versa, but this occurred less than 20 percent of the time for all groups. Not surprisingly, residents had greater experience in terms of Africa trips, whereas foreigners had greater experience with trips elsewhere. On average, foreigners had greater past experience with Africa trips including South Africa than with other Africa trips, which indicates a degree of repeat visitation to the country.

Foreigners were asked what other countries they were visiting on this trip; the results are shown in table 3.3. The number of visitors also traveling to Swaziland or Lesotho is not surprising, given their proximity. When one excludes these two countries, relatively few overnight foreigners are making a multicountry trip. The proportion is higher for day visitors.

Table 3.3 Countries Being Visited by Foreign Respondents on Current Trip

Country	Overnight (minimum 1%)	Day (minimum 2%)
Swaziland	35	37
Lesotho	12	13
Botswana	4	10
Namibia	6	9
Zimbabwe	4	7
Mozambique	2	5
Kenya	1	5
Tanzania		3
Zambia		3
Malawi		2

Note: Blank cells indicate less than 1 percent.

Source: On-Site Visitor Survey.

Table 3.4 Average Time Spent in Various Parks by Overnight Visitors

	Foreigners		Residents	
Park	Nights	Day Visits	Nights	Day Visits
Of those surveyed in KwaZulu-Natal (KZN)				
Hluhluwe-Umfolozi Park	1.87	0.00	2.14	0.00
Ithala	0.33	0.02	0.42	0.00
Other public parks in NE KZN	0.63	0.13	0.43	0.04
Kruger	1.11	0.06	0.13	0.01
All other in South Africa	1.09	0.36	0.13	0.00
KZN visitor total	*5.03*	*0.58*	*3.25*	*0.05*
Of those surveyed in Kruger National Park				
Southern KNP	3.15	0.15	3.66	0.31
Northern KNP	2.77	0.06	4.27	0.17
Blyde River Canyon	0.29	0.08	0.10	0.04
HUP	0.09	a	a	0.01
Other public parks in NE KZN	0.06	a	0.02	0.00
All other in South Africa	0.17	0.03	0.10	0.00
Kruger visitor total	*6.54*	*0.31*	*8.15*	*0.54*

a. Included in next category.

Source: On-Site Visitor Survey.

The foreign and resident overnight visitors were asked to specify how many nights and day visits were spent in each of several parks; the results are shown in table 3.4 ("day visits" refers to visits that were not associated with an overnight stay in the park).

Those visiting Kruger are spending more total nights, on average, in parks than those visiting KZN (especially for residents). However, these days are very concentrated on Kruger, whereas KZN visitors on average spend more time in a variety of parks. Also of note is that the average time spent by KZN visitors in KNP is greater than the reverse, reflecting Kruger's stronger pull as a primary attraction.

Travel Motivations and Considerations

Foreigners were asked to identify the most important reason for coming to South Africa, using the South Africa Tourism Board (SATOUR) survey categories. Responses were, in percent:

Overnight:

Wildlife	51
Visiting friends and/or relatives	21
Scenic beauty	15

Day:

Wildlife	56
Visiting friends and/or relatives	14
Business/professional activities	11

Given that the surveys were conducted at game reserves, it is not surprising that wildlife is dominant among both groups. The values indicate that the parks benefit from the visiting friends and relatives market and, to a lesser degree, the business market.

Residents were asked, in an open-ended format, their main consideration when deciding on the itinerary for their trip. Responses were categorized as follows, in percent:

Overnight:

Opportunity to see wildlife and nature	29
Escaping the city life or relaxing	12
Facilities in the area	8
Proximity to home	8

Day:

Opportunity to see wildlife and nature	41
Escaping the city life or relaxing	12
Proximity to home	7
Show relatives or foreigners the parks	6

Again, wildlife is the dominant motivation, though "escape" is also important. Responses reflect both general considerations, such as the above, as well as reserve-specific considerations, such as proximity to home.

Foreign respondents rated a set of factors in terms of their importance in deciding which countries to visit on the trip (on a scale of 1 to 5, 5 being extremely important). Resident respondents did the same, but with the focus on which areas to visit. Results are shown in Figures 3.1 through 3.4, in which the average rating is shown for each variable.

Results are similar across day and overnight visitors within each market (foreigners and residents), but there are some differences across the markets. Foreigners rate "see Big Five" the most highly, followed by "experience different cultures," "variety of attractions," "reputation

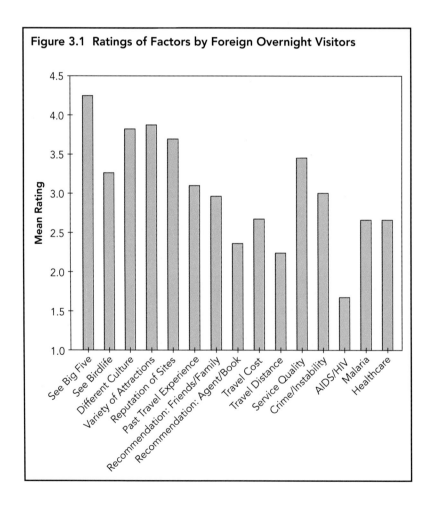

Figure 3.1 Ratings of Factors by Foreign Overnight Visitors

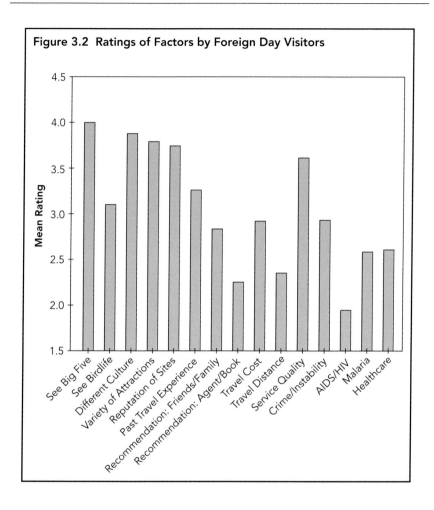

Figure 3.2 Ratings of Factors by Foreign Day Visitors

of specific sites," and "service quality." Relative to foreigners, residents tended to place greater emphasis on seeing birdlife and less emphasis on the variety of attractions, and, especially, recommendations from travel agents or guidebooks. Relative to other factors, travel costs tended to be of average importance across the four groups.

When foreign overnight visitors were asked in an open-ended format the most important reason for coming to KZN (or the Greater KNP Area) in particular, the most frequent responses were as shown in table 3.5. Again, results are consistent with Kruger being a primary attraction. It is well known for wildlife, whereas visitors to KZN choose to visit for a broader variety of reasons.

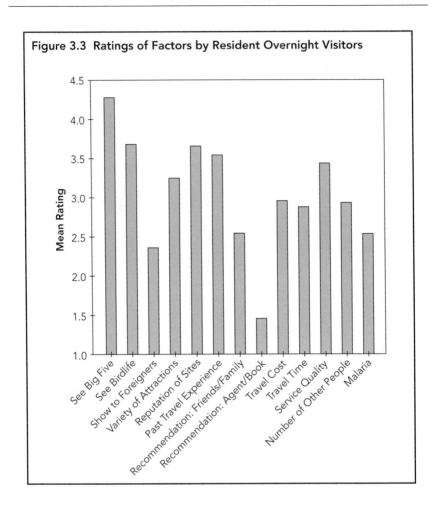

Figure 3.3 Ratings of Factors by Resident Overnight Visitors

Park Name Recognition and Past Visits

Foreign respondents were asked whether they knew selected parks by name before they started planning their trip. By far the best known was Kruger, as is illustrated in table 3.6. Data for Ithala and Pilanesberg are only for visitors surveyed in KZN and KNP, respectively. Residents were asked how many visits they had made to selected parks in the past five years; the results are shown in table 3.7.

Nor surprisingly, most visits have been to the region or park in which visitors were surveyed, indicating repeat visitation. As was noted in the context of current trip itineraries, there is an asymmetry in past visits

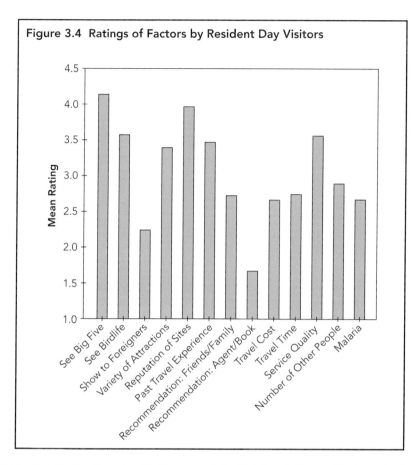

Figure 3.4 Ratings of Factors by Resident Day Visitors

Table 3.5 Motivations for Visiting KwaZulu-Natal and Kruger National Park (percent; minimum 5%)

Reason	Surveyed in KZN	Surveyed at Kruger
Recommended by friends or family	17	
Wildlife and nature	17	54
Visiting friends or relatives	10	
Reputation or heritage of park	8	15
Planned by tour guide (no choice)	8	
On our route	6	
Business or professional activities	5	
Scenic beauty	5	5
Comparing this park with others	5	
Rustic or African bush experience		6

Note: Blank cells indicate that those reasons were given less than 5 percent of the time (e.g., 0 to 4.9 percent of the time).

Source: On-Site Visitor Survey.

Table 3.6 Name Recognition before Trip Planned (percentage of foreign respondents, sorted by overnight percent)

Park Recognized by Name	Overnight	Day
Kruger	98	97
Natal Drakensberg	62	56
Hluhluwe-Umfolozi Park	54	46
Kalahari Gemsbok	44	50
Saint Lucia Wetland	39	42
Addo	33	27
Tsitsikama	31	27
Pilanesberg	29	29
Ithala	17	13
Londolozi	16	9
Phinda	9	6

Source: On-Site Visitor Survey.

Table 3.7 Visits to Selected Parks during the Past Five Years (average by park for resident respondents, sorted by overnight average)

Park Visited	Overnight	Day
For those surveyed in KwaZulu-Natal		
Hluhluwe-Umfolozi Park	3.64	3.61
Natal Drakensberg	1.94	2.15
Kruger	1.85	2.62
Saint Lucia Wetland	1.62	3.76
Ithala	0.91	1.37
Tsitsikama	0.37	0.32
Kalahari Gemsbok	0.23	0.27
Addo	0.21	0.18
Phinda	0.14	0.05
Londolozi	0.03	0.08
For those surveyed at Kruger National Park		
Northern KNP only	3.20	2.96
Southern KNP only	3.12	4.64
Both Northern and Southern	1.54	1.17
Pilanesberg	1.11	0.38
Natal Drakensberg	0.93	0.64
Hluhluwe-Umfolozi Park	0.76	0.16
Saint Lucia Wetland	0.56	0.37
Tsitsikama	0.50	0.46
Addo	0.26	0.22
Kalahari Gemsbok	0.24	0.24
Londolozi	0.17	0.29
Phinda	0.07	0.22

Source: On-Site Visitor Survey.

between KZN parks and Kruger, with KZN visitors going to Kruger more frequently than the reverse.

Appropriate Fees and Past Fee Experience

At the time of the survey, entrance fees of R9 were charged for HUP and R30 for KNP. These fees are the same for residents and foreigners, and are paid only once (on entry), not on a daily basis. The exchange rate varied over the phases, with rates at the 15th of each month during the three phases being R6.4750, R6.9420, and R7.6890 to $1. Thus, $1 = R7 is an appropriate "average" value, though the current (April 2002) exchange rate is $1 = R11.1400.

Respondents were asked what they considered to be the appropriate fee for their group (that is, for residents, for foreigners) at public parks in South Africa. In addition, they were asked about their past experience paying fees, with the expectation that those paying fees in the past would be more willing to pay fees at the study sites. The results are shown in table 3.8.

Both foreigners and residents felt that "appropriate fees" were higher than those being charged at the time of the survey. In addition, actual fees

Table 3.8 Appropriate Fees and Fees Paid Elsewhere by Type of Visitor

Fee	Resident Day	Resident Overnight	Foreign Day	Foreign Overnight
Appropriate fee, in Rand, average (separately by location, residents)	20 (KZN)[a] 44 (KNP)[b]	26 (KZN) 44 (KNP)	86	77
Appropriate fee, in Rand, most frequent (percentage in parentheses)	10 (20)	30 (21)	50 (18)	50 (16)
Appropriate fee, in Rand, second most frequent (percent)	20 (17)	50 (16)	100 (11)	100 (13)
Percentage of respondents that paid fees elsewhere in Africa	69	75	47	59
Average fee paid, in Rand, elsewhere in Africa	44	60	73	68
Percentage of respondents that paid fees outside Africa	14	15	59	54
Average fee paid, in Rand, outside Africa	68	63	102	109

a. KwaZulu-Natal
b. Kruger National Park

Source: On-Site Visitor Survey.

at the study sites were lower than the average paid elsewhere in Africa and, especially, outside Africa. As is shown in table 3.8, those surveyed at Kruger reported higher appropriate fees than those surveyed at KZN parks.

Though the fee system is more complex than can be presented easily in surveys (for example, with vehicle and community levy fees), results indicate general support for current, and even increased, fees. Of course, any people who were not willing to pay current fees were not in the sample of respondents.

DEMAND ANALYSIS

This section evaluates changes in quantity demanded in response to the imposition of a departure tax, changes in entrance fees, and increased crowding in the reserves, using contingent valuation and contingent behavior methods.

Contingent Valuation of a Departure Tax: Foreign Overnight Visitors

Foreign overnight visitors were asked how the existence of a departure tax would affect their decision about whether to visit South Africa. A split sample was used, in which half the respondents were presented the tax in the form of directly paying the amount on departure and half were presented the tax in the form of an increase in their airline ticket price (or package price, if the ticket price was included in the package). In phase 1, the wording of the first half was as follows:

> Many countries have departure taxes that are paid by visitors at airports when leaving the country. If South Africa had implemented a departure tax of (A) $10—(B) $25—(C) $50—(D) $100—(E) $250—(F) $500 prior to your visit, such that you would have had to pay that amount upon departure, would you have cancelled your visit to the country?

Each respondent was presented one of the values, on an alternating basis. This was changed for phase 2 and 3, to be as follows:

> Many countries in Africa and elsewhere have departure taxes that are paid by visitors at airports when leaving the country. If South Africa had had in place a departure tax of (A) $25—(B) $50—(C) $100—(D) $250—(E)

$500—(F) $750, such that you would have had to pay that amount upon departure, would you have visited South Africa on this trip, visited another country instead, or stayed at home?

The following reflects the combined data set. An initial logistic regression analysis was undertaken, with the probability of still visiting South Africa modeled as a function of the departure tax (bid), the phase (and thus the wording above), the version (direct versus in ticket), the number of people respondent was paying for, and household income. The only significant coefficient was for bid, which was both negative and highly significant. In other words, responses did not differ based on whether the tax was paid on departure or as part of the ticket, nor did it differ depending on the phase, and thus the difference in wording shown above. The effect can be seen visually in figure 3.5.

The figure illustrates the modest effect of departure taxes at levels at all close to those that are common (for example, $25 or less). A tax of more than $250 would be necessary before visitation would be cut in half. This evaluation is based on stated intended behavior, rather than actual behavior, and thus may underestimate price responsiveness. Conversely, the survey contained explicit information that prices would increase because of the tax, whereas an actual departure tax may be incorporated into the price of international tickets and never noticed, such that results may overestimate price responsiveness. In any case, the results indicate the high value that nature tourism visitors in South Africa place on their experience, as well as the consumer surplus they retain from their visit.

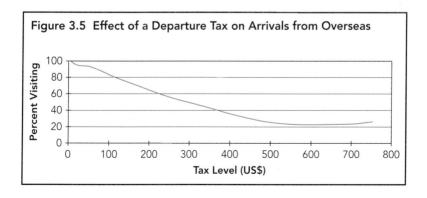

Figure 3.5 Effect of a Departure Tax on Arrivals from Overseas

Responsiveness of Tourists to Changes in Entrance Fees: A Contingent Behavior Model

A contingent behavior model was used to evaluate the effect that price and crowding changes would have on the itineraries of overnight visitors. Contingent behavior is a relatively new modeling technique, but it has been applied frequently in the United States (for example, Englin and Cameron 1996; Siderelis, Moore, and Lee 2000). As noted in the introduction to part 2, only one application in a developing-country context has been found in the literature (Chase and others 1998). Because it combines data on both actual and contingent behavior, it possesses the strengths of both revealed and stated preference methods.

Data and Methods

Overnight respondents were first asked to describe their actual itinerary in terms of the number of nights (and, separately, day visits) they were spending in each of the following public parks in South Africa on this trip.

For visitors at HUP and Ithala:

- HUP
- Ithala
- Other public parks in northeastern KZN
- KNP
- Other public parks in South Africa
- Total

For visitors at KNP:

- Southern KNP
- Northern KNP
- Blyde River Canyon
- HUP
- Other public parks in northeastern KZN

- Other public parks in South Africa

- Total

They were then presented with a scenario and asked whether their itinerary would have been different if the scenario features had been in effect, and, if so, what their itinerary would have been; the latter is their itinerary contingent on the scenario features (a sample scenario is presented in appendix 3-B). In order to make responses as realistic as possible, respondents were first asked when they would have been aware of the features (for example, when they planned their itinerary or only on arrival at the park). The features were price increases at HUP and other parks in northeastern KZN, price increases at KNP, and a crowding increase. The crowding increase applied only to the region in which the visitor was surveyed.

Contingent behavior allows one to estimate how scenario features would affect visitation at the parks on which data are gathered. For example, if a visitor currently was spending three nights in HUP and four nights in KNP, but the fee at HUP was increased by $20, would the visitor cancel their visit to HUP—and would they spend more days at KNP?

The amount of the fee and crowding increases varied across respondents, on the basis of a fractional factorial design. The range of fee increases also varied across the phases, but the highest levels were $80 for KZN and $100 for Kruger in the case of foreigners and R100 and R120, respectively, for residents. The highest crowding level was 100 percent (a doubling). As part of the scenario, respondents were also presented reference information on current fee levels.

Because prices vary across parks in KZN, the project team was asked to use two related fee increases for the region in which the surveys were administered, in addition to the unrelated fee increase in the other region (for example, KNP for those surveyed in KZN). For respondents surveyed in KZN, the main fee increase was at HUP and the secondary fee increase was at other public parks in northeastern KZN. For those surveyed in KNP, the main fee increase was at southern KNP (SKNP) and the secondary fee increase was at northern KNP (NKNP). The increase at the secondary site was always half the increase at the main site. This relationship should be kept in mind when interpreting the results given below.

The fee increases are expected to lead some visitors to substitute away from HUP and SKNP, the main sites, while not affecting other visitors (those who value the experience sufficiently to pay the higher fee). In other words, the expected net effect is negative. In the case of the secondary sites, the expected effect is less clear. Because the fee increases at these sites were half as great as for their local "competitors" (the main sites), the fee increase might lead some visitors to substitute away from the secondary sites, some to substitute to them from the main sites, and some not to be affected. This mixed effect is supported by a review of changes in nights at these secondary sites (some increase, some decrease, some remain unchanged in response to the scenarios), and is the most likely explanation for the nonsignificant coefficients in the Ithala models and the resident NKNP model, as well as the relatively low level of significance in the foreign NKNP model.

In the following models, the number of nights at each site is modeled as a function of entrance fees, crowding, demographic characteristics, and other relevant variables. Because responses are all non-negative integers (that is, 0, 1, 2, 3), count data models such as Poisson and Negative Binomial (NegBin) are preferred over basic linear regression (ordinary least squares, or OLS). Except for the HUP OLS models, which are provided for comparison with the Poisson, all models were first estimated with Poisson. The limitation with Poisson is that it assumes that the variance and mean of the dependent variable (number of nights) are equal. If the variance is greater than the mean, overdispersion exists and the NegBin model is more appropriate. The following models were first estimated using Poisson. When overdispersion was indicated, the NegBin approach was used instead.

In each case, an initial model with a full set of variables was estimated—the sets for foreigners and residents are listed below. Variables that were not significant at the $p = 0.10$ level were removed. In the case of the OLS model, the set of significant variables from the Poisson model was used, rather than starting with an initial model. The overall resident model for HUP was significant at 0.0008, whereas all other models were significant at 0.0000000.

The data sets reflect a small amount of exclusion of observations. Visitors surveyed at KZN parks stayed 11 or fewer days at any given park. However, some visitors surveyed at KNP stayed for particularly

Table 3.9 Exclusion of Observations from Data Sets by Type of Visitor (number of respondents)

Observations	KZN Foreign	KNP Foreign	KZN Resident	KNP Resident
Original	216	124	158	169
Outliers	0	2	0	2
Positive change	1	1	1	1
Final	215	121	157	166

KZN = KwaZulu-Natal; KNP = Kruger National Park.
Note: Each respondent generated two observations.
Source: On-Site Visitor Survey.

long periods. These visitors are considered outliers and are excluded from the contingent behavior analysis. In the case of foreigners, the cutoff was set at 15 nights in KNP (southern and northern sections combined), whereas for residents it was set at 31 nights.

The different cutoffs reflect differences in the pattern of visitation, with each cutoff occurring at the "breakpoint" in the distribution. In each case, two KNP respondents were removed on the basis of outlier status. In addition, a small number of visitors reported that they would increase the total number of nights in nature reserves as a result of the scenarios. Though one might expect increases in nights at individual reserves (for example, visitors might substitute away from HUP in favor of Ithala because the price rise at HUP was greater), one would not expect total nights to increase because the scenarios included only price rises and crowding increases, both of which generally would be considered negative. It is assumed that these respondents did not understand the scenario. The modest effect of exclusion on the size of the data sets is shown in table 3.9.

A comparison of model results both before and after exclusion of these observations indicates that the exclusion had only a minor effect on results. There is a modest amount of additional loss of data for each model because of missing values on independent variables.

Two additional methodological considerations are worth noting. First, because each observation has two responses (number of days at current fee and crowding levels + number of days at scenario levels), panel models such as random or fixed effects ideally should be used. However, several of the panel models attempted here failed to estimate, a result that has occurred elsewhere as well (for example, Chase and others 1998, in the case of Tobit analysis). Therefore, the following results are based on simple pooled models. The pooled approach, which does not account for panel effects, has been used elsewhere (for instance, Eiswerth and others 2000) and is considered acceptable here because each respondent generated only two observations (rather than several, as is sometimes the case).

Last, the data set is from on-site surveys, and thus is truncated and endogenously stratified. Truncation refers to the lack of information on people who do not visit the reserves, whereas endogenous stratification refers to the likelihood of a person being sampled depending on the frequency of his or her visit, which may lead to "avidity bias." There are approaches for dealing with these issues (for example, Englin and Shonkwiler 1995). However, in the present case the scenarios involve increases in price and reductions in quality. This would not be expected to attract current nonvisitors, so truncation is not considered a problem.

With respect to endogenous stratification, if "person X" takes two trips per year to a given park and "person Y" takes only one, X is twice as likely to be surveyed. However, any scenario response by X also has twice the impact—for example, if X would substitute away from the park because of a price increase, this would lead to a two-visit reduction per year as opposed to a one-visit reduction per year for Y. Therefore, endogenous stratification is not considered a problem here.

The list of initial independent variables is given in table 3.10. Independent variables that were nonsignificant at $p = 0.10$ were dropped from the models. The resulting final models are shown in tables 3.11 through 3.14. The absence of variables and the blank cells in specific models reflect the nonsignificance of those variables, and thus their omission. "Nights" and "days" are used interchangeably here, but the dependent variable being evaluated is nights spent at the listed locations (it does not include day visits).

Results: Foreign Overnight Visitors to HUP and Ithala

Table 3.11 presents results of models with the number of nights at HUP, Ithala, and KNP as the dependent variables. When interpreting coefficients, it should be kept in mind that the independent variables are predicting both the actual and contingent number of nights, except in the case of the scenario variables (fees and crowding). Thus, the positive sign on *#paid for* can reflect a positive relationship between the

Table 3.10 Independent (Predictor) Variables Used in Contingent Behavior Analysis

Variable	Residents	Foreigners	Description
Fee KZN	✓	✓	The fee level at KZN parks, set at R9 for current resident itineraries (R8 + R1 community levy) and at $1.40 for foreigners, and at this price plus the scenario increase for contingent itineraries.
Fee KNP	✓	✓	Same as above, although, for KNP, with current itineraries set at R30 for residents and $4.60 for foreigners.
Crowds KZN Crowds KNP	✓	✓	The crowding attribute, set at 0 for current itineraries and at the scenario level for contingent itineraries.
Ithala			Whether the visitor was surveyed at Ithala, in the case of the Ithala model.
#Paid for	✓	✓	The number of people the respondent is paying for on this trip.
Trips RSA Trips, Africa Trips, Other	✓	✓	For foreigners, the number of international wildlife or nature-oriented trips the respondent has taken during the past five years (between 1995 and 1999) to (1) Africa including South Africa, (2) Africa not including South Africa, and (3) Asia, Latin America, Australia, and New Zealand, respectively. For residents, trips to South Africa drop out. This does not include the present trip.
Countries	×	✓	Number of countries respondent is visiting on this trip, not including South Africa.
Big Five	✓	✓	The importance rating for "Opportunity to see the Big Five" in deciding which places to visit on the present trip. For KNP, the ratings for "Past experience" (only residents), "Reputation," and "Malaria" were also used.
Wildlife	×	✓	Whether wildlife was the most important reason for coming to South Africa.
Past_HUP Past_Ita Past_KNP	✓	×	The number of trips to each park made in the past five years.

(continued)

Table 3.10 (*Continued*)

Variable	Residents	Foreigners	Description
Self-Org	✓	✓	Whether the respondent organized the trip himself or herself, rather than via an operator, friend, or relative.
HUP name	✗	✓	Whether respondent knew of the
Ithala name	✓	✓	respective park by name before he or she started planning the trip (in the case of Kruger, all respondents knew the park by name, so this variable was not included in the analysis).
Fee prior	✓	✓	Whether the respondent would have
Crowds prior			known about the entrance fees and levels of crowding, respectively, prior to arriving at the reserve.
Certain	✓	✓	How certain the respondent was of his or her response to the scenario (1 = not at all, 2 = somewhat, 3 = very).
Price	✓	✓	Whether price or crowding was the most
Crowding			important scenario attribute when responding to the scenario ("both," "none," and missing value set to zero).
Fees, Africa	✓	✗	Whether respondent has paid entrance
Fees, other			fees at other parks in Africa or outside Africa, respectively.
Appropriate fee	✓	✓	Appropriate entrance fee at public parks such as Ithala/HUP or KNP (depending where survey was administered). Residents reported fee for residents and foreigners for foreigners.
Age	✓	✓	Raw number.
Male	✓	✓	Whether male.
Education	✓	✓	Educational level, 5-point scale.
Income	✓	✓	Gross household income in 1999, for residents scored on a 7-point scale. For foreigners, in millions of rand.
Household size	✓	✗	Number of people in household.
Residence	✗	✓	Dummy variables were used for the following countries of residence: Benelux countries, France, Germany, United Kingdom, and United States. The base is visitors from all other countries.

HUP = Hluhluwe-Umfolozi Park; KNP = Kruger National Park; and KZN = KwaZulu-Natal. RSA = Republic of South Africa.

Source: On-Site Visitor Survey.

Table 3.11 Foreign Visitors Surveyed at HUP and Ithala

| | Dependent Variable Is Number of Nights Spent at Each of the Following: | | | | | | | |
| | HUP—Poisson | | HUP—OLS | | Ithala—Poisson | | KNP—NegBin | |
	Coefficient	Significance Level	Coefficient	Significance Level	Coefficient	Significance Level	Coefficient	Significance Level
Constant	0.565	0.000	1.656	0.000	-3.002	0.000	-0.672	0.040
Fee KZN	-0.010	0.000	-0.013	0.000				
#Paid for	0.076	0.014	0.160	0.006	0.144	0.062		
Countries	-0.201	0.000	-0.253	0.000			0.351	0.004
Crowding	0.177	0.026	0.283	0.015			-0.470	0.034
Fee prior	-0.180	0.023	-0.288	0.014	-0.357	0.041		
Ithala					2.715	0.000		
Ithala name					0.724	0.001		
Wildlife					0.647	0.001	0.881	0.000
Trips Africa					0.365	0.000	0.295	0.045
Trips RSA							-0.149	0.061
Self-org					0.462	0.025		
Germany							0.674	0.010
Benelux					-0.849	0.009	0.626	0.028
US							1.207	0.002
UK	-0.198	0.059	-0.302	0.043				
Income							-0.662	0.087

HUP = Hluhluwe-Umfolozi Park; KNP = Kruger National Park; and KZN = KwaZulu-Natal. OLS = ordinary least squares. RSA = Republic of South Africa.
Note: A blank cell indicates that an independent variable was not significant at $p = 0.10$. These variables were dropped from the model.

Source: On-Site Visitor Survey.

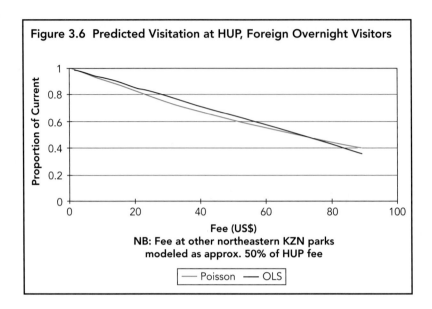

Figure 3.6 Predicted Visitation at HUP, Foreign Overnight Visitors

number of people paying for and either or both the actual number of days or the contingent number of days.

One can isolate the effect on the contingent number of days (for instance, how a given variable affects whether, and by how much, the respondent will change the number of days in response to the scenario) by having it statistically interact with the scenario features. For simplicity, this was not done at this stage. The following discussion focuses on scenario variables, especially fees, and those variables that are significant across multiple models.

In both the HUP models, the *fee KZN* coefficient was highly significant and had the expected sign. A review of the summary statistics indicates that quite a few people would not change their itinerary in response to the scenario features, but those that did substantially reduced the number of days in HUP. As was noted by Englin and Cameron (1996, 142), the Poisson specification is log-linear, with elasticity calculated by multiplying the coefficient by the price. For example, elasticity for HUP at current fee levels would be: $-.0100 * 1.40 = -0.014$. At \$10, it would be $-.100$.

The effect of HUP fees on visitation levels there is also illustrated in figure 3.6. In Poisson models, the predicted values for the dependent variable (in this case number of days) are calculated as $e^{(\alpha+\beta X)}$, where e is the base for natural logarithms and $\alpha+\beta X$ represents the constant and vector of coefficients multiplied by the values for each independent variable. Means are used for all variables except price, which is varied across the range shown.[2]

As is illustrated by figure 3.6, fees would have to be substantially higher than current levels to have a dramatic effect on the number of visitors to HUP.

Fee KZN was not significant for either the Ithala or KNP models. As was noted above, a likely explanation for this result at Ithala is that substitution away from Ithala because of fee increases there may be balanced by substitution to Ithala from HUP because of the fee increase at HUP being twice as high. The reason for nonsignificance in the KNP model is less clear, but it suggests that visitors generally do not see KZN and KNP as substitutes for each other. This is supported by the nonsignificance of the *fee KNP* variable in any of the models (and thus its omission from table 3.11). That is, an increase in fees at KZN parks will not lead to an increase in visitation at KNP, nor will an increase in fees at KNP lead to an increase in visitation at KZN parks. Though the above models are based on surveys of visitors in KZN, the results for KNP visitors below are consistent with this conclusion insofar as *fee KZN* was nonsignificant in those models.

The crowding feature was not significant in any of the models, suggesting that it generally was not a major concern to visitors. Conversely, the positive sign for *crowding* in the HUP model and negative sign in the KNP model suggests that those who are concerned about crowding are likely to spend more days at HUP and fewer days at KNP.

The variable *#paid for* is significant and positive in most models, which suggests that larger groups tend to spend longer periods at a given site, at least for HUP and Ithala. The negative signs on the *countries* coefficient in the HUP models indicate that the more countries one visits, the fewer days spent at HUP. With respect to prior knowledge of fee levels (*fee prior*), the negative signs for HUP and Ithala suggest that those who are likely to know about fee levels are also those that are more likely to care about them—and to displace away as they increase. Last, visitors from the United Kingdom are likely to spend fewer days at HUP relative to other visitors.

Results: Foreign Overnight Visitors to KNP

Turning now to results of the surveys of visitors at KNP, models for southern, northern, and total KNP (SKNP, NKNP, and TKNP, respectively) are shown in table 3.12. A model for HUP nights among Kruger visitors was estimated, but the resulting model fit poorly. The lack of significance may be explained by what appears to be the one-sided nature of visitation between HUP and KNP. That is, many HUP visitors also go to KNP, but few KNP visitors go to HUP. This may be an anomaly of the data set, but it supports the belief that KNP is a primary attraction and HUP is a secondary one. For example, only 6 percent of surveyed visitors at KNP had actual itineraries that included HUP, and only 4 percent had contingent itineraries that did (the net effect of the scenarios presented at KNP was to reduce, rather than increase, visitation at HUP). All KNP models were negative binomial.

As expected, the coefficient on *fee KNP* is negative and highly significant, though least significant for NKNP. The price elasticity for TKNP at current fee levels is $-.006 * 4.60 = -.028$. The resulting predicted visitation at KNP is shown in figure 3.7, although the values for northern KNP and total KNP are so close that they mostly appear as one line.

The differences between southern KNP and northern KNP can be explained by the fact that scenario fee increases at the former were twice as great as at the latter—the coefficients and graph indicate that visitors responded to this difference as predicted (the drop in visitation at SKNP is roughly twice as great as at NKNP). That the TKNP line is essentially the same as the NKNP line is surprising, because one would expect it to be between the SKNP and NKNP lines. That is, the faster decline in SKNP should "pull-down" the TKNP line. However, there were no errors in the data—the change in TKNP equals the sum of the changes in SKNP and NKNP.

A comparison of this graph with the equivalent one for HUP (as well as the respective coefficients in the tables) indicates that visitors at SKNP are more price-responsive than in HUP. This may be due to the availability of NKNP as a better substitute for SKNP than Ithala or other northeastern KZN parks are for HUP.

The *fee KZN* variable was not significant for any of the models. The crowding variable was significant only for NKNP, and then only marginally. The positive sign presumably is because SKNP is more crowded

Table 3.12 Foreign Visitors Surveyed at Kruger National Park

	Dependent Variable Is Number of nights Spent at Each of the Following:					
	Southern KNP		Northern KNP		Total KNP	
	Coefficient	Significance Level	Coefficient	Significance Level	Coefficient	Significance Level
Constant	−0.285	0.457	−2.328	0.000	0.128	0.685
Fee KNP	−0.014	0.000	−0.006	0.010	−0.006	0.000
Crowds KNP			0.004	0.054		
Trips RSA	−0.110	0.035				
Trips other	−0.104	0.081				
Countries			0.185	0.032		
Self-org			0.489	0.001	0.264	0.004
Certain			0.406	0.011		
Big Five	0.203	0.013			0.141	0.010
Fee prior	0.801	0.000	0.642	0.001	0.583	0.000
Age			0.020	0.003	0.010	0.019
Education			0.131	0.089		
France	−0.444	0.078				
Income	0.207	0.035				

RSA = Republic of South Africa.
Note: A blank cell indicates that an independent variable was not significant at $p = 0.10$. These variables were dropped from the model.

Source: On-Site Visitor Survey.

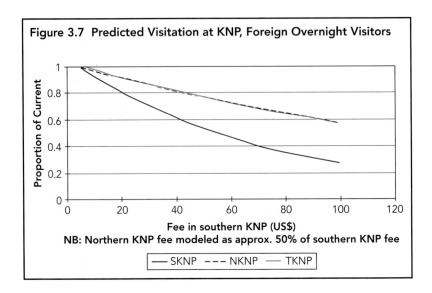

Figure 3.7 Predicted Visitation at KNP, Foreign Overnight Visitors

than the northern section (Ferreira and Harmse 1999), such that increased crowding for the park as a whole might displace some visitors from southern to northern KNP. The only other variable that was significant in all models was *fee prior*. Unlike for KZN parks, it was positive in the KNP models. This may be because it represents familiarity with, and thus commitment to, KNP as a destination.

Results: Resident Overnight Visitors to HUP and Ithala

Model results for resident HUP and Ithala visitors are shown in table 3.13. As before, the coefficient on *Fee KZN* had the expected sign and was significant in the HUP models, but was not significant in the Ithala or KNP model. Elasticity at current HUP prices is $-.004 * 9 = -.036$.

The relationship between price and visitation is shown graphically in figure 3.8. As expected, price-responsiveness (allowing for conversion to dollars) is greater among residents than among foreigners. Nonetheless, the results indicate that fees can be increased above their current level with only modest effect on visitation. For example, fees would have to be raised to approximately R40 before visitation would fall below 90 percent of its current level.

Again, neither the importance rating of fees nor crowding is significant. Few other variables were significant across models. *Self-org* was

Table 3.13 Resident Visitors Surveyed at Hluhluwe-Umfolozi Park and Ithala

| | Dependent Variable Is Number of Days Spent at Each of the Following: | | | | | | | |
| | HUP—NegBin | | HUP—OLS | | Ithala—Poisson | | KNP—Poisson | |
Variable	Coefficient	Significance Level	Coefficient	Significance Level	Coefficient	Significance Level	Coefficient	Significance Level
Constant	0.3895	0.076	1.6569	0.000	-2.6921	0.000	4.5650	0.000
Fee KZN	-0.0040	0.003	-0.0074	0.005				
#Paid for Ithala							-0.4148	0.001
Trips Africa					4.1782	0.000	0.0516	0.001
Self-org	0.3636	0.021	0.6191	0.040	-0.7732	0.002		
Big Five					-0.1439	0.047		
Certain							-2.2788	0.000
Fee prior							2.1084	0.000
Fee	-0.2528	0.064	-0.5497	0.049			-2.0781	0.000
Crowding	-0.3671	0.004	-0.7752	0.002			-2.8287	0.000
Appropriate fee					0.0140	0.000		
Fee Africa	0.3572	0.011	0.6054	0.021				
Household size							-0.4222	0.006
Income							0.5154	0.000

OLS = ordinary least squares; KNP = Kruger National Park.
Note: A blank cell indicates that an independent variable was not significant at $p = 0.10$. These variables were dropped from the model.

Source: On-Site Visitor Survey.

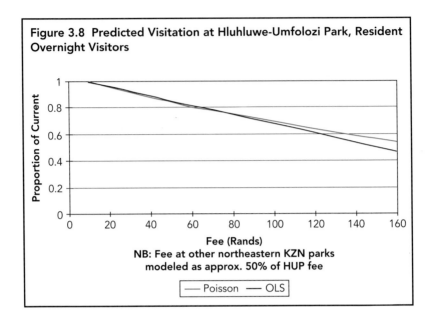

Figure 3.8 Predicted Visitation at Hluhluwe-Umfolozi Park, Resident Overnight Visitors

significant at both HUP and Ithala, but positive in the former and negative in the latter. The significance of *fee Africa* in HUP suggests that those with experience paying fees in other countries stay longer and/or are less responsive to fee increases, but this result should be treated with caution because 86 percent of the respondents fall into this category (there is little variability in responses).

Results: Resident Overnight Visitors to KNP

Results for resident overnight visitors at KNP are shown in table 3.14, but a data limitation should be noted. As in the surveys of foreign visitors, residents surveyed at KNP were presented a scenario that involved a fee increase in the northern section that was 50 percent of the increase in the southern section, such that the final fee in the north was approximately half of that in south. However, for scenario E, presented to 11 (6.5 percent) of the 169 respondents, a typographical error resulted in presentation of the value R250 rather than R25 for the northern section—in these cases, the increase in the northern section was 500 percent, rather than 50 percent, of that in the southern section. Nonetheless, it is the

Table 3.14 Resident Visitors Surveyed at Kruger National Park

| | Dependent Variable Is Number of Days Spent at Each of the Following: | | | | | |
| | Southern KNP | | Northern KNP | | Total KNP | |
Variable	Coefficient	Significance Level	Coefficient	Significance Level	Coefficient	Significance Level
Constant	1.4643	0.001	0.8586	0.081	1.8963	0.000
Fee KNP	-0.0079	0.000			-0.0042	0.000
#Paid for					-0.1215	0.007
Trips other	-0.2665	0.086				
Big Five	0.1571	0.093	-0.1643	0.036		
Past experience			-0.1223	0.069	-0.1193	0.011
Malaria			-0.1295	0.009		
Past KNP					0.0177	0.002
Fee					-0.2828	0.001
Crowding	0.5827	0.001				
Appropriate fee	-0.0096	0.003	0.0047	0.098		
Fee Africa			0.5439	0.000	0.4448	0.000
Age			0.0263	0.000	0.0137	0.000
Household size	-0.1510	0.006				

Note: A blank cell indicates that an independent variable was not significant at $p = 0.10$. These variables were dropped from the model.

Source: On-Site Visitor Survey.

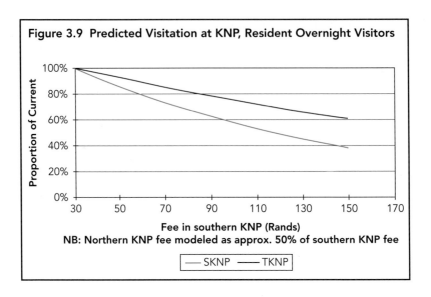

Figure 3.9 Predicted Visitation at KNP, Resident Overnight Visitors

value in the southern section (the main site) that is used in the data set. The error should enhance the significance of the KNP fee coefficient, because the respondents in these cases were presented a fee much higher than that contained in the data set. Despite this, the coefficient is non-significant in the NKNP model, presumably because of the mixed-substitution effect noted above. All models were estimated using the negative binomial approach.

The Fee KNP coefficients for SKNP and NKNP were highly significant, as expected. The price elasticity for total KNP is $-.0042 * 30 = -.126$. The effect of fees is shown graphically in figure 3.9. Neither the *fee KZN* nor the KNP crowding coefficients were significant. None of the remaining variables are significant in all of the KNP models, though several are significant in two of the three. The negative sign on the malaria coefficient is as expected, given the malarial risk at KNP. However, the negative signs on *past experience* and *Big Five* are not as expected.

Analysis of Congestion Effects on Day Visitors

Day visitors were not presented with CB scenarios, but they were asked about crowding—specifically, they were asked whether a doubling of visitors to the parks would have reduced the quality of their experience.

Table 3.15. Responses to a Doubling in Crowding

Option Selected	Percentage of Those Answering Question	
	Foreigners	Residents
Pay current entrance fee and go to zone that is twice as crowded	17	8
Pay current entrance fee plus an extra fee for zone with current crowding	67	71
Not come to the park, but spend days at parks elsewhere in South Africa	17	17
Not come to the park, and not spend days at parks elsewhere in South Africa	0	3

Source: On-Site Visitor Survey.

The 42 percent of foreign and 49 percent of resident respondents who said it would were then presented with a scenario involving zones in parks with differing degrees of crowdedness, and the requirement that an additional fee be paid for the zone representing the current level of crowding (rather than the doubling). The additional fee varied across respondents. Table 3.15 presents the summary information.

Because the overall samples of day visitors are small, and fewer than half reported that the doubling would reduce experience quality, the number of observations in this survey component is small—only 59 residents and 42 foreigners. Therefore, results broken down by fee levels are unreliable and are not reported here. However, broadly, in the case of residents the percentage willing to pay the extra fee remained stable across fee levels, which ranged from R10 to R60. In the case of foreigners, the percentage declined at higher fee levels, with drops occurring in the transition from $20 to $30 and $30 to $45.

DISCUSSION

This section summarizes the above results, with a focus on managerial variables such as price and crowding. Starting with importance ratings for considerations when choosing where to travel, the features of the

Table 3.16 Own-Price Elasticity at Original and Current Fee Levels

Respondent Category	HUP—at Fee Levels in Place		Total KNP at Sampling (R30 and $4.60)
	At Sampling (R9 and $1.40)	As of Nov. 2001 (R30 and $3.00)	
Residents	−0.036	−0.120	−0.126
Foreigners	−0.014	−0.030	−0.028

HUP = Hluhluwe-Umfolozi Park; KNP = Kruger National Park.

Note: The different dollar values for R30 are due to exchange rate changes between the sampling period and November 2001.

Source: On-Site Visitor Survey.

attractions themselves rate highest (for example, opportunity to see the Big Five). Overall, travel cost was rated "average" as a consideration, and for all four groups service quality was rated as more important than cost.

Turning to specific evaluations of price-responsiveness, the contingent valuation responses indicate very high willingness to pay for the overall trip to South Africa, with a departure tax of $250 being needed to reduce visitation by 50 percent. As one might expect, price responsiveness was greater for individual parks. Nonetheless, responses to the contingent behavior scenarios indicate that fees would have to be raised to fairly high levels before having a major impact on the number of visitors. The elasticity results are summarized in table 3.16.

In all cases, signs are as expected and demand is inelastic. Also as expected, elasticity is lower for foreigners than for residents. Somewhat surprisingly, for both markets elasticity at KNP at the time of sampling is greater than at HUP. However, this is partly because of the (then) higher fees at KNP—mathematically, as was illustrated above, higher fees lead to greater elasticity for a given coefficient in the Poisson and negative binomial formulation.

Several considerations should be kept in mind when interpreting the results. First, a reminder that the values presented here are conditional on the main-secondary differences in fee increases (for example, it assumes that price increases at HUP will be twice as great as at other KZN parks). Second, the CB models were only estimated using data from overnight visitors, and day visitors may react more dramatically.

Third, any past visitors who no longer visited because of fee levels charged at the time of sampling would not have been surveyed. Fourth, results are based on respondent reaction to hypothetical scenarios, rather than actual behavior in response to fee changes. Reactions to actual fees may be either greater or lesser than those indicated here. However, results from evaluations of both actual and hypothetical fee increases in Costa Rica (Chase and others 1998; Lindberg and Aylward 1999) suggested that actual responses may be less than those reported here—that is, that people would be even less price responsive than these results indicate. However, Lindberg and Aylward's evaluation involved actual fee levels only up to $15.

A related consideration is that visitation is determined not only by the decisions of visitors but also by the decisions of tour operators. Relative to visitors, operators generally have a greater knowledge of available attractions and may choose to bring their clients to alternate parks when one park raises fees and similar parks are available at lower price. Nonetheless, when there are no good substitutes or when all parks raise their fees by similar amounts, substitution may not be a problem.

Despite these qualifications, the results indicate that fees can be increased significantly without a major impact on visitor numbers, particularly for foreigners (the differential price-responsiveness noted above is one reason for establishing a two-tiered pricing structure, with higher fees for foreigners). Such a conclusion is based not only on the CV and CB results but also on responses to the "appropriate fee" question and experience with fees elsewhere.

Last, crowding does not appear to be a major problem at the moment. The crowding variable was not a good predictor in the CB models, even though in some scenarios the number of visitors was doubled. In addition, fewer than half the day visitor respondents said that a doubling of visitors would reduce the quality of their experience. Interestingly, of those who said they would be bothered by such a doubling, most would prefer to pay an extra fee to avoid the increased crowding. Thus, if visitor numbers continue to grow, it may be worthwhile to disperse visitors and increase fees to cover associated costs—or to use crowding (or lack thereof) as one basis for differential fees across or within parks.

Appendix 3-A. Demographic Characteristics of Types of Visitors (percent)

Demographic Variable	Resident Day	Resident Overnight	Foreign Day	Foreign Overnight
Gender				
Male	77	71	71	70
Female	23	29	29	30
Highest level of education				
Some years of high school or less	7	6	2	2
High school graduate or equivalent	29	27	14	15
Some years at university, college, or technical school	16	15	18	16
Diploma or degree from university, college, or technical school	34	35	34	37
Postgraduate diploma/degree/studies	16	17	30	30
No answer			1	1
Age (years)				
18–30	21	14	34	19
31–40	30	23	25	36
41–50	22	23	18	19
51–65	22	30	21	23
Older than 65	6	10	1	3
Gross annual income (thousands of rand)				
50 or less	8	4	4	2
51–100	19	20	7	2
101–150	21	23	8	4
151–250	29	24	15	12
251–350	7	13	14	15
351–500	6	7	13	20
More than 500	3	4	24	29
Volunteer	1	0	1	1
Student loan	0	0	3	1
Pensioner	0	0	0	2
Don't know	0	0	1	1
Refused to answer	7	5	9	14
Number of people in household				
1	7	8	21	17
2	35	43	51	55
3	13	14	11	9
4	25	22	11	13
5	14	9	3	4
6	5	2	2	2
7	1	1	1	0
More than 7	0	1	0	0

(continued)

Appendix 3-A. (*Continued*)

Demographic Variable	Resident Day	Resident Overnight	Foreign Day	Foreign Overnight
Province of residence				
Gauteng	36	36		
KZN	35	36		
Eastern Cape	0	1		
Western Cape	3	9		
Northern Cape	0	1		
Free State	0	2		
North West Province	3	2		
Northern Province	7	4		
Mpumalanga	16	9		
Country, region, or continent of residence				
United Kingdom			12	15
Germany			24	35
Benelux			14	20
Scandinavia			5	2
Other Europe			21	10
United States			7	10
Canada			1	2
South America			3	0
Australasia			3	3
Asia			1	1
Africa			2	2
Other			6	0

Note: This table shows demographic variables for each of the four categories of tourists, in percentages within each category: for example, 77 percent of the resident day visitors surveyed were male, 23 percent female.

Source: On-Site Visitor Survey.

APPENDIX 3-B. SAMPLE SCENARIO, FOREIGNERS SURVEYED IN KZN, SCENARIO A

In this scenario, the following features would exist:

Entrance fees at Hluhluwe-Umfolozi would be R75 ($10) higher than they are today.

Entrance fees at other public parks in northeastern KZN, including Ithala, would be R37 ($5) higher than they are today.

Entrance fees at Kruger National Park would be R0 ($0) higher than they are today.

The number of people in KZN parks, and thus the number of vehicles you would see, would increase by 0 percent. There would be no change in the number of people in Kruger National Park.

For reference, entrance fees at public parks in KZN currently are R9 ($1.20) per entry, plus a community levy, as well as vehicle fees at some parks.

For example, HUP and Ithala charge R30 ($4.00) per vehicle.

The entrance fee at Kruger National Park currently is R30 ($4.00) per entry plus R25 ($3.33) per vehicle.

NOTES

1. In reporting results, percentages are rounded to the nearest whole number, so totals do not always equal 100. In some cases (for example, countries visited and travel motivations), only response categories that represent a minimum percentage of the sample are reported. When the terms "significant" and "nonsignificant" are used in the context of data analysis, they refer to whether a variable is statistically significant at the $p = 0.05$ level, unless otherwise noted. All respondents were weighted equally in this analysis, regardless of visit frequency or the size of the group they represented or paid for (thus, a respondent answering on behalf of a family of four traveling together was treated the same as a respondent traveling alone).

2. Although price-quantity graphs in economics generally are presented with price on the y-axis, the CB graphs are presented with price on the x-axis to make them more intuitive to noneconomists.

REFERENCES

Chase, L. C., D. R. Lee, W. D. Schulze, and D. J. Anderson. 1998. "Ecotourism Demand and Differential Pricing of National Park Access in Costa Rica." *Land Economics* 74:466–82.

Eiswerth, M. E., J. Englin, E. Fadali, and W. D. Shaw. 2000. "The Value of Water Levels in Water-Based Recreation: A Pooled Revealed Preference/Contingent Behavior Model." *Water Resources Research* 36(4):1079–86.

Englin, J., and T. A. Cameron. 1996. "Augmenting Travel Cost Models with Contingent Behavior Data: Poisson Regression Analyses with Individual Panel Data." *Environmental and Resource Economics* 7:133–47.

Englin, J., and J. S. Shonkwiler. 1995. "Estimating Social Welfare Using Count Data Models: An Application to Long-Run Recreation Demand under Conditions of Endogenous Stratification and Truncation." *Review of Economics and Statistics* 77:104–12.

Ferreira, S. L. A., and A. C. Harmse. 1999. "The Social Carrying Capacity of Kruger National Park, South Africa: Policy and Practice." *Tourism Geographies* 1(3):325–42.

Lindberg, K., and B. Aylward. 1999. "Price Responsiveness in the Developing Country Nature Tourism Context: Review and Costa Rican Case Study." *Journal of Leisure Research* 31(3):281–99.

Seymour, J. 1998a. *KwaZulu-Natal's Domestic Tourism Market: June '98–September '98.* Durban: KwaZulu-Natal Tourism Authority.

———. 1998b. *KwaZulu-Natal's International Tourism Market: January '98.* Durban: KwaZulu-Natal Tourism Authority.

Siderelis, C., R. Moore, and J.-H. Lee. 2000. "Incorporating Users' Perceptions of Site Quality in a Recreation Travel Cost Model." *Journal of Leisure Research* 32(4):406–14.

CHAPTER 4

PREFERENCES FOR DEVELOPING-COUNTRY NATURE TOURISM IN OVERSEAS MARKETS

A Case Study of the Netherlands

Kreg Lindberg and Benedict G. C. Dellaert

ndividual countries and international organizations such as the World Tourism Organization (WTO) have long conducted evaluations of overseas tourism source markets. Because recognition of nature or ecotourism as a distinct market segment is relatively recent, there have been few evaluations of that source market segment. However, the information base is growing, with the WTO's recent studies of seven ecotourism-generating markets being an important contribution.[1]

This chapter contributes to that information base by providing an analysis of the Dutch market for developing-country nature tourism, based on a national survey of households in the Netherlands. It provides data on past and intended future trips and how demand is affected by cost and other factors. It should be read in conjunction with the international visitor component of chapter 3, which contains additional detail on foreign visitors to nature reserves in the study region (as well as to Kruger National Park).

After a brief description of sampling and survey versions, the chapter discusses recent and intended future trips, including trip and entrance fee costs. Next, ratings for South Africa relative to other African countries are presented for a set attributes. This is followed by an evaluation of World Heritage name recognition and effect on travel plans.

The second half of the chapter focuses on demand analysis, using site selection (SS) and choice models (CMs).[2]

SAMPLING, SURVEY ADMINISTRATION, AND SURVEY VERSIONS

This survey was conducted as part of the research company Gfk's ongoing national program of surveying Dutch households. The first stage of the survey was a "screener," in which respondents were asked about their past travel to the developing-country regions of Central and South America; West, Central, and Southern Africa; and Asia, with the regions identified on a map (these regions are referred to as the Americas, Africa, and Asia from here on). They were then asked about future travel plans to these regions. The screener was part of Gfk's regular survey process and was sent to 4,129 people, of whom 3,890 (94 percent) responded.

On the basis of responses to the screener, respondents were sorted into five categories:

- Past nature tourists to Africa: Those stating that they (1) had gone to Africa during the past $3^1/_2$ years and (2) went to a nature reserve in that region.

- Past nature tourist to the Americas: Those stating that they (1) had not gone to Africa on a past trip (during the past $3^1/_2$ years), but (2) had gone to the Americas, and (3) went to a nature reserve in that region.

- Past nature tourists to Asia: Those stating that they (1) had not gone to Africa on a past trip, but (2) had gone to Asia, and (3) went to a nature reserve in that region.

- Future nature tourists to Africa: Those stating that they (1) had not gone to any of the regions on a past trip, but (2) planned to go to Africa in the next 2 $^1/_2$ years, and (3) probably or certainly would go to a nature reserve in that region.

- All other respondents.

A second-stage "full survey" was sent to respondents in the first four categories in January 2001. There were four base versions of the survey questionnaire, with the number of completed questionnaires as indicated:

- Past nature tourists to Africa received a version of the questionnaire asking about their past trip to Africa and their preferences for a hypothetical future trip to Africa. Past trip details were used for the site selection model, whereas future trip responses were used for the choice model (see below). The number of completed questionnaires (N) in this group = 35 (group 1).

- Past nature tourists to the Americas received a questionnaire asking about their past trip to the Americas and their preferences for a hypothetical future trip to Africa. $N = 50$ (group 2).

- Past nature tourists to Asia received a questionnaire asking about their past trip to Asia and their preferences for a hypothetical future trip to Africa. $N = 64$ (group 3).

- Future nature tourists to Africa received a questionnaire asking about their preferences for a hypothetical future trip to Africa. $N = 53$ (group 4).

In short, the survey covered past trip behavior for each of the three regions, as well as stated preferences for future travel to Africa. A pilot test of the full survey was conducted, followed by the final administration. All of the 10 pilot surveys were completed and returned. Of the 248 final surveys sent out, 212 (86 percent) were returned.

Because the sample for the full survey was relatively small, and because the pilot version was almost identical to the final version, the pilot surveys were included in the full data set. As a result, the sample size for past nature tourists to Africa is 45. Despite the inclusion of the pilot surveys, the data set remains small, and the results should be interpreted with appropriate caution, especially when it comes to regional or country breakdowns.

The very high response rates for both the screener and the full survey suggest that nonresponse bias is not a problem. Weighting factors calculated by Gfk allow extrapolation of results to the Dutch population as a whole, and these were used in the analysis of screener results discussed below. However, given the small size of the full survey sample, as well as the way in which it was selected (based on past and intended future travel behavior, as described above), the weighting factor was not used to extrapolate results for the full survey. It needs to be stressed that the results for the full survey are not representative of all Dutch people, but rather only of those who meet the criteria of past or planned future trips to the regions used for the project.

DUTCH NATURE TOURISM TRAVEL TO DEVELOPING COUNTRIES

This section summarizes past trip behavior and attribute ratings for nature tourism in developing countries.

Screener Survey Results

The results of the screener survey were weighted to reflect estimated proportions for the Dutch population as a whole. Respondents were asked, for each of three regions, to state (1) whether they had gone on vacation to that region during the past $3^{1}/_{2}$ years (from January 1997 to the date of the survey), (2) whether they had gone to a nature reserve during that trip, (3) whether they were seriously planning to go to the region in the coming $2^{1}/_{2}$ years (June 2000 through December 2002), and (4) whether they planned to go to a nature reserve during such a trip. Results are shown in tables 4.1 and 4.2 (all tables in this chapter are based on data from the Dutch survey).

The responses indicate that Africa was the least popular of the three regions, but that nature reserves played a greater role as attractions

Table 4.1 Travel to Various Regions in the Past 3.5 Years

Region	Traveled to Region (percentage of sample)	Went to Nature Reserve? (percentage of those traveling to region)		
		Yes, It Was Main Attraction	Yes, But It Was Not Main Attraction	No
The Americas	2.9	20	49	32
Africa	1.5	26	59	15
Asia	3.4	8	52	40

Source: Data from Dutch Survey.

Table 4.2 Planning Travel to Various Regions

Region	Planning Travel to Region (percentage of sample)	Planning Travel to Nature Reserve? (percentage of those traveling to region)				
		Certainly	Probably	Probably Not	Certainly Not	Don't Know
The Americas	4.1	18	54	12	1	13
Africa	3.4	33	51	4	0	10
Asia	3.8	16	57	14	0	10

Source: Data from Dutch Survey.

there than in the other regions. Nonetheless, only in a quarter of the cases were nature reserves the main attraction. When extrapolated to the Dutch population as a whole, an estimated 223,000 Dutch people visited Africa during this period, of whom 58,000 went to a nature reserve as the main attraction.

As with past travel, responses indicate that Africa is the least popular of the three regions for planned future travel, though differences across regions are less noticeable. Also, nature reserves continue to play a greater role as attractions in Africa than in the other regions.

Though they are not directly comparable, the percentage of "yes" responses for past visits to nature reserves can be compared with the percentage of "certainly" and "probably" responses for planned travel. Only in the case of Asia does the proportion planning to visit nature reserves substantially exceed the proportion from past visits (16 + 57 = 73 percent versus 8 + 52 = 60 percent). Extrapolating to the whole Dutch population, 503,000 Dutch people are estimated to travel to Africa in the next 2 $\frac{1}{2}$ years, of whom 422,000 probably or certainly will visit a nature reserve. Keeping in mind that not all planned travel actually occurs, and that travel is affected by terrorism and other unpredictable factors, the expectation is that travel to Africa (as well as the other developing-country regions) is likely to increase in the future.

Summary of Most Recent Trip

The full questionnaire versions applied in the second stage included several questions about the respondents' most recent trip. The results, broken down by region, are shown in table 4.3.

Table 4.3 Countries Seriously Considered and Actually Visited in Most Recent Trip

Region and Country	Considered Visiting (percent)	Actually Visited (percent)	Conversion Rate (actually visited as percentage of considered)	Average Days	Median Days
Africa (including pilot) (n = 45)					
Kenya	33	13	40	15	14
Tanzania	29	7	23	9	10
Senegal	7	4	67	3	3
Gambia	13	11	83	13	10
South Africa	73	69	94	22	22
Zimbabwe	29	16	54	8	6
Botswana	24	9	36	6	6
Namibia	33	2	7	11	11
The Americas (n = 50)					
Mexico	62	40	65	16	15
Ecuador	12	4	33	14	14
Guatemala	20	10	50	7	10
Costa Rica	22	4	18	11	11
Venezuela	26	10	38	16	18
Brazil	32	14	44	20	20
Dominican Republic	24	2	8	14	14
Suriname	12	6	50	21	21
Asia (n = 64)					
India	28	14	50	35	24
Nepal	20	9	46	14	9
Sri Lanka	27	17	65	16	17
Thailand	53	36	68	19	18
Malaysia	30	14	47	14	9
Indonesia	53	27	50	29	25
Vietnam	11	3	29	31	31
China	28	16	56	15	10

Source: Data from Dutch Survey.

As indicated by the results in this table, South Africa does well on all measures, particularly within the African region. Almost three-quarters of respondents who went to Africa in the past 3.5 years (group 1 + pilot) considered going to South Africa on their most recent trip, and 94 percent of these actually went. The average days spent in the country was 22. This advantage holds when it comes to those planning to go to Africa in the future (group 4, not shown in the table). Of these, 79 percent were seriously considering South Africa, with the nearest competitor being Kenya, with 38 percent.

Various trip details were then gathered, and for those traveling to Africa (group 1) they are as follows. Roughly half (49 percent) traveled on a fully organized tour, 34 percent made all arrangements themselves, and the rest used a combination. More than half (57 percent) traveled in a party of two (including the respondent), whereas 26 percent traveled by themselves. On average, there were 3.57 people per party if a large group of 40 is retained in the data, and 2.50 people per party if it is excluded. A "party" was defined in the survey as including people known to each other before the start of the trip and excluding those met during the trip (for example, respondents might travel by themselves as part of a tour group).

Trip and Entrance Fee Costs

For the full data set, the average total trip cost by region is shown in table 4.4. The results indicate that the Americas are the most expensive in total cost. However, when one divides by the number of people paid for, which is the more appropriate measure, Africa is the most expensive. All monetary figures are in U.S. dollars, unless otherwise noted, and were converted from Dutch guilders at 1 euro = $0.8795 = NLG 2.2.

Total trip costs and entrance fee costs were then broken down by countries. Many respondents visited multiple countries on their trip, and in these situations it is difficult to allocate costs across the countries. Therefore, trip costs shown in table 4.5 are only for those who visited a single country during their trip. In addition, respondents who reported a zero cost or a missing value for cost were excluded. The costs include amounts paid both in advance and locally. Table 4.5 also shows average entrance fees paid across countries.

Table 4.4 Trip Costs and Advance Payment by Region (US$)

Region	Total Cost	Percentage Paid in Advance	Cost per Person
Africa (including pilot)	3,100	61	2,012
The Americas	3,273	64	1,631
Asia	2,621	52	1,557

Source: Data from Dutch Survey.

Table 4.5 Average Total Trip Costs and Entrance Fees Paid (US$, the number of observations on which the figures are based is shown in parentheses)

| Country | Costs | | Entrance Fees |
	Per Person	Per Person per Day	
Africa	*2,242*	*104*	*10*
Kenya	1,330 (3)	95	30 (1)
Tanzania	1,995 (1)	125	22 (2)
Senegal			6 (1)
Gambia	1,164 (2)	67	4 (4)
South Africa	2,487 (21)	107	6 (6)
Zimbabwe			18 (2)
Botswana			10 (1)
Namibia			
Other			8 (5)
The Americas	*1,562*	*90*	*12*
Mexico	1,649 (13)	96[a]	13 (8)
Ecuador	1,995 (2)	158	1 (1)
Guatemala			10 (3)
Costa Rica	1,995 (1)	100	8 (1)
Venezuela	1,189 (4)	68	22 (2)
Brazil	1,450 (5)	73	25 (2)
Dominican Republic	1,247 (1)	89	
Suriname	1,539 (3)	74	
Other			8 (5)
Asia	*1,371*	*80*	*10*
India	1,197 (3)	41	2 (3)
Nepal	2,993 (1)	120	14 (2)
Sri Lanka	1,185 (6)	93	4 (1)
Thailand	1,327 (11)	65	5 (5)
Malaysia	1,132 (4)	98	40 (1)
Indonesia	1,374 (9)	57	11 (4)
Vietnam	1,995 (1)	95	
China	1,537 (5)	132	
Other			15 (3)

Note: See text for data limitations; blank cells indicate lack of data.
[a]In the Mexico per-person-day calculation, one outlier observation was removed.

Source: Data from Dutch Survey.

As shown by the numbers of observations, the country-level figures are based on few observations and should be interpreted with caution—given the exclusions noted above, the trip cost averages are based on a total of only 98 observation across the three regions combined. Indeed, some of the results are based on a single observation, and for some countries there were no data at all. Only three countries (Mexico, South Africa, and Thailand) generated at least 10 observations on cost, and within Africa only one country (South Africa) had more than 3 observations.

One can have more confidence in the regional averages, but even these are based on small sample sizes. In addition to the sample size problem, there may be recall errors, especially in the case of entrance fees—in many cases, respondents reported going to nature reserves but did not report a fee, which may be because of either lack of recall or lack of fee.

South Africa Relative to Other African Countries

Respondents who had visited Africa in the past or were planning a trip to Africa in the future were asked to rate eight countries on 12 different attributes. For each attribute, respondents rated each country relative to others in the region. For 7 of the attributes, the scale was from "much worse than average" (–3) to "much better than average" (+3):

1. Quality of the natural sites (for example, the possibility of seeing wildlife and experiencing unspoiled nature).

2. Quality of cultural sites (for example, the possibility of experiencing other cultures or to see historic sites).

3. Variety in sites (that is, both natural and cultural sites, as well as beaches, nice shopping, and so on).

4. How familiar you are with the local sites.

5. Quality of tourist facilities (such as accommodation, guides, excursions, and roads).

6. How quiet and unspoiled nature, sights, and the facilities are.

7. Recommendations by friends, family, and travel agents.

For the other 5 attributes, the rating scale was from "much higher than average" (–3) to "much lower than average" (+3) (because these are "negative" attributes, higher = worse):

8. Cost of traveling to the country (for example, flights from Amsterdam).

9. Cost of local transportation (for example, bus or domestic flights).

10. Local costs (such as accommodation, meals, and souvenirs).

11. Risk of catching malaria.

12. Risk of being robbed or mugged.

Figure 4.1 shows the ratings for South Africa, with the values representing average (mean) ratings for those tourists who had visited Africa in the past (group 1 + pilot).

Keeping in mind the small sample size, and the dominance in the data set of people who actually visited South Africa (table 4.3), the ratings shown in figure 4.1 indicate that respondents generally viewed South Africa in positive terms relative to other countries in the region.

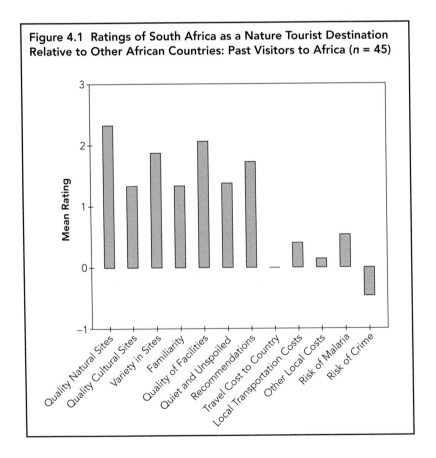

Figure 4.1 Ratings of South Africa as a Nature Tourist Destination Relative to Other African Countries: Past Visitors to Africa (n = 45)

South Africa was rated particularly well in terms of quality of natural sites and quality of tourist facilities. The only attribute for which South Africa rated worse than average was risk of being robbed or mugged.

Figure 4.1 shows means (averages), but one might expect variability across respondents. This is shown in the box-whisker plot of the same data in figure 4.2. This plot illustrates the substantial variability in ratings for some attributes, particularly for crime risk.

Average ratings for those respondents planning to go to Africa (group 4) are shown in figure 4.3. The ratings show the same general

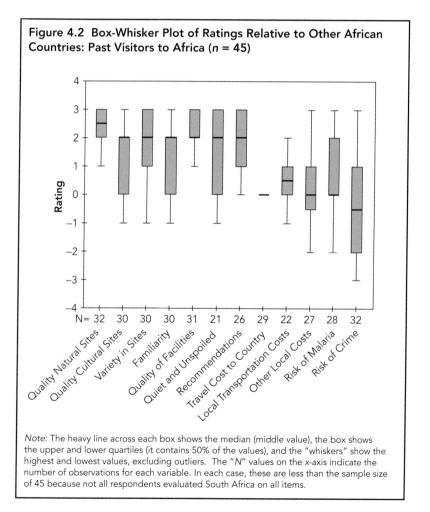

Figure 4.2 Box-Whisker Plot of Ratings Relative to Other African Countries: Past Visitors to Africa (*n* = 45)

Note: The heavy line across each box shows the median (middle value), the box shows the upper and lower quartiles (it contains 50% of the values), and the "whiskers" show the highest and lowest values, excluding outliers. The "*N*" values on the x-axis indicate the number of observations for each variable. In each case, these are less than the sample size of 45 because not all respondents evaluated South Africa on all items.

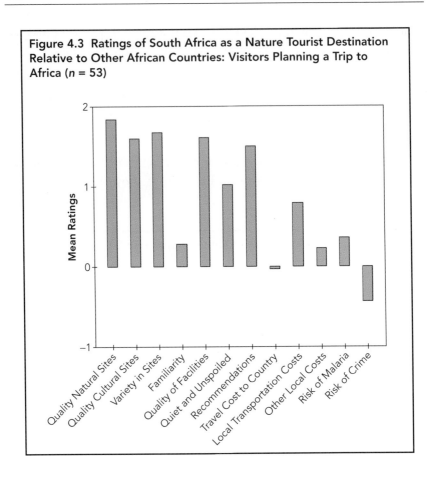

Figure 4.3 Ratings of South Africa as a Nature Tourist Destination Relative to Other African Countries: Visitors Planning a Trip to Africa (n = 53)

pattern, with the exception that the rating for familiarity with local sites is lower.

World Heritage Name Recognition and Effect on Travel Plans

Anecdotally, designations such as "national park" or "World Heritage Site" are thought to enhance the reputation of sites and to increase visitation. However, this effect has not been well studied empirically, in part because it is difficult to isolate the effect of designation from other factors. For example, sites that have such designations already tend to be attractive to visitors, and increased infrastructure or other spending associated with designation may be more important than designation per se.

As a limited evaluation of the awareness and role of World Heritage designation, respondents were asked:

> Natural and cultural sites can have various official names and designations, such as "national park." In this study, we are interested in how well known the status "World Heritage" is. Do you know this term?

Approximately half (49 percent) did not know the term; 7 percent selected "I have seen the term, but don't know what it means"; 34 percent selected "I know roughly what it means"; and 11 percent selected "I know exactly what it means." Those in the latter three categories, who had at least seen the term, were asked:

> Thinking back on your trip, can you remember if you knew which sites in the countries you considered visiting had the "World Heritage" designation? If so, did this designation affect your decision to visit these sites?

More than half (57 percent) did not know which sites had the designation, 20 percent knew and were more inclined to visit those sites, and 23 percent knew but this knowledge did not affect their decision to visit the sites (a "knew and less inclined to visit" category was also provided, but nobody selected that one).

The population for this survey was Dutch people who have traveled to developing countries and/or who planned to travel to Africa in the near future. Therefore, it is not representative of the general population. However, it is broader than the population of visitors who are surveyed at World Heritage sites, and thus more representative of the general population. The results indicate that a minority, but a substantial proportion, of the population had some concept of World Heritage. In addition, it does affect the travel decisions of a substantial number of people—in this case, 20 percent of those who had at least seen the term, or just under 10 percent of the survey population as a whole.

DEMAND ANALYSIS AND MODELS

Related to the question of how well South Africa performs on a set of attributes is the question of which attributes affected a person's decision regarding what country to visit. In the On-Site Survey (OSS), importance ratings were asked directly to address this issue (see chapter 3).

In the Origin Country Survey, site selection and choice models were used. These are described in the following sections.

Factors Affecting Trip Decisions: Site Selection Model

As was mentioned in chapter 2, Loomis (1995) noted that there are four steps in the recreation choice process: (1) whether to participate in an activity, (2) which site to visit if one chooses to participate, (3) how many trips to take to the site, and (4) how long to stay at the site. These steps arose in the context of outdoor recreation in the United States, a context in which it is common for respondents to make more than one trip per year. For that reason, participation models that estimate trips per year are typically combined with site selection models of which site to visit on a given trip.

The focus here is on selection of a site or destination, in this case which country to visit on a given trip. In the U.S. recreation context, the probability of choosing a particular site from a set of possible sites is modeled as a function of the travel cost and quality attributes of the various sites. Travel cost is typically based on travel distance multiplied by the cost per mile or per kilometer, with the assumption that respondents drive to the sites. The quality variables vary across studies but can include factors such as lake water levels or fish catch rate.

In this study, travel to countries was by plane, though internal travel may be by various modes. Given the small size of the origin country, most or all flights would be from the same airport—Schiphol in Amsterdam. It is important to note that airfares may vary more to a particular destination than between destinations in a region (the cost to a given destination depends on whether the ticket was purchased individually or as part of a package, as well as on the class and subclass traveled). Therefore, rather than calculate an average cost of travel based on distance, the intention was to use the actual price paid by respondents visiting the various countries. However, as was noted above, the data set was too small to confidently estimate average travel cost, or entrance fees, across the eight countries for each region. Therefore, the independent variables were limited to respondent rating of the 12 attributes given above.

Because the number of observations for individual regions was low, the regions were combined into a pooled data set. That is, the data are from the combined groups 1 through 3, plus the pilot. Each respondent was modeled as choosing from a set of nine countries—the eight rated for the region in which he/she traveled and a null "all other" country that takes on the value 0 (average) for all the attributes. Those respondents who visited a country in the region other than the eight rated were modeled as having chosen "country 9."

Respondents were asked to rate all eight countries in their region on all 12 attributes. However, respondents generally rated only a subset of the eight, presumably because of lack of knowledge about the others. When actual ratings were available, those values were used. When values were missing, two different approaches (and thus analyses) were utilized. In the first, the series mean for that country * attribute combination was used, controlling for region. For example, if respondent 103 did not rate Senegal on the quality of natural sites, the average rating given to Senegal for this attribute by others was used. In the second, 0 (average performance) ratings were used when the respondent did not rate the country on the first attribute (quality of natural sites, which was not only the first task but also likely a salient one).

The second (average performance) approach is based on the assumption that if a respondent cannot rate a country, then the country was not part of his or her "choice set" when deciding which country to visit. This assumption does not always hold true, because some respondents did not rate all countries they reported visiting, let alone the ones they said they considered. Conversely, the first (series mean) approach assumes that all eight countries were part of a respondent's "choice set," and that also does not always hold true, because the results presented in table 4.3 indicate that most countries were considered by fewer than one-third of the respondents. Indeed, the "average" model generated a much better fit to the data, so that model is presented here.

Of the 159 respondents who traveled to one of the three regions, 9 did not report a total trip cost or reported a cost of 0. These observations were deleted on the assumption that the respondent did not personally choose the destination (that is, the trip was a gift or for business). In addition, 30 respondents visited multiple countries. Although one might create country groupings to allow for such multiple destination trips (see, for example, Mendelsohn and others 1992), only one grouping (Mexico and Guatemala) was visited by more than two respondents.

Table 4.6 Site Selection Model of Factors Affecting Country Choice

Variable (attributes and country dummy variables)	Coefficient	Significance Level
2. Quality of cultural sites	0.416	0.020
3. Variety in sites	0.469	0.014
4. How familiar you are with the local sites	0.715	0.000
6. How quiet and unspoiled are nature, sights, and the facilities	0.497	0.005
9. Cost of local transportation	0.555	0.008
10. Local costs (for example, accommodation, meals, and souvenirs)	0.343	0.081
South Africa	1.570	0.005
Ecuador	−1.801	0.089

Note: As described in the text, the ratings for the cost variables are reversed, such that a higher rating reflects lower costs. Thus, a positive coefficient indicates that perceptions that a country has low cost levels increase the probability of that country being visited.

Source: Data from Dutch Survey.

Moreover, it is difficult to incorporate such groupings in the present case where responses across regions are pooled. Therefore, these 30 observations were deleted, leaving a data set with 120 observations.

A multinomial logit (MNL) model was estimated, with country choice as the dependent variable. This model evaluates the probability that a given country is selected as a function of the ratings of that country and the ratings of other countries. An initial model including the 12 attributes was estimated, but coefficients that were nonsignificant at $p = 0.10$ were deleted. This generated the model shown in table 4.6.

The model fit the data well, with an adjusted McFadden's rho-squared (constants only) of 0.34. Familiarity was the most important attribute in terms of both coefficient magnitude and significance. The quality of natural sites was not significant, but further evaluation indicated that this is because of combining data across the three regions. In particular, Mexico was the most visited country in the Americas region, but it also was rated the lowest in that region on natural sites.

This finding illustrates the variety of attributes that are valued by tourists in determining which country to visit. The quality of cultural sites appears more uniformly significant across the regions, as does the variety in sites. Local transport costs and, to a lesser degree, local costs generally are significant, but the cost of traveling to the country is not. Neither crime nor malaria risk is significant.

Although these 12 attributes were selected on the basis that they would be most likely to affect destination choice, it is recognized that many additional factors are involved. The inclusion of dummy variables for each country allows one to estimate, in combination, "country brand effects" (for example, travel to countries based on their overall reputation) and specific attributes that were not rated and thus not included in the above model.

Of the 24 countries, only the dummy variables for South Africa and Ecuador were significant. Ecuador has a negative sign, which indicates a negative brand image—given its individual attribute ratings, it "deserves" greater market share than it receives. Conversely, South Africa has a positive image, indicating that its market dominance exceeds what one would expect from its ratings on attributes (or that there is another attribute or set of attributes on which South Africa rates well, and/or Ecuador rates poorly, and which was not included in the model). South Africa's positive image may be a result of historical and family connections with the Netherlands and/or a "post-apartheid" effect of goodwill and media coverage leading to a greater awareness of the country.

A key benefit of site selection models such as this one is that they are based on actual behavior—the choices respondents have made regarding which sites to visit. However, there are also drawbacks. One of these is that, depending on how much information is requested per trip, it can be burdensome on respondents to provide information on multiple trips, which limits the sample size.

In addition, the independent variables often will be colinear. In this data set, the largest bivariate correlation was 0.679 between quality of cultural sites and variety of sites. However, several correlations, using both Pearson and Spearman methods, were 0.500 or greater. Though well under the common rule of thumb for colinearity (0.800), these correlations are high enough to keep in mind. A complementary modeling approach, choice modeling, was also used to increase the sample size and avoid the potential problem of colinearity. The results of that analysis are presented in the next section.

Factors Affecting Trip Decisions: Choice Model

Choice modeling is described in the introduction to part 2 and its application is also illustrated in chapter 2. Like the SS approach, CM focuses on site choices, but in this case using hypothetical sites characterized by specified attributes and levels (for example, specific entrance fee or natural quality levels). CM is used to estimate the probability that consumers will choose a particular product (country, nature reserve, and so on) on the basis of the attributes of that product relative to those of others in the market.

This survey contained CM scenarios in which respondents were asked to choose among five countries that they could select as the main destination for their next trip to Africa (the five included the East African countries of Kenya and Tanzania, as well as Nambia, South Africa, and Zimbabwe). For each country, the scenarios contained specific levels for travel costs, malaria and crime risks, and natural attractiveness. A sample scenario and instructions is provided in appendix 4-A.

Two different levels were used for Quality of Natural Attractions ("good" or "very good"), and for the two attributes related to health and crime risk. The latter two were described as the risk of catching malaria (higher than average [1 in 500] or lower than average [1 in 5,000]) and the risk of crime (higher than average [1 in 500] or lower than average [1 in 5,000]), respectively. Monetary values are in Dutch guilders (NLG), and four different levels were used for local cost per day (150, 225, 300, or 375) and flight cost (1,000, 1,500, 2,000, or 2,500). The levels for the cost attributes were selected based on realistic ranges for travel to Africa at the time of data collection. In addition, all attributes were evaluated for perceived realism with travel experts and regular travelers. Nonetheless, the scenario levels may not reflect actual risk or cost levels for any given country.

Namibia was used as a "base" option, with constant levels across all choices. For the other countries, these levels were systematically varied. By observing respondent choices across the varying levels, the effect of each of the attributes can be estimated.

In the model presented here, the choice of the most attractive country was evaluated using multinomial logit. In each scenario, the respondent chose one of the five countries. Respondents then indicated whether they would actually visit the country in the next two years if the description were accurate. Those saying "no" were treated as choosing "Other"—that is, a country other than these five, or no country at all.

A value of good natural attraction quality was set equal to 1, whereas very good was set equal to 2. Thus, the coefficient reflects the benefit of change from good to very good quality. For both malaria and crime, low risk was set at 1, whereas high risk was set at 2. Thus, the coefficients are expected to be negative, indicating the negative effect of an increase in malaria or crime risk. "Other" was given a value of zero for each attribute. Demographic variables were used to predict the likelihood of choosing one of the five African countries (instead of the "Other" option). Thus, a positive coefficient on income indicates that those with higher income are more likely to travel to one of these Africa countries than are those with lower income.

All respondents (groups 1 through 4 plus the pilot) were presented the CM scenarios, so the data set contained 212 respondents. Each was presented four scenarios, so there were 848 choice occasions. However, 27 of the choices were missing values, so the data set contained 821 choices. In the model shown in table 4.7, there was also the item "nonresponse," which led to 766 observations being included in the analysis. The model had an adjusted McFadden's rho-squared (constants only) of 0.14 (relative to constants only) and was significant at $p = 0.00000$.

As expected, the coefficients on malaria and crime are highly significant and negative. The value for crime is higher than for malaria, which indicates that respondents were more concerned about crime risk. The coefficients for the two main price variables (local costs and flight) were

Table 4.7 Choice Model

Variable	Coefficient	p-Value
Malaria	−0.670	0.000
Crime	−1.010	0.000
Local costs (NLG per day)	−0.006	0.000
Local costs = NLG375 ("highest cost level" dummy variable)	0.690	0.018
Flight cost (thousands of NLG)	−0.436	0.001
Income	0.118	0.001
Female	0.354	0.031
Plan to go to Africa	1.695	0.000
South Africa	2.038	0.000
Zimbabwe	0.799	0.069
Kenya	1.369	0.002
Tanzania	0.872	0.046
Namibia	0.565	0.378

Note: NLG = Dutch guilders.

Source: Data from Dutch Survey.

also negative, as expected, indicating that respondents preferred lower prices to higher prices. Nonetheless, the local costs = NLG375 dummy variable indicates that price-responsiveness decreases at the high end of the market.[3]

The positive signs for income and female indicate that female respondents and those with a higher income are more likely to choose one of the five African countries than are male respondents and those with a lower income. The Africa plan variable was included as a consistency test. Before the presentation of the scenarios, respondents were asked whether they intend to travel to Southern or Central Africa in the next two years. The positive sign on the Africa plan variable indicates that those who said they were intending to travel to the region indeed were more likely to choose one of the five countries relative to the "all other" base.

All country variables are significant except Namibia, which served as the base. South Africa has the largest coefficient, which is consistent with its domination of past trips in the data set (shown in table 4.3). Zimbabwe had somewhat more past trips than Kenya and many more than Tanzania, but both of these countries had a larger coefficient than Zimbabwe's in the choice model. This may reflect decreased interest in traveling to Zimbabwe because of political instability there at the time of the survey.

Several variables were included in the initial model and then removed because of nonsignificance (at $p = 0.10$). The natural attraction quality attribute was one of these, and its nonsignificance was unexpected. It may be due to the effect noted in the site selection model above, in which natural attractions were not the main criterion for respondents in country choice. However, it was more important for those traveling to Africa in the site selection model. Another possible explanation is that it is difficult to be specific about different levels of quality because "quality" can incorporate many different attributes. The resulting generic specification of a good versus very good "quality of natural attractions" may not have been sufficiently meaningful to respondents (or respondents simply may have been satisfied with a good rating).

Neither age nor education was a significant predictor of whether one would select from the group of five rather than all other countries. Moreover, the variable from the screener survey reflecting whether respondents had traveled to Africa during the past 3.5 years also was nonsignificant. This suggests, in this context, that past travel behavior does not consistently predict future behavior, either positively (repeat visitation) or negatively (variety seeking).

The significance of local costs = NLG375 was noted above. Additional cost dummies for local costs = NLG300, flight costs = NLG2000, and flight costs = NLG2500 were nonsignificant, indicating that the leveling off of price-responsiveness only occurs at the highest level of local cost and does not occur in either of the two highest levels of flight cost. Interaction variables were estimated for combinations of South Africa and each of the attributes. None of the coefficients was significant, which suggests that South Africa has a brand effect, but that this is independent of the attributes—that is, visitors prefer South Africa over the other four named countries, but do not respond to prices, crime, or malaria differently in South Africa than in other countries.

CM can be used to calculate the choice probability or "market share" of destinations given a specified set of attribute levels. For example, using the results shown above, the estimated market share of South Africa, the four other destinations, and the rest of the world is shown in table 4.8.

Table 4.8 Market Share across Options (percent)

Scenarios	South Africa	Other Four African Countries Combined	Other Countries or Don't Travel
Base			
All five African countries have the same levels: low malaria and crime risk, NLG225 ($90) per day local costs, and NLG1,500 ($600) flight costs	27	36	37
Changes			
Higher local costs for South Africa: NLG300 ($120) per day	18	40	41
Higher flight costs for South Africa: NLG1,750 ($700)	25	37	38
Lower local costs for South Africa: NLG150 ($60) per day	37	31	32
High malaria risk for South Africa	16	42	43
High crime risk for South Africa	12	44	45

Note: NLG = Dutch guilders. $ = US$.

Source: Data from Dutch Survey.

As was noted above, after indicating their preference over the five African destinations, respondents were asked whether they would actually visit the country chosen. Across all scenarios, 45 percent said they would visit the destination selected. This is higher than the 35 percent of respondents who, in the Africa plan question, said they intend to travel to Southern or Central Africa in the next two years. This may reflect the hypothetical nature of the choice scenarios and/or the information presented in them (for example, attributes were limited in number, and presented attribute levels may not reflect actual levels in those countries). In any case, the market share results should be treated with some caution when it comes to absolute percentages. More confidence can be placed on relative percentages (for example, across countries, and changes in percentages caused by changes in attribute levels).

As a starting point, a base was specified that represented the same levels for each attribute across each of the five countries: low malaria and crime risk, NLG225 per-day local costs, and NLG1,500 flight costs. For reference, the results shown in table 4.5 indicate actual average per-day costs (both local and paid in advance) of NLG269 ($107) for South Africa, NLG238 ($95) for Kenya, and NLG313 ($125) for Tanzania. In other words, once one adjusts for nonlocal costs such as airfares, actual per-day costs were lower than most of the levels used in the CM scenarios (because they came from the same survey, the data on per-day costs were not available at the time the CM scenarios were developed).

In the base case, all levels are equal across the five countries, so market share between them is determined only by the country constants. The simulation illustrates clearly the effects of changes in the attributes. If local or flight costs for South Africa are increased (the first two changes), while holding costs in other countries at base levels, South Africa's market share decreases—there is a loss of market share to the other four countries and the rest of the world. Conversely, if local costs are decreased (third change) South Africa achieves a gain in market share, from 27 percent to 37 percent. Higher malaria or crime risk lead to dramatic losses in market share, from 27 percent to 16 percent and 12 percent, respectively.

Simple elasticity calculations illustrate price responsiveness, using the change from the base to the higher local and flight costs shown in table 4.8. For local costs, the price elasticity is –1.0, whereas for flight costs it is –0.44. For a local cost decrease (from NLG225 to NLG150), the elasticity is –0.54. These values are inelastic, with the exception of the unitary elasticity figure, but are much higher than those found in other study components, notably the On-Site Survey (chapter 3). In that component, price elasticity among foreigners for entrance fees was estimated at –0.014 for Hluhluwe-Umfolozi Park. However, entrance fees are a different type of cost and are relatively small in magnitude.

CONCLUSION

This concluding section briefly compares the results of the site selection and choice modeling models with each other and with the ratings by foreigner on-site respondents (chapter 3). Any such comparison is inherently limited by the differences in the two approaches within the Dutch survey, and by the fact that the On-Site Survey was (1) completed by all foreigners, rather than just Dutch residents, and (2) completed at specific nature reserves in one country, rather than at the variety of locations and countries visited by the Dutch respondents. Nonetheless, it can shed light on areas of agreement, or lack thereof.

The responses to the OSS importance rating indicated that five attributes were most important: the likelihood of seeing the Big Five species, the opportunity to experience a different culture, the variety of attractions, the reputation of sites, and the quality of the services and facility. This rating is partly consistent with the Dutch SS results, where site variety and cultural site quality were significant. Familiarity was important in the SS model, whereas in the OSS reputation was very important and past travel experience was of medium importance. Natural site quality would be closest to the Big Five attribute, but it was not significant in the SS model, nor was the quality of tourist facilities and services.

Turning to the CM analysis, natural attractiveness again was non-significant. As with the SS model, this presumably reflects the wide range of countries visited by the Dutch respondents, and the variety of motivations for doing so.[4] With regard to cost, both local costs and flight costs were significant in the CM model. Local costs, but not flight costs, were significant in the SS model. Travel cost was of medium importance in the OSS ratings.

Last, the risk of crime was significant in the CM model, but not in the SS model; it was of average importance in the OSS ratings. Malaria was important in the CM model, though the coefficient was of lower magnitude than for crime. It was not significant in the SS model, and it was of average to below average importance in the OSS ratings.

In summary, the positive features that attract visitors emerge as the most important attributes. It is notable that South Africa rates well on those features, as is indicated by the figures above (ratings for natural and cultural sites, variety in sites, and unspoiled nature). South Africa also rates well on service quality (attribute 5). The country is close to average in the three travel cost attributes, and indications are mixed about the importance of these attributes.

In other words, cost does not appear to be a priority issue for tourism in South Africa. Despite the presence of malaria in Kruger National Park and portions of KwaZulu-Natal Province, South Africa was rated better than its African competitors on this feature. In addition, it does not appear to be a major consideration for visitors, perhaps because prophylactics such as mefloquine are available. Crime risk is considered important, and this is the only attribute for which South Africa rates poorly. As the tourism industry already knows well, South Africa's crime problem can, and presumably already does, have an important impact on demand for the country's tourism product.

APPENDIX 4-A. SAMPLE SCENARIO FROM THE CHOICE MODEL

Please assume that due to factors such as political developments and shifts in fuel prices, future circumstances differ from those in the past. In each of the following choices a different scenario is presented. Please indicate which destination you would choose for a trip to Africa. After each choice you can indicate whether you would really like to travel to the country that you chose.

In every choice, 5 countries are presented. The characteristics of the first four destinations vary, while the fifth destination remains the same. The first four countries are described using the following 5 characteristics (Note: f = Dutch guilders, or NLGs):

1. Quality of natural attractions: good or very good.

2. Risk of catching malaria: higher than average (1 in 500) or lower than average (1 in 5,000).

3. Risk of crime: higher than average (1 in 500) or lower than average (1 in 5,000).

4. Local costs per person per day: $f150, f225, f275, f300$, or $f375$.

5. Flight cost: $f1,000, f1,500, f1,750, f2,000$, or $f2,500$.

The fifth destination is Namibia, which has the fixed characteristics of: quality of natural sites = good, risk of malaria = high, risk of crime = high, local costs are $f275$ and flight cost is $f1,750$.

Please tick the destination that you find most attractive given these characteristics.

NB: Tick only one country per choice.

Choice 1

	Destination				
	South Africa	**Zimbabwe**	**Kenya**	**Tanzania**	**Namibia**
Quality of natural attractions	Very good	Very good	Good	Good	Good
Risk of catching malaria	Low	High	Low	High	High
Risk of crime	Low	Low	High	High	High
Local costs (per day)	$f150$	$f375$	$f375$	$f150$	$f275$
Flight cost	$f1,000$	$f1,500$	$f2,000$	$f1,500$	$f1,750$
Please tick the most attractive destination	[ ]	[ ]	[ ]	[ ]	[ ]

NOTES

1. The markets were Germany, United States, United Kingdom, Canada, Spain, France, and Italy (World Tourism Organization 2002).

2. In reporting results, percentages are rounded to the nearest whole number, so totals do not always equal 100.

3. Decreasing price-responsiveness has also been found elsewhere (Dellaert and Lindberg, forthcoming).

4. As noted in the SS section, Dutch travel to South Africa may be affected significantly by family and historical connections, rather than predominantly by the types of natural and cultural features that attract other visitors.

REFERENCES

Dellaert, B. G. C., and K. Lindberg. (Forthcoming). "Variations in Tourist Price Sensitivity: A Stated Preference Model to Capture the Joint Impact of Systematic Utility and Price Response Consistency. *Leisure Sciences*.

Loomis, J. B. 1995. "Four Models for Determining Environmental Quality Effects on Recreation Demand and Regional Economics. *Ecological Economics* 12:55–65.

Mendelsohn, R., J. Hof, G. Peterson, and R. Johnson. 1992. "Measuring Recreation Values with Multiple Destination Trips." *American Journal of Agricultural Economics*, pp. 926–33.

World Tourism Organization. 2002. *The U.S. Ecotourism Market*. Madrid: World Tourism Organization.

CHAPTER 5

ARE THERE LATENT MARKETS FOR NATURE TOURISM IN SOUTH AFRICA?

An Evaluation of Non-Whites' Participation and Preferences

Kreg Lindberg, Aki Stavrou, Erica Wilson, and Shandir Ramlagan

Research conducted to date indicates that park visitation (participation) varies across racial and ethnic groups (Cordell, Betz, and Green 2002; Floyd 1999)[1] Goldsmith (1994) observed that minorities are largely absent in most national parks in the United States. As was noted by Floyd (1999), the U.S. National Park Service 1997 *Strategic Plan* states that the low participation of minorities "is an important cultural and social issue … and many parks do not attract and offer park experiences meaningful to visitors from varied ethnic backgrounds, or have not yet made their park values relevant to them" (U.S. National Park Service 1997, 55).

Floyd continues by noting that the National Park Service must ensure that its management policies promote equal access to parks. Similarly, Driver and others (1996, 5) observed that "if public land managers are to be responsive to the changing needs and values of an increasingly multicultural citizenry in management planning, they must work toward a fuller understanding of those needs and values" (see also Ewert 1999). Research can contribute to this understanding.

Although the academic literature on this topic is almost entirely dominated by studies from the United States, the issues are relevant to many countries. In South Africa, Africans (Blacks) are not a numerical minority, as they are in the United States, but they, Asians, and Coloureds are minorities in terms of status. Moreover, visitation at South African parks historically has been dominated by White South Africans and White foreigners. In the "New" (postapartheid) South Africa, efforts have been made to increase the participation of non-Whites in all aspects of society, including park visitation.

This chapter extends the "race, ethnicity, and recreation" literature geographically, utilizing a combination of quantitative and qualitative methods and exploring not only marginality and ethnicity but also discrimination and other issues. It next describes the concepts and literature in the field, and it then discusses the South African context and lists a set of research questions. It continues with sections describing the methods and results, followed by a discussion. When used here in the South African context, "Africans" refers to Black South Africans, "Whites" refers to South Africans and Americans of European ancestry, "Asians" refers to South Africans of South Asian ancestry, "Coloureds" refers to South Africans of mixed race ancestry, and "non-Whites" refers to Africans, Asians, and Coloureds as a group.

CONCEPTS AND THE LITERATURE

In his seminal work, Washburne (1978) introduced the concepts of marginality and ethnicity. The central tenet of marginality is that low levels of non-White participation are caused by a lack of socioeconomic resources, which in turn may be due to historical discrimination within society generally (as opposed to that at parks in particular) (Floyd 1999; Washburne 1978). Lower income hinders the ability of non-Whites to participate given the costs involved in visiting parks, as well as the basic lack of transport in many cases (West 1989).

The ethnicity (subcultural) hypothesis explains differing participation rates as a result of differing norms, value systems, and socialization practices. These differences may involve preferences for recreational experiences and style of park use in terms of location, social group, activity, desired facilities, and so on. At the most fundamental level, non-Whites may be averse to parks or simply indifferent to them. According to Meeker (1973) and Taylor (2000), national parks in the

United States historically have been established for predominantly White, middle-class members of the population.

As a result, park recreation suited the culture and style of this group. For example, Taylor (2000) noted the Western social construction of wilderness as empty, pristine areas for Whites to escape the ills of modern society, to seek peace and quiet and solitude. However, for minorities these spaces can mean loneliness, threat, fear, and prejudice. Meeker (1973, 203) noted that "the deeper emotional and cultural needs of both groups [American Blacks and Indians] are unlikely ever to be satisfied in the sense that the parks satisfy Americans of European ancestry." Parks may not only fail to satisfy the needs and motivations of non-Whites, but may be viewed as hostile due to past or current discrimination (discussed below).

Participation may also be connected to broader issues of environmental awareness and activism. Taylor (1989) reported a lack of environmental awareness and activism on the part of Black Americans, explaining that Blacks were heavily involved in the civil rights movement in the 1960s and 1970s, a time when the modern environmental movement began to establish a stronghold on the public scene. Civil and human rights were put before the protection of nature, and environmental issues were often perceived as "White issues."

Regardless of the underlying cause, there are indications that African Americans and White Americans have different levels of preference for, and actual participation in, trips to natural areas. For example, in his study of 20 leisure activities, Philipp (1995) found that African Americans gave lower ratings than did White Americans of the same social class for both the appeal and comfort of "camping in mountains."

Given a decision to participate, the style of participation also may differ across groups. For example, Gramann (1996) found that mean party size at Yosemite National Park for Hispanics was 4.4, whereas for non-Hispanics it was 3.1; this is consistent with a greater family orientation among the former. Likewise, Baas, Ewert, and Chavez (1993) reported from their study of Mecca Hills, California, that Hispanics were more oriented toward group sports than were non-Hispanics.

The former also placed more importance on infrastructure and were more likely to use informal channels to gather information about the site. Thapa, Graefe, and Absher (2002) similarly found that Whites generally reported using all available information sources to a greater extent than either Hispanics or "other minority groups." Floyd (1998) found that Hispanic and African Americans were less likely than White Americans to use print media provided by a state parks department, but were more likely to view television programs produced by the agency.

Philipp (1997) found that African Americans were more likely than White Americans of the same social class to prefer the leisure benefit of activities that provide opportunities for social interaction (although they were also more likely to prefer those oriented toward relaxation, self-expression, and self-esteem). Likewise, Philipp (1994) found that Blacks are more likely than Whites to prefer large groups.

Dwyer and Hutchison (1990) found that African Americans were more strongly oriented toward social interaction and facility development than were White Americans, with 53 percent of African Americans preferring developed facilities and conveniences, but only 24 percent of White Americans preferring the same. Virden and Walker (1999) found that, relative to Whites and Hispanics, Black Americans preferred greater levels of development and management presence. Although such preferences fit within the concept of recreation style, Virden and Walker (1999, 223; referring to Johnson and others 1998) observed that their preferences "may be related to safety concerns, which may in turn be based on affective and perceptual/cognitive meanings involving fear, anxiousness, or real or perceived threats." Safety concerns may be caused by fear of wildlife (Taylor 1989; Wallace and Witter 1992), but to the extent they are due to treatment by agency personnel or other visitors, it reflects discrimination.

Although the above suggests that cultural orientation develops passively, a process of differentiation from other ethnic groups and preservation of ethnic identity may also occur (Floyd 1999; Washburne and Wall 1980). Such processes would reinforce existing differences in participation and recreation style.

The marginality and ethnicity concepts have underpinned the majority of studies in this field, but assimilation and discrimination have also been put forward as factors. Yinger (1981, 249; cited in Floyd 1999) described assimilation as "the process of boundary reduction that can occur when members of two or more societies or of smaller cultural groups meet." In the context of participating in recreation, this typically has involved two aspects: cultural assimilation, in which minority groups take on the cultural characteristics of the majority; and structural assimilation, in which minority and majority groups interact (for example, through family, friend, work, residential, or school relationships) (Floyd and Shinew 1999).

One expected outcome of assimilation is that minority groups acquire the behavioral patterns of the majority group, including its rate of participation in recreation. However, as Floyd (1999) noted, the assimilation process may be selective, with some aspects of minority culture being maintained or even accentuated despite broader assimilation (Shaull and Gramann 1998). Unlike marginality and ethnicity, assimilation theory has been fruitful in exploring intra-ethnic differences in participation, motivation, and style.

The effect of discrimination within society broadly, which may affect socioeconomic status, is covered within marginality. Discrimination may also occur during interaction with other visitor groups or management personnel, thereby negatively affecting participation. Floyd (1998, 1999) noted that this hypothesis often is seen as a major explanatory factor yet has not been the focus of substantial theoretical or empirical evaluation. In particular, the role of institutional discrimination (due, for example, to management agency culture) has been largely neglected.

As was noted above, parks in the United States historically have been dominated by Whites and their culture. Whereas Whites went to parks, and nature generally, to escape the ills of modern society, to seek peace and quiet and solitude, for Blacks and other minorities these spaces could be threatening. Taylor (1989) described several cases of Blacks and Hispanics being attacked while visiting "White" areas in the 1930s and 1940s (see, for example, Philipp 1999; Virden and Walker 1999). West (1989) noted that Blacks may continue to feel that outdoor recreation areas are for White people only, that they are "White territory" (see, for example, Johnson and others 1998).

This perception is based on implicit segregation, and is shared by both Blacks and Whites. For example, Philipp (1999) found that American Whites recognize differing levels of "welcome" for Black Americans across leisure activities. It is important that despite common perceptions that Blacks would be more welcome in some contexts than in others, his results suggest that middle-class African Americans feel much less welcome in most leisure activities than middle-class White Americans believe.

As is common, this categorization into four approaches or concepts is useful but limited, with several issues cutting across these categories. For example, awareness might be classified as part of marginality, because low levels of awareness may be due to low levels of educational attainment. Johnson and others (1998) classified lack of awareness as a marginality issue and found that rural African Americans were more likely than the White Americans in their sample to report lack of awareness as the reason for not visiting natural recreation areas. However, variation in awareness may also have origins in ethnicity.

Likewise, past exposure, particularly in childhood, may affect participation rates. Though not a focus of their study, the results presented in Virden and Walker (1999) indicate that higher levels of childhood experience are correlated with higher rates of current participation. Philipp (1995, 1999) also noted the potential importance of childhood exposure, but the relationship between childhood and adult visitation has not been a focus of the debate on race, ethnicity, and recreation. Past exposure is partly a function of the participation rate for a respondent's parents, and the perceptions and behavior of the parents may be due to multiple factors, including marginality, ethnicity, and discrimination.

Variations in recreation location have also been noted in the literature. For example, Juniu (2000, 358) summarized research results as indicating that "ethnic minorities tend to recreate closer to home, use city parks, be more family oriented, and utilize local facilities rather than national, state, or regional sites" (see also West 1989). Locational preferences may reflect familiarity; Philipp (1994) found that Blacks were more likely than Whites to prefer locations, lodging, and restaurants that were personally familiar or generally well known. Locational issues may also be a function of marginality (for example, lack of transport), ethnicity (for example, local sites may cater best to recreation styles), and/or discrimination (for example, local sites may be more welcoming).

THE SOUTH AFRICAN CONTEXT

As with parks in the United States, park systems in South Africa generally were established on the basis of White values, with Blacks often being excluded from these areas. Floyd (1999) reported that conflicts surrounding subsistence use and access to sacred sites within parks have led to a contentious relationship between Native Americans and the National Park Service in the United States. Likewise, the establishment of parks in South Africa has led to a loss of access to resources, and Whites and Blacks have differing views of natural heritage and its conservation (Ranger 1989).

In South Africa, parks have a political history that involved displacement of people, and the parks often served as buffer zones for the military. Colonizers in southern Africa set about "protecting" wildlife for the benefit of tourists by displacing large sections of the indigenous population to create national parks. Relocation was often violent and typically resulted in loss of livestock, and in some instances loss of life as well. Homes were destroyed, and the alternatives were usually barren plots in overcrowded "reserves."

Furthermore, extended families were not necessarily sent to the same reserve but often were dispersed across the country. Rarely was any compensation paid to the affected families. Local people were thus deprived not only of their homes and their land, but also of access to the areas on which they depended for survival. Protected areas and the wildlife they supported therefore came to be viewed in a negative light. The legacy of apartheid remains. As Wells (1996, 322) observed:

> National parks and most other protected areas in South Africa are firmly associated with the former apartheid regime. Earlier governments' policies of setting aside large natural areas amidst a sea of black rural poverty for the enjoyment of an affluent white minority have been strongly challenged as inconsistent with the new democratic goals of South Africa. Many rural people were forcibly resettled when parks were established. Others were denied access to natural resources and ancestral burial sites without any consultation, let alone compensation.

Since the transition from apartheid to a democratic society, an effort has been made to encourage visitation by non-Whites. An increase among non-Whites could not only create more public acceptance and support for nature conservation, but could also broaden the market for parks, with concomitant benefits for park revenue and local employment opportunities.

Mirroring Taylor's (1989) observation that American Blacks have been involved in civil rights issues, thereby limiting their involvement in environmental issues, Magi (1999, 293) observed that South African Blacks "perceived issues of local empowerment and socioeconomic benefit as far more important than environmental sustainability." Before the election of the democratic government in 1994, Wilson and Hattingh (1992) used in-depth interviews and surveys to explore recreation preferences within Black townships. They report a low preference for natural environment activities, with one explanation being that Blacks normally viewed natural resources as means of subsistence rather than for preservation or aesthetically based activities. However, they also noted that education was correlated with environmental preference, with higher educational levels leading to greater recreational use of the natural environment.

Magi's (1999) results supported American research findings that Blacks prefer recreation activities closer to home, rather than in remote, natural settings. Indeed, nature-based outdoor facilities were the least visited of the four facility types, largely because they were not as accessible as other types of facilities, such as swimming pools and cinemas. He stressed the potential for African demand for natural resource recreation and noted that institutional changes (such as in the education system) and spatio-recreational changes (for example, better access to resources) would be needed to achieve increases. Wells and Magi both mention that the legacy of apartheid continues to have an effect on outdoor recreation behavior, with both urban facilities and parks often being seen as "White" areas.

Though focused on beach recreation, Booth's (2001, xiii) observation of recreational style differences across race may also be relevant in the park context:

> I discerned different cultural attitudes towards the beach. White beachgoers in Durban [KwaZulu-Natal's largest city] displayed solitariness and specialized interests. Individuals (as well as couples and small family units) blocked themselves off from others by burying themselves in newspapers, magazines and books, barricading themselves behind headphones, and marking out their territories with defensive arrangements of towels, umbrellas and deck chairs. Space is paramount. "I don't care what color skin sits or swims next to me," explained one White beachgoer, "as long as I have enough space to do my own thing." By contrast, Africans viewed the beach as a site of entertainment, a place to unite as a crowd, and to

enjoy social interaction. … It was a place of activity, movement and noise; a place of "all in" games, singing, dancing, and partying; a place to express one's emotions. … Spreading large blankets on the ground and eating from communal pots enhanced sociability.

Though the literature from elsewhere in Africa is limited, Helleiner (1990) reported on a study of domestic tourism in Nigeria. Of the six attraction categories, wildlife and game reserves received the lowest level of visits. On the basis of an evaluation of demographic character-istics, he observed that those visiting such reserves "were an intellectu-ally elite group, whose penchant for this kind of tourist attraction was not typical of the majority of Nigerians interviewed but more akin to the tastes of foreigners, like the thousands who flock every year to Tanzania and Kenya." In other words, there appears to be a limited process of assimilation at a global scale. Likewise, Husbands (1989) found that perceptions of general tourism differ across educational levels, with many Zambians associating "tourist" with "foreigner."

In his study of domestic tourism in Kenya, Sindiga (1996, 25, 24) observed that

Kenyans do not participate in domestic tourism because of economic reasons. … If the majority of Kenyans cannot afford the accommodation expenses, the high cost of transportation further compounds the prob-lem. Tourism is about travel and travel is about money.

He went on to say that "other incentives such as lower entry fees to parks and reserves are merely secondary concerns. Such fees are frequently not the most expensive part of a tour" (1996, 24). He also mentioned the Wildlife Clubs of Kenya, a nonprofit organization created to stim-ulate interest in wildlife and the natural environment, which facilitates park visitation among members.

RESEARCH QUESTIONS

Several research questions emerge from the U.S. experience and the South African context. First, do non-Whites visit parks less frequently than do Whites? Second, if so, what are the reasons for this lower level of participation? Specifically, what are the respective roles of:

a. Marginality, and particularly lack of financial resources relative to cost of transport and other expenses (for example, non-Whites would like to go but cannot afford the time or money)?

b. Ethnicity in the broad sense of explaining variability in participation after controlling for socioeconomic factors? This includes recreation style, safety concerns, and lack of interest due to a mismatch between the experience offered by South African parks and the experience desired by non-Whites (for example, non-Whites would not like to visit as frequently as Whites in the same socioeconomic class).

c. Lower participation in all forms of leisure (for example, as a percentage of total leisure trips, non-Whites go as frequently as Whites, but the former take fewer total trips)?

d. Lack of awareness due to one or more related factors, including lack of information, never having thought about it, or lack of childhood visits/exposure (for example, non-Whites might want to go there, but do not know about the opportunity)?

e. Lack of interest due to concerns about being unwelcome or discriminated against (for example, Whites do not want non-Whites to go there)?

Factors c and d often are grouped within ethnicity or marginality, but are treated separately here.

Third, what might be done to increase participation among non-Whites? Fourth, should the actions identified in response to the third question be implemented? Some authors in the U.S. context (such as Dwyer and Hutchison 1990 and Floyd and Johnson 2002) have questioned the implicit, and sometimes explicit, objective of having minorities mimic the recreational behavior of the majority. As was noted above, parks have evolved to provide the experiences desired by the dominant group(s) within society. Minorities may or may not desire these experiences. If they do not, the question arises as to whether (or how far) parks should evolve to provide experiences desired by non-Whites, or indeed Whites not desiring current park opportunities.

Although equal access to recreational opportunities is assumed as an objective, it is not assumed that these opportunities should be limited to parks. In South Africa, as in the United States, it may be appropriate to subsidize different types of recreation sites and opportunities, with the goal not of encouraging all citizens to enjoy the current set of offerings but of providing a set enjoyed by all citizens. This follows the logic of such management planning approaches as the recreation opportunity spectrum. The intention is not to maintain historical segregation but to match preferences and opportunities.

As stressed by Taylor (2000), concerns about a park's "carrying capacity" should not be used to justify excluding nontraditional (for example, non-White) users. In addition, expanding visitation by nontraditional users may be critical in increasing political and financial support for parks. Nonetheless, it is appropriate to question whether parks can or should be "all things to all people." If there is a mismatch between visitor preferences and the recreation opportunities parks can provide within their mandate, one should consider other means for satisfying those preferences. The challenge, particularly in countries like the United States with a limited role for government, is that public funding of parks is more or less accepted, whereas public funding of other types of recreation sites may not be.

Fifth, though not a primary focus of this research, the issue of park visits leading to change in environmental attitudes was explored.

METHODOLOGY

As noted by Floyd (1999, 18), "to better understand minority use of national parks, it is necessary to utilize multiple methodological approaches." In this study, a combination of quantitative and qualitative methods is used. The quantitative approach provides an overview of participation across a relatively large sample. The qualitative approach provides richer information per respondent and is particularly valuable in exploratory studies like this one, with a limited research foundation on which to build (in the non–United States context). Indeed, even the quantitative component of this study involved several open-ended questions. Though it is easiest and common to use closed-ended questions (see, for example, Johnson and others 1998), open-ended questions allow for greater richness and are less prone to leading (West 1989).

Richins (1999, 98) suggested that "mixed methods have been shown to assist in confirmation or unity of results, to provide a fresh insight and detail, to enhance understanding, or may even suggest a new or paradoxical result to the research findings" (see also Henderson 1991). These benefits are particularly important in the context of research on minority groups, as they help capture the richness, nuance, and subtlety in the personal meaning of experience, recreation, and so forth (Henderson 1998; Henderson and others 1999; Virden and Walker 1999).

Quantitative Component: Household Survey in KwaZulu-Natal and Gauteng

This component involved an in-person survey of households in the provinces of KwaZulu-Natal and Gauteng during February and March 2001, as described in chapter 2. A sample of enumerator areas (EAs— physical areas used in the census) was taken, with exclusion of those EAs that contained fewer than 50 households and those in which less than 50 percent of households had an annual household income of R42,000 or more (at the time of the survey $1 = R7.8). Low-income EAs were excluded because it is unlikely that a significant number of residents would have visited parks. However, because Whites tend to have higher incomes than non-Whites, this exclusion generated a proportion of Whites greater in the sample than in the South African population as a whole. Of the 841 observations, the percentage breakdown by race is as follows: Africans, 22; Whites, 68; Asians, 8; and Coloureds, 2.

The questionnaire was in English, but interviewers were able to conduct the interview in the main languages of the region, including Afrikaans, Zulu, and Sotho. In about 95 percent of the cases, respondents were able to participate in their mother tongue, whereas the remainder generally were happy to respond in a second language. There were three versions of the survey questionnaire (see chapter 2). Effectively respondents were grouped according to whether they were Past visitors, Likely future visitors, or Unlikely future visitors to game or nature reserves in South Africa or neighboring countries. Details on the questions asked are provided in the "Results" section below, and copies of the surveys are available from the authors.

It should be noted that parks in South Africa are diverse in their natural and facility features. Several are game parks, containing most or all of the wildlife Big Five, whereas others are known more for their scenery than for large wildlife. It is quite common to drive several hours to get to parks. For example, from Durban it is 250 kilometers to Hluhluwe-Umfolozi Park (HUP) and 725 kilometers to Kruger National Park.

Qualitative Component: Focus Group Survey of Asians and Africans

The qualitative component was a Focus Group Survey involving Asians and Africans from KwaZulu-Natal (KZN) that consisted of (1) a pre-trip focus group meeting, (2) a field trip to HUP, the main park in the northeastern part of the province, and (3) a one-year, post-trip focus group. This process was completed with three separate sets of participants.

The first was African youth, selected because they would form a logical nucleus for the next generation of visitors. These were young adults under the age of 30, either single or in a relationship but not yet married, who were either students or had just started working. The pre-trip session was conducted in Durban separately with two sets of 10 respondents, the first being mainly students and the second being employed. From these 20, 5 males and 5 females were selected to go on the field trip. One male and 2 females canceled at the last-minute, so 7 members were in this field trip group. The post-trip session, at a participant's home, was held with 4 participants.

The second set was African adults, consisting of couples over the age of 30, married with children, with a combined annual household income exceeding $12,000. The pre-trip session was conducted separately, with 4 couples in one case and 2 couples in the other. In both cases, they were held at a respondent's home. From this group, 3 couples, with their children, were selected to participate in the field trip, though one of the adult males had to cancel at the last minute. The post-trip session, at a participant's home, was held with 2 couples.

The third set was made up of Asian young adults under the age of 30 who were either students or had just started working, comprising a mix of 2 married and 3 unmarried couples. All 10 participated in the pre-trip session, held at DRA Development, and in the field trip. The post-trip session, at a participant's home, was held with 2 couples.

Thus, from an initial pool of 213 people interviewed for the project, 42 adults participated in the pre-trip sessions, 22 participated in the field trip, and 12 in the post-trip session. Participants were selected on the basis of being "good contributors" (forthcoming with opinions) or because they introduced diversity (for example, they had originally come from a rural homestead). As with the Household Survey, respondents in the Focus Group Survey had incomes and educational levels higher than the national average. They were selected as representative of the most likely "potential future visitors," but their experiences and attitudes may not reflect those in other social classes.

Each of the three sets participated separately in the following process. A pre-trip session of 90 to 120 minutes was held during February 2001. This was followed in March by a three-day field trip to HUP. Each group stayed at a variety of accommodations and was taken on game drives and game walks (due to the presence of rhinos and other dangerous wildlife, the game walks are led by an armed park ranger). During the field trip, participants spent up to three hours a day in focus groups and individual one-on-one interviews with the researchers. Last, a post-trip session of approximately 90 minutes was held in February 2002. Two members of the project team, the second and fourth authors, moderated all sessions and were participant observers during the field trips. They are Greek and Asian South Africans, respectively.

In the pre-trip focus group sessions, topics included current and ideal vacations, and perspectives on nature and parks. During the field trip, topics included reactions to the visit, differences between expectations and actual experience, and suggestions on how to attract more non-Whites. During the post-trip sessions, topics included whether respondents had returned to HUP or other parks as a result of their field trip experience, additional discussion of previous park visitation (or nonvisitation), attitudes toward conservation, exposure to park-related information sources, and preferences for use of public funds for development of recreation opportunities. In each case, a semistructured interview approach was used.

RESULTS

The results are presented according to the research questions noted above, which are somewhat more specific than the broad marginality, ethnicity, and discrimination categories often used. Partly for this reason, a given result or quote often relates to more than one question. Indeed, the quantitative participation model cuts across questions 1, 2a, and 2b (do rates differ, and is this due to marginality or ethnicity?). When interpreting results, it should be remembered that the Household Survey involved respondents of all races, whereas the Focus Group Survey only involved Africans and Asians. Quotes from the Focus Group Survey are identified with the person's group membership and gender.

Question 1: Do Non-Whites Visit Parks Less Frequently Than Do Whites?

Reported visitation from the Household Survey, shown in table 5.1, supports anecdotal evidence that non-Whites do visit less frequently than Whites (all tables in this chapter are based on data from the Household Survey).

As is indicated in table 5.1, the majority of respondents across all races took no trips to reserves during the period. However, Whites clearly visited more frequently than non-Whites. One African respondent visited parks 72 times during the period. This observation is an outlier relative

Table 5.1 Number of Trips (in Past Three Years) by Race (percent)

Park Visits	African	White	Asian	Coloured	Total
0	88.4	61.2	81.3	83.3	69.3
1	7.9	20.0	12.5	11.1	16.5
2	1.1	5.4	4.7	5.6	4.4
3	0.5	2.6	0	0	1.9
4	0	1.8	0	0	1.2
5	0	1.1	1.6	0	0.8
6	1.1	2.1	0	0	1.7
8	0	0.5	0	0	0.4
9	0	0.5	0	0	0.4
10	0	1.6	0	0	1.1
12	0.5	0.7	0	0	0.6
15	0	0.5	0	0	0.4
16	0	0.4	0	0	0.2
18	0	0.4	0	0	0.2
20	0	0.5	0	0	0.4
25	0	0.2	0	0	0.1
30	0	0.2	0	0	0.1
40	0	0.4	0	0	0.2
72	0.5	0	0	0	0.1

Source: Data from the Household Survey.

not only to the sample as a whole but also, in particular, to the African subsample. Therefore, it is deleted from further analysis and the results shown below. The average number of trips by race, with the African outlier omitted, was:

African	0.24
White	1.51
Asian	0.30
Coloured	0.22

Because the issue of interest is White versus non-White participation, all non-Whites were grouped together and a *t*-test conducted. The mean number of trips was statistically different at $p = 0.000$.

Question 2a: Is Low Participation Due to the Marginal Status of Non-Whites?

To address the issue of whether low participation among non-Whites is due to marginality, a participation model was developed from Household Survey data. As noted in the introduction to part 2, participation and site selection models are often used in combination to evaluate recreation demand. The participation model estimated here complements (and uses results from) the site selection model in chapter 2. Participation models typically do not specify race as an explanatory variable, but Bowker and Leeworthy (1998) provided an example and review of race inclusion in recreation demand models more broadly.

Participation Model

In this context, the primary issue in the participation model is whether race affects the frequency of reserve visitation. However, it is important to control for other demographic factors, such as age, gender, education, income, and household size, that might affect trip frequency. In addition, there may be locational factors that affect frequency—for example, if Whites tend to live closer to attractive reserves than do non-Whites, one would expect they would visit more often, independent of race.

To control for locational factors, the results of the site selection model estimated in chapter 2 were used to estimate price-quality index values using equation 2.1.9 in Hausman, Leonard, and McFadden (1995, 9).

Table 5.2 Variables Used in the Participation Model

Variable	Description
Price-quality index	Controls for locational advantages, as described in text
First child	Whether respondent's first trip to a park was before age 10 years (21% of full sample, 29% of those who have ever been to a reserve)
First teen	Whether first trip was between the ages of 10 and 19 years, inclusive (25% of full sample, 34% of those who have ever been to a reserve)
First adult	Whether first trip was as an adult (age 20 years or older)
Age	Ordinal, five categories
Male	Female = 0, male = 1
Race	Dummy (dichotomous) variables for African, Asian, and Coloured (White is the base)
Education	Ordinal, six categories
Income	Ordinal, seven categories
Household size	Combined number of adults and children in household (one outlier observation with 25 adults was set to missing value)

Source: Data from the Household Survey.

The index values vary across enumerator areas and incorporate both (1) the distance to reserves, and thus the price of traveling to them; and (2) the quality of the reserves, as reflected by the coefficients on the reserve dummy variables in table 2-4. For example, Pongola EA had the highest index value due to its location in northern KwaZulu-Natal and thus proximity to popular reserves. Van der Bijl Park is located in Gauteng and had the lowest index value. All else being equal, one would therefore expect residents of Pongola to visit reserves more frequently than do residents of Van der Bijl Park.[2] Table 5.2 presents the variables used in the participation model, including demographic and locational variables.

As a group, the three "first" variables are a measure of whether previous visits affect the number of trips in the past three years. In comparison with each other, they are a measure of the relative effect of first visits occurring at different times in the respondent's life. Ten respondents reported they had been to a reserve but did not report an age, and these are excluded from the above three variables.

The participation model was estimated with negative binomial regression, and the results are shown in table 5.3. The number of trips to nature reserve in the past three years was the dependent variable, and the model was significant at $p = 0.000$. In addition to the exclusion of the outlier noted above, 96 observations were excluded due to item nonresponse, leaving a total of 744 observations.

Table 5.3 Participation Model: Park Visits in Past Three Years

Variable	Coefficient	p-value
Constant	−5.971	0.000
Price-quality index	0.003	0.020
First child	3.214	0.000
First teen	2.674	0.000
First adult	2.833	0.000
African	−0.970	0.000
Asian	−0.932	0.024
Education	0.244	0.000
Household size	−0.177	0.002
Income	0.303	0.000

Source: Data from the Household Survey.

The participation model confirms a difference in visitation rates between Whites and non-Whites. Age and gender (whether male) were nonsignificant at $p = 0.10$ and therefore were dropped from the model. As expected, the sign on the price-quality index is positive, with those living closer to reserves generally, and attractive reserves in particular, making more visits. Past experience does increase the number of trips in the study period. The effect of first visits during teenage and adult years does not differ greatly, but the effect is larger for first visits during preteenage years. This suggests that childhood exposure can increase participation later in life. It should be kept in mind that the causal link remains uncertain, because a different factor may be leading to both high participation and early first visits. However, given that demographic factors such as education and income are controlled for in the model, the result does support the importance of childhood visits.

Turning to income, education, and race, the significance of the first two is consistent with the marginality hypothesis. In the sample, Whites had the highest mean levels of both education and income. Given that these factors are positively correlated with participation, the lower levels among non-Whites partly explains their lower level of participation. However, the negative signs for African and Asian indicate that marginality is only part of the explanation. After controlling for differences in income and education, Africans and Asians still participated less, thus supporting ethnicity as a predictor of participation (the coefficient for Coloureds was nonsignificant at $p = 0.10$ and was thus dropped from the model; this suggests that ethnicity is not an issue for Coloureds, but the small number of Coloureds in the sample means that this should be interpreted with caution).

Focus Group Responses

As is shown in table 5.3, the participation model supports the role of marginality as one explanation for lower levels of participation among non-Whites. Indeed, although one Asian respondent noted that "I think if you love nature you will pay," cost and transportation constraints came out clearly in the focus group results, as is indicated by the following quotes:

> I think what can hold people back is the budget and the planning. (African youth, female)

> We don't have cars, but we'd like to go back there. So if you don't have transport of your own and you'd like to go there, where can you get transport that can take you from Durban to that particular area? (African youth, female)

Even when respondents have their own car, it can be sufficiently valued, and sufficiently at risk of damage in a park, that the respondent would not want to use it for a park visit—especially because motor vehicles are often important status symbols. For example, one of the Asian couples had been planning to vacation at a game reserve but did not want to take its own vehicle due to concern that it would be damaged by one or more of the following: dirt road conditions (for example, potholes), fauna (for example, charged by an elephant or rhinoceros), or flora (for example, scratches from tree branches). As one participant stated:

> If we didn't pay so much for our cars, I promise you we would take it there. (Asian, male)

The alternative was to rent a car, ideally a four-wheel drive with high clearance to enhance the view, but that would significantly add to costs.

Perceptions of cost tended to be higher than actual costs, and these perceptions are in part associated with the belief that parks are for rich Whites or foreigners. For example, participants stated:

> Game reserves are very expensive because it is based to people coming from overseas. (African youth, female)

It is also a cost factor. I've never been to one, also I understand that some of them charge only in U.S. dollars. It is fine to charge U.S. dollars to international tourists, but is it fair to charge local people in dollars? (Asian, female)

These responses provide an indication that actual or perceived cost, together with lack of transportation, are constraints for non-White park visitation. However, cost relative to disposable income is an issue for all races and for all types of travel—not just for minorities traveling to parks. For example, past destination choices for the Indian couples were heavily influenced by cost considerations: Two of the vacations were free, one was a timeshare, another received discounts, and the final vacation was paid for by parents, and therefore could also be considered as being free.

Results from the Household Survey support the role of cost across races. In the Unlikely future survey, respondents were asked if there was a reason they had not gone to a reserve in the past three years and do not plan to go in the future, and in the Likely future survey, respondents were asked why that had not gone to parks in the past three years but plan to go in the future. In both cases, responses were open-ended and could reflect multiple constraints. On the basis of a review of responses, the survey research company (DRA Development) created 19 categories and grouped responses accordingly. Two of these reflect cost constraints (for example, parks are/were too expensive) and two reflect time constraints (for example, too busy at work).

Whites were more likely to report cost and time constraints than were non-Whites. However, Whites were also more likely to report constraints generally (many respondents did not report a constraint). To control for different overall reporting frequencies, only observations with at least one reported constraint were analyzed; the results are shown in table 5.4.

Table 5.4 Constraints on Visiting Parks (percentage reporting each constraint)

Constraint	Non-Whites	Whites
Cost	42	39
Time	27	29

Source: Data from the Household Survey.

The results are similar across races, and do not differ statistically (using a chi-square test). Given that non-Whites tend to have lower incomes than do Whites, and thus also fewer transportation options, marginality clearly plays a role in participation rates. Nonetheless, the constraints data remind us that cost is a limitation for Whites as well.

Question 2b: Is Low Participation Due to Ethnicity (Broadly)?

As is shown in table 5.3, the participation model based on the Household Survey also supports the role of ethnicity as an explanation for lower levels of participation among non-Whites. It should be stressed that this reflects visitation rates, not necessarily appreciation of the experience or desire to visit. Non-Whites did visit less frequently than Whites, but statements during the field trip, and the post-trip sessions, reflect their significant interest in their experience.

As one tangible illustration, a group of three couples shared a camera during their trip, which involved two days on-site. Between them, they used four rolls of 36-exposure film. Indeed, they ended up buying additional film while at the park. The field trip experience is illustrated by the following quotes:

> Seeing the lion itself to me it was an experience of a lifetime. (African youth, female)

> It was very impressive, nothing I could have imagined. (African youth, female)

> I thought [before the trip that] all the animals were aggressive, and very dangerous. I never thought I would see a kudu or wildebeest so damn close, and it didn't even attack. (African youth, female)

Household Survey

One gauge of the level of desire for park experiences comes from the "ideal trip" question as answered by Unlikely and Likely future visitors (that is, those who have not gone on a trip in the past three years). Respondents were asked to describe their ideal holiday, assuming unlimited time and money, in terms of what they would do, where they would go, and with whom they would travel. Responses were classified as

Table 5.5 Ideal Trips: Preferences for Nature Tourism across Regions (percent)

Group	In South Africa	Elsewhere in Africa	Elsewhere in World	Total
Unlikely	16	3	3	22
Likely	23	3	1	27

Source: Data from the Household Survey.

Table 5.6 Ideal Trips across Races (number and percent)

Type of Trip	Non-Whites	Whites
Nature tourism	44 (19%)	92 (26%)
Other	190 (81%)	257 (74%)

Source: Data from the Household Survey.

Table 5.7 Ideal Trips across Races, Not Including Asians (number and percent)

Type of Trip	Africans + Coloureds	Whites
Nature tourism	36 (20%)	92 (26%)
Other	146 (80%)	257 (74%)

Source: Data from the Household Survey.

nature tourism, reflecting a desire to visit parks or similar natural attractions, or as "other." Nature tourism interest for all races combined is shown in table 5.5.

Combining the data for Unlikely and Likely versions, as well as grouping non-Whites together, the results across races are shown in table 5.6. Focusing on the percentage within each race, the results indicate that Whites are somewhat more likely to select nature tourism activities than are non-Whites. This difference is statistically significant ($p = 0.034$) using a chi-square test.

Responses to the choice modeling scenarios (see chapter 2) indicate that Asians may be less likely than Africans or Coloureds to choose nature tourism trips. Given this result, the cross-tabulation shown in table 5.6 was also performed with Asians removed, and the results are shown in table 5.7.

A comparison of the two tables indicates that exclusion of Asian respondents from the analysis reduces the difference. Statistically, the chi-square value diminishes in significance from $p = 0.034$ to $p = 0.092$.

If one uses $p = 0.05$ as a cutoff, the difference is no longer significant. In summary, the quantitative results indicate that differences in broad activity preferences across races are not as great as one might expect. For both Whites and non-Whites, only a minority would choose nature tourism activities. However, there is some difference between Whites and non-Whites, particularly Asians.

Focus Group Study

The Focus Group Study provides further information regarding the cause of the difference. Some of the factors associated with ethnicity that may affect non-White preferences and hinder participation include recreation preferences and styles that may be inconsistent with park opportunities, and concerns about safety. With respect to recreational styles and preferences, Asian focus group participants noted that older Indians prefer to visit resort and gambling destinations like Sun City and the Wild Coast. The cost of a park visit is much cheaper, but the socialization of older Indians means that they will not consider parks. When asked whether their families did not travel to parks because they were seen as "White places," one participant noted:

> No, I think Indian people choose not to go there. They like to be pampered, and like the luxury of living in a hotel, and room service. Whereas in the bush you got to do everything yourself, and I think the security as well. People tend to feel a bit intimidated out in the wild. (Asian, male)

Despite this indication that some segments within the non-White population prefer nonpark experiences, the focus group participants reported that they were highly satisfied with their experience during the field trip. In the post-trip session, they were posed a hypothetical scenario of being the minister in charge of tourism and nature reserves. They were "given" R10 million (approximately $880,000 at March 2002 exchange rates) to spend on improving recreation opportunities in South Africa, with the explanation that the money could be spent on nature parks, urban parks and facilities, or other purposes.

After they allocated their proportions to nature parks versus other recreation destinations or activities, they were asked how they would spend the portion spent on nature parks. None of them indicated they would develop new or different facilities, even though infrastructure was used as a sample expenditure item. The following excerpts from the discussion indicate that facility development was not an issue:

> Moderator: You feel the game reserve as you saw HUP was absolutely perfect. You don't need to change anything that might attract more African people?

> African youth, female (1): No, not to me. It was a very exciting experience. Right now I don't have anything that maybe I was able to change. To me everything was fine.

> [And:]

> African youth, female (2): I will say everything was fine. I think what was lacking for the people is information.

There were style differences across groups. For example, during the field visit it was observed that Africans tended to be most interested in the wildlife, and when there were no animals to be seen they tended to engage in conversation. Asians tended to value the scenery as well, and avoided conversation to avoid scaring away animals.

Moreover, one of the African youth males appeared focused as much or more on the social experience as the nature experience, and he preferred the more developed location (Hilltop) because of its (small) shops and other amenities. In his description of planning to return with friends, he mentioned that part of his motivation was to have fun and impress women (his and his friends' girlfriends). Conversely, he also expressed his desire to "relax" and, later in the session, his enjoyment of the "freedom" of being in the park. These latter are consistent with traditional (that is, dominant culture) motivations for park visits.

Satisfaction with the experience may be due in part to the variety of infrastructure already available. As in the U.S. literature, some non-Whites stressed the importance of infrastructure, often due to safety considerations, which revolved predominantly around fear of wildlife and especially snakes. For example, one African adult female noted that "I was so afraid, I couldn't sleep that night." Protection of self and other family members, especially children, was viewed as highly important, and a lack of safe facilities and accommodation was cited as a possible reason for nonvisitation to game parks in the future. It also explains preferences for specific types of facilities. Safety issues are illustrated in the following quotes:

> The safety factor—I know part of the allure in going there [to nature reserves] is living in the wild and I think to a lot of Indians, especially the safety factor would be sort of a deterrent. I know to the older generation, I'm talking personally from my family. … Maybe building accommodation—if they see a fence up or something like that, they might appreciate going there and feeling safe. Driving around in their car and then sleeping in a safe camp at night. 'Cause I've had nightmares, sleeping in those camps. (Asian, female)

> I would like to stay at the Hilltop because I'll be free to walk in the night without fear of the monkeys and elephants. (African youth, male)

> Near home, there is a game reserve but I've never been there, because when I thought of a game reserve, I also thought of danger because I heard all those stories about elephants trampling cars … so I had a fear of game reserves. (African youth, female)

However, some participants preferred staying at Mpila, which was more exposed to wildlife than Hilltop. Indeed, during one evening, the adult African group was "invaded" by more than 20 elephants, as well as numerous warthogs. This increased the desire among some to stay at Mpila. For the African adults and three of the four African youths in the post-trip session, the preference was for nature over safety:

> We want to really experience the nature reserve, you know you've got to accept that element of danger, you've got to be always alert, and I think you got to be excited by that you know. (African adult, male).

> It's exciting, you feel like you are right in the jungle and I think that it was really exciting. (African youth, female)

These African participants felt that staying at Hilltop was like staying at a generic resort, and if they were to come to a park they wanted to experience nature in its fullness, even if it was scary; fear was seen as part of the nature experience. Nonetheless, families with kids, and particularly the mothers, tended to prefer Hilltop for safety reasons.

It should be stressed that fear of animals is quite realistic in many contexts and is shared, to varying degrees, across races; in a private reserve nearby, two (White) visitors were killed in recent years in close proximity to their accommodation, one by a lion and the other by an elephant. However, there may be ethnic or racial differences due to mythologies and other factors. For example, Africans were much more afraid of snakes than were Asians.

One benefit of increased visitation is that exposure to feared animals without incurring harm can lead to fear reduction. For example, owls are considered evil in Zulu culture. On the field trip, the fear of owls was reduced, but this reduction appears to apply only to the "natural" owls in the reserve—in the post-trip focus group session, one respondent noted that he still felt other owls could be killed and used for medicine.

Question 2c: Is Low Participation Due to Less Frequent Travel?

Though general travel behavior was not a focus of the research, it was addressed in both the Focus Group and Household Surveys. In the focus groups, there was the perception that Whites not only visited parks more frequently than non-Whites but also traveled in general more frequently. For example, one of the African youth (male) observed that "I know mostly, the White people—they like traveling a lot."

In the Household Survey, respondents in the Unlikely and Likely future visitor categories were asked if they had taken any nonbusiness trips in the previous year (2000). Forty-six percent of those in the former category and 67 percent of those in the latter took at least one trip. The percentage of each race taking at least one trip was:

African	43
White	56
Asian	56
Coloured	47

Results indicate differences across race (chi-square is significant at $p = 0.031$), but the question is whether this is because of marginality or ethnicity. To evaluate this, a logistic regression was estimated using age, gender, race, education, income, and household size as predictors of whether the respondent took at least one trip in the previous year. Results are shown in table 5.8. The model was significant at $p = 0.000$, had a Nagelkerke R^2 of 0.097, and generated 62 percent correct predictions.

Table 5.8 General Travel in 2000

Variable	Coefficient	p-value
Constant	0.671	0.076
Age	−0.216	0.005
Income	0.337	0.000
Household size	−0.211	0.000

Source: Data from the Household Survey.

Most of the variables, including all the race variables, dropped out of the model as nonsignificant. As expected, higher income levels make it more likely that respondents will have taken a trip during the preceding year, whereas older age and larger household size make it less likely. As noted above, non-Whites tend to have lower incomes than Whites, so marginality is also an issue in general travel, not just park visits. However, there was no additional effect of ethnicity in this model. In other words, once differences in income, age, and household size are controlled for, Africans, Whites, Asians, and Coloureds were equally likely to travel in the preceding year.

Question 2d: Is Low Participation Due to Lack of Awareness?

Several related issues are combined in this section, including that of never considering parks, lack of information, and lack of childhood exposure. Again, these issues are relevant across all races, but may be particularly important for non-Whites. For example, if information about parks was presented in sources used by Whites more than by non-Whites, this could differentially affect participation across races. Likewise, if non-Whites did not visit parks as children because of racial restrictions at the time, this also could have differential effects.

With respect to never considering parks, this may be related to the spatial scope of a respondent's worldview. Parks generally are located a significant distance from residential areas, especially urban areas. If, for cultural, educational, income, or other reasons, respondents have a spatially limited worldview, they may simply never think about traveling far from home, to parks or any other type of destination.

However, responses to the ideal vacation scenario quite commonly included destinations far from home, including many intercontinental locations. This suggests that a spatially limited worldview is not a constraint. Indeed, there may be an element of the opposite among some

Table 5.9 Awareness of Parks (percentage of respondents able to name at least one reserve in the province and in the rest of the country)

Location	Non-Whites	Whites
Reserves in KwaZulu-Natal	52	70
Reserves in the rest of South Africa	59	90

Source: Data from the Household Survey.

respondents—the parks are relatively proximate and familiar, whereas some felt that holidays should be spent exploring more distant and exotic locations.

Another potential constraint is lack of information, in which respondents either do not know of a park's existence or lack information about the park's attraction, how to get there, and so on. In the Household Survey, respondents completing the Unlikely future version were asked to name two parks in KwaZulu-Natal (applied to respondents in both KZN and Gauteng provinces) and two in the rest of South Africa. The intention was not to "test" respondents but to gauge their level of awareness, using a basic measure. The results are shown in table 5.9.

With respect to both geographic regions, there were substantial and significant differences (chi-square results were significant at $p = 0.000$ for each). There is clearly greater awareness among Whites than non-Whites.

This finding is consistent with focus group results, in which the African respondents indicated that the main reason for them not visiting the parks after the removal of apartheid-era restrictions was lack of information. As one participant observed:

> [Black people] do not know about these nice places, like Hilltop, where they can relax and have some fun. … People don't have information for those things, so I think what is lacking is information. (African youth, male)

Part of the lack of information results from lack of exposure to parks during childhood. As is illustrated in the participation model results, a childhood visit is a positive predictor of more recent visits. Within the Asian focus group, only one participant spoke of a childhood that included park visitation:

> We've been to lots of nature reserves and [it's] something we've been doing as we've grown up. … It stemmed from my grandparents—I was

born in the Transvaal, my dad was born in the Transvaal and it was a regular family outing for them to go to a game park. ... They obviously had a love for it, something just drew them to it and from that I think—just came down into the generations. (Asian, female)

As this participant later noted in the context of discussing what images and information to include in a park marketing campaign:

I think to a lot of people it would be hard to capture in an advert the thrill of actually seeing something in the wild as opposed to seeing it in a zoo. ... Based on past experience I mean if you go once that's when you get the feel to go back again. (Asian, female)

However, the other Asian participants had different upbringings, in which exposure to natural areas was not evident. For one of the Asian participants, the trip to HUP was the first time he had seen animals in the wild. Both Africans and Asians noted the lack of childhood exposure:

When we were growing up, our parents never really exposed us to—or we were never really taken on holidays to—game parks or things like that. When we went away it was always I think more for my parents to just relax—to get away from work where they really didn't want to do anything. ... It wasn't really part of my culture. ... Maybe if my parents exposed us to game parks and wildlife we would have shown a greater interest when we became income earners, and gone on trips like that on our own. So maybe if you start from a young age, it just breeds interest. (Asian, female)

I think it's lack of exposure, because I grew up in the townships. There were no animals at all. I remember during my young age my parents used to take me to the circus—that's where I grew interested with animals, you know ... all along we've been the victims of ignorance. (African adult, male)

The Asian participant who had spent much of her childhood visiting game parks stressed the importance of educating and exposing children to natural areas at a young age—this was a potential method of reaching out to Asians and increasing their awareness:

You've got to stimulate interest amongst the youth because that's how it spreads the word. ... So I think you would have to go to youth groups, maybe churches and temples and things like that and use promotions. ... Most youth groups are looking for ways—positive ways—to encourage

186   NATURE TOURISM, CONSERVATION, AND DEVELOPMENT IN KWAZULU-NATAL

kids, and I think nature is one of the good alternate ways to. … I'd love my son to grow up one day and to go to a game park and have the experiences we do. (Asian, female)

An African participant noted:

Whites bring their kids up with that culture and we never had that experience. If you don't have that experience and background, you will not pursue it. Maybe now, our younger generation is getting the experience, and will go to nature reserves. (African adult, male)

Questions 2e: Is Lack of Interest Due to Being Unwelcome and/or Discriminated Against?

Focus group participants clearly indicated that parks were seen as "White areas," because Whites were the ones who historically had the opportunity to visit the areas, and thus were an established clientele:

If you look at it on TV all they show is White people driving around in the game reserve. You never see an Indian family driving around. So you always thought White people go to game reserves. (Asian, male)

We thought we were not allowed to go there. (African adult, female)

Mostly when you see adverts of places, you normally see White people, but when you are Black—I think most Black people will be attracted once you see that place. (African youth, male)

Respondent comments indicate that perceptions of parks being White areas are not only a legacy of apartheid but also of current images. As participants noted, perceptions can be changed by changing the images that are presented:

I think the advertisements, they should use Black people because we find that Black people have this idea that nature reserves are for White people only, because on the ads, you find that they only show White people on the reserve. (African youth, female)

Though past discrimination and ongoing images clearly convey parks as White areas, respondents did not report concerns that they would be discriminated against if they were to visit parks:

When I was there, I never felt like a minority as such. (African youth, male)

I had a feeling that it was a White people's thing to go there, but I thought about it and said to myself, well since it is in KwaZulu-Natal, most Black people are working there. I agreed I might even communicate with the Black people there … but when you get there you notice that everything was cool, there was no White person, there were no Black people. We were all treated in the same way. So I really enjoyed myself there. (African youth, male)

Nobody is looking at you if you're Black or White or anything like that. It's just everybody is minding his or her own business. (African youth, female)

The lack of discrimination experienced by participants should be tempered by the observation that most of their interaction was with each other and park staff. They had less interaction with other park visitors. However, there was at least the expectation that they would be accepted by other visitors. Indeed, the African respondents in particular wanted to interact with foreigners in order to enhance their knowledge of them.

Question 3: What Could Be Done to Increase Non-White Participation?

Realistically, park agencies are not able to affect some important participation constraints, notably income and overall travel rates. However, research results indicate that there are opportunities for parks to stimulate participation. In the Household Survey, Unlikely future visitors were asked what managers of South Africa's parks could do to make them more attractive as places to visit.

As with the constraints question, responses were open-ended and were grouped into 15 categories. Two of these relate to reducing costs and two to advertising and providing more information. Again, only those reporting at least one action were included in the analysis, with results shown in table 5.10.

Table 5.10 Opportunities for Increasing Visitation (percentage of respondents by race recommending cost reduction or advertising / more information)

Recommendation	Non-Whites	Whites
Cost reduction	30	39
Advertising / more information	50	9

Source: Data from the Household Survey.

It is interesting that Whites were more likely to report cost reduction than non-Whites. This reflects the fact that cost is a constraint across races (see table 5.4). However, when it comes to advertising, there is a clear indication that non-Whites consider this a priority. The difference between races is both large and statistically significant (chi-square, $p = 0.000$), and is consistent with the qualitative results reported above.

Perhaps the most dramatic step parks can take is sponsorship of trips among targeted groups—essentially repeating the process utilized in the focus group field trip. Participants clearly enjoyed the visit, and they are potentially increasing demand by word of mouth, as indicated by the following quotes in the context of discussing the trip with friends and colleagues:

> And then they were very excited about the place because most of them, they never even seen an elephant. So they were very impressed, so they also wanted to go there and see the place. (African youth, male)

> We actually talk about it at work all the time. … I try to explain to them it is like seeing an elephant or seeing a hyena walking in front of your car or coming up close to a giraffe. You just can't explain it, you've gotta see it for yourself. (Asian, male)

When asked if he still felt, post-visit, that the parks were "a White thing," one respondent stressed:

> I believe it's for everyone it's only that like we said earlier we lack exposure to such things like nature reserves and all along we've been the victim of ignorance. … I'm saying when I'm with my friends enjoying relaxing I talk about Hluhluwe, you find that they don't even know like [a different respondent] has just said anything about the warthogs so I had to explain to them how they eat, how they live, how they feed, about everything and elephants and the rhinos and everything. (African adult, male)

The children also continue to speak enthusiastically about their experience. None of the participants in the post-trip sessions had actually returned to HUP or gone to other parks. And, as noted by Helleiner (1990) in his study of Nigeria, a high level of awareness does not necessarily translate into a high level of visitation. However, several post-trip participants reported specific or general plans to return, with their field trip experience being a major motivation for these plans.

The results indicate that a mismatch between desired experiences and the opportunities offered by parks is not a problem. It will be important to offer, as is common in South Africa, a range of accommodation so that visitors can choose along the wildness-safety continuum. Though cooking and other facilities were provided in the accommodation, televisions were not, and this was well received. As noted by one respondent:

> We don't need a TV here. It's better without a TV and the noise. It's good to listen to the noise of the wildlife. (African youth, female)

However, there was some disappointment that the lights were turned off at 10:30 p.m. and that some of the accommodation involved communal bathroom facilities, although this was tied to safety concerns (the danger of roaming animals between the accommodation and the toilets). The main suggestion relating to accommodation was to fence off certain areas for safety reasons, particularly areas that kids would commonly use. There was also periodic concern about the quality of roads in the parks and concern about resulting damage to cars due to potholes. Nonetheless, several respondents noted that they did not feel the parks should pave the roads.

Though parks are seen as historically White areas, discrimination was neither expected nor experienced. Two marginality issues did come across as important: cost and transport. Feedback from respondents in both the Household and Focus Group Surveys indicates that perceptions of accommodation and other costs associated with park visits tend to be higher than actual costs. Thus, if information campaigns provide information on costs, as well as on practicalities, they may be able to enhance participation:

> It's very, very important the problem is the approach should be to promote and if you going to be promoting you need to dispel this misconception that people cannot afford, and I think what [a different participant] has actually said it's so, so true because one of the perceptions that we had especially with [a different participant] was we couldn't actually afford to go and I think that was the most dominant perception which actually discouraged us even from inquiring about the information. (African adult, male)

Other content suggested as important in an information campaign includes attractions (for example, whether the park offers the Big Five), services and facilities (for example, shops and restaurants), types of accommodation, facilities for children, and advice about how to obtain more information. It was noted that women are the ones who often decide where to travel, so campaigns should be targeted toward them.

Asian respondents tended to stress cinema advertisements, and even provided suggestions about what shows (times) and locations (specific cinemas) could be used to target specific market segments. They also noted that the popularity of some parks, notably Drakensberg, among Asians could provide ideas about attracting Asians to other parks, including HUP. Both Africans and Asians recommended radio and newspaper ads, as well as specific radio stations and papers, which tend to cater to different racial and age markets. There was also general agreement among respondents that youth should be targeted, because they not only influence their parents but also can translate exposure into demand for the rest of their lives. Schools currently take children on yearly school excursions, and parks could be an option for such trips.

One respondent noted that ordinary people should be used in information campaigns because:

> If you use ordinary people, you will say, oh, even ordinary people can afford it—well, maybe I can also afford it. (African youth, male)

Celebrities, as an alternative to ordinary people, were considered inappropriate both because viewers may not trust them (for example, may feel they are endorsing a park without ever having been to it) and because they may feel the celebrities are wealthy and can afford the visit, while the viewers cannot. It is not surprising that it was also suggested that Africans and Indians appear in the campaign material, depending on the market targeted:

> They should also use Black people because we find that Black people have this idea that nature reserves are for White people only because on the ads you find that they only show White people on the reserve and all that. (African youth, female)

The importance of inertia and word-of-mouth advertising reinforces the natural tendency to identify with one's own racial group. If an

African sees only Whites depicted in park images and does not hear about visits from African friends and colleagues, it may be difficult to overcome the inertia caused by historically White use of parks.

Throughout the focus group process, a common theme among Africans was that of the African Renaissance. Part of this movement involves a return to one's roots. In the case of the Zulu, this involves rural areas and hence a strong link with nature. Apartheid and urbanization are seen as having broken this link. Thus, a connection to nature is part of their effort to develop their identity. As one respondent stated:

> Tell people to go back and identify with their roots. We need to identify our differences and values and culture. We need to reconcile with ourselves first before you can expect the Coloured, the Indian, and White man to understand you. (African adult, male)

Last, there was a clear impression that lack of transportation hindered participation, as did the perceptual hurdle of planning and information acquisition. Perhaps because past travel appears mostly to have been organized by family or others, respondents found it intimidating to initiate trip planning. They desired substantial information regarding the practicalities, yet seemed unsure of how to obtain this information. If this hurdle can be overcome, participation may increase noticeably:

> I think taking a vacation like going to Hluhluwe really needs a lot of time and planning. … I think what can hold people back is the budget and the planning but after that is done, I think that it could be much easier for everybody to go. (African youth, female)

The broader information campaign described above can help reduce this hurdle. However, it may be desirable for park agencies, or an agent acting in conjunction with them, to develop packages that include transport and/or accommodation and can easily be purchased. One specific proposal from participants was to arrange a bus connection from Durban, as exists for the Wild Coast. This might be particularly popular, and thus profitable, during weekends (for example, leaving Durban Friday evening, returning Sunday evening) or seasonal periods of heavy travel such as summer holidays.

Question 4: Do Parks Need to Change (and Should They Try) to Increase Non-White Participation?

The preceding discussion indicates that non-Whites appear to value the experience that currently is offered, without a desire to develop facilities and services that differ from traditional norms for parks. In that sense, there is no indication that parks need to change dramatically to reach an expanded non-White market—they just need to overcome, when possible, the constraints noted above.

Nonetheless, several respondents noted that parks would not meet the recreational needs of all South Africans. To stimulate discussion on the topic, the "R10 million" hypothetical scenario (described above) was presented to respondents in the Focus Group Survey. As noted above, the second stage of that scenario was to identify expenditure items within the proportion that was allocated to parks. The first stage was to allocate proportions to nature parks versus other recreational opportunities, notably more urban or mass recreation activities such as barbecue facilities and swimming pools.

In the African adult group, there was a consensus that the majority of the money (65–70 percent) should go to parks, primarily for such general conservation purposes as antipoaching patrols. When prompted about what should be done to enhance the visitor experience, responses were to bring in more animals and to promote the parks, especially among Africans. Among African youth, the consensus centered on 50 percent going to parks, whereas for Asians the proportion was somewhat under 50 percent. Asians focused to some degree on the role of parks in attracting foreign tourists, which contributed to the local economy. Both groups recognized that not all South Africans are interested in parks, or able to visit them. As the following quotes illustrate, both groups were concerned about others in society and systematic in their approach to the issue:

> I wouldn't allocate most of it to improving game reserves because I think if you look at demographics and the population as a whole, I don't think many people in the lower rungs of society have income or money left over at the end of the month to make a trip to the game reserve. ... Maybe about 30 percent of it could be used toward improving game reserves, but I think if you were to take into account the best interests of

the population—maybe I would use more of it towards improving picnic spots and beaches and parks. (Asian, male)

Firstly before spending my money [the R10 million], I'll do a survey because what I've noticed that most people, from the rural areas, they like to come to the urban areas in most cases. So before I spend these monies and allocate them, I will do a survey on the people, from all the urban and rural areas to see what they really like, and then I'll spend my money but I think I'll like make it like 50/50. (African youth, male)

Though not directly comparable, Magi (1999) reported that respondents in his study in KZN were least likely to support additional nature-based facilities (for example, fishing areas, bird sanctuaries, and township parks), and most likely to support home- or community-based facilities like radio, television, museums, community halls, and shebeens/taverns.

Question 5: Do Park Visits Lead to Change in Attitude toward Conservation?

Respondents were asked whether their visit to the HUP had affected their attitude toward conservation. Although there is the potential for social desirability or interviewer bias in questions of this type, such bias was not apparent in responses. Moreover, it is difficult to isolate the effect of a visit from preexisting attitudes or personality generally. Nonetheless, there are clear indications that the visit did raise awareness among participants. As one participant noted in the context of being disturbed by warthogs while cooking at a barbecue:

We actually appreciated the fact that we were more like intruding in their own territory so we were very much conscious not to retard their freedom whilst also we were sort of enjoying seeing the natural habitat. (African adult, male)

As part of the discussion, two respondents noted:

I think that [the visit] has actually created a deep, a deeper sense of appreciation of nature. (African adult, male 1)

[And:]

I'll say in me and also sharing it with my family and then also with my friends—we seem to have developed a far more keener interest you know just to get more and more in touch with information on various aspects of nature. (African adult, male 2)

Not only was appreciation deepened, but also understanding. Respondents generally, but particularly the African adults, expressed interest in ecological issues, such as the relationships between animals and their environment.

DISCUSSION

Two theories have been widely tested as a means of explaining inter-racial and inter-ethnic variations in outdoor recreation participation: marginality and ethnicity. However, most studies have shown weak support for both, indicating that new methodologies and theories are required (Philipp 1999). The goal of this study was to extend previous research geographically and contextually, while using a combination of methodologies and addressing discrimination and other aspects that go beyond the basic marginality-ethnicity focus.

Starting with that initial focus, results clearly illustrate that marginality plays a role. The participation model indicates that education, income, and household size (which affect per-person income) are significant predictors of participation. Relative to Whites, non-Whites in the quantitative sample have lower levels of education and income, and larger household sizes. In the related analysis of nonbusiness travel generally, education was not significant, but income and household size were significant. Taken together, these analyses support the marginality hypothesis with respect to travel both in general and to parks in particular.

There is also some support for ethnicity in the sense of "everything left over after the effect of marginality." The negative signs for Africans and Asians in the participation model show that visitation rates for these groups were lower than for Whites even after controlling for socioeconomic and locational factors. However, this appears to be due only in part to what one might traditionally view as ethnic issues—notably recreational preferences or styles and variation in safety concerns across race.

When it came to preferences for "ideal trips," differences across races were modest. Asians do appear to be significantly less interested in nature-oriented destinations, but differences among Whites, Africans, and Coloureds were not statistically significant at $p = 0.05$. There do appear to be racial differences in on-site recreational styles, as well as safety concerns. Nonetheless, these differences are not dramatic, and results indicate a surprising degree of uniformity in desired experiences and facilities. This implies that park facilities do not need to undergo major change to appeal to a greater number of non-White visitors than they currently attract.

Non-Whites consistently reported seeing parks as "White areas." However, it was promising that they neither expected nor experienced discrimination during the field trip. In other words, the "White area" perception reflects past discrimination and historic visitation patterns, as well as current media images, but it does not appear to reflect current discrimination.

The above suggests that ethnicity may play a relatively large role in Asian nonparticipation but that it plays a relatively small role in African nonparticipation. Discrimination apparently plays little or no role. The two remaining factors that came across in both the qualitative and Household Surveys are cost and information. Africans had lower income and higher household size levels than both Asians and Whites, so they may be most affected by reductions in cost. However, as is shown in tables 5.4 and 5.10, cost reductions would benefit all races.

The problem is that park agencies typically are already underfunded and need to generate revenue to cover their costs, including the costs of accommodation and other visitor-related infrastructure. In addition, to some degree the issue appears to be one of perceived rather than actual cost levels. Moreover, results from other study components indicate that transport cost, or transport unavailability, is more important than on-site cost, such as entrance fees and accommodation. Thus, targeted subsidies, such as for school groups, may be both desirable and feasible, but a general reduction in entrance or accommodation cost may not be the most effective means of enhancing participation.

A more effective means, particularly among non-Whites, is the provision of information and a reduction in the practical hurdles needed to visit. It is important that this provision be targeted to its intended demographic market (by race, age, income, and so on) in terms of substantive content, presenters, and outlet. Given the transportation challenge, combined with concerns about logistical hurdles, development of park package trips may also be important in enhancing visitation.

In summary, current low levels of park visitation among non-Whites are due to a variety of related factors, including lack of resources, historical prejudice and access restrictions, lack of childhood exposure, inertia, and lack of information. Park agencies cannot reverse past prejudice or lack of childhood visits among non-Whites, nor can they realistically affect national employment and income levels. However, they can stimulate current visitation among non-White adults and children and in so doing can generate a new, more racially balanced visitor mix for South African nature reserves.

NOTES

1. The focus of this study is visitation involving an overnight stay at nonurban natural areas such as national parks and nature reserves; the term "park" is used to refer to such areas. Nonetheless, the literature review includes studies of a range of leisure activities, including visits to urban parks. The terms "race" and "ethnicity" are used interchangeably here; the categories evaluated in this study are described in the section below.

2. The index values are the same across races within a given EA. One might imagine that races might respond differently, for example, to distance (the price component of the index). Therefore, a distance-multiplied-by-race term was included in the site selection analysis to determine if respondents of different races did react differently. It is interesting that only Coloured respondents differed statistically from Whites in this regard, and they were less sensitive to distance than were Whites; this diverges from the findings of Bowker and Leeworthy (1998), in which Hispanics are more price-responsive than are non-Hispanic Whites. However, the small number of Coloured respondents in the sample suggests that care should be taken when interpreting this result.

REFERENCES

Baas, J. M., A. Ewert, and D. J. Chavez. 1993. "Influence of Ethnicity on Recreation and Natural Environment Use Patterns: Managing Recreation Sites for Ethnic and Racial Diversity." *Environmental Management* 17:523–29.

Booth, D. 2001. *Australian Beach Cultures: The History of Sun, Sand and Surf.* London, Frank Cass.

Bowker, J. M., and V. R. Leeworthy. 1998. "Accounting for Ethnicity in Recreation Demand: A Flexible Count Data Approach." *Journal of Leisure Research* 30(1):64–78.

Cordell, H. K., C. Betz, and G. T. Green. 2002. "Recreation and the Environment as Cultural Dimensions in Contemporary American Society." *Leisure Sciences* 24:13–41.

Driver, B. L., D. Dustin, T. Baltic, G. Elsner, and G. Peterson. 1996. "Nature and the Human Spirit: Overview." In B. L. Driver, D. Dustin, T. Baltic, G. Elsner, and G. Peterson, eds., *Nature and the Human Spirit: Toward an Expanded Land Management Ethic.* State College, Pa.: Venture.

———. 1990. "Outdoor Recreation Participation and Preferences by Black and White Chicago Households." In J. Vining, ed., *Social Science and Natural Resource Recreation Management.* Boulder, Colo.: Westview.

Ewert, A. W. 1999. "Managing for the New Forest Visitor: The Impact of Changing Demographic Variables." In J. Aley, W. R. Burch, B. Conover, and D. Field, eds., *Ecosystem Management: Adaptive Strategies for Natural Resources Organizations in the 21st Century.* Philadelphia: Taylor and Francis.

Floyd, M. F. 1998. "Getting Beyond Marginality and Ethnicity: The Challenge for Race and Ethnic Studies in Leisure Research." *Journal of Leisure Research* 30(1):3–22.

———. 1999. "Race, Ethnicity, and Use of the National Park System." *Social Science Research Review* 1(2):1–24.

Floyd, M. F., and C. Y. Johnson. 2002. "Coming to Terms with Environmental Justice in Outdoor Recreation: A Conceptual Discussion with Research Implications." *Leisure Sciences* 24:59–77.

Floyd, M. F., and K. J. Shinew. 1999. "Convergence and Divergence in Leisure Style among Whites and African Americans: Toward an Interracial Contact Hypothesis." *Journal of Leisure Research* 31:359–84.

Goldsmith, J. 1994. "Designing for Diversity." *National Parks* 68:20–21.

Gramann, J. H. 1996. "Ethnicity, Race, and Outdoor Recreation: A Review of Trends, Policy, and Research." Miscellaneous Paper R–96–1. Vicksburg, Miss.: U.S. Army Engineer Waterways Experiment Station.

Hausman, J. A., G. K. Leonard, and D. McFadden. 1995. "A Utility-Consistent, Combined Discrete Choice and Count Data Model: Assessing Recreational Use Losses Due to Natural Resource Damage." *Journal of Public Economics* 56:1–30.

Helleiner, F. M. 1990. "Domestic and International Tourism in Third World Nations." *Tourism Recreation Research* 15:18–25.

Henderson, K. A. 1991. *Dimensions of Choice: A Qualitative Approach to Recreation, Parks, and Leisure Research.* State College, Pa.: Venture.

———. 1998. "Researching Diverse Populations." *Journal of Leisure Research* 30(1): 157–70.

Henderson, K. A., B. E. Ainsworth, L. M. Stolarzyck, J. M. Hootman, and S. Levin. 1999. "Notes on Linking Qualitative and Quantitative Data: The Cross Cultural Physical Activity Participation Study." *Leisure Sciences* 21(3):247–55.

Husbands, W. 1989. "Social Status and Perception of Tourism in Zambia." *Annals of Tourism Research* 16(2):237–53.

Johnson, C. Y., J. M. Bowker, D. B. K. English, and D. Worthen. 1998. "Wildland Recreation in the Rural South: An Examination of Marginality and Ethnicity Theory." *Journal of Leisure Research* 30(1):101–20.

Juniu, S. 2000. "The Impact of Immigration: Leisure Experience in the Lives of South American Immigrants." *Journal of Leisure Research* 32:358–81.

Magi, L. M. 1999. "Township Recreation Patterns and the New Order in South Africa." *Tourism Geographies* 1(3):293–312.

Meeker, J. W. 1973 (revised 1992). "Red, White and Black in the National Parks. In G. E. Machlis and D. R. Field, eds., *On Interpretation: Sociology for Interpreters of Natural Resource and Cultural History*. Corvallis: Oregon State University.

Philipp, S. F. 1994. "Race and Tourism Choice: A Legacy of Discrimination?" *Annals of Tourism Research* 21:479–88.

———. 1995. "Race and Leisure Constraints." *Leisure Sciences* 17:109–20.

———. 1997. "Race, Gender, and Leisure Benefits." *Leisure Sciences* 19:191–207.

———. 1999. "Are We Welcome? African American Racial Acceptance in Leisure Activities and the Importance Given to Children's Leisure." *Journal of Leisure Research* 31:385–403.

Ranger, T. 1989. "Whose Heritage? The Case of Matobo National Park." *Journal of Southern African Studies* 15(2):217–49.

Richins, H. 1999. "Utilizing Mixed Method Approaches in Tourism Research." *Pacific Tourism Review* 3(1):95–99.

Shaull, S. L., and J. H. Gramann. 1998. "The Effect of Cultural Assimilation on the Importance of Family-Related and Nature-Related Recreation among Hispanic Americans." *Journal of Leisure Research* 30:47–63.

Sindiga, I. 1996. "Domestic Tourism in Kenya." *Annals of Tourism Research* 23(1):19–31.

Taylor, D. E. 1989. "Blacks and the Environment: Toward an Explanation of the Concern and Action Gap between Blacks and Whites. *Environment and Behavior* 21(2):175–205.

———. 2000. "Meeting the Challenge of Wild Land Recreation Management: Demographic Shifts and Social Inequality." *Journal of Leisure Research* 32(1):171–79.

Thapa, B., A. R. Graefe, and J. D. Absher. 2002. "Information Needs and Search Behaviors: A Comparative Study of Ethnic Groups in the Angeles and San Bernardino National Forests, California." *Leisure Sciences* 24:89–107.

U.S. National Park Service. 1997. *National Park Service Strategic Plan*. Washington, D.C.: U.S. Department of the Interior.

Virden, R. J., and G. J. Walker. 1999. "Ethnic/Racial and Gender Variations among Meanings Given to, and Preferences for, the Natural Environment." *Leisure Sciences* 21:219–39.

Wallace, V. K., and D. J. Witter. 1992. "Urban Nature Centers: What Do Our Constituents Want and How Can We Give It to Them? *Legacy* 2:20–24.

Washburne, R. F. 1978. "Black Under-Participation in Wildland Recreation: Alternative Explanations. *Leisure Sciences* 1(2):175–89.

Washburne, R. F., and P. Wall. 1980. *Black-White Ethnic Differences in Outdoor Recreation.* U.S. Department of Agriculture Research Paper INT–249. Ogden, Utah: U.S. Department of Agriculture Forest Service, Intermountain Forest and Range Experiment Station.

Wells, M. P. 1996. "The Social Role of Protected Areas in the New South Africa." *Environmental Conservation* 23(4):322–31.

West, P. C. 1989. "Urban Region Parks and Black Minorities: Subculture, Marginality and Interracial Relations in Park Use in the Detroit Metropolitan Area." *Leisure Sciences* 11:11–28.

Wilson, G. D. H., and P. S. Hattingh. 1992. "Environmental Preferences for Recreation within Deprived Areas: The Case of Black Townships in South Africa." *Geoforum* 23(4):477–86.

PART III

BUSINESS AND THE ENVIRONMENT IN NATURE TOURISM: SUPPLY STUDIES

CHAPTER 6

TOURISM'S CONTRIBUTION TO CONSERVATION IN ZULULAND

An Ecological Survey of Private Reserves and Public Protected Areas

Kreg Lindberg, Barry James, and Pete Goodman

More than 25 years ago, Budowski (1976, 27) noted the "[virtual] explosion of tourism concerned with wildlife." Visitor levels have continued to rise since that time, especially in developing countries. He observed that tourism and environmental conservation could exhibit relationships based on conflict, coexistence, or symbiosis, and expressed concern that in most cases the tendency was toward conflict, despite the potential for symbiosis.

More recent articles have expressed support for tourism's actual or potential contribution to conservation, but also concern about its negative effects, failure to achieve expected benefits, and potential to distract attention from more permanent means of environmental protection (Bookbinder and others 1998; Durbin and Ratrimoarisaona 1996; Goodwin and Swingland 1996; Gössling 1999; Isaacs 2000; Mendelsohn 1997; Yu, Hendrickson, and Castillo 1997). Though opinions on the impact of tourism have often been polarized, and evidence to support

This research benefited from the input of project team members Ernst Lutz, Geert Creemers, and Bruce Aylward. The authors thank the game ranch owners and managers, as well as the field and scientific staff of KZN Wildlife, for their assistance. They also thank Marc Hero for reviewing an earlier version of the chapter.

such opinions have often been anecdotal, there is a growing empirical literature that is leading to more informed and balanced views of tourism's role within conservation (as used here, "tourism" incorporates recreation, as well as both consumptive and nonconsumptive activities).

Much of this literature occurs within the field of recreation ecology, which evaluates the ecological changes caused by visitors and associated activities (for example, clearing of trails or construction of facilities). Liddle (1997) and Hammitt and Cole (1998) provided overviews of principles and findings, and relevant articles can be found regularly in the conservation and environmental management journals (see, for example, Buerger and others 2000; Cilimburg, Moonz, and Kehoe 2000; De-la-Torre, Snowdon, and Bejarano 2000; Duchesne, Cote, and Barrette 2000; Hawkins and others 1999; Kutiel, Eden, and Zhevelev 2000; Miller and Hobbs 2000; Steidl and Anthony 2000; Thurston and Reader 2001). In addition, there is a smaller literature on the effectiveness of management strategies for reducing undesirable effects (for example, Medio, Ormond, and Pearson 1997).

Recreation ecology focuses on anthropogenic changes that generally are viewed as negative, but tourism can also contribute to conservation. The next section briefly reviews such contributions. The remainder of the chapter describes the particular contribution of private natural areas, using the example of private game reserves in KwaZulu-Natal Province of South Africa.

TOURISM'S CONTRIBUTION TO CONSERVATION

Tourism can contribute to conservation through several often-overlapping mechanisms. Perhaps the broadest, and most difficult to quantify, is tourism's role in the creation and maintenance of public protected areas. Anecdotally, it is clear that the number of such areas would be far smaller if visitors were not allowed (Dabrowski 1994). As Butler (1991, 202) noted, "There are many examples of the establishment of national parks and other heritage properties because of the real or perceived benefits which would accrue to a country through their expected encouragement of tourism." These benefits accrue to visitors, tourism enterprises, local communities, and others, and each group is a potential supporter of establishing parks.

Additional contributions can be grouped into three categories: educational, political and local community, and financial. Conservation education associated with natural area tourism has the potential not only to mitigate negative on-site ecological effects and provide local employment but also to change visitor attitudes and off-site conservation behavior (Jacobsen and Robles 1992). Taking a broader view of education, tourism can also contribute to research (and site maintenance) as visitors and tour companies assist academic or agency staff in their research endeavors.

Tourism can generate political support for conservation through several mechanisms. In many countries, visitors to natural areas have formed strong lobby groups to preserve those areas. In addition, benefits from nature tourism accruing to other groups, notably the tourism industry and local communities, have enhanced political support for the areas on which this tourism depends. Moreover, in many cases the fee revenue generated by tourism at public natural areas goes to governmental treasuries (rather than remaining with the park or management agency), and this can increase political support for the areas. In some cases, this political support can lead to financial support for the protected area (Lindberg, Enriquez, and Sproule 1996). Last, visitors may join or otherwise support conservation organizations that in turn help fund protected area management.

Recently, there has been substantial research on local community attitudes and behavior toward natural areas, and tourism can play an important role in this context (see Durbin and Ratrimoarisaona 1996; Fortin and Gagnon 1999; Lindberg, Enriquez, and Sproule 1996; Young 1999). In many parts of the world, local residents have borne significant costs when natural areas have been protected, because the establishment of these areas has often led to reduced access to resources, and in some cases translocation. Tourism can provide local benefits that counterbalance local costs, and thereby lead to more favorable attitudes. As Walpole, Goodwin, and Ward (2001, 219; citing Goodwin 1996, 288) put it, "Ecotourism forms a link between protected areas and the livelihood of local people, 'providing revenue to the local community sufficient for local people to value, and therefore protect, their wildlife heritage as a source of income.'" As Yu, Hendrickson, and Castillo (1997, 137) put it,

> Significant environmental conservation in the Peruvian Amazon will necessarily run counter to the interests of local inhabitants. Ecotourism can bring about temporary truces in the conflict between development and conservation by transferring some of the benefits of conservation to local inhabitants, at least over the short term.

This potential should be tempered by the realization that (1) in some cases, employment benefits will be modest; (2) residents may not make the conceptual link between conservation and income (and, in reality, the link may not be as strong as some might believe or wish); and (3) income from tourism may actually increase local resource use by enabling the use of newer technology and additional labor (Alexander 2000; Yu, Hendrickson, and Castillo 1997; Langholz 1999). Local communities, and thus conservation attitudes, can also benefit through revenue-sharing programs, in which a portion of fees paid to protected area management agencies is distributed to local communities. Such programs exist in Nepal and several African countries (see Bookbinder and others 1998; Durbin and Ratrimoarisaona 1996; Lewis and Alpert 1997; Lindberg 1998).

Perhaps the most obvious contribution that tourism can make is financial. Several researchers have noted the severe lack of protected area financing relative to funding levels considered necessary to properly manage the areas (Vaughan 2000; James, Green, and Paine 1999; Wilkie and Carpenter 1999; Wilkie, Carpenter, and Zhang 2001). Government funding can be, and has been, supplemented by international donations (Boza 1993; Wilkie and Carpenter 1999; Wilkie, Carpenter, and Zhang 2001). Shortfalls remain, however, and nature tourism is often seen as a means for raising further revenue. The U.S. recreational fee demonstration program has generated substantial revenue benefits for the relevant agencies, including the National Park Service and the U.S. Forest Service. In fiscal year 2000, the agencies collected $176 million from the program, which is in addition to the $22 million collected at nonprogram sites (U.S. Department of the Interior and U.S. Department of Agriculture 2001). Few systems will generate such funding levels, but in many countries public protected area agencies depend, often substantially, on direct and indirect visitor fees (Lewis and Alpert 1997; Wilkie and Carpenter 1999).

At many sites, and in some protected area systems, visitor demand is inadequate to generate sufficient revenue to cover a significant portion of management costs. Furthermore, the revenue that is collected often is not earmarked for the site or the system, and thus may be "lost" in the central government's treasury. In addition, tourism generates both financial and nonfinancial costs, so revenue does not necessarily represent a net benefit.

Finally, tourism can be a fickle industry, subject to declines due to factors outside the control of natural area managers, which means that funding dependent on tourism can also be fickle (Durbin and Ratrimoarisaona 1996 Goodwin and others 1998; Lindberg, Enriquez, and Sproule 1996; Walpole, Goodwin, and Ward 2001; Wilkie, Carpenter, and Zhang 2001). These concerns must be balanced with the reality that other sources of funding, from governmental allocations to donations, can also be fickle, as well as traditionally insufficient.

THE ROLE OF PRIVATE NATURAL AREAS

Although the above discussion centers on public natural areas, the visitor demand that leads to financial and economic benefits at such areas can also be captured, often more efficiently, by private areas. In brief, tourism provides an incentive to establish and maintain private natural areas. The role of private natural areas has been discussed in the academic, "grey," and popular media (for example, anonymous 2001). However, detailed evaluations of their contribution to conservation have not appeared; most studies focus on economic and/or managerial issues.

For example, Price Waterhouse (1994) evaluated the financial and economic desirability of cattle ranching versus wildlife and associated tourism for conservancies in Zimbabwe (see Richardson 1998 for a similar analysis of Namibia). They found that a small wildlife operation with tourism, hunting, and culling generated much greater gross revenue per hectare than did cattle, even at a high stocking rate. In the Latin American context, Hoogesteijn and Chapman (1997) noted the potential conservation gains from Venezuelan ranches expanding the sale of capybara (*Hydrochaeris hydrochaeris*) and caiman (*Caiman crocodilus*), alongside traditional cattle production, with tourism noted as an additional option. Aylward and others (1996) reported on the financial viability of tourism at the Monteverde Cloud Forest Reserve in Costa Rica.

Such detailed economic evaluations are complemented by broader "managerial" evaluations that typically fall within one of two extremes: case study evaluations of one or a few reserves or mail surveys of multiple reserves. Yu, Hendrickson, and Castillo (1997) provided a case study history of three lodge properties in the Peruvian Amazon region, including the encroachment and legal and administrative challenges they have faced.

Langholz and others (2000) and Langholz (1996) gave examples of the mail survey approach. On the basis of surveys of owners and managers of private areas in Latin America and Africa, they found that motivations for establishing private reserves are often dominated by conservation goals; this is fortunate for conservation, for Wilkie and Carpenter (1999) reported that even in "high value" nature tourism locations like East Africa and Southern Africa, tourism will not always be the most financially attractive land use. Profitability is the second most important motivator, but many reserve owners do not depend on their reserves for revenue generation. Indeed, though profitability was on the increase, Langholz (1996) reported that in his study only 59 percent were profitable. Such reserves often provide other revenue-generating goods and services beyond nature tourism (such as game sales), but nature tourism is the dominant revenue component, generating an average 67 percent of operating income.

Intuitively, it is evident that private areas that maintain largely natural conditions on their property contribute to conservation, and in some studies the spatial extent of these areas is reported. For example, Alderman (1994) reported that the 63 Latin American and African reserves in her study own 493,850 hectares and manage additional land totaling 496,044 hectares. Watkins and others (1996) provided the most comprehensive evaluation to date of private area contributions to conservation. Their study of several countries in Africa yielded data on the extent of total country area contained in private natural areas and brief case-study descriptions of specific contributions to conservation.

For example, Watkins and his coauthors reported that in South Africa, private protected areas (that is, game ranches registered with the authorities) are both more numerous and more extensive in area than legally designated sites. The private areas cover 6.85 percent of the country's area, compared with 6.26 percent for public natural areas. With respect to species conservation, the authors noted that Ol Ari Nyiro Ranch holds almost 10 percent of Kenya's remaining 500 black rhinoceroses, that all but one of the 65 white rhinos imported from South Africa are located on private land, and that the Kenya Wildlife Service continues to encourage efforts by private landowners to breed and protect this and other species. The authors noted the importance of further evaluation of private protected areas and their contribution to biodiversity; such an evaluation is presented here, using the example of KwaZulu-Natal Province, South Africa.

Study Region

The study region is the northeastern portion of the province of KwaZulu-Natal (KZN), South Africa, lying between 26 045′ and 31 010′ S, 28 045′ and 32 050′ E. The province covers an area of 9,485,855 hectares and the study region 2,496,000 hectares (26.3 percent of the province). KZN contains a wide diversity of landscapes and vegetation communities, ranging from the easterly coastal plains with coastal forests, sandy bushveld, and sandforest, through to savanna woodlands, grasslands, and high-lying alpine heath. It is an important subtropical agricultural and plantation forestry region, and the Drakensberg escarpment is the source of much of the country's water. It is also the most populous province of South Africa. Some 34 percent of the province has been transformed, with major agents of transformation being sugarcane (4.4 percent), commercial plantation forestry (6.8 percent), and subsistence farming (8.8 percent).

The provincial conservation agency at the time of the study was the KwaZulu-Natal Nature Conservation Service (NCS), now known as Ezemvelo KZN Wildlife (as of 2002). Protected areas managed by NCS are referred to here as "public areas." "Commercial game ranches" are defined by the Natal Conservation Ordinance 15/1974 as "any area of privately owned land on which game are propagated, kept or maintained for business purposes and in respect of which a permit has been issued in terms of this ordinance."

Registered commercial game ranches are required to have a game fence of an acceptable standard surrounding the property. Nonregistration does not prevent a landowner from commercializing game on the property, but registration confers certain advantages, such as legal ownership of the game and permission to hunt without having to apply for a permit each time. Game on all land outside commercial game ranches has the status of *res nullius* (no private ownership). For the purposes of this analysis, all private properties that utilize game or have nature tourism as the primary form of land use, regardless of whether they are registered as commercial game ranches, are referred to as "game ranches."

Public areas in KZN are not as large or spectacular as the large game reserves of East Africa, but they have made some important contributions to the conservation of biodiversity—the most notable being the white rhino success story and the fact that today they provide protection for the dwindling population of black rhinos. In recent years, populations of elephants have been reestablished in the three major public areas: Hluhluwe-Umfolozi Park (HUP), Mkhuze Game Reserve, and Ithala Game Reserve.

The Moçambique coastal plain, which forms the northeastern edge of the province, is located at the point of transition between tropical and temperate regions and thus has a variety of plant and animal species from both. Partly because of the avifauna diversity in the province and partly because of its unique zoographic position, KZN is the single most important region for conserving Red Data bird species in South Africa. Of the 62 Red Data bird species currently listed, 49 occur regularly in KZN, and the province makes a major, or the only, contribution to the existence of 26 of them.

Nine magisterial districts (local government areas) in northeastern KZN form the study region, with four of these districts being within the Uthungulu Regional Council and five within the Zululand Regional Council. The study sample comprises 30 properties located in this region, of which 27 are game ranches and the remaining 3 the above-mentioned public areas. One of the properties is located on the western boundary of the study region, but it was included because it is the largest game ranch in the region.

Public areas cover 798,349 hectares (8.4 percent) and game ranches 238,604 hectares (2.5 percent) of the province, while in the study region public areas cover 415,000 hectares (16.6 percent) and game ranches 167,396 hectares (6.7 percent). Thus, the combined area under game management for the province is 1,036,953 hectares (10.9 percent) and for the study region 582,396 hectares (23.3 percent). The remaining land in the study region consists of 607,604 hectares (24.3 percent) of commercial farmland and urban areas, and 1,306,000 hectares (52.3 percent) of communally managed land.

An important contextual issue in the study region is that the number and areal extent of game ranches increased dramatically in the 1990s, due in part to increases in international visitor arrivals to the country, together with decreasing beef prices and the withdrawal of beef subsidies (Richardson 1998 reports similar effects in Namibia). Thus, cattle farming was becoming less economically viable at the same time that tourism growth provided new income opportunities. There is some indication that game ranch expansion "overshot" these opportunities, because occupancy rates are low at several ranches (only 3 of the 20 "tourism ranches" that provided rates reported occupancy of 50 percent or higher, and many reported occupancy of 10 percent or less). Thus, the long-term maintenance of the contribution described below may depend on continued growth in visitor numbers.

METHODS

The evaluation is based on a stratified (based on property size) random sample of 27 (45.7 percent) of the 59 private areas in the study region, as well as the three main public areas listed above. Information gathering involved three activities: a landowner questionnaire, a physical assessment, and a geographic information system (GIS) query of landscape, ecosystem, community, and species coverage.

To promote participation in the project, a presentation was made at the Natal Game Ranchers' Association Annual General Meeting in September 1999, and a letter of introduction was sent to all members of the association. Appointments were then made with landowners or managers of the selected properties (from here on, landowners and managers reporting on their behalf are referred to collectively as landowners). A pilot study of three properties, two private and one public, was undertaken in November 1999, and the questionnaire was subsequently refined.

The landowners of the three properties that formed the pilot study were later contacted to obtain the additional information for the final questionnaire, and the remaining 27 properties were assessed between January and April 2000. In some instances, an appointment was made but canceled at the last moment by the landowner. On these occasions, landowners of the closest properties that were in the size range on the list were contacted. The first property with a landowner who was prepared to have a meeting at short notice then replaced the original selection.

The questionnaire was administered in person. After the interview, the property was assessed by means of driving or walking around the property. During this assessment, note was taken of the condition of roads, condition of animals, grass species composition and basal cover, evidence of erosion, bush encroachment, and alien plant invasion. In addition, a general discussion on management philosophy and attitudes was conducted. Within the time allocated (1.5 days per property), it was not possible to conduct detailed veld condition assessments, and game species numbers had to be based on landowner counts or estimates. The questionnaires and site visits were supplemented by GIS analysis of existing data.

As was noted above, there are varied and often interwoven motivations for landowners to maintain private areas, with tourism being but one. Indeed, 23 (85.2 percent) of the 27 landowners included in their reasons for going into nature tourism that they had a personal interest or love for wildlife. Because this analysis is concerned with tourism's contribution to conservation, land uses "with and without tourism" were compared in an effort to isolate the effect of tourism in particular. Specifically, landowners were asked:

> Think back to when you converted to nature tourism [referred to the earlier item involving this information]. Now assume that tourism hadn't been an option—for example, that visitors and/or hunters simply did not come to the region. If that were the case, what would you currently be doing with the land? For example, would it be in sugar cane, plantation forest, cattle, or ...?

Landowners were reminded that the issue was not simply one of land use before conversion, because land use may have evolved over time without tourism.

Of the 27 private areas, 5 landowners (18.5 percent) stated they still would have purchased and/or retained the property for hobby or other reasons. Therefore, the conservation benefits generated by these ranches cannot be attributed to tourism, and these ranches are excluded from this analysis, except where noted. The remaining 22 ranches (81.5 percent of those surveyed) are included. For most of these 22, cattle would have been the land use "without tourism," though the sale of venison and other activities were also noted. For the purposes of this analysis, it is assumed that such land uses would not have contributed to conservation, such that each included property's current contribution is due to tourism. This is a nonconservative assumption that should be borne in mind when interpreting results. Conversely, inclusion in the "tourism group" was conservative (that is, in borderline cases, the property was excluded).

The results from public areas are also presented here, both for comparison purposes and because tourism plays a role in their ongoing existence. We do not assume that the nontourism default is a set of pristine public areas of their current size. In this context, Yu, Hendrickson, and Castillo's (1997, 136) observation is worth noting (see also Czech and Krausman 1997; Makhdoum and Khorasani 1988):

> The recent ecotourism literature concerns itself largely with the deleterious effects of tourism on local cultures and ecosystems of visited areas. ... [However,] in the face of alternatives like farming, logging and oil drilling, tourism is a remarkably benign way to balance the sometimes contradictory goals of biological conservation and economic development.

For ease of reference, "public sample" refers to the three public areas sampled, "game ranch sample" refers to the 27 private areas sampled, and "tourism ranch sample" or "tourism ranches" refers to the 22 areas within the game ranch sample whose existence is credited to tourism.

Various types of results are presented in the next section; the methods used to obtain them vary. The following describes these methods across result types, together with relevant background information.

Representation of Priority Landscapes

The landscapes of KwaZulu-Natal have been classified and mapped, and each untransformed remnant allocated a priority rank in terms of its potential contribution to landscape conservation (Fairbanks and Benn 2000). Using the mapping software program ArcView, all public areas and game ranches in the study region (not just those in the sample) were overlaid with the landscape coverage, and a GIS query was performed to determine how many hectares of each landscape were found on each property. The total number of hectares in each priority class by property type was then totaled.

The estimated tourism contribution to the study region was calculated by adjusting (1) the study region game ranch figures by (2) the proportion of the game ranch sample's coverage represented by the tourism sample. For example, 97.7 percent of the game ranch sample land in class 3 is contained in properties in the tourism sample, so the region's tourism contribution (97,572) is calculated by multiplying the region's game ranch contribution (99,910) by 0.977.

Infrastructural Footprint

The areal contribution to conservation is reduced by the infrastructural "footprint" resulting from tourism. This footprint was divided into two categories: (1) roads and tracks and (2) tourist accommodation and management facilities. An estimate of the length of the road network was obtained from the landowner, from GIS queries or hand-drawn maps when available, from orthophotos, or (as a last resort) from subjective comparisons with other properties. The area of impact was calculated as length times average width, with the latter assumed to be a constant (and somewhat conservative) five meters for roads. The properties had few or only very short sections of paved road, and only one property allowed off-road driving. The vast majority of roads were gravel or dirt.

Facility area for the smaller properties was measured by pacing the outside length and breadth of each facility. For the larger properties, where it was not possible to pace out each facility, the landowner was asked to estimate the size. Because nearly all the facilities are unfenced, and there are areas of untransformed vegetation within the perimeters, most footprints are "porous." For example, a camp may have four accommodation units, a dining area, and an administrative area. The footprint of the camp was estimated by measuring its outer boundaries rather than by measuring the size of each individual unit. The vegetation between units was largely intact, and animals were free to move between units. Airfields that are simply mown areas are not included in the footprint.

Landscape Connectivity

Game ranches not only increase the absolute amount of land available for conservation but can also contribute to landscape connectivity. The potential linkages between the five public areas in the study area—Ithala, HUP, Mkhuze, Pongola Nature Reserve, and the Saint Lucia Wetland Park—can be seen in map 1.4. The Greater Saint Lucia Wetland Park is already linked to Mkhuze Game Reserve via a narrow band of formally conserved land on the Mkhuze floodplain, but this is further enhanced by a collection of large and small game ranches to the south of Mkhuze.

The linkage is almost complete between Mkhuze Game Reserve, through state land and some private and communal land, to the Lebombo Mountain Reserve and to the Pongola Nature Reserve, which incorporates the Pongolapoort Dam. The Magudu game ranches between the Pongola Nature Reserve and Ithala create a further potential link, although incomplete. There are also potential links developing between HUP and the Greater Saint Lucia Wetland Park. The extent to which all game ranches (not just those in the sample) reduce the overall distance to be traveled between protected areas was calculated. Each reduction may result from one or more game ranches and is not necessarily along a straight line.

Representation of Vegetation Communities

The contribution of game ranches to vegetation community representation is based on Camp's (1999) Bioresource Groups. The coverage of each community in public areas and game ranches for the whole province (not just those in the sample or study region) was estimated using GIS queries. Using the same method, the areal coverage within the tourism sample was estimated for each community represented in the sample.

Contribution to Herbivory

The contribution that tourism ranches make to restoring ecosystem and community processes is evaluated in three contexts: herbivory, predation, and parasitism. For herbivory, the current number of herbivores on each property was counted relative to the historical number of species. In addition, the contribution to the process of herbivory was assessed. Because ecosystem processes have been disturbed by the predominance of domestic bulk grazers, it follows that the reestablishment of browsers onto a property would contribute to restoring the grazer–browser balance and enhance seed dispersal. Therefore, the balance between browsers and grazers was also evaluated.

Contribution to Predation

As for herbivory, the total number of "in-range" predators on each property was counted relative to the historical number of species. In addition, landowner attitudes toward predators were obtained.

Parasitism

The introduction of indigenous animal species generally means that landowners do not have to concern themselves with control of either ecto- or endo-parasites, because indigenous species have a long history of coevolution with them and usually only succumb if they are ill or infirm. All the game ranches had at one time been cattle ranches, which means that all of them dipped their cattle. When commercial cattle ranching was first introduced in the study area, the dips that were used were arsenic based and tended to kill off many nontarget species, including dung beetles and oxpeckers. In recent years, so-called oxpecker-friendly dips have been developed that are not as detrimental to nontarget species.

However, there is a tendency among some landowners to introduce out-of-range herbivore species, which are not adapted to the local parasites. To prevent these species from succumbing, some have devised methods to dip or dose their game. Because game cannot be handled in the same way as cattle, landowners have to buy or construct devices to dip the game when they come to drink, or they place drugs for the control of endo-parasites into supplementary feed. Landowners were asked the extent to which they (1) still had cattle and dipped only the cattle regularly with oxpecker-friendly dips, (2) dipped their game, and (3) treated game for internal parasites.

System Resilience

Resilience can be decreased by artificial water and supplementary feeding, because both factors artificially elevate carrying capacity. The availability of water on game ranches is far in excess of what it was historically. The prevailing tendency to create many closely spaced, permanent water sources on game ranches, coupled with the relatively small size of most game ranches, results in losses in both resilience and biodiversity.

Given that the provision of artificial water allows a greater animal biomass than is typical of other areas with similar rainfall, the effects of droughts will be more keenly felt because reserve stands of lightly grazed grassland further from water will not be available, and animals can thus neither migrate to reserve forage within the game ranch nor migrate to areas outside the ranch. The loss of plant biomass also means that at the end of the drought, recovery of grass cover will be slower on game ranches, with a higher density of artificial water points. In terms of biodiversity, a high density of water points also results in loss of spatial heterogeneity (Walker and others 1987). The extent of artificial water provision and supplementary feeding was assessed through queries to the landowners.

Species Conservation

Species presence was based either on game count details supplied by the landowner or, in the absence of landowner knowledge, on records of known distribution of that species. Because not all landowners had accurate counts for different species, in many cases a species was recorded simply as present or absent.

Demographic and Genetic Uncertainty

Game ranch contributions to species populations are constrained by the lack of connectivity between properties. Ultimately, a game ranch's contribution to the conservation of a species will be a function of the persistence of the species population on the ranch. Demographic viability refers to the likelihood that a local population will or will not become extinct. There is no single "magic" population size that will guarantee the persistence of a population, because extinction is a probabilistic phenomenon; the larger the size of each population, the lower the probability of extinction. Four factors influence the likelihood of population extinction (Meffe and Carroll 1994): demographic uncertainty, environmental uncertainty, natural catastrophes, and genetic uncertainty. Genetic and demographic uncertainty are considered here.

The maintenance of populations of animals in parks and wildlife sanctuaries in limited numbers has some genetic consequences, the most important of which is inbreeding depression. However, even in a population that is large enough to escape serious inbreeding, a gradual loss of genetic variability may limit future evolutionary change. In randomly mating populations, such as most mammals and birds, inbreeding considerations alone require that populations should not consist of fewer than 50 individuals, but genetic variability will only be maintained if the population sizes are an order of magnitude higher.

Genetic variability is important because it allows animal populations to adapt to and survive changes in their physical or biotic environment (Franklin 1980). Of all the animal species, mammals and birds are most vulnerable to inbreeding depression. Franklin (1980) suggested that, in the short term, the effective population size should not be less than 50 and, in the long term, the minimum effective population size should be 500. Below this latter value, it is likely that genetic variance for complex traits is lost at a significantly faster rate than it is renewed by mutation. It must be noted that these figures are merely guidelines, because the number can be influenced by the breeding strategy of an individual species.

Demographic uncertainty is usually taken to mean uncertainty resulting from the effects of random events on the survival and reproduction of individuals. As a general guideline, populations of 10 to 50 individuals are often said to be too small because they result in a rapid loss of genetic variability or they are prone to extinction by a single natural catastrophe. Populations of 1,000 to 10,000 individuals are considered to be adequate to ensure long-term persistence. The possibility that individuals can migrate between populations increases the demographic viability of populations, and in small populations active metapopulation management actions become important. Using $N \geq 1,000$ for long-term viability and $N \geq 50Q$ for short-term viability (where N = population size estimate), we assessed the viability of important larger species usually constrained by fences and for which estimates of population size could be obtained.

Genetic Integrity

The contribution to viability can be mitigated by threats to the genetic integrity of species populations arising from two sources: (1) cross-breeding with the same species from different bioclimatic regions and thus with different adaptations; or (2) hybridization with another species, subspecies, or race. These two possibilities are addressed as follows. For each of the species on each game ranch that could be or is usually captured and translocated, the source of the present population was ascertained from the landowner. If the population has always been on the property or the founder population or supplementary population was translocated from the same veld type found in KwaZulu-Natal, it was not considered.

RESULTS

In some cases, there will be minor discrepancies across computations of land area (for example, between the totals in tables 6.2 and 6.5). Some calculations were based on landowner reports and others on GIS queries; discrepancies result from errors in property sizes given by landowners, from inaccuracy in digitizing boundaries, or where the fenced boundary is not the same as the legal boundary (in, for example, protected areas). In addition, the inclusion of the large (approximately 30,000 hectares) game ranch on the western boundary of the study region inflates the "percentage of regional total" values in table 6.1.

Table 6.1 Contribution of Public Areas, Game Ranches, and Tourism Ranches to the Representation of Priority Landscapes in the Study Region

Priority Class	Study Region Total by Class (hectares)	Public Area Contribution		Game Ranch Contribution		Tourism Ranch Contribution (estimated; subset of game ranches)	
		Area (hectares)	Percentage of Regional Total	Area (hectares)	Percentage of Regional Total	Area (hectares)	Percentage of Regional Total
1	151,554	25,096	16.6	3,743	2.5	3,743	2.5
2	356,546	13,556	3.8	26,164	7.3	26,164	7.3
3	910,348	128,927	14.2	99,910	11.0	97,572	10.7
4	1,062,301	241,232	22.7	64,315	6.1	55,855	5.3
5	0	0	0.0	0	0.0	0	0.0
Total	2,480,749	408,811	16.5	194,132	7.8	183,333	7.4

Note: Priority class 1 is the most important and class 5 the least important.

Sources: See the "Methods" section of this chapter.

Representation of Priority Landscapes

The total number of hectares in each priority class by property type is shown in table 6.1. As these data illustrate, the tourism contribution represents the vast majority of the game ranch contribution. Moreover, the tourism contribution significantly complements the public contribution and in one case (class 2) exceeds it. It is also in this class that tourism brings the combined public plus game ranch contribution above the World Conservation Union (IUCN) goal of 10 percent representation across landscape classes. (The sources for data in this and following tables are described in the Methods section.)

Infrastructural Footprint

The footprint results are shown in table 6.2. Percentages are values per property, and average percentages are not weighted by property size. Because larger properties generally have lower densities, overall density (the sum of footprints divided by sum of areas) for the tourism sample is lower than the average across properties reported here.

The results indicate that tourism ranches contain greater infrastructural intensity, with both road and facility average density being more than eight times greater than in public areas. This may result from several factors, including that (1) tourism ranch road density is in part a legacy of cattle farming operations and (2) public areas are larger than tourism ranches. For example, the average public area in the sample contained 17.7 hectares of facilities. Only 2 of the 22 tourism ranches have facilities covering more land in absolute terms—but tourism ranch property sizes are relatively small, so intensity is high. The data also indicate that roads account for the bulk of the footprint in both types of areas. Though not directly comparable, results are generally consistent with studies elsewhere, insofar as the tourism footprint represents only a small proportion of the areas. For example, Cole (1982) noted that less than 2 percent of the land area around two very popular subalpine lakes in the Eagle Cap Wilderness in Oregon (United States) was substantially disturbed by recreation.

Landscape Connectivity

The extent to which game ranches in the study region reduce the overall distance to be traveled between public areas is summarized in table 6.3.

Table 6.2 Summary of Infrastructural Footprint for Tourism and Public Samples

Category	Total Land Area (hectares)	Roads		Facilities		Combined Footprint	
		Area (hectares)	Percentage of Land Area (min/max/average)	Area (hectares)	Percentage of Land Area (min/max/average)	Area (hectares)	Percentage of Land Area (min/max/average)
Tourism ranches	99,188	1,149	0.24	180	0.04	1,329	0.46
			4.05		0.82		4.46
			1.86		**0.34**		**2.20**
Public areas	163,639	388	0.14	53	0.02	441	0.16
			0.32		0.07		0.39
			0.23		**0.04**		**0.27**

Sources: See the "Methods" section of this chapter.

Table 6.3 Reduction in Distance between Large Protected Areas Facilitated by Game Ranches

Public Areas	Distance Between Public Areas (kilometers)	Distance with Game Ranches Included (kilometers)	Percentage Decrease
HUP to Mkhuze	25.7	15.3	40.5
HUP to Ithala	82.0	69.6	15.1
Mkhuze to False Bay	13.5	2.4	82.2
Mkhuze to Ithala	66.3	40.2	39.4
Mkhuze to Pongolapoort	8.24	1.74	78.9
Pongolapoort to Ithala	42.0	15.8	62.4

HUP = Hluhluwe-Umfolozi Park.

Sources: See the "Methods" section of this chapter.

The reduction varies between 15.1 percent (HUP to Ithala) and 82.2 percent (Mkhuze to False Bay Park). Game ranches, therefore, make a significant contribution toward the improvement of connectivity between protected areas; although not all of these ranches exist because of tourism, the sample results described above suggest that tourism is largely responsible for this gain.

The contribution of game ranches is mitigated by the fact that both private and public areas have perimeter fencing (and in some cases also internal fencing), which reduces the connectivity benefit; indeed, game fences are less permeable than cattle fences, such that the transition from cattle to game ranch may reduce the mobility of some species. Because many plants are animal-dispersed, they are also restricted. Nonetheless, animal movements have to some extent improved, especially among birds and mammal species that are not restricted by fences. Such species include some antelopes and predators, such as leopards.

Representation of Vegetation Communities

Table 6.4 shows the results for the whole KZN Province. To varying degrees, game ranches in the province contribute to 19 of the 23 vegetation communities. Two of these vegetation communities (sour sandveld, 14, which is endemic, and coast hinterland thornveld, 17) do not occur in public protected areas.

Predictably, the number of communities and the land area covered by each is lower among the tourism sample in the study region than

Table 6.4 Percentage of Vegetation Communities within KwaZulu-Natal Province That Occur in Public Areas and on Game Ranches

Vegetation Community[a]	Percentage in Public Areas	Percentage on Game Ranches
1. Moist Coast Forest, thorn and palm veld (NE)	12.61	0.05
2. Dry Coast Forest, thorn and palm veld (NE)	0.54	0
3. Moist Coast Hinterland Ngongoni veld (NE)	0.44	0.01
4. Dry Coast Hinterland Ngongoni veld (NE)	0.87	0.04
5. Moist Midlands mistbelt (E)	2.11	0.22
6. Dry Midlands mistbelt (E)	0.83	0
7. Northern mistbelt	11.41	5.12
8. Moist Highland sourveld	3.76	0
9. Dry Highland sourveld	0.17	0.21
10. Montane veld	72.88	0
11. Moist transitional tall grassveld (E)	2.24	0.87
12. Moist tall grassveld (NE)	0.84	2.36
13. Dry tall grassveld (NE)	1.23	1.93
14. Sour sandveld (E)	0	0.47
15. Moist Lowland tall grassveld (E)	5.86	2.55
16. Dry Lowland tall grassveld (E)	2.27	5.05
17. Coast Hinterland thornveld	0	2.38
18. Mixed thornveld	0.73	0.39
19. Moist Zululand thornveld	7.98	0.59
20. Dry Zululand thornveld	12.85	15.99
21. Valley bushveld (E)	0.31	0.68
22. Lowveld	13.33	12.19
23. Sandy bushveld	14.53	7.15

[a]Communities that are endemic or near endemic to the province are denoted (E) and (NE), respectively.

Sources: See the "Methods" section of this chapter.

among all game ranches in the whole province. As is shown in table 6.5, the tourism ranches contribute to eight of the communities. Although lowveld (22) is the best represented, the most important community in the sample is moist tall grassveld (12), which is more than 30 percent transformed and less than 1 percent protected in the province. Also important is sandy bushveld (23).

Contribution to Herbivory

Table 6.6 summarizes the contribution of tourism ranches and public areas to herbivory, broken down by browsers, grazers, and herbivores as a whole. Many of the original herbivore species are present on the tourism ranches, and reestablishment is an ongoing process. Browsers form an

Table 6.5 Representation of Vegetation Communities within the Tourism Sample

Vegetation Community[a]	Area within Properties in Tourism Sample (hectares)
7. Northern mistbelt	128
11. Moist transitional tall grassveld (E)	2,420
12. Moist tall grassveld (NE)	2,114
15. Moist lowland tall grassveld (E)	557
16. Dry lowland tall grassveld (E)	6,122
20. Dry Zululand thornveld	32,795
22. Lowveld	40,968
23. Sandy bushveld	13,360
Total	98,464

[a]Communities that are endemic or near endemic to the province are denoted (E) and (NE), respectively.

Sources: See the "Methods" section of this chapter.

Table 6.6 Contribution to Herbivory (species per property)

Type of Property	Measure	Browsers		Grazers		Total Herbivores	
		Historical	Current	Historical	Current	Historical	Current
Tourism ranches	Min.	5	4	11	7	19	12
	Max.	8	8	17	16	23	23
	Avg.	7.64	5.59	13.00	11.09	20.64	16.68
Public areas	Min.	5	8	13	13	21	22
	Max.	8	9	16	15	22	24
	Avg.	6.67	8.67	14.67	14.00	21.33	22.67

Sources: See the "Methods" section of this chapter.

important part of these introductions. Elephants are the largest of the herbivores and those that have the most dramatic effect on their habitat—they are one of the most important species to have been removed completely from the study region. All three public areas have reestablished populations of elephants (there are 300 in HUP, 54 in Ithala, and 26 in Mkhuze), and four of the tourism ranches have elephants in populations of 8, 42, 65, and 2, respectively. There is thus a considerable contribution in terms of restoring grazer–browser balance and thereby restoring one of the factors controlling woody plant density.

Most of the herbivores that originally occurred in the study area have been returned to most tourism properties, with exceptions including elands, elephants, klipspringers, black rhinos, and white rhinos. Black rhinos, primarily due to their high cost, have not been reestablished, except for one property, which has only one male. White rhinos are also

Table 6.7 Contribution to Predation (large species per property)

Type of Property	Measure	Historical	Current
Tourism ranches	Min.	5	3
	Max.	8	9
	Avg.	**6.27**	**4.55**
Public areas	Min.	6	6
	Max.	9	8
	Avg.	**7.33**	**7.00**

Sources: See the "Methods" section of this chapter.

costly, but not as expensive as black rhinos, and they have been available to game ranches for a longer period. Klipspringers are restricted by having specific habitat needs and, consequently, their reestablishment has not been widespread.

Contribution to Predation

Table 6.7 summarizes the current and historic presence of large predators. As with herbivores, the tourism ranches lag behind public areas with respect to current presence, but the majority of the large predators are represented on tourism properties. Only free-ranging predators are included in these figures; captive animals are excluded. Many landowners do not know the smaller predators and, for this reason, it is not certain whether they occur on properties unless their distribution is so wide that they would be certain to occur. Only HUP has a resident pack of wild dogs, but there is a pack that moves around the Magudu area and is not confined to any particular ranch. Seven landowners, plus Mkhuze Game Reserve, reported seeing the pack, and the species is included in their property tabulation.

Caracals are seen from time to time, although they did not originally occur over much of the study region. Two public areas and two tourism properties have cheetah. Cheetahs were never common in the province, due mainly to their preference for drier, open plains, such that the increasing bush encroachment in the area does not favor them. Crocodiles are found on 11 of the tourism properties, which is five more than their historical distribution.

Brown hyenas have always been rare in the study area, and attempts were made to reestablish them in both HUP and Ithala. However, they never established themselves in HUP, are rare in Ithala, and are only occasionally seen in the Lower Mkhuze area. Spotted hyenas have always been common in the study area but were heavily persecuted in the past. They occur on 19 of the tourism properties. Black-backed jackals have always been relatively common in the region, although their populations have declined due to disease. They occur on all tourism properties, though not in great numbers. Side-striped jackals would have only occurred on the coast in the past and not on any of the properties in the study region. However, they have been seen on one of the properties close to False Bay. Leopards have always been in the region despite being persecuted. They are found on all 22 tourism properties but are an elusive species and seldom seen. Lions previously were common throughout the study region but were completely eradicated in the past. Only one public area and two of the tourism properties now have lions.

Many landowners tolerate predators such as eagles and jackals, and smaller predators such as mongooses are not considered a problem. Leopards are also generally left alone, but some landowners still feel that the larger predators are unwelcome. Nonetheless, game ranching contributes to conservation of predators through reduced persecution, and the larger predators such as lions, cheetahs, and crocodiles have been deliberately reestablished on some game ranches.

Parasitism

Of the game ranches assessed, (1) a small number still had cattle and dipped only the cattle regularly with oxpecker-friendly dips, (2) most did not dip their game, and (3) none treated game for internal parasites. Therefore, the natural animal–parasite relations that occurred in the past are generally being left to continue, though the danger remains that injudicious use of tick dips on out-of-range species may result in dip-resistant ticks.

System Resilience

The availability of water on game ranches is far in excess of what it was historically. In the tourism sample, the minimum distance that an animal needs to travel to water is 426 meters, and the maximum distance is 2 kilometers (2,131 meters). One landowner in particular wants to build additional dams because he feels that two portions of his farm are too dry, yet animals have to walk no further than 750 meters on average to get water. The farm was seriously eroded, with large dongas in some areas, and the grass basal cover and species composition was low.

With respect to supplementary feeding, of the 22 tourism properties, 2 landowners fed their animals every winter and 9 provided supplementary feed only in extreme conditions, although 2 of these provided this feed only for selected species (white rhinos and ostriches).

Stocking rate and carrying capacities were estimated for each property. Of the 22 tourism properties, 11 (50 percent) were evaluated as overstocked, with one property having more than three times as much stock as the natural carrying capacity for the property. One landowner recorded 79 mortalities for 1999 (mostly impalas, warthogs, and nyalas). Thirty-eight of the deaths occurred in a cold, wet spell in late August. This property was heavily stocked, and the mortalities could be an indication of food-related stress.

Product moment correlation coefficients were calculated between measures of (1) degree of supplementary feeding; (2) stocking rate divided by natural carrying capacity (CC); and (3) veld condition, based on a rating of eight variables (bare ground, erosion, grass basal cover, herbaceous species composition, vigor, woody plant encroachment, alien plant invasion, and animal condition); with higher scores indicating better condition. There was a positive correlation between supplementary feeding and stocking rate as a ratio of CC (significant at $p = 0.10$), and negative correlations between veld condition and both stocking rate as a ratio of CC and supplementary feeding (both significant at $p = 0.01$). Though the direction of causality cannot be determined statistically, it is plausible that supplementary feeding leads to overstocking, which leads to reduction in veld condition.

Species Conservation

Tables 6.8 and 6.9 show the presence of important mammal, bird, and reptile species by property. Several of the larger mammals found on the tourism properties were ranked either specially protected or protected in the *Provincial Gazette* of KwaZulu-Natal of October 15, 1998. Species classified as specially protected include black rhinos, oribi, suni, and wild

Table 6.8 Summary of Important Mammal Species by Property

Common Name	Tourism Ranches																						Public Areas		
	1	2	3	4	5	6	9	11	12	15	16	17	18	20	21	22	23	24	25	26	27	29	HUP	Ithala	Mkhuze
Aardvark[a] +	✓	✓	✓	✓	✓	✓	!	✓	✓	7	✓	✓	✓	✓	✓	✓	✓	✓	✓	✓	✓	✓	✓	✓	✓
Aardwolf[b]+	!	✓	✓				!	✓	!	!		✓										✓	✓	✓	✓
African wild cat[a] +																							✓		
Buffalo[c]												14		34	32	23		34					4,530	80	
Bushbuck[c]	6	20	10		20	27		15	10	✓	35	6	✓	150	✓	✓		✓	14	✓	✓	✓	✓	✓	50
Cheetah[c]													✓	2		22			✓				✓		<5
Duiker, Blue[c]													✓						✓				✓		
Duiker, Red[c]	12	30	30		10	✓		✓	✓	✓	30	25	✓	60	✓	✓	✓	✓	20	✓	20	✓	✓	54	200
Elephant[c]												8		42	10	65		2					300		26
Hartebeest, red[c]				3	8		2									7								106	
Hippopotamus											✓	✓		10		5		9					✓		80
Hyena, Brown[c]													✓			✓					✓	✓		✓	
Klipspringer[c]												✓		10		✓		✓	✓		✓	✓	✓	✓	10
Leopard[c]	✓	✓	✓	✓	✓	✓	✓	✓	✓	4	✓	✓	✓	✓	✓	25	✓	✓	✓	3	✓	✓	✓	✓	30
Lion[c]														3		19							65		
Monkey, Samango[b]																							✓		
Oribi[a]																								✓	
Pangolin[a] +	!	!	–	–	–	–	–	–	–	–	–	–	–	–	–	–	–	–	–	–	–	–	!	!	!

(continued)

229

Table 6.8 (Continued)

Common name	Tourism Ranches																						Public Areas		
	1	2	3	4	5	6	9	11	12	15	16	17	18	20	21	22	23	24	25	26	27	29	HUP	Ithala	Mkhuze
Ratel (Honey badger)[a] +	!	✓	✓	✓	✓	!	!	✓	✓	✓	✓	✓	!	✓	!	✓	!	✓	!	✓	✓	✓	✓	✓	✓
Rhino, Black[a]			5	3										1									283	45	80
Rhino, White[c]						1			1		17	1		20	7	50		7					1,542	60	100
Serval cat[c] +		✓		✓	!	!	!			!	✓	5	✓	✓	!	✓	✓	✓		✓	✓	✓	✓	✓	✓
Suni[c]	6			50			✓	✓		✓	✓		✓		✓	✓		✓		✓	✓		✓	✓	✓
Waterbuck[c]		12	30	20		50	12		20		90	10		60	10	25			2	70		12	653	61	50
Wild dog[a] +		✓			✓						✓	✓		✓				✓					7		

HUP = Hluhluwe-Umfolozi Park.

✓ = present but numbers unknown; ! = within range but not seen.

+ = Species not counted as most landowners uncertain whether they occur. Wild dog are not confined to any particular farm; a pack moves around the north of the study area.

Note: Blank cells indicate the absence of the species.

[a]Specially protected.

[b]Unprotected in Kwazulu-Natal.

[c]Protected.

Sources: See the "Methods" section of this chapter.

Table 6.9 Summary of Important Bird and Reptile Species by Property

Birds (common name)	Tourism Ranches																						Public Areas		
	1	2	3	4	5	6	9	11	12	15	16	17	18	20	21	22	23	24	25	26	27	29	HUP	Ithala	Mkhuze
White pelican (49)	✓																	✓					✓		✓
White stork (83)		✓	✓	✓	✓	✓			✓	✓	✓	✓	✓	✓	✓	✓	✓	✓	✓	✓	✓	✓	✓	✓	✓
Woolly necked stork (86)	✓	✓	✓	✓	✓	✓	✓	✓	✓	✓	✓	✓	✓	✓	✓	✓	✓	✓	✓	✓	✓	–	✓	✓	✓
Openbill stork (87)	✓	–	✓	✓	–			✓	✓	✓	✓	✓	✓	–	✓	✓	–	✓	✓	✓	✓	–	✓		✓
Marabou stork (89)	✓	✓	✓	✓	✓	✓		✓	✓	✓	✓	✓	✓	✓	✓	✓	✓	✓	✓	✓	✓	–	✓		✓
Sacred ibis (91)	✓	✓	✓	✓	✓	✓	✓	✓	✓	✓	✓	✓	✓	✓	✓	✓	✓	✓	✓	✓	✓	✓	✓	✓	✓
Pygmy goose (114)	✓	–	✓	✓	✓			✓	✓	✓				–	✓	✓	–	✓	✓	✓	✓		✓		✓
Cape vulture (122)	✓	✓	✓	✓	–	✓	✓	✓	✓	✓	✓	✓	✓	✓	✓	✓	✓	✓	✓	✓	✓	✓	✓	✓	✓
Lappet faced vult. (124)	✓	✓	✓	✓	✓	✓	✓	✓	✓	✓	✓	✓	✓	✓	✓	✓	–	✓	✓	✓	✓	✓	✓	✓	✓
Whiteheaded vult. (125)	✓	✓	✓	✓	✓	✓	✓	✓	✓	✓	✓	✓	✓	✓	✓	✓	✓	✓	✓	✓	✓	✓	✓	✓	✓
Bathawk (129)								✓															✓		✓
Martial eagle (140)	✓	✓	✓	✓	✓	✓	✓	✓	✓	✓	✓	✓	✓	✓	✓	✓	✓	✓	✓	✓	✓	✓	✓	✓	✓
Sthn bnd snake eagle (144)	✓	✓	✓	✓	✓	✓	✓	✓	✓	✓	✓	✓	✓	✓	✓	✓	✓	✓	✓	✓	✓	✓	✓	✓	✓
Bateleur (146)	✓	✓	✓	✓	✓	✓	✓	✓	✓	✓	✓	✓	✓	✓	✓	✓	✓	✓	✓	✓	✓	✓	✓	✓	✓
Palmnut vulture (147)						✓						✓											✓		
Peregrine falcon (171)							✓				✓							✓					✓		
Rock kestrel (181)		✓			✓	✓	✓						✓	✓			✓	✓	✓			✓	✓	✓	
Stanley's bustard (231)		–			–		✓				✓			–			–					✓	✓	✓	
Lsr blkwinged plover (256)				✓																			✓		✓
Redwinged pratincole (304)				✓																			✓		✓
Delagorgues pigeon (351)				✓															✓				✓		✓
Grey lourie (373)	✓	✓	✓			✓	✓	✓	✓	✓	✓	✓	✓	✓						✓			✓	✓	✓

(continued)

Table 6.9 *(Continued)*

Birds (common name)	Tourism Ranches																						Public Areas		
	1	2	3	4	5	6	9	11	12	15	16	17	18	20	21	22	23	24	25	26	27	29	HUP	Ithala	Mkhuze
Black coucal (388)				✓							✓													✓	✓
Pels fishing owl (403)			✓	✓								✓												✓	✓
Lemon brstd canary (871)	✓	✓	✓	✓	✓	✓		✓	✓	✓	✓	✓	✓	✓	✓	✓	✓	✓	✓	✓	✓	✓	✓		✓

Reptiles (common name)	Tourism Ranches																						Public Areas		
	1	2	3	4	5	6	9	11	12	15	16	17	18	20	21	22	23	24	25	26	27	29	HUP	Ithala	Mkhuze
Crocodile				✓		1				✓	✓	✓	✓	9	1	✓	✓	✓	✓	✓	✓	✓	8	13	19
Python	✓	✓	✓	✓	✓	✓	✓	✓	✓	✓	✓	✓	✓	✓	✓	✓	✓	✓	✓	✓	✓	✓	✓	✓	✓

HUP = Hluhluwe-Umfolozi Park.

✓ = present but numbers unknown; ! = no bird list, but within range. Bird presence is based on bird lists obtained from landowners, and where not available, from Harrison and others (1997a, 1997b).

Note: Blank cells indicate the absence of the species.

Sources: See the "Methods" section of this chapter.

dogs, whereas protected species include brown hyenas, cheetahs, leopards, lions, servals, elephants, white rhinos, giraffes, black wildebeests, red hartebeests, tsessebes, blue duikers, klipspringers, hippopotamuses, buffaloes, and waterbucks.

Additional species are seen infrequently, including specially protected species such as aardvarks (antbears), pangolins, and ratels (honey badgers). Various species of specially protected and protected bats, mongooses, and rodents are likely to benefit from the protected habitat afforded to the larger species, but to determine the extent to which they are present would require a dedicated study beyond the scope of this evaluation. In the analysis, only species that were important within the study region and likely to be found within it were considered. Smaller, more elusive species were excluded.

The contribution that game ranches make to the conservation of these species varies from poor in the case of African wild cats, black rhinos, and wild dogs, to good in the case of bushbucks, red duikers, leopards, and waterbucks. It is not surprising that there is a positive relationship between number of species and property size, with a significant (at $p = 0.05$ or better) correlation coefficient between size and numbers of important animal species in each of four groups: the Big Five, birds and reptiles, mammals, and all species.

Demographic and Genetic Uncertainty

As is illustrated in table 6.8, the only viable long-term populations are white rhinos and buffaloes in HUP, a public area. More species are viable in the short term, but larger species such as buffaloes, elephants, hippopotamuses, lions, black and white rhinos, and wild dogs do not occur in viable numbers on private land. Only one of the tourism ranches has a (short-term) viable population of white rhinos and elephants. Numbers for the other species are unknown for many properties, so their viability cannot be assessed.

Genetic Integrity

Table 6.10 lists introductions and source of species for all 27 game ranches (not just the tourism sample). Most animals on game ranches in the study area are purchased from either NCS auctions or the Game Marketing Association, a part of the Natal Game Ranchers' Association.

Table 6.10 Introduction to and Source of Species for Game Ranches during the Past Five Years

Species	Local (within 50 km)	KZN (rest of province)	Northern Province	Mpumalanga (excluding Kruger)	Kruger National Park	Eastern Cape	Namibia	Zimbabwe	Can't Remember or Never Knew	Total
Blesbok	100	94							7	201
Buffalo, African		158								158
Bushbuck		38								38
Caracal		1								1
Cheetah		2					17			19
Eland			20						15	35
Elephant, African					100			2	12	114
Gemsbok									10	10
Giraffe		40	10	6					85	141
Hartebeest, red		30	6						38	74
Hippopotamus		6		17					11	34
Hyena, brown									1	1
Impala	256	1,150							550	1,956
Jackal, black backed		4	2						3	9
Jackal, side striped									8	8

(continued)

Species						Total
Kudu	34	59	13		44	150
Lion		3		12		15
Nyala	29	101	17		13	160
Ostrich	30		16		11	57
Reedbuck, common	31	70			9	110
Reedbuck, mountain	33			20		53
Rhino, black		1				1
Rhino, white		29			7	36
Serval		1				1
Warthog	109	19				128
Waterbuck	29	10	53	21	38	151
Wildebeest, blue	83	374	7		407	871
Zebra, Burchell's	38	330	42	122	163	695

KNZ = Kwazulu-Natal.

Note: Blank cells indicate that none of the indicated species were introduced from those source areas in past five years.

Sources: See the "Methods" section of this chapter.

However, some animals have been purchased from Mpumalanga and the Northern Province. Lions mostly originate from game ranches and Kruger National Park in Mpumalanga Province. Other species purchased from Mpumalanga include giraffes, hippos, waterbucks, and zebras. Species purchased in the Northern Province include kudus, elands, giraffes, ostriches, waterbucks, and blue wildebeests. All of the cheetahs in the study area originate in Namibia, and most of the elephants come from Kruger National Park.

Landowners generally did not consider that species from other provinces could be a threat, but apart from mountain reedbucks (37.7 percent), waterbucks (65.5 percent), and zebras (30.8 percent), the proportion of animals coming from other provinces is small (less than 15 percent). However, it should be stressed that although most game for reestablishments is sourced within the province, there is no record of where the founder populations of those sources originated.

Potential threats to genetic integrity from hybridization of subspecies are blue and black wildebeests, or blesboks and bonteboks, on the same property. Others could be the bushveld group of black rhinos (*Diceros bicornis minor*), which is found naturally in KwaZulu-Natal, the Namibian desert black rhino (*D. b. bicornis*), and the East African black rhino (*D. b. michaeli*) on the same property. Only one of the game ranches had black rhinos, a single male (*D. b. minor*), and the three protected areas have populations of only *D. b. minor*. None of the sample properties had both blue and black wildebeests or both blesboks and bonteboks. These results indicate that within the sample properties, there is no threat to genetic integrity from hybridization.

Response to Future Increase in Demand

To evaluate the likely ecological effects of a future increase in demand, landowners were asked how they would respond to a 100 percent increase (doubling) in the number of visitors to the area. The quality of responses varied, with some landowners having very clear ideas, on the basis of existing plans, of how they would respond, and others having less clear ideas. Nonetheless, the following provides at least a general indication of how existing landowners would respond, though one would expect some new entrants into the sector as well.

Because of the current low occupancy rates, many landowners would simply increase occupancy, and thus revenue, without building additional facilities. However, several landowners would build additional facilities, and 2 (9 percent) landowners would expand the road network. Eight (36 percent) landowners would purchase more land, with the intended acquisitions averaging 2,671 hectares for the 7 landowners who had particular properties in mind; these properties currently are predominantly in cattle use, such that land purchase would represent conservation gains. Seventeen (77 percent) would introduce additional game (increase stocking), with buffaloes being the species to increase in greatest number.

SUMMARY AND CONCLUSIONS

Relative to a base of pristine nature, tourism clearly has a negative impact on both the biotic and abiotic environment. Moreover, the concerns expressed by critics (such as Isaacs 2000) should be heeded: Tourism should not be the sole basis for conservation. Nonetheless, the example of private game reserves in KwaZulu-Natal illustrates the important contribution that tourism can make to conservation by providing incentives to private landholders to maintain their properties in a largely natural state.

Game ranching, or any other form of wildlife utilization on private land, has the potential to contribute significantly to conservation at all levels of the biodiversity hierarchy, with this contribution depending on the geographical position of the land, the position of the property in relation to that of public areas, the size of the property, the management philosophy, and the quality of management. At the landscape level, the study region covers 2,496,000 hectares, of which public areas cover 415,000 (16.6 percent) and game ranches 167,396 (6.7 percent). On the basis of sample results, tourism ranches account for the vast majority (94 percent) of the game ranch contribution. This contribution is particularly great in landscape priority classes 2 and 3 (see table 6.1), with the tourism ranch contribution in the former class representing almost twice as much as the public area contribution to the class.

To some degree, this contribution is reduced by roads and facilities. However, the current footprint is modest, with most of the properties being less than 2 percent transformed. Responses to the "100 percent increase in demand" scenario indicate that future growth would not dramatically change footprint density. Most landowners have self-imposed limits on tourist numbers, based on a personal perception of the carrying capacity of their ranches, with capacity being based on their ability to provide personal service and a sense of exclusivity or privacy.

Though some new facilities were built in the transition from cattle to game ranching, many landowners noted that this transition led to the demolition and removal of old houses and staff quarters, cattle handling facilities, dips, water reservoirs, irrigation pipes, power lines, windmills, and related facilities. In addition, large quantities of scrap metal were removed, which before conversion to game ranching had been allowed to accumulate on the farms.

Tourism ranches also reduce distances between public areas, and thus they contribute to landscape connectivity. However, this benefit is limited by game-proof fences, which inhibit landscape-scale, large herbivore movement. The establishment of game ranches has done little to reinstate historical fire regimes in terms of the timing, scale, and pattern of burning. Most landowners stated that they adhered to the burning guidelines as laid down by the Department of Agriculture, which were designed for maximum agricultural productivity rather than the maintenance of biodiversity, and which tend to favor productive fire-climax grasses like *Themeda triandra*.

Similarly, artificial water point density and distribution on sampled game ranches are a legacy of cattle ranching and do not relate to historical distribution. The current pattern of surface water development leads to a loss of system resilience and an increased risk of population collapse and biodiversity loss during times of stress, such as drought.

At the vegetation community level, game ranches contributed to the representation of 19 vegetation communities out of 23 in KZN Province; the tourism sample, which contains fewer properties and is more localized, contributes to 8 vegetation communities. Two of these 19 vegetation communities do not occur within public protected areas, and thus their protection on game ranches is extremely significant.

With respect to ecosystem and community level processes, the most notable change caused by game ranching is the reestablishment of many of the original large herbivore species. The most significant of these are the megaherbivores, such as elephants and black rhinos, which can have a disproportionately large impact on the environment. Large predators such as lions, leopards, and cheetahs have also been reestablished. Many important species, such as aardvarks, aardwolves, African wild cats, blue duikers, klipspringers, leopards, pangolins, ratels, and servals, are very seldom seen and are therefore difficult, if not impossible, to count. However, the high-quality habitat that is required for the successful reestablishment of the larger, charismatic species will benefit these and a host of other species. The larger species are umbrella species, which can serve as a conservation proxy for protecting other species.

Despite the gain from the reestablishment of species, from a demographic and genetic perspective, larger herbivore species such as black and white rhinos, elephants, and buffaloes, as well as large predators such as lions, cheetahs, and wild dogs, generally do not occur in viable numbers on the tourism sample properties. However, if collaborative partnerships were developed between groups of landowners, and between landowners and the NCS, viable populations might be possible. In addition to potential substantial gains from dropping fences, populations of all larger species across both private and public areas could be maintained as one large metapopulation, with the occasional exchange of individuals between them (artificial migration). At the moment, however, metapopulation management is only occurring in the public areas with selected rare species, such as black and white rhinos, and not within game ranches.

In short, tourism makes a substantial contribution to conservation in the study region through the incentives it provides to establish game ranches. However, as with the other mechanisms described in the overview above, this contribution is potentially fickle and also falls short of its potential. It is fickle insofar as it depends on exogenous factors that are largely beyond the control of conservation managers, including beef prices and demand for "safari tourism" experiences generally and in South Africa in particular.

It is encouraging that many of the landowners participate in the industry "out of a love for it" and are not driven purely by financial motives. Nonetheless, financial viability is important, and conservation managers and others can support policies and activities that contribute to it. For example, tax or other incentives might be provided, especially when landowners contribute to identified conservation goals, including protection of specified priority vegetation communities or species. Likewise, diversification of game ranch revenue could be facilitated through provision of relevant information and endorsement of sustainable harvesting of indigenous medicinal plants, grass and reeds for basket and mat weaving, and wood for carvings.

Perhaps the single most important step for enhancing the current contribution would be the removal of fences, with the resulting management of game and tourism at a landscape scale rather than on the scale of the individual property. The barriers to such a step can be substantial, but current efforts are promising, including the Greater Saint Lucia Maputaland Biosphere Reserve initiative, the Space for Elephants initiative, and other initiatives among various landowners to create unbroken corridors of private land between the major protected areas. Such efforts would benefit from the evaluation and dissemination of feasible partnership models.

Removal of fences would not only enhance connectivity, with associated benefits for demographic and genetic viability, but also facilitate more natural fire regimes and other objectives. In public protected areas, process-based management principles are applied to the fire regime, and almost all fires are point source burns, which burn until they reach a natural barrier. Such a regime is more feasible at the landscape level than at the property level, especially for smaller properties.

Other information dissemination efforts would contribute in more specific ways, including in the evolution to more natural fire regimes and in the removal of artificial water points. Landowners were receptive to new ideas, and many landowners reacted positively to the idea of a training course or "game farmers' day," possibly modeled on the Department of Agriculture's "farmers' days," which were generally well attended.

REFERENCES

Alderman, C. 1994. "The Economics and the Role of Privately Owned Lands Used for Nature Tourism, Education, and Conservation." In M. Munasinghe and J. McNeely, eds., *Protected Area Economics and Policy: Linking Conservation and Sustainable Development*. Washington, D.C.: World Conservation Union–IUCN and World Bank.

Alexander, S. E. 2000. "Resident Attitudes towards Conservation and Black Howler Monkeys in Belize: The Community Baboon Sanctuary." *Environmental Conservation* 27(4):341–50.

Anonymous. 2001. "Private Nature Reserves: Freelance Conservationists." *The Economist*, Aug. 25, 62–63.

Aylward, B., K. Allen, J. Echeverria, and J. Tosi. 1996. "Sustainable Ecotourism in Costa Rica: The Monteverde Cloud Forest Reserve." *Biodiversity and Conservation* 5:315–43.

Bookbinder, M. P., E. Dinersteinh, A. Rijal, H. Cauley, and A. Rajouria. 1998. "Ecotourism's Support of Biodiversity Conservation." *Conservation Biology* 12(6):1399–1404.

Boza, M. A. 1993. "Conservation in Action: Past, Present, and Future of the National Park System of Costa Rica." *Conservation Biology* 7(2):239–47.

Budowski, G. 1976. "Tourism and Environmental Conservation: Conflict, Coexistence, or Symbiosis?" *Environmental Conservation* 3(1):27–31.

Buerger, R., J. Hill, J. Herstine, and J. Taggart. 2000. "The Impact of Recreation on Barrier Islands: A Case Study on Masonboro Island." *Coastal Management* 28(3):249–59.

Butler, R. W. 1991. "Tourism, Environment, and Sustainable Development." *Environmental Conservation* 18(3):201–9.

Camp, K. 1999. "The Bioresource Groups of KwaZulu-Natal." Cedara Report N/A/99/6 and N/A/99/11-13. Natural Resource Section, Cedara, KwaZulu-Natal Department of Agriculture.

Cilimburg, A., C. Moonz, and S. Kehoe. 2000. "Wildland Recreation and Human Waste: A Review of Problems, Practices, and Concerns." *Environmental Management* 25(6):587–98.

Cole, D. N. 1982. "Controlling the Spread of Campsites at Popular Wilderness Destinations." *Journal of Soil and Water Conservation* 37:291–95.

Czech, B., and P. R. Krausman. 1997. "Distribution and Causation of Species Endangerment in the United States." *Science* 277:1116–17.

Dabrowski, P. 1994. "Tourism for Conservation, Conservation for Tourism." *Unasylva* 45:42–44.

De-la-Torre, S., C. T. Snowdon, and M. Bejarano. 2000. "Effects of Human Activities on Wild Pygmy Marmosets in Ecuadorian Amazonia." *Biological Conservation* 94(2):153–63.

Duchesne, M., S. D. Cote, and C. Barrette. 2000. "Response of Woodland Caribou to Winter Ecotourism in the Charlevoix Biosphere Reserve." Canada. *Biological Conservation* 96(3):311–17.

Durbin, J. C., and S-N. Ratrimoarisaona. 1996. "Can Tourism Make a Major Contribution to the Conservation of Protected Areas in Madagascar?" *Biodiversity and Conservation* 5:345–53.

Fairbanks, D. H. K., and G. A. Benn. 2000. "Identifying Regional Landscapes for Conservation Planning: A Case Study from KwaZulu-Natal, South Africa." *Landscape and Urban Planning* 50:237–57.

Fortin, M.-J., and C. Gagnon. 1999. "An Assessment of Social Impacts of National Parks on Communities in Quebec, Canada." *Environmental Conservation* 26(3): 200–11.

Franklin, I. R. 1980. Evolutionary Change in Small Populations. In M. E. Soule and B. A. Wilcox, eds., *Conservation Biology: An Evolutionary-Ecological Perspective.* Sunderland, Mass.: Sinauer Associates.

Goodwin, H. J. 1996. In Pursuit of Ecotourism." *Biodiversity and Conservation* 5:277–92.

Goodwin, H., I. J. Kent, K. T. Parker, and M. J. Walpole. 1998. *Tourism, Conservation, and Sustainable Development.* London: International Institute for Environment and Development.

Goodwin, H., and I. R. Swingland. 1996. "Ecotourism, Diversity and Local Development." *Biodiversity and Conservation* 5:275–76.

Gössling, S. 1999. "Ecotourism: A Means to Safeguard Biodiversity and Ecosystem Functions?" *Ecological Economics* 29:303–20.

Hammitt, W. E., and D. N. Cole. 1998. *Wildland Recreation: Ecology and Management,* 2d ed. New York: Wiley.

Harrison, J. A., D. G. Allan, L. G. Underhill, M. Herremans, A. J. Tree, V. Parker, and C. J. Brown, eds. 1997a. *The Atlas of Southern African Birds. Volume 1: Non-Passerines.* Johannesburg: Birdlife South Africa.

———. 1997b. *The Atlas of Southern African Birds. Volume 2: Passerines.* Johannesburg: Birdlife South Africa.

Hawkins, J. P., C. M. Roberts, T. Van't Hof, K. De Meyer, J. Tratalos, and C. Aldam. 1999. "Effects of Recreational Scuba Diving on Caribbean Coral and Fish Communities." *Conservation Biology* 13(4):888–97.

Hoogesteijn, R., and C. A. Chapman. 1997. "Large Ranches as Conservation Tools in the Venezuelan Ilanos." *Oryx* 31(4):274–84.

Isaacs, J. C. 2000. "The Limited Potential of Ecotourism to Contribute to Wildlife Conservation." *Wildlife Society Bulletin* 28(1):61–69.

Jacobsen, S. K., and R. Robles. 1992. "Ecotourism, Sustainable Development, and Conservation Education: Development of a Tour Guide Training Program in Tortuguero, Costa Rica." *Environmental Management* 16(6):701–13.

James, A., M. Green, and J. Paine. 1999. *A Global Review of Protected Area Budgets and Staffing.* WCMC Biodviersity Series 10. Cambridge, England: World Conservation Monitoring Centre.

Kutiel, P., E. Eden, and Y. Zhevelev. 2000. "Effect of Experimental Trampling and Off-road Motorcycle Traffic on Soil and Vegetation of Stabilized Coastal Dunes, Israel." *Environmental Conservation* 27(1):14–23.

Langholz, J. A. 1996. "Economics, Objectives and Success of Private Nature Reserves in Sub-Saharan Africa and Latin America." *Conservation Biology* 10(1):271–80.

———. 1999. "Exploring the Effects of Alternative Income Opportunities on Rainforest Use: Insights from Guatemala's Maya Biosphere Reserve." *Society and Natural Resources* 12:139–49.

Langholz, J. A., J. P. Lassoie, D. Lee, and D. Chapman. 2000. "Economic Considerations of Privately Owned Parks." *Ecological Economics* 33:173–83.

Lewis, D. M., and P. Alpert. 1997. "Trophy Hunting and Wildlife Conservation in Zambia." *Conservation Biology* 11(1):59–68.

Liddle, M. 1997. *Recreation Ecology: The Ecological Impact of Outdoor Recreation and Ecotourism.* London: Chapman & Hall.

Lindberg, K. 1998. *Economic Aspects of Ecotourism.* In K. Lindberg, M. Epler Wood, and D. Engeldrum, eds., *Ecotourism: A Guide for Planners and Managers*, vol. 2. North Bennington, Vt.: Ecotourism Society.

Lindberg, K., J. Enriquez, and K. Sproule. 1996. "Ecotourism Questioned: Case Studies from Belize." *Annals of Tourism Research* 23(3):543–62.

Makhdoum, M. F., and N. Khorasani. 1988. "Differences between Environmental Impacts of Logging and Recreation in Mature Forest Ecosystems." *Environmental Conservation* 15:137–42.

Medio, D., R. F. G. Ormond, and M. Pearson. 1997. "Effect of Briefings on Rates of Damage to Corals by Scuba Divers." *Biological Conservation* 79:91–95.

Meffe, G. K., and C. R. Carroll, eds. 1994. *Principles of Conservation Biology.* Sunderland, Mass.: Sinauer Associates.

Mendelsohn, R. 1997. "The Role of Ecotourism in Sustainable Development." In G. K. Meffe, and C. R. Carroll, eds., *Principles of Conservation Biology.* Sunderland, Mass.: Sinauer Associates.

Miller, J. R., and N. T. Hobbs. 2000. "Recreational Trails, Human Activity, and Nest Predation in Lowland Riparian Areas." *Landscape and Urban Planning* 50(4):227–36.

Price Waterhouse. 1994. *The Lowveld Conservancies: New Opportunities for Productive and Sustainable Land-Use.* Report to the Save Valley, Bubiana, and Chiredzi River Conservancies. Harare.

Richardson, J. A. 1998. "Wildlife Utilization and Biodiversity Conservation in Namibia: Conflicting or Complementary Objectives?" *Biodiversity and Conservation* 7:549–59.

Steidl, R. J., and R. G. Anthony. 2000. "Experimental Effects of Human Activity on Breeding Bald Eagles." *Ecological Applications* 10(1):258–68.

Thurston, E., and R. J. Reader. 2001. "Impacts of Experimentally Applied Mountain Biking and Hiking on Vegetation and Soil of a Deciduous Forest." *Environmental Management* 27(3):397–409.

U.S. Department of the Interior and U.S. Department of Agriculture. 2001. *Recreation Fee Demonstration Program: Progress Report to Congress Fiscal Year 2000.* Washington, D.C.

Vaughan, D. 2000. "Tourism and Biodiversity: A Convergence of Interests?" *International Affairs* 76(2):283–97.

Walker B. H., R. H. Emslie, R. N. Owen-Smith, and R. J. Scholes. 1987. "To Cull or Not to Cull: Lessons from a Southern African Drought." *Journal of Applied Ecology* 24:381–401.

Walpole, M. J., H. J. Goodwin, and K. G. R. Ward. 2001. "Pricing Policy for Tourism in Protected Areas: Lessons from Komodo National Park, Indonesia." *Conservation Biology* 15(1):218–27.

Watkins, C. W., A. M. Barrett, R. Smith, and J. R. Paine. 1996. "Private Protected Areas: A Preliminary Study of Private Initiatives to Conserve Biodiversity in Selected African Countries." World Conservation Monitoring Centre, Cambridge, U.K.

Wilkie, D. S., and J. F. Carpenter. 1999. "Can Nature Tourism Help Finance Protected Areas in the Congo Basin?" *Oryx* 33(4):332–38.

Wilkie, D. S., J. F. Carpenter, and Q. F. Zhang. 2001. "The Under-Financing of Protected Areas in the Congo Basin: So Many Parks and So Little Willingness-to-Pay." *Biodiversity and Conservation* 10(5):691–709.

Young, E. H. 1999. "Balancing Conservation with Development in Small-Scale Fisheries: Is Ecotourism an Empty Promise? *Human Ecology* 27(4):581–620.

Yu, D. W., T. Hendrickson, and A. Castillo. 1997. "Ecotourism and Conservation in Amazonian Peru: Short-Term and Long-Term Challenges." *Environmental Conservation* 24(2):130–38.

CHAPTER 7

MARKETS DERIVED FROM NATURE TOURISM IN SOUTH AFRICA AND KWAZULU-NATAL

A Survey of the Sale of Live Game

Lisa Scriven and Theuns Eloff

In the African context, land-based nature tourism relies heavily on game viewing involving large mammal species. In the 1990s, demand for an African game viewing experience grew rapidly. This trend came into conflict with another, more pervasive, set of long-term trends in African countries. The expansion of livestock and agricultural activities combined with poor management of protected areas and the growth in poaching of trophy animals had led to a long-term decline in populations of many game species of value in nature tourism. As protected areas sought to capitalize on the tourist boom and as the private sector more and more converted land from livestock uses to game ranching and game viewing, the demand for live game for the purposes of stocking properties rose significantly. In South Africa, state-run protected areas—particularly

The authors would like to extend their thanks to all of the individuals and organizations that so graciously provided their assistance in the completion of this document. Their contributions in providing game sales data and communicating their personal experience in the game industry are very much appreciated. They include KwaZulu-Natal Wildlife, Pieter Mulder, Professional Hunters Association of South Africa, South African Game Ranchers Association, Stock Owners Cooperative, Vleissentraal Auctioneers, and various game capture companies and private ranch owners (who cannot be named for reasons of business confidentiality).

those in northeastern KwaZulu-Natal Province (NE KZN)—with a long history of successful species and population management seized the opportunity to service this market by selling "surplus" game.

This chapter provides a summary and comparative analysis of developments in live game markets in South Africa and KwaZulu-Natal. The objectives of the chapter are to:

- Assess the economic contribution of the trade in live game to the private game ranches and public conservation agencies in South Africa and, specifically, the province of KZN

- Analyze the game sales market in South Africa and, specifically, in KZN (that is, quantities, species, and prices) and trends therein

- Relate the market conditions and trends in KZN to that of game sales in South Africa more generally, and

- Assess what policy and other influences have affected trends in these markets over time and report on factors expected to influence future market conditions.

Market data and interviews with market participants provide an adequate if not complete set of observations for responding to these questions. In the 1990s the market expanded rapidly at both the national and provincial levels. Revenue from live game sales is now an important component of receipts for protected area systems fortunate enough to be well endowed with game—and particularly so for KZN Wildlife, which has a comparative advantage in high-value species such as rhinoceroses and elephants. Market and institutional barriers still limit the extent and efficiency of the market, however, and it remains unclear what level of demand the market will ultimately support, given that new entrants into the game "industry" often drive demand.

The chapter begins by summarizing the history of live game sales in South Africa and then moves on to explore the current status of game sales in the country as a whole and in KZN. Trends in the market during the past decade, in quantities, prices, and revenues, are then presented and discussed, again comparing and contrasting national and provincial experience. Finally, a discussion of the factors influencing the market for live game is provided.

HISTORY OF THE GAME INDUSTRY IN SOUTH AFRICA

Financing conservation is of increasing concern for those with an interest in ensuring that a sustainable level of global biodiversity is maintained. Conservation land uses are in continual competition with other economic uses of the same land. At the same time, state conservation budgets are under constant pressure, with funds being reallocated to departments of higher political priority. This is the case particularly in the developing world, where matters such as poverty, job creation, and health have a much greater sense of urgency.

Not only are state conservation budgets being restricted more and more, but conservation is also being put under pressure to actually make money. "Sustainable use" is the strategy for the twenty-first century, and society now demands that nature pay its way—at least to a certain extent. Protected areas, traditionally seen as the only way to conserve, are now perceived as just one piece of the puzzle. The others must be made up of innovative mechanisms to utilize—and still conserve—natural resources.

South Africa's new sociopolitical dispensation has not escaped these global trends and pressures. Intense competition for government funds is prevalent, leading to dwindling budgetary allocations for nature conservation and environment portfolios. It has been suggested that, until recently, a lack of understanding of the strategic, economic, and social value of South Africa's natural treasures may have contributed to a lack of effort to avoid such cutbacks without sourcing and securing alternate conservation financing mechanisms. As such, conservation priorities have faced serious threats due to a lack of finance options.

More recently, however, a shift in these trends has been evolving, resulting in more emphasis on finding options for sustainable resource use. South Africa's biodiversity is, after all, among the richest in world; although it is appreciated for its intrinsic value, it is evident that, when appropriate, ways can be found for it to provide tangible economic benefits to the country as well.

South Africa's game industry has acknowledged the economic value of some of the country's most valuable natural resources. In fact, wildlife has been recognized as having economic value since the 1960s, when hunters began to pay to stalk game. Trophy hunting businesses evolved out of this demand and make up but one part of the ever-expanding and diversifying game industry in the country today. A central tenet of both this industry and the wildlife management strategies of some conservation agencies in the country is the exchange of game. Game sales will thus be examined to determine the extent of their contribution to both the South African economy and conservation-related activities.

Motivation for Trading Game

Today, trading in game facilitates the realization of practical game ranching and conservation objectives, enabling both public and private reserve managers to deal with surplus game while simultaneously providing a method for generating income to offset management costs of the reserves.[1] For example, *boma* auctions and catalogue auctions held by KZN Wildlife (the nature conservation body in KZN) in 2001 have generated enough revenue for the organization to offset management costs by as much as 15 percent (KZN Wildlife website, http://www. kznwildlife.com/auction2001.htm).

Many conservation objectives can be met by trading in game. Trading facilitates the reintroduction of species into areas from which they may have been removed, it provides options for genetic diversification within species, and it offers opportunities to strengthen population sizes (for example, to achieve balanced predator–prey ratios). Trading has been practiced with such success, in fact, that South Africa is one of the few countries in the world where the numbers of rare and endangered species are increasing. This is due, in part, to the value and commercial utilization of these renewable resources (Peter Mulder, personal communication, 2000).

One such case had been demonstrated convincingly by the efforts of the (then) Natal Parks Board (now part of KZN Wildlife) to save the in situ white rhino population, which had dwindled to a mere 25 animals in the early 1900s. After decades of protection and management, the numbers had risen to about 650 in the 1960s ('t Sas-Rolfes 1996, 1), when the idea of Operation Rhino emerged as a means to translocate and reintroduce these animals to both public and private reserves. Initially, the Parks Board sold the animals at highly subsidized, set purchase prices. Although this achieved the objective of starting the process of restocking South Africa's land with white rhinos, auctioning eventually took over as the preferred method of trade. Allowing the sale of rhinos in a manner that more accurately reflected their value on the market led to the realization of the potential benefits of selling live game. Due, in large part, to such efforts, the white rhino population is now more than 7,000 ('t Sas-Rolfes 2000).

Game Sales and Related Industries

Various industries in South Africa support the sale of game including trophy hunting, biltong hunting, venison sales, and tourism. Some of these complement one another to a certain degree, allowing game ranchers to engage in more than one activity simultaneously and offering opportunities for diverse sources of income generation.

Although this chapter examines the sale of live game from public and private areas, the role of such sales needs to be placed in the larger context. Public areas typically sell only surplus game to subsidize conservation goals; their primary objectives are to serve conservation objectives and to provide game viewing opportunities to visitors. Private game reserves, however, may tend to be driven more by market principles.

These private players derive economic benefits from the activities available in the industry while ultimately still benefiting conservation on a larger scale. It should not, however, be understood that the sale of live game necessarily constitutes the largest financial draw to the game industry. For example, tables 7.1 and 7.2, respectively, estimate the amount of money a game farmer would receive for various species sold at auction as opposed to selling them through hunting activities.[2]

Table 7.1 Approximate Price, Commission, Costs, and Net Income from the Sale of Live Game

Species	Auction Price (rand)	Minus Commissions	Minus Capture Costs (rand)	Equals Farmer's Net Income (rand)
Giraffe	12,000		5,000	6,500
Blue wildebeest	2,300	5–7% to auctioneer	400–600	1,600–1,800
Impala	550		200	300

Source: Natal Game Ranchers Association.

Table 7.2 Approximate Income from Consumptive Use (Hunting) of Game

Species	Local or Biltong Hunter (rand)	Foreign or Trophy Hunter (rand)	Income Relative to Farmer's Net Income from Table 7.1
Giraffe	8,000	30,000 (US$2,300)	Consumptive use income is higher
Blue wildebeest	2,200	10,000 (US$750)	Consumptive use income is higher
Impala	550	4,000 (US$350)	Consumptive use income is higher

Source: Natal Game Ranchers Association.

In general, the same game sold to a biltong hunter or a trophy hunter (obviously dependent on the quality of the individuals of each species) would yield more income than that obtained from the sale of live animals. In addition, consumptive uses of game enable the game farmer to receive not just the hunting fee but also income from accommodations paid for by the hunter. According to the Natal Game Ranchers Association (NGRA), local hunters' lodging expenditures are reputed to account for as much as 50 percent of some game farmers' yearly income. Foreign hunters pay up to about $400 a night for lodging; plus the game ranchers keep the meat, providing them with yet another source of income.

A general estimate of the total income generated by game industry activities (not including game sales) in South Africa in 2000 would include:

- Trophy hunting (overseas hunters)—between R153 and R175 million. This includes revenue generated by both private-sector and government hunting activities

- Biltong hunting (local hunters)—R450 million

- Venison sales—R20 million

- Tourism—R40 million (this estimate refers only to the money actually spent on the game reserves).

The above game industry activities (excluding game sales) alone generated more than R660 million for the South African economy. Although this summary excludes the contribution of the sale of game itself, it provides an indication of the market size of the different potential participants in the game sales market, as well as the potential and actual network of activities that have contributed to the development of the industry in general.

Selling live game, by comparison, may be less attractive financially; it does, however, provide an extremely viable and potentially lucrative option for managing excess game. For example, if a private reserve's impala numbers are too high, they can either be hunted or relocated. A combination of the two may be required by farmers to achieve their desired total game numbers when a game rancher is unable to hunt as many individuals of a species as required to maintain an optimal (optimal for the game rancher, not necessarily the ecological optimum) carrying capacity. This is due in part to the limited hunting seasons and the practical limitations of hunting. In these cases, game sales—along with game ranchers who opt for no hunting on their land—can provide a significant source of income.

Participation in the Game Industry

The area of land under a specified use can be used as an indicator of participation in this industry. For this study, "exempted game farms" will provide the required relevant information. These farms are registered as a land use under each provincial conservation authority and can be measured with a certain degree of accuracy. They refer to areas that are fenced for game and exempt from laws pertaining to the hunting and capture of animals; permit requirements are, thus, relaxed on these matters. (Note: Although game ranch owners do have this exempt status regarding the use of game once it is on their land, additional permit requirements apply to other activities, such as the transport of these animals outside these areas.) In terms of exempted game farms, the game industry in South Africa increased by an average rate of 5.6 percent a year between 1993 and 2000 (table 7.3), and investments in these privately owned game ranches are estimated to be in excess of R15.5 billion.

Additional areas are under similar land uses, but it is difficult to obtain data on them because not all these areas are registered in the same official manner as exempted game farms. Furthermore, other farms or ranches may not be as active in the game industry and are not, as such,

Table 7.3 Exempted Game Farms in South Africa

Characteristic	1993	2000
Number of farms	3,357	5,061
Total area occupied (hectares)	7,039,992	10,364,154
Percentage of agricultural land under farm use	8.49	12.5

Source: T. Eloff, Center for Wildlife Economics, University of Potchefstroom, South Africa.

critical to this discussion. Having said that, estimates including these additional areas amount to between 8,000 and 9,000 game farms in South Africa (Falkena 2000, i; Peter Mulder, personal communication, 2000). These estimates reflect private game reserves in addition to the approximately 444 conservation areas under state management.

As table 7.3 shows, many groups and individuals have become involved in the game industry during the past decade. Their motivations for doing this are difficult to isolate but are likely due to a number of factors. For example, the nearly 4 percent shift in the use of agricultural land may be explained, in part, by various obstacles and disincentives that have surfaced in agriculture. Traditional agricultural activities have been faced with challenges including recent regulatory changes, increasingly volatile climate conditions resulting in drier, less fertile soil conditions, and theft of livestock (cattle and sheep).

Another motivation may be the perceived relative profitability of the game industry. The previous section outlined how game ranching offers opportunities to participate in various game-related industries. In addition to the diversification of income-generating potential, the lure of foreign exchange from tourism-related activities is proving to be quite significant.

Even if motivations are not profit driven, many people have become involved in the game industry for more philanthropic reasons. They may simply have a love of nature, they may want to secure a place for escaping the stress of larger cities, or they may even be interested in engaging in the establishment of environmental educational facilities. This is supported by the findings from NE KZN as presented in chapters 6 and 8. Whatever the reason, it is clear that there has been an influx of participants in this industry, and this goes some way toward explaining the higher profile and level of activity in game sales, as will now be discussed.

CURRENT STATUS OF THE SOUTH AFRICAN GAME INDUSTRY

Methods for Trading Game

There are three primary methods for trading live game in South Africa. The two that account for the largest portion of game sales activity are sales made at game auctions (this includes both live and catalogue auctions) and sales made independently of an auction environment by game capture companies. A third option involves private buyers and sellers negotiating and completing a deal themselves, but this takes place on a much smaller scale.

Game Auctions

Game auctions are conducted in two different ways. One is by live sale at what is known as a live, or *boma* auction (named for the type of animal holding pen used), at which animals are exhibited to potential buyers. The second is by catalogue auctions, when animals are bid on and purchased without being seen.

Live auctions tend to have the "best" animals (they are of high quality and tend to be scarcer, more highly-sought-after species), with buyers having the added advantage of being able to see what they are getting before they bid on and purchase them. In catalogue auctions, by contrast, buyers are not able to select the exact animal they want. They can, for example, request a certain age and sex ratio of a herd of bushbuck, but this will not necessarily be exactly what is delivered due to the random nature of capturing herds of antelope.

Another advantage of live auctions is that because the animals are held in *bomas* for a period of time, they tend to be calmer than those just captured. As a result, they will have a better chance of surviving transport because they will tend to be less agitated when in confined spaces. This is particularly the case with certain kinds of antelopes, which tend to excite easily.

Catalogue auctions may, however, be preferable for buyers seeking to purchase animals that are difficult to capture and relocate (such as giraffes), because of the reduced transport requirements and lower chances of mortality en route to their game farms (see Ebedes 1994 for a comprehensive discussion of the advantages and disadvantages of auction types).

The auctions themselves are usually conducted and advertised by an auctioneering company, with catalogue and live auctions often taking place in succession at the same venue. The auctioneering company generally bases its commission on the auction turnover, with additional charges being paid by game farmers to the game capture companies to transport the animals.

Although state organizations generally have their own in-house capture unit (for example, KZN Wildlife Game Capture Unit), private game capture companies provide their services to most private game ranchers for transporting game to and from auctions. Game capture companies buy the game from the ranchers and transport them to holding pens, from where they will be sold in the live *boma* auctions. The companies may then offer to provide their services to the purchaser of the game for relocation to the destination game ranch. After a few auction-related deductions, the game capture company collects the balance of the selling price at auction. In this capacity, game capture companies fulfill the vital role of intermediary between the game ranchers and the buyers at auctions.

Species prices tend to vary between *boma* and catalogue auctions. Depending on the species being purchased, prices tend to be higher at the live auctions. There are exceptions to this, making it difficult to establish a general trend. For example, the auctions in KZN in 2001 fetched a higher average price for nyalas and waterbucks (by approximately 10 percent and 8 percent, respectively) at live auctions, whereas average prices for giraffes and zebras were slightly higher (about 5 percent and 22 percent, respectively) for catalogue auctions in the same year.

Game Capture Company Sales

Game capture companies also have opportunities to trade game outside of auctions. The companies facilitate the trading of game by matching up buyers and sellers. For example, a game farmer may have a hunting package booked by a foreign client who is interested in hunting kudus. If the farmer does not have any suitable individuals on his property, he could contact a game capture company, which would perhaps know where to obtain such an animal. Alternatively, the game capture company may contact various game ranches to see if they are interested in selling.

The game capture company would then facilitate the trade, providing capture and transport services.

Selling live game in this manner accounts for a large proportion of South Africa's game industry. In fact, one of the main game capture companies in KZN reported that its out-of-auction, or direct, sales make up about 90 percent of its business, with the remaining 10 percent made up of auction activity. In 2001, this company claims to have sold approximately 100,000 individual animals in direct sales. An exact figure for this type of activity on a broader level is difficult to determine, primarily due to the private nature of these businesses and the fact that they are under no obligation to disclose confidential financial information.

An estimate of the activity level of this business may, however, be made on the basis of a recent survey conducted by one of the authors (Eloff). The results of this survey suggested that, depending on the size of the operation, sales made by game capture companies outside auctions likely amount to approximately double the annual auction turnover. This is a rough estimate and is intended only to provide a guide as to the extent of sales taking place in this manner on a larger scale. This estimate is supported by the Stockowners Cooperative in KZN, which, among other services, assists game ranchers in sourcing and selling game outside auctions. In 2001, it was reported that the Cooperative coordinated the sale of more than R30 million ($3.5 million) in game sales both at and outside auctions—R20 million in direct (out-of-auction) sales and R10 million in auction sales (they provided services for the Natal Game Ranchers Association Auction).

A straightforward doubling of auction turnover (according to Eloff's findings) without considering influencing factors may, however, be inaccurate. For example, in 2001 the amount of game sold by game capture companies outside auctions was estimated to be about R120 million. Obviously, this is not double the R82.3 million turnover at the 2001 auctions (see below), and is explained by the fact these auctions sold a significant number of high-value game such as rhinos.[3] Simply doubling the amount would provide a poor estimate because the game capture companies are not involved in a large portion of the high-value rhino trade; KZN Wildlife sold all of the black rhinos and 68 of the 140 white rhinos at the 2001 auctions. In any case, even if one makes a conservative estimate on the basis of the survey mentioned, it is apparent that

Table 7.4 Average Prices for Sale of Selected Species by Game Capture Companies, 2001 (rand)

Species	Average Direct Sale Price in KZN[a]	Average KZN Auction Price[b]
Black wildebeest	2,912	3,667
Blesbok	809	607
Blue wildebeest	2,481	2,648
Eland	5,393	4,315
Giraffe	15,099	13,537
Impala	701	684
Kudu	1,941	2,749
Nyala	9,167	7,384
Ostrich	1,294	2,118
Red hartebeest	3,559	3,502
Springbuck	539	774
Warthog	1,294	738
Waterbuck	5,393	6,030
Zebra	3,559	3,303

KZN = KwaZulu-Natal.
[a]Direct sale prices include value-added tax (VAT) as well as capture and transport costs.
[b]KZN auction prices include VAT, but exclude capture and transport costs.

Source: Direct sale prices (to be read as approximations only) provided by a large game capture company in KZN (to remain anonymous for business confidentiality reasons). KZN auction prices based on detailed data for private and public KZN auctions in 2001 provided by T. Eloff, Center for Wildlife Economics, University of Potchefstroom, South Africa.

game sale activities conducted in this manner generate a significant amount of economic activity.

Prices for game traded directly by game capture companies tend to be somewhat lower than at auctions. This is, obviously, an attraction. But buyers must also have the flexibility to be able to wait until the species has been sourced and is available in the quantity they desire. Table 7.4 provides a summary of average prices for direct sales in 2001 for selected species as supplied by one of the largest game capture companies in KZN, along with comparisons with KZN auction prices for the same year.

Private Sales

Game may also be traded between private ranchers without the intervention of an independent game capture company. Due to the high level of expertise and care required to capture and transport game, not to mention the equipment and transport containers needed, this activity is unlikely to make a significant contribution to the game sales market in South Africa. This conclusion is also based on the impressions of a number of private game ranchers and game capture companies consulted.

As outlined above, some activities of the game sales industry are difficult to assess. Although an effort was made to provide an estimate of the total contribution of each to the South African game sales market, the only tangible data available pertain to auction activities. The auctions in South Africa do, nonetheless, account for a large part of game traded in the country. It will be assumed that trends in these activities can be used to indicate the general status of the industry on a broader level. As such, the remainder of this chapter will utilize these data to analyze the status and trends in the South African game sales market.

First Auctions

There is a lack of consensus as to exactly when the first auctions in South Africa took place. This is partly because there was (and there still is) no central organizational authority for such events and because the first auctions were quite small and relatively informal. There are claims that auctions began as early as 1965 in the then–Northern Transvaal (Ebedes 1994, 74), whereas others have suggested that they may have started a few years later (Vleissentraal Auctioneers, personal communication, 2001).

In any case, there does seem to be agreement that the first formal auctions took place in the middle to late 1960s. These did not, however, occur without a certain amount of resistance from state conservation agencies. It was the perception at that time (and may still be for some) that the conservation of wildlife was the exclusive business of the state and that private-sector involvement was not a desirable option to encourage. Not only was the private sector perceived to be incompetent when it came to wildlife affairs, but it was presumed that it would have a negative impact on conservation due to its profit-seeking (and thereby "exploitative") nature.

Despite any initial resistance, private auctions have continued during the past 35 years. More recently, state conservation agencies from the former Orange Free State, Transvaal, and Natal Parks Board have also begun selling live game at auctions (Ebedes 1994, 74).

Game Sales Market in South Africa

South African auctions generated record turnovers for the industry in 2001. For the 17,282 head of game sold at the 43 auctions held around the country (including catalogue and *boma* auctions), the turnover totaled more than R82.3 million ($9.6 million). The most commonly traded species in terms of numbers sold were

Impala	3,932
Blue wildebeest	1,700
Common blesbok	1,520
Common springbuck	1,314
Nyala	1,053
Kudu	1,003
Common eland	891
Burchell's zebra	815
Red hartebeest	699
Gemsbuck	563

Highest average prices at auctions in 2001 went for the following species (in rand):

Black rhino	($60,000) 520,341
White rhino	160,170
Roan	100,959
Black impala	95,868
Buffalo (disease free)	77,019
Sable	62,946
Tsessebe	14,461
Lion	14,191
Giraffe	12,411
Livingstone's eland	($1,200) 10,744

Game Sales Market in KwaZulu-Natal

As was mentioned above, KwaZulu-Natal (and specifically its conservation authority) has played a unique role in the game sales industry in South Africa.[4] This historical position has put the province in a good position to benefit from the growing industry.

Study Area Synopsis
The specific area selected for examination within KwaZulu-Natal, Zululand, is one of the most active provinces for game sales activity

in South Africa. The study area occupies 2,496,000 hectares or 26.3 percent of KZN territory (the entire province covers 9,485,855 hectares), with the individual properties selected for the study constituting approximately 272,392 hectares of the study area. Twenty-seven private properties (totaling 108,753 hectares, or 39.9 percent of the study area) as well as the three state-protected areas of Hluhluwe-Umfolozi Park (HUP), Ithala Nature Reserve, and Mkhuze Game Reserve (totaling 163,639 hectares, or 60.1 percent of the study area) were selected for in-depth analysis.

Activities on study area properties. The findings of the Ecological Survey (see chapter 6) indicated that the focus of activities on these private properties ranged across the game industry options. Primary goals for these game ranches included various combinations of trophy hunting, game viewing, biodiversity conservation, and venison or biltong hunting. Only two of the property owners allowed no hunting whatsoever. This would lead one to believe that, apart from the two properties mentioned, hunting constitutes a significant component of income from game industry activities.

Consistent with the general findings stated above regarding participation in game ranching, 26 of the 27 private properties in the study area had previously been used for raising cattle. Eight of these also raised some cattle at the same time. One of the primary reasons stated for conversion was that cattle had become less economically viable. Many (23) also stated that their personal interest in, or love for, wildlife was also a reason for converting to nature tourism through game ranching.

Only 8 of the game ranchers had been involved in nature tourism for a significant length of time (more than 20 years). The other 18 (who previously used the land for cattle) had converted to nature tourism during the past 10 years. This means that almost two-thirds of the game ranchers in the area likely would have been actively buying game during the past decade to stock their ranches. The others may have been in the market for game as well, but more likely would have had their game levels relatively well established by the time the others became involved. It is this influx of game ranchers and land use conversion that has been one of the contributing factors to the increasing prices for game.

Game on study area properties. Current values of game on the private ranches in the study area are considerable (see the data collected in the

Producer Survey and discussed in chapter 8). Game values were reported by 23 of the 27 private properties, the total estimated value being R99.2 million. This calculates to a per-hectare value of R1,300. If the state-owned protected area of HUP—occupying an area of more than 96,000 hectares—is included, the value of game on the properties jumps to more than R586 million and increases the per-hectare value to R3,400. The most likely reason for this increase with the addition of the protected area is that high-value species, such as white rhinos, black rhinos, and nyalas, are more numerous on state-owned areas like HUP and increase the game value figures substantially.

Game acquisition and use in study area properties. The Ecological Survey also found (table 7.5) that most animals purchased by the private game ranches in the study area come from local (that is, KZN) sources. Although some game populations tend to be less abundant in this province and, hence, are more easily sourced elsewhere (for example, cheetahs, giraffes, and waterbucks), often fewer than 15 percent of the game sold to these game ranchers originated in other provinces.

Various use options have been deployed by the game ranchers in the study area for the species on their farms including nonconsumptive uses such as tourism, as well as consumptive uses such as trophy hunting, biltong hunting, and live capture (either for private and direct sales or auction sales). During a five-year period, the 27 private properties reported income for 1,123 individual game for trophy hunts and 4,171 for biltong hunts. The three state-owned protected areas had 930 individuals taken through trophy hunts and 2,032 through biltong hunting. The most common trophy and biltong species on both the private and state-owned properties are shown in table 7.6.

The third revenue-generating use of game examined among these properties was that of live capture. The private properties reported the live capture of 1,612 individual game animals during the five-year period, whereas the three protected areas reported the live capture of 10,868 animals during the same period. The highest quantities of various species captured are provided in table 7.7.

Although information was not provided by those interviewed regarding the destination of these animals, the most likely answer is that they would either be for out-of-hand and direct sales or auction sales. In the case of the three protected areas, some species may also go toward

Table 7.5 Origin of Species Purchased by Study Area Properties

Species	Number from Geographical Source			Total Number	Percentage from "Other"
	Local	KZN	Other		
Blesbok	100	94	7	201	3.5
Buffalo, African	0	158	0	158	0
Bushbuck	0	38	0	38	0
Caracal	0	1	0	1	0
Cheetah	0	2	17	19	89.5
Eland	0	0	35	35	100
Elephant, African	0	0	114	114	100
Gemsbok	0	0	10	10	100
Giraffe	0	40	101	141	71.6
Hartebeest, red	0	30	44	74	59.5
Hippopotamus	0	6	28	34	82.4
Hyena, brown	0	0	1	1	100
Impala	256	1,150	550	1,956	28.1
Jackal, black backed	0	4	5	9	55.6
Jackal, side striped	0	0	8	8	100
Kudu	34	59	47	150	31.3
Lion	0	3	12	15	80
Nyala	29	101	30	160	18.8
Ostrich	30	0	27	57	47.4
Reedbuck, common	31	70	9	110	8.2
Reedbuck, mountain	33	0	20	53	37.7
Rhino, black	0	1	0	1	0
Rhino, white	0	29	7	36	19.4
Serval	0	1	0	1	0
Warthog	109	19	0	128	0
Waterbuck	29	10	112	151	74.2
Wildebeest, blue	83	374	414	871	47.5
Zebra, Burchell's	38	330	327	695	47.1
Total	772	2,520	1,925	5,227	36.8

KZN = KwaZulu-Natal.

Source: James and Goodman (2000).

meeting the state priorities of internal translocations of game or providing founder populations by way of once-off donations to Community Conservation Areas and Reserves.

Game Auctions in the Province of KZN

The reputation of KwaZulu-Natal's auctions, both for game quality and variety available, brings in a large audience of buyers from around

Table 7.6 Commonly Hunted Species on Study Area Properties

Relevant Study Area	Trophy Hunting (most common)	Biltong Hunting (most common)
Private ranches	Bushpig, grey duiker, red duiker, elephant, giraffe, red hartebeest, impala, kudu, nyala, common reedbuck, white rhino, suni, warthog, waterbuck, blue wildebeest, Burchell's zebra	Bushpig, grey duiker, impala, kudu, nyala, common reedbuck, steenbok, warthog
State-owned properties	Bushpig, grey duiker, red duiker, impala, kudu, nyala, white rhino, suni, warthog, blue wildebeest, Burchell's zebra	Impala, kudu, nyala, white rhino, suni, warthog, blue wildebeest, Burchell's zebra

Source: James and Goodman (2000).

Table 7.7 Common Species for Live Capture in the Study Area

Relevant Study Area	Live Capture (most common)
Private ranches	Bontebok, cheetah, giraffe, red hartebeest, impala, kudu, leopard, lion, nyala, white rhino, warthog, blue wildebeest, Burchell's zebra
State-owned properties	Buffalo, giraffe, impala, kudu, leopard, lion, nyala, white rhino, black rhino, warthog, waterbuck, blue wildebeest, Burchell's zebra

Source: James and Goodman (2000).

Southern Africa as well as overseas. This favorable reputation contributes to the fact that current game auctions in the province account for a significant proportion of South Africa's total annual game sales turnover (this will be explored further in the following section). Tables 7.8 and 7.9 provide data from the 2001 live and catalogue auctions in KZN regarding the greatest number of a particular species sold and the highest average price received for a species.

Both the private sector (through the Natal Game Ranchers Association) and KZN Wildlife conduct their own auctions in the province, but the vast majority of species sold and turnover generated takes place at the annual KZN Wildlife auction (figures 7.1 and 7.2). In fact, the auction held by KZN Wildlife in 2001 set a new turnover record for the organization; the R20.7 million surpassed the record of R15.1 million in 2000

Table 7.8 Greatest Number Sold at KZN Auctions, 2001, by Species

Species	Number Sold
Impala	960
Nyala	814
Warthog	340
Blue wildebeest	279
Blesbok	165
Zebra	136
Red hartebeest	99
Kudu	86
Eland	81
Springbuck	80

Source: T. Eloff, Center for Wildlife Economics, University of Potchefstroom, South Africa.

Table 7.9 Highest Average Price at KZN Auctions, 2001, by Species (rand)

Species	Live	Catalogue
Black rhinoceros	520,341	—
White rhinoceros	167,252	—
Giraffe	11,447	11,983
Nyala	6,965	6,285
Bushbuck	5,873	3,843
Waterbuck	5,676	5,251
Common reedbuck	—	4,316
Eland	3,693	3,817
Zebra	2,926	3,580
Red hartebeest	—	3,072

— Not available.

Source: T. Eloff, Center for Wildlife Economics, University of Potchefstroom, South Africa.

(see appendix 7-A for details of species traded, quantities, average prices, and turnover). The NGRA auctions have, however, been running only since 1999 and could increase their share of game sold and turnover generated as their auction builds its own reputation.

Key Species at KZN Auctions

Game sold in the province of KwaZulu-Natal, as briefly mentioned above, are of very high quality, and the variety of species available are not readily available at many other auctions in the country. A result of this is manifested in the share of species sold and turnover generated from these sales; these reveal a heavily weighted distribution in favor of

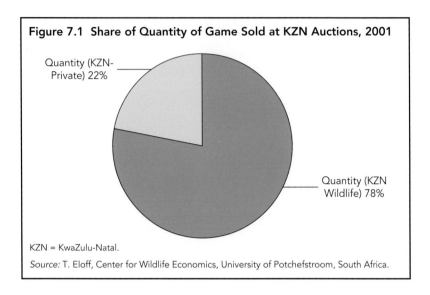

Figure 7.1 Share of Quantity of Game Sold at KZN Auctions, 2001

Quantity (KZN-Private) 22%

Quantity (KZN Wildlife) 78%

KZN = KwaZulu-Natal.

Source: T. Eloff, Center for Wildlife Economics, University of Potchefstroom, South Africa.

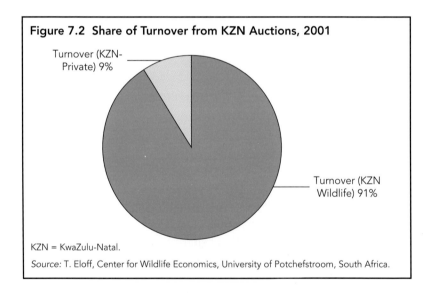

Figure 7.2 Share of Turnover from KZN Auctions, 2001

Turnover (KZN-Private) 9%

Turnover (KZN Wildlife) 91%

KZN = KwaZulu-Natal.

Source: T. Eloff, Center for Wildlife Economics, University of Potchefstroom, South Africa.

three species in particular—the nyala, the white rhino, and the black rhino. As shown in figure 7.3, these three species alone accounted for more than one-quarter of the total number of species sold in KwaZulu-Natal in 2001 (public and private auctions combined). Figure 7.4 illustrates an even more extreme relationship in that these three species

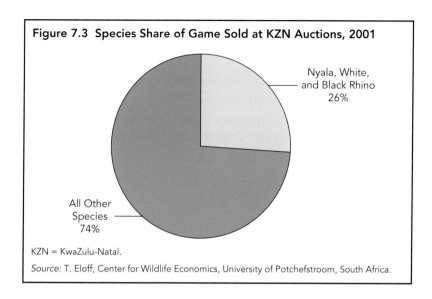

Figure 7.3 Species Share of Game Sold at KZN Auctions, 2001

Nyala, White,
and Black Rhino
26%

All Other
Species
74%

KZN = KwaZulu-Natal.
Source: T. Eloff, Center for Wildlife Economics, University of Potchefstroom, South Africa.

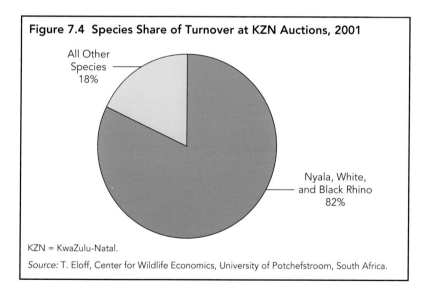

Figure 7.4 Species Share of Turnover at KZN Auctions, 2001

All Other
Species
18%

Nyala, White,
and Black Rhino
82%

KZN = KwaZulu-Natal.
Source: T. Eloff, Center for Wildlife Economics, University of Potchefstroom, South Africa.

brought in more than 80 percent of the almost R22.7 million in turnover generated in the province.

If the focus is on black and white rhino sales exclusively, it is clear that their symbolic importance (due to the success of Operation Rhino) and practical significance (due to their conservation and economic value) are justified. These species constitute a substantial portion of auction turnover in KZN; in 2001, KZN sold almost half of the country's white rhinos (68 of the 140) and all of its black rhinos (6 of them). These two species alone account for R13.4 million for KZN, or almost 60 percent of the province's total auction turnover of almost R22.7 million. This is just under 53 percent of the entire country's auction turnover in these species, and 16 percent of the total auction turnover for South Africa.

TRENDS IN GAME SALES MARKETS

South African Trends

The growing number of auctions held in South Africa, as well as the quantity of game sold and turnover generated, all show a considerable escalation in auction activity during the past 11 years (figure 7.5). In comparison with the 9 auctions held in 1991, at which 8,290 head of game were sold, generating R18,351,165 in turnover (approximately $8.4 million), statistics for the more than 43 auctions in 2001 denote a remarkable increase and reflect a growing demand for game and the willingness to pay a market price for it.

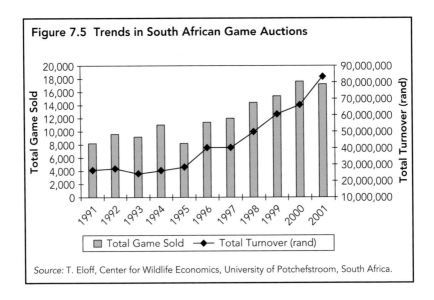

Figure 7.5 Trends in South African Game Auctions

Source: T. Eloff, Center for Wildlife Economics, University of Potchefstroom, South Africa.

It is interesting to note that with respect to average auction prices since 1994, the total number of game sold during the previous year has decreased on two occasions (1995 and 2001). Despite this fact, the total annual turnover for these periods always increased. As figure 7.5 shows, the number of game sold decreased from 11,096 in 1994 (generating R17.5 million) to 8,171 in 1995 (generating R19.8 million), and from 17,702 sold in 2000 (generating R63 million) to 17,282 in 2001 (generating R82.3 million). This suggests that there is an overall increase in prices paid for game at auctions, or at least that some species are increasing in value enough to offset any minor decrease in value for other species.

The general price increase for individual species during the past 11 years, as shown in figure 7.6, is fairly significant. This can be attributed, at least in part, to the increased demand from the expanded participation

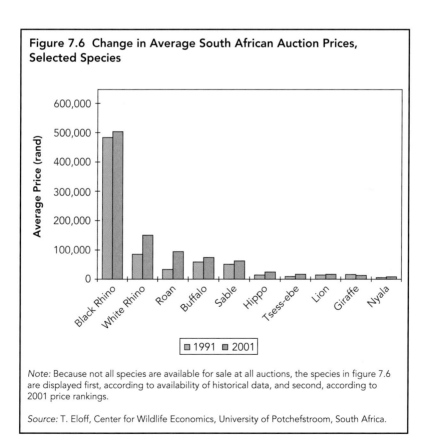

Figure 7.6 Change in Average South African Auction Prices, Selected Species

Note: Because not all species are available for sale at all auctions, the species in figure 7.6 are displayed first, according to availability of historical data, and second, according to 2001 price rankings.

Source: T. Eloff, Center for Wildlife Economics, University of Potchefstroom, South Africa.

in the game industry (as was shown above). More participants will result in higher demand, which generally leads to higher prices—basic market principles apply.

Another reason for increasing game prices is because of the strong buying power of many wealthy game ranchers and game ranching companies. Money poses less of an obstacle to many of these individuals and consortiums, causing auction prices to be pushed up because of their willingness to bid and pay a higher amount.

Very few individual species have consistently brought in higher average auction prices every year during the past decade. In general, game auction prices seem to respond to variations in supply and demand in a manner similar to almost any other market. For example, the average selling price for a Hartwater springbuck went from R713 in 1996, when 97 were available for sale, to R3,005 in 1997, when only 39 were available at auction. There are cases, however, where simple supply and demand principles do not seem to apply. Prices for many species seem to keep increasing, despite the fact that available supply is also generally increasing. These include (among others) gemsbucks, Livingstone's elands, impalas, and red hartebeests.

Other cases reflect a reverse relationship to what one might expect to find with respect to how prices respond to available supply. Lions, for example, sold on average for R8,200 in 2000 when only 2 were available, whereas auctions in 2001 saw the average price for the 15 lions available rise to R14,191. These prices likely reflect that the quality of these animals was much better than at previous auctions. It is also possible that, in the case of lions, the policies of provincial conservation authorities are having an impact on prices. Until recently, the tendency was to resist granting permits for lions on small, enclosed areas. There now appears to a greater willingness to consider this arrangement as a viable option, thereby expanding the potential buyers' market for this species. Despite variations in the reasons for price increases, the fact remains that auction prices in the country have shown an overall increase during the past decade for the vast majority of species.

In addition to increasing auction prices in South Africa, there has been an overall positive change in the quantity of individual species sold during the past decade. Apart from the reductions in 1995 and 2001 discussed above, the total number of species sold at auction has increased

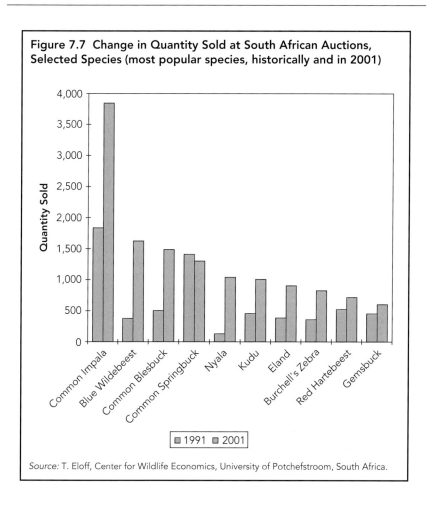

Figure 7.7 Change in Quantity Sold at South African Auctions, Selected Species (most popular species, historically and in 2001)

Source: T. Eloff, Center for Wildlife Economics, University of Potchefstroom, South Africa.

annually. This change is reflected in selected individual species, as is shown in figure 7.7. Species included in the figure were selected according to which were the most popular (in number sold). It is interesting that these species were the most highly traded in 2001 and have been among the most highly traded during the past decade.

KZN Trends

Game auctions in KZN itself have a significant history as well and demonstrate trends similar to those of the country in general. The results of these sales demonstrate that the province's game sales industry is well developed

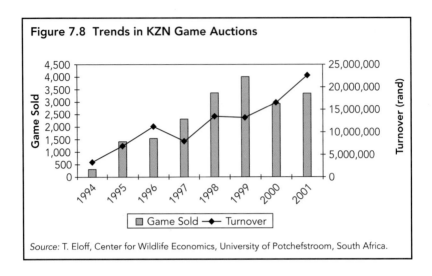

Figure 7.8 Trends in KZN Game Auctions

Source: T. Eloff, Center for Wildlife Economics, University of Potchefstroom, South Africa.

because they have been increasing turnover steadily throughout their existence. Figure 7.8 illustrates the province's success at achieving higher annual turnovers and its efficiency in obtaining these levels without flooding the market by dramatically increasing numbers of game sold.

The earlier days of auction game sales in KZN seem to be characteristic of a "new" industry and show slow or inconsistent growth. As the industry matures and develops, however, turnover is shown to increase at a faster, and seemingly more stable, rate. This is demonstrated in figure 7.5.

Trends in KZN auctions (since 1994) with respect to the highest average auction prices and highest quantity of species sold (as per the results of the 2001 auctions) are shown in figures 7.9 and 7.10, respectively. The complete data for trends in specific species sales in KZN since 1994 can be found in appendix 7-B.

Comparison of Trends in South Africa with Those in KwaZulu-Natal

Auctions in KZN have generated a significant proportion of the country's total live game sales revenue during the past decade (figures 7.11 and 7.12). This has been accomplished although only 2 of the 43 auctions held in South Africa in 2001 took place in KZN.[5] The fact that fewer than 5 percent of the auctions that took place in the country generated

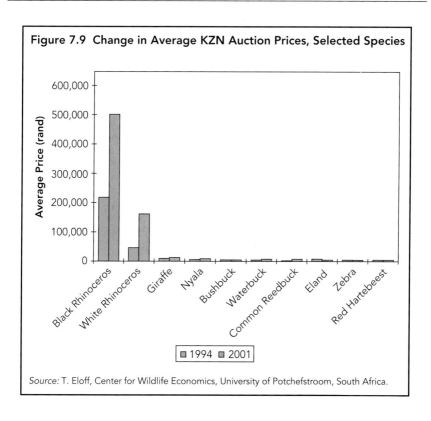

Figure 7.9 Change in Average KZN Auction Prices, Selected Species

Source: T. Eloff, Center for Wildlife Economics, University of Potchefstroom, South Africa.

28 percent (almost R22.7 million) of the total turnover (R82.3 million) highlights how significant the game sales in KZN are to the national economy.

There has been a slight decrease in the proportion of the national market captured by the KZN auctions since 1991 (from 36 percent down to 28 percent; see figures 7.11 and 7.12). Although this is only a relatively small decrease and should not detract from the important contribution of KZN's auctions, it might suggest that the industry is growing at an even faster rate elsewhere in the country.

Trends in KZN's auction activity with reference to its share of the country's total auction activity have been broken down according to quantities sold as well as turnover, comparing 1991 data with the most current auction results (2001). These data are shown in figures 7.13 and 7.14.

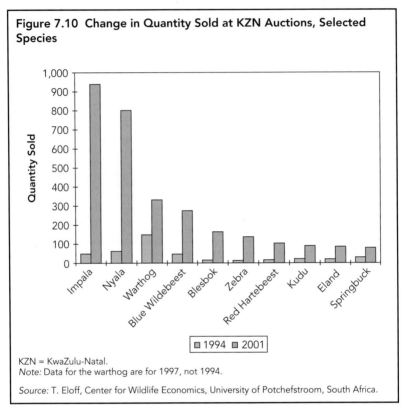

Figure 7.10 Change in Quantity Sold at KZN Auctions, Selected Species

KZN = KwaZulu-Natal.
Note: Data for the warthog are for 1997, not 1994.

Source: T. Eloff, Center for Wildlife Economics, University of Potchefstroom, South Africa.

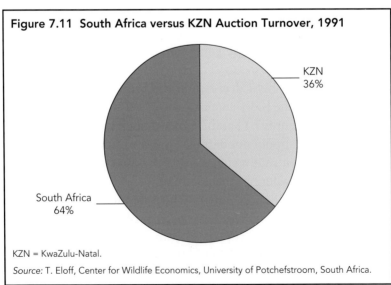

Figure 7.11 South Africa versus KZN Auction Turnover, 1991

KZN = KwaZulu-Natal.

Source: T. Eloff, Center for Wildlife Economics, University of Potchefstroom, South Africa.

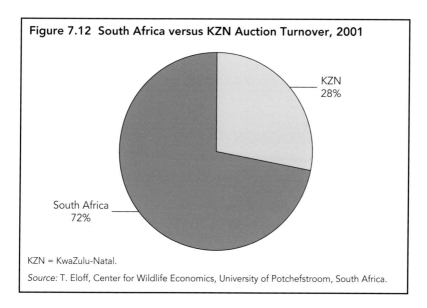

Figure 7.12 South Africa versus KZN Auction Turnover, 2001

KZN
28%

South Africa
72%

KZN = KwaZulu-Natal.

Source: T. Eloff, Center for Wildlife Economics, University of Potchefstroom, South Africa.

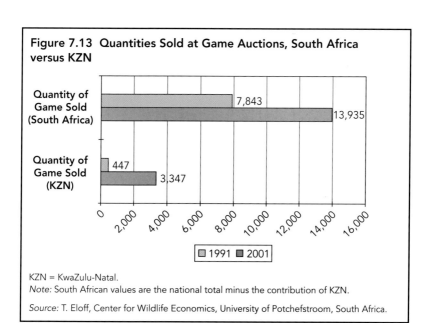

Figure 7.13 Quantities Sold at Game Auctions, South Africa versus KZN

Quantity of Game Sold (South Africa): 7,843 / 13,935

Quantity of Game Sold (KZN): 447 / 3,347

☐ 1991 ■ 2001

KZN = KwaZulu-Natal.

Note: South African values are the national total minus the contribution of KZN.

Source: T. Eloff, Center for Wildlife Economics, University of Potchefstroom, South Africa.

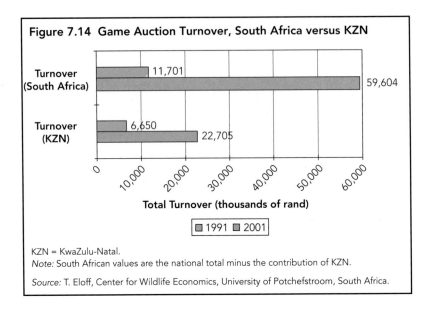

Figure 7.14 Game Auction Turnover, South Africa versus KZN

Turnover (South Africa): 11,701; 59,604
Turnover (KZN): 6,650; 22,705

Total Turnover (thousands of rand)

☐ 1991 ☐ 2001

KZN = KwaZulu-Natal.
Note: South African values are the national total minus the contribution of KZN.

Source: T. Eloff, Center for Wildlife Economics, University of Potchefstroom, South Africa.

FACTORS INFLUENCING GAME SALES

As with any market, internal and external factors will influence its positive or negative growth. Some of the factors that either already have, or may in the future, influence the game sales industry (either positively or negatively) in South Africa are summarized in this section.

Supply and Demand

The growth in game sales, both in terms of quantities sold and turnover generated, has been partly a result of the influx of both the quantity and type of game ranchers to the industry. As the number of game ranchers entering the industry increases, so does the need to stock land with game. The increase in the quantity of demand likely constitutes at least part of the reason for increasing game prices, both in KZN and in South Africa in general. What is meant by the "type" of game rancher now participating in the industry has to do with their level of purchasing power. According to various game industry organizations, both foreign and non-farming-dependent individuals are becoming more and more involved in the game industry.

Foreign participants have stronger currencies with which to buy game; this certainly gives them an advantage as buyers, particularly with the decreasing value of the rand relative to stronger foreign currencies. Individuals who are not dependent on their game ranches often have more buying power as well. For example (and as mentioned above), many of the newer entrants into the game ranching arena in the study area have other sources of income on which to rely. In fact, 63 percent (17 of the 27) of the private property owners had other business interests, and almost half (44.4 percent) do not live on these properties permanently. These cases imply that these property owners have other financial resources and would suggest that they may have the option of paying higher prices for game.

Ranch sizes, another factor having to do with demand, may also be affecting the price of game. According to the Natal Game Ranchers Association, fences are being dropped between many game ranch properties in KZN at an unprecedented rate. This also increases the buying power of the game ranchers involved because they can combine their resources to purchase game that will potentially benefit all of them.

Although this increase in demand is clearly affecting game sales, some argue that once this land has reached its production potential and once it is believed that existing stocks will be sustained through natural reproductive rates, demand will likely decrease. This argument suggests that further injections of game will not be required to the same extent that they have been recently. This reduced demand could have a negative impact on the games sales industry and should be borne in mind as an obstacle to organizations that rely on sustained demand of their surplus game to subsidize the costs of reserve management.

Conversely, the depth of the game industry in general must be considered. The argument from this perspective, in contrast to that above, suggests that due to the diversity of the game industry activities available to game ranchers, reaching saturation point will be unlikely. As long as the industry is well rounded and well developed (in other words, there is not too much emphasis on one activity, especially at the expense of all others), the various options should tend to sustain a healthy market for a long time.

Effects of Climate Fluctuations

Another factor influencing demand pertains to changes in climate conditions and the weather patterns in South Africa that have proven to influence the game industry directly. Dry conditions make it more difficult for game to adjust to their new habitat, increasing the chances for mortalities. In times of drought, auction prices have responded accordingly. In 1999, the dry conditions resulted in an overall decrease over 1998 auction prices (reflecting a decrease in demand due to less hospitable environments for introducing game) for many species. Some of these included buffaloes, nyalas, bushbucks, reedbucks, springbucks, and zebras.

When considering the potential impact of drought and how it might affect game sales, it is important to also consider the characteristics of the various regions being affected. With KZN, for example, the characteristics of its landscape (veld type) make it relatively resilient with respect to drought. In the event of a very dry season or year, KZN therefore would be in a stronger position to pick up the industry, whereas other, drier regions might have larger losses of species more sensitive to climate fluctuations. This is particularly the case with overstocked reserves or reserves that stock species that are not indigenous to the region. A species unable to adapt to a change in the region because of fodder shortages would be the first to show signs of stress, and their numbers would decrease.

Some individuals and organizations predicted that 2002 would be an extremely good year for game sales in KZN. The cold temperatures and snow in parts of KZN over the winter of 2001 killed off some of the supply of game. This loss of game meant that many game farms were in the process of breeding up again. Because the previous years had been good with respect to rainfall, the carrying capacity was quite high, creating positive conditions for buyers at the 2002 auctions. At the same time, however, potential losses of excess game over the previous winter may affect the supply side of the market, driving numbers of species available down and prices up.

When changes in weather patterns are the cause of an increase or decrease in demand for game, one must remember that there will be a time lag for game ranchers within which to respond. For example, in postdrought periods, it will take some time for prices to recover. Landowners will not immediately go out to replace lost game for fear of losing them as well. Once the rains return, however, and the ranchers are more comfortable, then the prices (driven by increased demand) will likely increase.

Disease

Animal diseases and an inability to control or contain them will also negatively affect game sales. For example, giraffes were excluded from KZN Wildlife's *boma* auctions in 2001 due to a rare illness (usually only found in cattle) that some had contracted. More common animal diseases include foot and mouth and tuberculosis (currently one of the leading causes restricting buffalo sales). Further reductions in government funding for agricultural research and inadequate preventative regulations regarding animal diseases could have serious implications for the game industry. (The source of the nonviral, nonbacterial problem in the giraffe was reported to have been isolated, and it is not expected to affect future game sales.)

Institutional Influences

Auction organizers might, themselves, have a certain amount of influence on game prices. Although there are practical limitations on the number of game that can be provided at auction, flooding the market for a certain species will certainly have an influence on the price. In KZN, an expressed desire on the part of local ranchers to have more influence on game auction prices led the Natal Game Ranchers Association to initiate its own auctions in 1999. It was felt that by having a second local auction (in addition to the one held by KZN Wildlife) and by increasing options for buyers, prices would more accurately reflect the market.

Crime has a negative impact on the game sales industry in general. If tourists and hunters (both local and overseas) perceive an area to be too unstable, there will be a reduction in demand for the relevant game activities in that area. As has been demonstrated in this chapter, the game industry makes a significant contribution to the South African economy and will depend on the ability of the government to manage the crime level in a manner that will not negatively affect its day-to-day business. Conversely, if crime can be controlled, the game sales industry will benefit from the increase in demand for game-related experiences.

Poaching has been a problem for game managers and owners for decades. There is a history to this activity that involves political as well as socioeconomic aspects, and efforts are being made to curb its effects. Unfortunately, it remains an active concern for game managers. Reductions in the numbers of species, and their respective reproduction rates, could have an impact on the quantity of game available for sale, and consequently on the game sales industry in general. A recent variation on poaching is the practice of poaching with dogs. This activity has received media attention lately, and though its effect is not currently significant for the larger game industry, in combination with more traditional poaching techniques it could be a factor for future market activities.

Institutional barriers (with respect to policymaking) that discourage participation in the game industry will also have a negative impact on game sales. As found by Pearce (1996, 7), because wildlife use in South Africa has demonstrated that it has an economic value, one should "avoid, wherever possible, conservation practice which bans or prohibits the utilization of wildlife products. Such bans take economic value away from the wildlife and render it an asset with limited economic value."

Some provincial regulations exist in South Africa that hinder trade in wildlife. For example (and in addition to examples already mentioned above), under the nature conservation ordinance for each of the nine provinces of South Africa, a permit is required to transport game to and from game reserves. Therefore, if a nyala is purchased at a game auction in KZN and is to be relocated to the Northern Province, a permit will be required for each province entered and exited. Although this does not directly affect prices or turnover at auctions, it is a time-consuming and bureaucratic process whose streamlining would enable more efficient trade. Equalizing provincial nature conservation ordinances wherever possible would benefit the game industry.

Market Development

A positive impact on the game industry will result from the expansion of currently underdeveloped facets of the game market, such as venison export. Venison is not only popular (in terms of palatability) with many people, but it also offers numerous health benefits, including low fat content, an absence of antibiotics and growth stimulants, a high protein content, and the benefits of having been fed a natural diet.

Those species that are currently less expensive (for the most part) are precisely those species used for venison (for example, impalas and spring-bok ewes, waterbucks, elands, and kudu cows). These species are not viable for the trophy market due to their relatively low trophy value. Furthermore, their reproductive rates are quite high, thereby mini-mizing the negative impact of increased harvesting. Finally, adding value to a species has, as has been discussed in this chapter, been recorded as having resulted in an increase in the overall number of species, thereby benefiting conservation efforts.

Influences in KZN

Some factors exist that will influence game sales and are specific to KZN. One factor that could certainly influence turnover has to do with prior game commitments by which KZN Wildlife is bound. This will be particularly significant in years where there may be a shortage of excess game due to natural reductions in game numbers (such as par-ticularly dry or cold seasons or an outbreak of disease). For example, according to KZN Wildlife authorities, the priorities for excess game from protected areas in KZN are:

1. Internal translocations

2. Donations to Community Conservation Areas (CCAs) and Community Conservation Reserves (CCRs)

3. KZN Wildlife auctions (both *boma* and catalogue), and

4. Direct (out-of-hand) sales.

If excess game levels are low and if the number of preexisting game com-mitments taken on by KZN Wildlife is high, turnover from annual auc-tions may be negatively affected. This may, in fact, be seen in auctions in 2002 because both buffalo and black rhino numbers have been affected by precisely such a situation.

The official establishment of the Greater Saint Lucia Wetland Park (GSWP) and its status as its own authority will also have an impact on KZN Wildlife's game sales revenue. Any auction revenue generated from the sale of game that originates in GSWP goes back to the authority itself. In the past, a significant amount of game for KZN Wildlife's auctions has come from this area and, given the size and substantial game populations of GSWP, it is highly probable that it will continue to provide large quantities of game for the auctions. The resulting impact on revenue returned to KZN Wildlife will certainly be affected. The Greater Saint Lucia Wetland Park Authority has officially been proclaimed, so this impact will also likely be felt at the 2002 auctions as well.

CONCLUSIONS

Finding innovative methods for financing the costs of meeting conservation objectives presents difficult challenges to every nation. South Africa's rich biodiversity provides it with a wealth of assets and potential opportunities at its disposal for this purpose. Shifting attitudes toward the opportunities available through the sustainable use of these resources stand to benefit the country in many ways. South Africa's game sales activities demonstrate one way in which it has proactively addressed conservation finance issues.

The game industry in South Africa has proven its significance as an economic contributor, through the influx of participants and the quantity of revenue generated by its numerous activities. The level of activity at auctions, in particular, has seen a significant increase in turnover since 1991, with a doubling in the number of game sold during the same period. Putting aside any moral reservations with respect to "putting a price on an animal," these activities provide a tangible illustration of valuing wildlife—one that proves that their value is escalating at a significant rate.

Levels of game sales activity in KwaZulu-Natal are very high and have been shown to constitute a considerable proportion of the entire game sales industry in the country. The reasons for this have to do with KZN's reputation for having game available of a very high quality and also for having a variety of species at its auctions that are only found in smaller quantities and far less frequently at other auctions around the country. The significance of these species, particularly in their economic contribution, is substantial and should be borne in mind when looking at KZN's role in the sale of live game.

Specific details available on the KZN study area examined provide substantiating evidence of some of the more general trends in the province and in the country as a whole. The growth of participation in the game industry is significant in this area, as is the economic contribution of the various game industry activities on the game farms and reserves. The properties examined in this area benefit from consumptive and nonconsumptive uses of wildlife, and they are active in both the supply and demand sides of the game sales markets.

Although the economic activities of the game industry are substantial, it is still vulnerable to external factors, just like any other market. Some of the potential effects on game sales, in particular, may be foreseeable, and there may be opportunities to mitigate negative effects, whereas other effects may be beyond the control of industry stakeholders. In either case, these factors should be acknowledged as relevant to the future of the industry and should be assimilated into the management plans of relevant parties, whether they are private or public.

Although the game sales market in South Africa currently shows clear signs of being very healthy and should continue to do so in the near future, the impact of a decrease in demand should be borne in mind. The extent of such an impact will depend on the time horizon being considered by the relevant parties (that is, if they are seeking short- or long-term benefits from the industry). In view of this potential impact, it is critical that efforts be continued to seek additional innovative mechanisms to finance conservation activities.

The contribution of game sales—as well as that of the larger industry supported by game sales—to the South African economy is evident. As such, efforts to provide security for its activities should be enhanced, and institutional barriers to the industry should be removed. This will enable the industry to maximize its potential and will further benefit the South African economy while providing a substantial means of financing conservation efforts.

Appendix 7-A. KwaZulu-Natal Game Auctions, 2001

Species	Quantity Sold	Average Price (rand)[a]	Total Turnover (rand)
Blesbuck	165	607	87,815
Bushbuck	32	5,249	147,351
Eland	81	4,315	306,623
Giraffe	47	13,537	558,136
Impala	960	684	576,159
Kudu	86	2,749	207,379
Nyala	814	7,384	5,258,940
Ostrich	28	2,118	52,034
Red hartebeest	99	3,502	304,163
Reedbuck, common	48	4,920	207,190
Reedbuck, mountain	25	1,294	28,382
Rhinoceros, white	68	283,248	10,293,283
Rhinoceros, black	6	593,188	3,122,044
Springbok, common	80	774	54,399
Warthog	340	738	219,962
Waterbuck	33	6,030	174,551
Wildebeest, black	20	3,667	64,333
Wildebeest, blue	279	2,648	648,250
Zebra	136	3,303	394,040
Total game sold	3,347	—	22,705,033

Note: This table combines private and public auctions and includes both live sale/*boma* and catalogue auctions.

[a]Average prices are corrected to 2000 constant values and include value added tax, but not capture and delivery costs. Prices were calculated according to a weighted value when individual data on each auction were available. Otherwise, a simple average calculation was made based on total turnover and quantity sold.

Sources: T. Eloff (unpublished data) and KZN Wildlife at http://www.kznwildlife.com/auction2001.htm.

Appendix 7-B. KwaZulu-Natal Game Auctions by Species, 1994–2001 (quantity sold and turnover, in rand)

Species	1994 Sold	1994 Turnover	1995 Sold	1995 Turnover	1996 Sold	1996 Turnover	1997 Sold	1997 Turnover	1998 Sold	1998 Turnover	1999 Sold	1999 Turnover	2000 Sold	2000 Turnover	2001 Sold	2001 Turnover	Total per Species Sold	Total per Species Turnover
Black Wildebeest	10	25,526	29	69,475			32	99,526	63	178,936	52	115,595			20	64,333	206	553,391
Blesbok	15	8,333	96	38,363	59	32,304	226	145,912	225	163,803	186	106,438	115	72,750	165	87,815	1,087	655,718
Blue Wildebeest	48	119,520	204	372,376	252	469,884	395	840,403	529	1,059,645	257	436,354	530	936,725	279	648,250	2,494	4,883,156
Buffalo									22	2,260,532	74	2,495,258					96	4,755,790
Bushbuck									19	63,082	19	51,949	25	67,000	32	147,351	95	329,382
Common reedbuck			30	58,011	196	475,676	96	236,019	96	264,745	116	279,663	120	423,600	48	207,190	702	1,944,904
Eland	12	73,123					23	114,336	10	87,805	25	113,066	25	124,650	81	306,623	176	819,603
Gemsbok											14	42,782					14	42,782
Giraffe	10	100,976	11	120,166	34	263,578	26	300,948	51	604,767	55	596,681	70	820,750	47	558,136	304	3,366,002
Grey Duiker											6	4,742					6	4,742
Hippo			4	82,873							2	52,687	4	102,000			10	237,560
Impala	45	21,652	658	260,048	278	148,880	569	323,815	1,160	629,712	1,620	734,299	970	458,000	960	576,159	6,260	3,152,565
Kudu	19	41,742	42	62,293	121	164,093	100	221,090	267	474,058	223	387,355	172	305,650	86	207,379	1,030	1,863,659
Mountain reedbuck											30	28,662	30	36,000	25	28,382	85	93,044
Natal red duiker											2	4,215					2	4,215

(continued)

Appendix 7-B. (Continued)

Species	1994 Sold	1994 Turnover	1995 Sold	1995 Turnover	1996 Sold	1996 Turnover	1997 Sold	1997 Turnover	1998 Sold	1998 Turnover	1999 Sold	1999 Turnover	2000 Sold	2000 Turnover	2001 Sold	2001 Turnover	Total per Species Sold	Total per Species Turnover
Nyala	61	175,826	110	299,309	282	852,317	367	1,158,531	275	898,226	622	1,866,175	325	1,656,100	814	5,258,940	2,856	12,165,424
Ostrich							10	32,701			10	22,550	46	98,300	28	52,034	94	205,586
Red Hartebeest	16	45,646	50	107,735	57	122,136	40	123,223	80	255,432	71	184,615	76	229,000	99	304,163	489	1,371,950
Springbok	23	17,267	26	30,249	38	18,919	95	53,614	140	95,898	155	61,697	76	44,600	80	54,399	633	376,642
Warthog							150	88,863	200	194,568	160	117,492	120	75,500	340	219,962	970	696,384
Waterbuck	13	56,607			17	66,281			29	159,368	29	127,766	45	254,900	33	174,551	166	839,472
White Rhinoceros	30	1,475,976	64	4,171,271	131	7,365,508	39	3,791,469	45	5,802,661	36	4,847,208	42	8,510,000	68	10,293,283	455	46,257,375
Black Rhinoceros	5	1,126,126	6	1,160,221	6	1,158,301							6	2,250,000	6	3,122,044	29	8,816,692
Zebra	8	20,120	90	181,077	81	150,193	141	286,493	153	378,049	240	459,431	124	284,000	136	394,040	973	2,153,403
Annual Totals	315	3,308,438	1,420	7,013,467	1,552	11,288,069	2,309	7,816,943	3,364	13,571,286	4,004	13,136,681	2,921	16,749,525	3,347	22,705,033	19,232	95,589,443

Note: This table combines private and public auctions and includes both live and catalogue auctions. The turnover is corrected to reflect 2000 constant values.

NOTES

1. The terms "game ranch/ing/er" and "game farm/ing/er" are used to refer to the private individuals (or their activities) who own properties stocked with game. The tendency is to use the term "game farmer" when discussing those who raise game on their land as they would do with cattle or sheep, for example. "Game rancher," on the other hand, usually refers to an individual who keeps game on a game-fenced area and intends to utilize this game for either consumptive or non-consumptive purposes. A rather loose referral system will be used in this chapter: "game rancher" is the more accurate term for this discussion, while the area stocked with game may be referred to as either a ranch or a farm. This is not to generate any confusion, but will reflect the most likely use of terminology in the game industry itself.

2. These prices are approximations only, as provided by the Natal Game Ranchers Association. They are meant to provide some perspective on income potential for game ranchers as opposed to exact income from various game industry activities.

3. From this point forward, all rand amounts have been converted to incorporate inflation and will reflect a value constant with 2000.

4. Unless otherwise noted all figures cited in this subsection come from James and Goodman (2000) and Porter, Ferrer, and Aylward (2002), which are summarized in chapters 6 and 8 of this volume, respectively.

5. These two auctions make up one *boma* and one catalogue auction each. Two *boma* and two catalogue auctions were held in the province in 2001, with one of each type being held on the same day and at the same venue. As such, the combined auction activity on a given day is counted as a single auction.

REFERENCES

Ebedes, H. 1994. "Going, Going, Gone—An Appraisal of Game Auctions." In W. Van Hoven, H. Ebedes, and A. Conroy, eds., *Wildlife Ranching: A Celebration of Diversity, Proceedings of the Third International Wildlife Ranching Symposium (1992)*. Pretoria: Promedia.

Falkena, Hans. 2000. *Bulls, Bears, and Lions: Game Ranch Profitability in Southern Africa*. Rivonia: South African Financial Sector Forum.

James, B. M., and P. S. Goodman. 2000. *Ecological Study*. Report to the World Bank Research Project on Nature Tourism and Conservation. Cascades, KwaZulu-Natal: Brousse-James & Associates and KZN Wildlife.

Pearce, David. 1996. "An Economic Overview of Wildlife and Alternative Land Uses." Presentation at the Overseas Development Administration, African Wildlife Policy Consultation, April.

Porter, S., S. Ferrer, and B. Aylward. 2002. *Producer Survey.* Report to the World Bank Research Project on Nature Tourism and Conservation. Cascades, KwaZulu-Natal: KZN Wildlife.

't Sas-Rolfes, Michael. 1996. "The Use of Auctions as an Incentive Measure for Wildlife Conservation." Paper presented at a workshop on incentives for biodiversity: sharing experiences, Montreal, Aug. 30–Sept. 1.

———. 2000. "Assessing CITES: Four Case Studies." In *Endangered Species, Threatened Convention: The Past, Present and Future of CITES.* London: Earthscan.

CHAPTER 8

THE PROFITABILITY OF NATURE TOURISM IN ZULULAND

A Survey of Private Reserves and Public Protected Areas

Sarah Porter, Stuart Ferrer, and Bruce Aylward

The game- and nature-based tourism industry in South Africa has shown extraordinary growth during the past 40 years and is currently the only growing livestock-based industry in the country. An estimated 9,000 commercial game farms exist, covering 14 percent of the country's surface, an area of more than 17 million hectares (Standard Bank AgriReview 2000). Another 5.4 percent of the country's territory is set aside in protected areas implying that some 20 percent of the country's land is managed primarily for game (World Bank 2001). In 1998 and 1999, the area surrounded by private game fences increased by 3.5 percent a year (about 300,000 hectares per year), leaving no doubt that the South African game industry is in a growth phase (Standard Bank AgriReview 2000).

This chapter provides a description of the game ranching industry in Northeastern KwaZulu-Natal (NE KZN) that is based on a cross-sectional survey conducted in 2000 of 3 public and 27 privately owned game ranches. A broad spectrum of game ranching and nature-based tourism operations was encountered in the study area. The businesses

The authors gratefully acknowledge contributions made to this research by Mark Darroch and Craig Hean, respectively senior lecturer and student in the School of Agricultural Sciences and Agribusiness, University of Natal, Pietermaritzburg. Darroch and Hean conducted refined analyses of data elicited in the Producer Survey.

differed in the products they provided, their size, and the extent of their market focus. Some properties offered both hunting and game viewing packages, whereas others relied specifically on only one of these packages. The operations differed greatly in size, from very small operations (less than 400 hectares) to reserves covering more than 10,000 hectares and considerably larger state-owned protected areas.

Though some properties assert that their objective is to maximize profits, a significant number are motivated by noneconomic objectives as well. The market remains largely in a start-up phase. Most of the properties surveyed had low occupancy rates and appear to be losing money. The public protected areas that have been established over a long period had higher occupancies and, though not covering their full costs, tourist operations provide a high degree of cost recovery for land and biodiversity management functions.

The chapter is structured as follows. The survey design and data collection are documented, followed by a report on the characteristics of the businesses surveyed. Descriptive statistics that are analyzed include business size (property area, number of tourist beds, and employment figures), business orientation, and competitive business strategies. The chapter then assesses the profitability of these enterprises, presenting the results for capital structure, revenues, cost structure, and returns on investment. A discussion of the significance of the findings concludes the chapter.

SURVEY QUESTIONNAIRE, SAMPLING, AND DATA COLLECTION

The survey questionnaire was designed to capture information to assess the profitability and management considerations of the reserves. In addition to introductory questions, the questionnaire included a set of questions regarding the management of the property. However, the bulk of the questionnaire was devoted to gathering financial information on the enterprise including:

Revenue

- Nonconsumptive uses (sale of game viewing safaris)

- Consumptive uses (sale of dead and live animals)

Costs

- Recurrent costs (salaries and wages, intermediate inputs)
- Capital costs (maintenance and depreciation)
- Opportunity costs

Assets

- Land, game, and physical infrastructure.

During July 2000, a pilot survey of two properties was conducted using personal interviews. Both survey questionnaires were successfully completed; however, survey interviews proved excessively lengthy (in excess of two hours each). The questionnaire format was revised to comprise three sections. Section A included general questions that did not require the presence of the survey enumerator. Section B elicited information that is available from standard business financial statements. Section C included questions for which the presence of the enumerator was considered necessary. The final survey questionnaires are available from the authors.

Sample

The study sample comprised 27 private and 3 public game reserves, including the same properties surveyed as part of the Ecological Study (chapter 6). All properties are located in the Zululand study area; 29 were in close proximity to the N2, the main North Coast road, around the towns of Hluhluwe, Mkhuze, and Pongola, and 1 was closer to Vryheid. Twenty-seven operations are privately owned, and 3 are KwaZulu-Natal Nature Conservation Services (KZNNCS) reserves. The extent to which financial and other information was obtained varied from property to property and across the data set. As a result, the sample size for the different questions varies, and this is indicated in the tables that present the results of the survey.

Data Collection

Each of the businesses in the survey sample was faxed, emailed, or hand delivered sections A and B in advance of the survey interview appointment. Managers were requested to self-complete section A before the interview was conducted. Managers were given an option to self-complete section B before the interview, to complete it during the interview, or to provide copies of financial statements so that the enumerator could complete it after the interview. Section C was completed during interviews for privately owned businesses; however, at their managements' insistence, all sections were self-completed by KZNNCS staff for the three public protected areas. Survey interviews were conducted in two waves, spaced two weeks apart. Managers unavailable for an interview during the first wave were, if possible, interviewed during the second wave. Telephones were used to interview managers who were not interviewed in person.

Responses to the survey by the managers varied. Two managers refused to participate in the survey, despite having participated in the Ecological Survey. One manager failed to attend an interview appointment. Several managers refused to furnish information from financial statements or did not have copies of their financial statements. Many managers did not complete sections A or B before the interview. If time constraints precluded completion of sections A or B in addition to section C during the interview, managers were requested to self-complete these sections following the interview and to return the completed questionnaire to the consultant.

Following completion of the second wave of survey interviews, businesses for which survey questionnaires were incomplete or outstanding were sent regular telephone and email reminders to complete and return the questionnaires. Overall response rates were less than ideal, which was not surprising given the sensitivity of the information involved and that a number of the properties were either still start-up operations (one was recovering from a devastating fire) or not being operated as a business per se. Ultimately, sufficient information was gathered to fully assess the operating profit of 15 properties, or half the original sample.

CONTEXT FOR THE GAME AND NATURE TOURISM INDUSTRY IN ZULULAND

In 1998 the total value of tourism in South Africa was estimated at R45 billion, of which ecotourism contributed approximately R2 billion a year (Falkena 2000). Falkena estimated that in 1998 approximately 80 percent

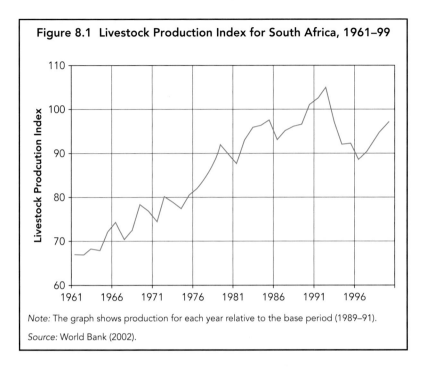

Figure 8.1 Livestock Production Index for South Africa, 1961–99

Note: The graph shows production for each year relative to the base period (1989–91).

Source: World Bank (2002).

of the income generated from game ranching was derived from hunting, 10 percent from game viewing and the export of venison, and 10 percent from live game sales. As was indicated above, the game industry in South Africa, and in the study area of Zululand, has grown rapidly during the past decade.

Several factors explain this growth in supply of privately owned game reserves. Possibly the most important factor, in line with world trends to liberalize markets, is that the agricultural sector has been increasingly subjected to the forces of the free market. Through the deregulation of agricultural control boards, including beef, the South African government has followed these trends. Figure 8.1 depicts the productivity of the livestock sector as a whole in South Africa over an almost 40-year time span. Deregulation of agriculture control boards, coupled with factors such as a decline in the real price of chicken relative to beef and changing health preferences, has resulted in the real price of beef showing a marked decline during the past decade.

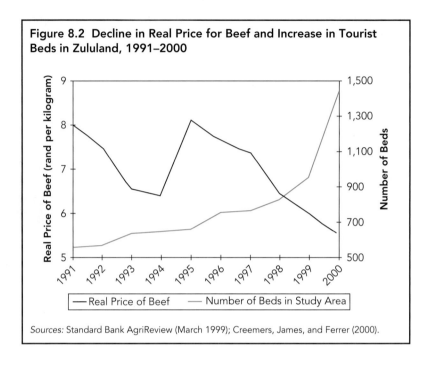

Figure 8.2 Decline in Real Price for Beef and Increase in Tourist Beds in Zululand, 1991–2000

Sources: Standard Bank AgriReview (March 1999); Creemers, James, and Ferrer (2000).

Figure 8.2 illustrates the trends of declining real beef prices and the simultaneous increase in number of tourist beds in the study area during the 1990s. The transformation of marginally profitable cattle land into game ranching areas was an attractive option for property holders in the region. Figure 8.3 shows the change in land area under reserves throughout the 1990s in Zululand. The public reserves saw no land being added to their area, yet the area under private reserves increased markedly during the decade. This land use transformation was supported by some experts' predictions that game- and nature-based tourism would be good performers in the economy and potentially large earners of foreign exchange (Falkena 2000). Thus the trend was away from cattle ranching and toward game ranching on privately owned farms. Ninety percent of the sample ranches included in the sample for this study were involved in raising cattle before transitioning to game ranching; of those, 15 percent continued to maintain a cattle operation alongside the game ranching at the time of the data survey.

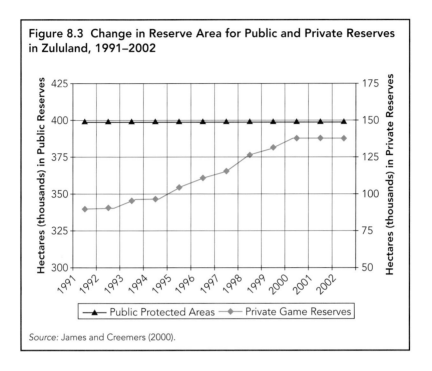

Figure 8.3 Change in Reserve Area for Public and Private Reserves in Zululand, 1991–2002

Source: James and Creemers (2000).

CHARACTERISTICS OF GAME RESERVES AND PROTECTED AREAS

A broad spectrum of game ranching businesses was encountered during the survey. Firms were found to vary considerably in size, business orientation, and business strategy. Accordingly, considerable variation was observed in businesses' capital structures, revenues, costs, and profits. The basic analysis provided in this section presents statistics describing the game business sampled in Zululand.

Size of the Enterprise

Measurements of size for game ranching businesses include property size, number of tourist beds provided, number of permanent employees, and business turnover. This section addresses the first three of these indicators of business size. Turnover is considered later in the chapter.

Table 8.1 Area of Game Reserves by Ownership and Size, 2000

Category	Number of Properties (N)	Mean Area of Properties (hectares)
Privately owned	27	4,028
Bed and breakfast	1	120
Small	8	682
Medium-size	12	1,782
Large	6	13,632
KZN Wildlife	3	54,546

KZN = Kwazulu-Natal.

Note: Small properties were classified as those less than 1,000 hectares, medium-size properties as those between 1,000 and 4,000 hectares, and large properties as those greater than 4,000 hectares.

Source: Data in this, and subsequent, tables are derived from the survey of public and private game reserves undertaken as part of the Producer Survey.

Property Area

The operations in the study area varied greatly in size, measured as area of land. To compare and contrast different game reserves in the study area, the properties were grouped into small, medium-size, and large farms (see table 8.1). Additionally, a fourth classification was used: bed and breakfast (B&B). This is for very small properties (under 200 hectares) that are unlikely to maintain any wild game on the property.

Of the 27 private operations, 30 percent were small properties, with an average area of 682 hectares. Medium-size properties made up the bulk of the private operations (44 percent), with a mean area of 1,782 hectares. The large properties (22 percent of privately owned properties) showed a marked increase in mean area to 13,632 hectares. The state-owned reserves had the largest mean area of land, with an average of 54,546 hectares. The overall mean area of the properties studied (9,080 hectares) is heavily biased upward by the extremely large areas of the three state-owned game reserves in the sample.

Mean farm area of land for all private game reserves surveyed falls just barely into the large size category (above 4,000 hectares), suggesting that large or larger medium-size properties predominate in the area. Reasons for this may be that large or larger medium-size game reserves are sizable enough to spread fixed costs over a sufficient area, but small enough to not require the level and intensity of management that small and very large properties require (Du P. Bothma 1996). Alternatively, it may simply reflect the size of the cattle farms that existed previously.

Table 8.2 Average Number of Beds and Beds per Hectare on Properties by Size Category

Category (N)	Beds per Property	Beds per Hectare
Bed and breakfast (1)	16	0.133
Small (8)	26	0.042
Medium-size (12)	24	0.017
Large (6)	41	0.004
KZN Wildlife (3)	270	0.006

Source: Producer Survey.

Under the current regime in South Africa, the sale of property provides the government the opportunity to purchase the property for the purposes of meeting land claims. This may create resistance, or a barrier, to the sale of property. Instead, properties may participate in leases and in joint ventures.

Number of Beds

A second measure of physical size of a game ranching operation is the number of tourist beds that it provides. Total number of beds on B&B, small, medium-size, large privately owned game reserves, and on state-owned game reserves differs both in terms of average number of beds per property and beds per hectare. Findings are reported in table 8.2.

As expected, beds per hectare decrease with property area. It would also be expected that average beds per property would increase with property area. The data show that as average property size goes up, so generally does the average number of beds per property in a size category. However, the difference in average bed numbers per property is rather small between small and medium-size properties. This implies that businesses on smaller properties are opting for more intensive tourism trade and are therefore catering for more tourists. Many of these smaller operations are partially reliant on state-owned game reserves for providing game viewing to clients. Figure 8.4 depicts bed densities across the private reserves based on the different sizes of properties.

On average, large properties have only about twice the number of beds as B&B and small properties, despite being about 17 times bigger in area. This may indicate that the larger businesses are keeping tourist densities low in order to provide a higher quality of service to their clients.

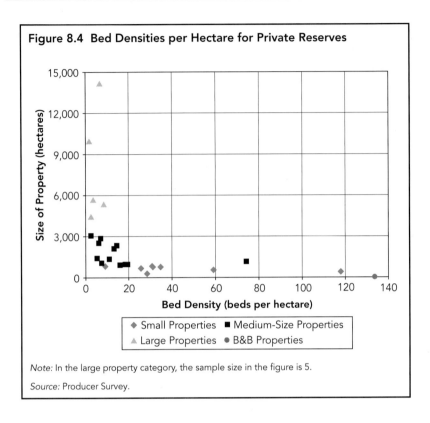

Figure 8.4 Bed Densities per Hectare for Private Reserves

Note: In the large property category, the sample size in the figure is 5.

Source: Producer Survey.

The lower the number of clients, the more personalized the service provided (personal communication, various survey respondents, 2000). Additionally, this lower tourism density is consistent with the type of tourism experience that is being marketed to the clients. A lower density of beds can foster more of a wilderness or adventure experience, or allow for more of a luxury experience. The state-owned reserves had the highest average number of beds per operation. The bed density per hectare at state-owned reserves was similar to those encountered at large privately owned reserves.

Job Creation

Job creation is another important indicator of economic size. Game ranching can potentially provide employment for all sectors of the community. Eloff (1999) estimated that 5,500 jobs are generated from foreign hunting in South Africa, with an average of 7 to 8 people

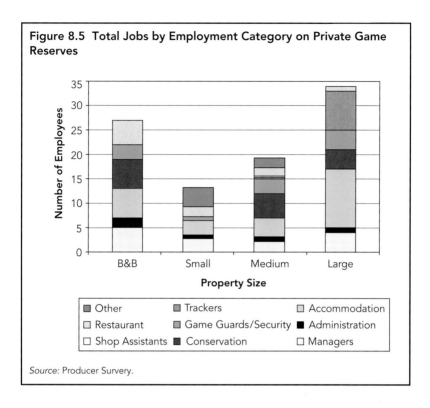

Figure 8.5 Total Jobs by Employment Category on Private Game Reserves

Source: Producer Survery.

employed per safari operator. In total, approximately 49,000 jobs are created on privately owned game reserves in the country, with an average of 7 employees per reserve.

Survey respondents were asked to classify laborers into a number of employment categories, as reported in figure 8.5. The total number of jobs created by game ranches was found to increase with property area. Larger operations tend to employ more labor. Average rates of employment on privately owned game reserves compare favorably with those reported by Eloff (1999) for South African hunting operations. This may be attributed to the partial game viewing focus of all the operations surveyed in this study. It is expected that game viewing is generally more service intensive than hunting.

Table 8.3 provides a breakdown of the employee numbers for each size of property. The B&B category stands out as an outlier, probably due to a factor indicated above, namely that the type of product or game reserve experience being offered to tourists would be a determinant

Table 8.3 Average Employment Levels and Employment Intensities on Private Reserves by Size Category

Size Category (N)	Average Number of Employees	Employees per Hectare	Average Number of Employees per Bed
Bed and breakfast (1)	27	0.225	1.69
Small (4)	13	0.019	0.49
Medium-size (7)	17	0.010	1.16
Large (1)	34	0.006	0.74

KZN = Kwazulu-Natal.

Note: Information on employment numbers were not received from KZN Wildlife.

Source: Producer Survey.

Table 8.4 Average Employment Levels and Employment Intensities on Private Reserves by Price Category

Price Category[a] (N)	Average Number of Employees	Employees per Hectare	Average Number of Employees per Bed	Average Price per Bed
Low (5)	11	0.012	0.70[b]	120
Medium (3)	18	0.009	0.61	319
High (5)	25	0.058	1.42	885

[a]Price per bed is as follows: low = less than R200 per bed per night, medium = R200–500 per bed per night, and high = more than R500 per bed per night.
[b]The average number of employees per bed on low-priced reserves includes a property that began operating in 1999 and is not yet operating at the planned number of beds. If this indicator is recalculated using this reserve's planned number of beds, the average number of employees per bed drops to 0.50.

Source: Producer Survey.

of the number of people employed. Table 8.4 reflects the employment intensity of an operation based on the price of its tourism product. Price can be seen as one indicator of the type of product offered. A "wilderness experience" tourism package can vary in quantity and quality of amenities and services included, and so package cost ranges from an inexpensive budget offering to a luxury product.

As the price of the tourism product goes up, so also does the average number of people employed on a property. It can be expected that a higher number and level of amenities and services included in a product will require more employment input. Though it could be expected that higher prices for tourism packages would support an increased

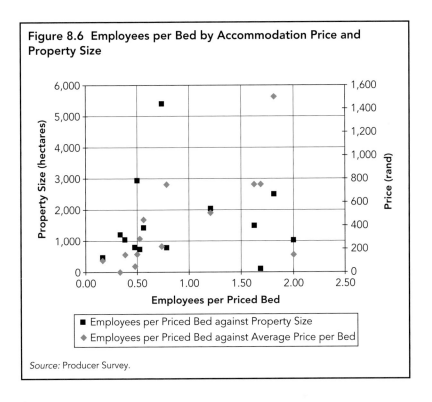

Figure 8.6 Employees per Bed by Accommodation Price and Property Size

Source: Producer Survey.

level of game and land management, not all of these amenities and services will be related to the game aspect of the package.

Thus, an increase in the product price may not correspond to a proportional increase in expenditures or employment in the conservation element of a game reserve. These data are represented graphically in figure 8.6, which shows that as the price goes up, the number of employees per bed also increases. The number of employees per bed, however, will not necessarily be directly related to property size because of a number of factors. A large property may choose to market a luxury product replete with a wide array of labor-intensive services and amenities.

On average, more managers are employed on smaller properties than on medium-size properties, with the most management staff being employed on large properties. From a conservation perspective, management requirements are expected to increase with property size. However, smaller game reserves tend to require more intensive management because natural conditions are harder to achieve on smaller properties (for example, natural movements of game may be restricted due to fences; Du P. Bothma 1996). This rate of increase is expected to be less than proportional.

The large proportion of accommodation services staff—cleaning, laundry, and gardening—in all property sizes reveals the strong emphasis on tourism in the game ranching industry in Zululand. As expected, large properties with more tourist beds employ relatively more of this staff category. The data show that as property size increases, more staff is devoted to conservation fieldwork. The average number of this staff category is higher for the medium-size property category (average conservation staff is 5) than for the large property category (average conservation staff is 4). The number of security staff also increases with property size.

The labor trends in the game ranching industry in Zululand suggest that in terms of employment, the industry is contributing significantly to economic uplift. However, if viewed in terms of jobs per hectare, the industry is relatively nonintensive. Small properties employ on average 0.019 people per hectare, medium-size properties 0.012 people per hectare, and large properties only 0.006 people per hectare. In comparison with other land uses in the area, such as sugarcane production, this represents a low utilization of labor per hectare.

Another comparison that should be investigated further is the level of relative employment on public versus private game reserves. The data given above cover only the private sector. If there is a difference in the employment intensity between public and private reserves, then it could be useful to also compare the income levels for employees across the public and private sectors. As far as the contribution that nature tourism can make to local economic development is concerned, it should be identified whether more people are employed on private reserves and at what wage level relative to the public reserves. It then needs to be established what will contribute relatively more to local development, few highly paid jobs or more low-paid jobs.

Business Orientation and Management Strategy

Another way to characterize the properties in the sample is on the basis of how the property holders view their game reserves as businesses. This is also of central importance when considering these operations as

Table 8.5 Managers' Description of Their Business Orientation, 2000

Description	Number of Managers	Percentage of Total
More a business than a way of life	9	39
Equally a business and a way of life	11	48
More a way of life than a business	3	13

Source: Producer Survey.

contributing to biological conservation, because profitability and conservation are unlikely to be fully compatible—although, as chapter 6 pointed out, private game reserves are providing important conservation benefits in the study area. Of the managers surveyed on private reserves, 39 percent saw their operations as being more of a business than a way of life. Of the other managers, 48 percent saw their operation as being equally a business and a way of life, whereas only 13 percent saw their operations as being more a way of life than a business (table 8.5). This latter category reflects those owners or managers who have invested in game ranching more as a hobby than as an investment.

Description of Farm Goals
Operational goals can be described as milestones that a business attempts to achieve, to gauge whether a not the business is moving toward its long-term mission or vision. Goals will differ according to the type of business and the long-term vision or mission.

Five important operational goals identified for the game- and nature-based tourism industry were to:

- Protect threatened species and natural habitats

- Maximize profitability and returns on investments

- Expand the size of the game- and nature-based tourism enterprise

- Reduce business risks—that is, risks that are inherent to the business independent of the way in which it is financed (for example, such social risks as labor problems), and

- Reduce financial risks—that is, variability in net cash flows due to fixed obligations associated with debt financing (for example, fluctuating interest rates).

Table 8.6 Importance of Operational Goals to Managers of Private Game Reserves (percentage selecting each ranking of importance)

Goal	Ranking of Importance (1 = highest)				
	1	2	3	4	5
Protect threatened species	61	9	4	17	9
Maximize profits	26	17	35	9	13
Expand operation	9	26	13	17	35
Reduce business risk	4	17	22	44	13
Reduce financial risk	0	31	26	13	30

Note: Rows sum to 100 percent.

Source: Producer Survey.

Managers of privately owned reserves were required to rank these goals in order of importance, where 1 represented the most important goal and 5 represented the least important goal. Table 8.6 reports the number of respondents, in terms of percentages, that ranked the goals at the different levels of importance. Protection of threatened species and natural habitat ranks as the most important farm goal for the majority of operations. Maximizing profitability seems to rank as the second most important (one of three most important goals for 78 percent of operations). It is of some concern that 26 percent of respondents ranked protection of threatened species as fourth or fifth most important, suggesting a willingness to sacrifice biological integrity for increased short-run profits.

Expansion of the operation and reducing business and financial risks ranked as relatively less important objectives. A reduction in business risk seems to be less important to game reserve managers than a reduction in financial risks. This can be expected since game farming operations are frequently financed initially with borrowed capital (Behr and Groenewald 1990b; Barnes and De Jager 1996). The greater the fixed obligations associated with debt financing, the more vulnerable the business is to financial risks due to fluctuating interest rates and variability in net cash flows, even in low-income years.

Description of Personal Goals

Personal goals of the principal decisionmaker and organizational goals should be closely related so that the long-term objectives of the business

Table 8.7 Importance of Personal Goals to Managers of Private Game Reserves (percentage selecting each ranking of importance)

Goal	Ranking of Importance (1 = highest)				
	1	2	3	4	5
Best game farmer	45	18	23	9	5
Best tourism operator	27	27	18	23	5
Community leadership	0	9	9	27	54
More free time	19	14	9	36	23
Pass farm on	9	32	41	5	13

Note: Rows sum to 100 percent.

Source: Producer Survey.

can be achieved. Five important personal goals identified that related to the game- and nature-based tourism industry were to:

- Become the best game farmer in the area
- Become the best tourism operator in the area
- Achieve community leadership positions
- Have more free time for family and leisure, and
- Pass farms on to future generations.

Respondents were asked to rank these goals in order of importance, where 1 is the most important goal and 5 is the least important goal. Table 8.7 reports the number of managers, in terms of percentages, that ranked the goals at the different levels of importance.

The majority of respondents (63 percent) ranked "becoming the best game farmer in the area" as their first or second most important personal goal. This correlates with the high ranking of conservation in the operational goals (table 8.6) and shows that operational goals and personal goals are related. "Becoming the best tourism operator in the area" also ranked high, with 54 percent of managers placing this goal in the two most important. This accords with "maximizing profitability" ranking high among organizational goals (table 8.6).

If a reserve provides the best tourism experience in the area, the reserve's competitiveness will increase, and therefore its profits will be maximized. The "achievement of community leadership positions" and

Table 8.8 Self-Rating of Management and Business Skills by Managers of Private Game Reserves

Management Skill	Mean Ranking by Size of Reserve[a]		
	Small	Medium-Size	Large
Interpersonal dealings with clients	4.7	4.3	4.0
Conservation	3.8	4.5	4.5
Marketing	3.2	2.5	2.5
Farm finance	3.5	3.9	3.5
Human resource management	3.8	4.1	4.0
Overall management	3.8	4.3	4.0

[a]In rankings, 1 indicates a very low rating and 5 indicates a very high rating.

Source: Producer Survey.

"having more free time" ranked as being relatively less important personal goals. The "passing on of game reserves to future generations" was found to be considered important as a secondary goal, with 73 percent of the managers interviewed ranking it as their second or third most important goal.

Ranking of Management Ability

Managers were required to rank certain management and business skills. The ranking of these skills provides an indication of management ability on the game reserves surveyed, although bias can be expected to accompany such self-reporting. Table 8.8 reports how the management skills were ranked in the different property categories.

The results indicate that smaller operations tend to be a lot more client oriented. Both interpersonal dealings with clients and marketing skills are ranked the highest out of the three privately owned property categories. The ranking of interpersonal dealings with clients decreased as operation size increased, implying that larger operations pay relatively less attention to clients than smaller operations. This is as expected, because larger operations have greater numbers of clients, and therefore it is more difficult to provide every client with personalized attention. Conversely, in smaller operations, the smaller numbers of clients allow managers to spend more time dealing directly with individuals.

Though the smaller operations seem to have a greater client focus, the medium-size and larger operations have better skills in conservation and human resource management. Generally, it is expected that conservation and human resource management skills are required as property area and labor force size increase.

Marketing and financial management skills tend to be ranked lower than other management skills. Smaller operations appear to have better marketing skills. The ranking of financial skills did not vary much among the three categories. The majority of managers interviewed consider their management teams to be competent in financial management. On the whole, managers of privately owned game reserves consider themselves competent in most aspects of reserve management, but they rank their marketing and financial skills below their conservation, interpersonal, and human resource management skills.

Main Competitive Strategies

The competitive strategy of a business can be defined as the approach that a business uses to build a sustainable advantage over its competitors to achieve its objectives and vision. The strategy chosen is based on the competitive advantage pursued and the scope of the target market. The competitive advantage is gained either through low-cost leadership (providing products at low prices), or through differentiation (providing unique products). The target market pursued can be broadly defined or focused.

The game reserves in Zululand use a number of different strategies to gain a competitive advantage. Due to the large number of operations in the area, competition is high in the game- and nature-based tourism industry. Therefore, the choice of strategy is pivotal to an operation's success.

Findings from the survey suggest that half of the small operations and the majority of medium-size operations are concentrating on broad market differentiation. This strategy entails marketing and selling unique tourism products to a broad cross-section of clients. Operations adopting this strategy will attempt to attract tourists from across the spectrum (for example, foreign and local) and offer different products (for example, horseback riding) to gain a competitive advantage.

The other half of the smaller operations and all larger operations adopted a best-cost strategy. This strategy is a hybrid of a number of other strategies, and operations adopting this strategy attempt to provide "value for money" to gain competitive advantage.

Focused differentiation is also commonly adopted by medium-size operations. This strategy differs from the previous strategy type only by the narrower scope of the target market; hence, these operations gain competitive advantage by focusing on niche markets, while providing unique products. In most cases, this strategy allows an operation to increases prices and therefore profits.

The medium-size property category showed the most differentiation in the types of competitive strategy adopted. This can be expected, because a majority of operations in Zululand fall into this category and therefore the achievement of a competitive advantage is made more difficult, leading to the adoption of several different strategies. Besides the strategies already discussed, focused, lowest-cost provider and customized strategies were adopted by some medium-size operations. The former strategy focuses on a niche market but attempts to gain a competitive advantage by keeping prices and costs low. The customized strategy provides "customized products" and attempts to gain a competitive advantage by providing clients with exactly the product that they desire. Of the other operations in this category, 11 percent had not given the strategy much thought, whereas another 11 percent would not divulge their strategy and were therefore classified as "other."

Main Sources of Risk

For reserve operators, risk consists of business and financial risk. Business risk refers to risks that are inherent in the business independent of the way in which it is financed (for example, labor problems, weather, and game prices). Financial risk refers to risks the business faces due to debt repayment obligations (for example, fluctuating interest rates). Both forms of risk play an extremely important role in the decisionmaking process. Managers of the game reserves in the sample were asked to identify important sources of risk to their operations. Table 8.9 reports the five most important identified sources of risk.

Clearly, crime and a declining tourist demand are considered to be the most important sources of risk for the game- and nature-based tourism industry in Northeastern KwaZulu-Natal. These sources of risk are related, because a crime increase in the region is likely to result in reduced tourism demand. Also, as will be shown in the following section (which reviews the capital structure of game reserves), investment

Table 8.9 Important Sources of Risk for Private Game Reserves

Source	Percentage of Reserves for which Source Is Important
Crime	91
Declining tourist demand	73
Risk of malaria outbreak	27
Land expropriation concerns	27
Changes in the cost of labor	27

Source: Producer Survey.

in land is a substantial portion of a property's overall investment. Thus, the risk of losing private land through expropriation could have an effect on a property owner's willingness to invest in game conservation. The direction of the effect will depend directly on the land policies set out by the government.

ECONOMICS OF THE GAME INDUSTRY

Data on financial inflows and outflows, as well as on fixed assets, were collected from private reserve operators via the questionnaire. Because data collection occurred in 2000, data were for that year or the most recent financial year for the operation. In the case of the public reserves, information on revenues and expenditures come from 2000–2001 financial year statements received after the data collection phase of the study. This was essential, because much of the information, in particular the land management and overhead expenditure amounts, are managed centrally and not by the reserves themselves. Asset information for the KZN Wildlife properties was drawn from material collected via the interview process.

Capital Structure

Reserve managers were interviewed regarding the fixed costs of capital input, primarily land, game, and physical infrastructure (roads, buildings, vehicles, and fencing). The variability in the quality of the physical infrastructure information, combined with sustained and significant local rates of price inflation, made it difficult to place much confidence in the figures obtained. As a result, the results are presented here only for land and game, which appear to make up about 60 percent to 70 percent of investment costs for these operations (on the basis of the rough estimates of physical infrastructure investment costs that were obtained).

Land

Land prices are expected to differ according to the potential tourism potential of the property (Falkena 2000). Other factors such as the location of the property and its ecological carrying capacity—which is directly related to the condition of the property—may also affect land prices. In general, it is expected that larger game reserves are more valuable but have lower per-hectare land values than smaller game reserves in a similar ecological area (Falkena 2000).

The survey of privately owned game reserves in Zululand found little difference in land prices between the different-size properties, with the exception of the one B&B operation, which predictably had a much higher land price. On average, quoted land prices were on the order of R3000 per hectare or about US$430 per hectare in 2000 dollars (table 8.10).

Livestock

Game ranching business is highly dependent on game species and stocking rates. Table 8.11 reports the value of game on game ranches by property size, calculated using KZN Game Auction prices for the year 2000. The average value of game generally increases with increasing property area, averaging from almost R3.1 million on smaller properties to R11 million on large properties and R490 million at Hluhluwe-Umfolozi Park (HUP).

Table 8.10 Land Values of Private Game Reserves

Property Size Category (N)	Average Land Price (rand per hectare)	Average Land Asset Value (rand)
Bed and breakfast (1)	12,500	1,500,000
Small (7)	2,864	2,037,371
Medium-size (12)	2,942	4,452,650
Large (5)	3,027	37,291,089

Source: Producer Survey.

Table 8.11 Value of Game on Reserves

Size Category (N)	Total Value of Game (millions of rand)	Value of Game per Hectare (rand per hectare)	Value of Game as a Percentage of Land Value
Bed and breakfast (1)	0.17	1,448	12
Small (7)	3.1	4,249	167
Medium-size (11)	2.6	1,659	55
Large (5)	11.0	1,142	51
KZN Wildlife (1)[a]	490.0	5,075	—

—Not applicable.
[a]The only property for which game values were calculated was Hluhluwe-Umfolozi Park.

Source: Producer Survey.

Game values per hectare were found to decline on privately owned game reserves as area increased, suggesting that smaller properties tend to be better stocked (or more overstocked) with more valuable game species than larger game reserves. On average, the value of game on small game reserves is well above 150 percent of the value of the operation's land, declining to approximately 55 percent on medium-size properties and 51 percent on large game reserves. The value of game in HUP, expressed on a per-hectare basis, exceeds that of all other game reserves surveyed due to the high densities of black and white rhinoceroses on this game reserve.

According to James and Goodman (2000), the private game reserves surveyed, and in particular the smaller properties, tend to be severely overstocked, while stocking rates at the state-owned game reserves are acceptable. This suggests that the privately owned operations are overstocking to provide more photographic and hunting opportunities (demonstrating an objective of increasing short-run profitability), whereas KZN Wildlife is primarily concerned with a conservation objective.

Revenue

Revenue from operations is discussed first in terms of the activity from which it is derived. Then the totals are assessed by property type.

Sources of Revenue

Revenue is generated in a number of ways on game reserves: through hunting, which includes both trophy or animal fees and daily rates;

Table 8.12 Annual Revenue Sources for Game Reserves in South Africa, 1999

Source of Revenue	Revenue Generated (rand)	Contribution to Total Revenue (percent)
Foreign hunting	182,299,656	23
Local hunting	450,000,000	57
Live sales	150,000,000	19
Sale of venison	10,000,002	1
Total	792,299,658	100

Source: Eloff (1999).

game viewing; the sale of tourism-related products (such as day trips to other attractions outside of the operation's boundaries); by retail outlets (such as a restaurant); and the sale of live game (Du P. Bothma 1996, Falkena 2000). Some properties will also generate revenue from outsourced activities, such as a charge for a professional hunter to bring clients onto a property and hunt. A survey by Eloff (1999) showed that in South Africa as a whole, hunting revenues were the major income source (see table 8.12); however, he did not consider revenues earned from game viewing.

Of the 29 operations studied in Zululand, 80 percent had hunting on the property. Of the privately owned properties, approximately 75 percent of the small game reserves offered hunting, and about 85 percent of medium-size game reserves and all of the large privately owned game reserves had some form of hunting. This contrasts with Barnes and De Jager's (1996) findings that in Namibia the trend was that larger game reserves were being used predominantly for nonconsumptive game viewing, whereas the smaller game reserves were devoted to hunting.

Behr and Groenewald (1990a), however, showed that in relation to the other provinces, Natal and Transvaal game farmers were more likely to provide hunting. This is probably related to the favorable climate, the vegetation, and the wide diversity of popular trophy species found in the area. The larger the farm, the greater the diversity of species and the more favorable it is to hunters. Furthermore, the focus on hunting is as expected, owing to the higher potential revenue it attracts.

Revenue sources for the properties in the sample are given in table 8.13, according to property size. Small, medium-size, and large game reserves in the KwaZulu-Natal study area had the highest percentage of revenue

Table 8.13 Sources of Revenue on Game Reserves According to Property Size (percent)

Size Category (N)	Game Viewing	Hunting	Other Tourist Products	Retail Operations	Live Game Sales	Outsourced Activities
Bed and breakfast (1)	72.0	0	20.0	8.0	0	0
Small (5)	27.6	34.3	5.0	14.3	9.3	9.3
Medium-size (7)	20.8	49.5	2.3	3.9	21.2	1.0
Large (4)	34.9	48.2	14.1	2.6	0.1	0.2
KZN Wildlife (1)	28.6	0	5.9	17.4	47.9	0.2

Note: Figures are expressed as percentage of total revenue, so rows total 100%.

Source: Producer Survey.

coming from hunting, followed closely by the income from game viewing. The very small B&B property relied overwhelmingly on game viewing for its revenue, and though the large state reserve did draw a bit more than 25 percent of its revenue from game viewing, the largest proportion of its revenue came from live game sales.

For all the privately owned game reserves surveyed, 29 percent of the revenue is generated by game viewing, 42 percent by hunting tourism, 7 percent by other products available to tourists and by retail outlets on the farms, 3 percent through outsourced activities, and the residual, 12 percent, through the sale of live game. For all game reserves surveyed, including the state-owned property, game viewing contributes almost one-third (29 percent) to total revenue generated; hunting contributes approximately 40 percent; tourist-related products, 7 percent; retail operations, 8 percent; and outsourced activities, 3 percent. The residual of 14 percent is generated through the sale of live game.

This result has a number of implications. First, it is evident that though game viewing is an important source of revenue for game reserves in Zululand, hunting is a very strong component overall. This is in line with results of studies conducted elsewhere in South Africa that identified hunting as the primary source of revenue in the game ranching industry (Du P. Bothma 1996; Eloff 1999; Behr and Groenewald 1990a). However, the overall averages do mask a wide variety across properties in different size categories.

Second, the contribution to total revenue from the sale of live game varies widely across different property sizes. Although medium-size

Table 8.14 Sources of Revenue on Game Reserves by Market Objective

Property Type (N)	Game Viewing	Hunting	Other Tourist Products	Retail Operations	Live Game Sales	Outsourced Activities
Strictly game viewing (5)	64.4	0.2	7.3	10.3	17.7	0.05
Strictly hunting (1)	0	93.0	0	0	7.0	0
Both (12)	16.8	51.4	7.2	6.9	12.3	4.5

Source: Producer Survey.

private reserves rely on live game sales for one-fifth of their revenues, the large private reserves surveyed showed an extremely low reliance on live game sales for revenue, though both property sizes do draw about half of their revenues from hunting. Larger reserves may see the revenue stream from hunting as a better option than live game sales and so maintain their stocks for hunting. For medium-size reserves and public reserves that have significant revenue streams from live game sales, this may reflect the ongoing growth of conservation as a land use in the region (and other parts of Southern Africa that source high-value species, in particular the rhinoceros, at the annual KZN Wildlife game auction).

An alternative way to view the breakdown in revenues is to consider the type of operation the property runs: strictly game viewing, a mix of game viewing and hunting, or strictly hunting. Table 8.14 provides a breakdown of revenue streams for different types of operations. Where both game viewing and hunting are offered, about half of total revenue comes from hunting. One element to consider in hunting revenue is that the income often depends on the value of the animal shot. High-value trophy species may bring in disproportionately more income from hunting, even with lower client numbers, than game viewing or low-value trophy species.

Occupancy

Occupancy rates for the properties, both private and public, are presented below. Three sources of occupancy rates exist for the set of properties in Table 8. 15. The first occupancy rate is taken directly from occupancy figures provided in the Ecological Survey. Here the state-owned property

Table 8.15 Occupancy Rates for Game Reserves (percentage of total bed nights) Compared with Accommodation Revenue (percentage of total gross revenue)

Size Category (N)	Occupancy Rate (source: Ecological Survey)	Occupancy Rate (source: Producer Survey Questionnaire)	Occupancy Rate (source: derived from revenue data of the Producer Survey Questionnaire)	Accommodation Revenue as Percentage of Total Gross Revenue	Gross Revenue per Hectare (rand)
Bed and Breakfast (1)	40	37	27	72	13,889
Small (4)	26	11	9	45	684
Medium (6)	8	24	16	47	254
Large (3)	45	37	33	61	1,094
KZN Wildlife (1)	82	15	47	29	455

Note: The occupancy rate derived from Producer Survey Revenue Data is calculated as (Accommodation Revenue/Average Price per Bed)/(Total Number of Beds * 365). The Accommodation Revenue equals revenues reported for only Phototourism and Hunting Packages in the Producer Survey.

Sources: Ecological Survey, appendix 3, table A3.29. Producer Survey; data on average price of accommodation is taken from the World Bank Database Report, appendix 6.

exhibits the highest occupancy rate of all properties. The Producer Survey also directly solicited information on occupancy rates; however, the explicit occupancy data were incomplete in some cases and not always provided along with types of accommodation and total bed numbers. Third, occupancy rates can be derived indirectly by using reported accommodation revenue. Accommodation revenue is divided by the average price per bed. In turn, this result is divided by the total number of bed nights on a property (number of beds multiplied by 365). This third set of data was more often available than direct occupancy numbers. However, there is substantial variability on occupancy rates for different-size properties across these three methods.

Table 8.15 also shows what percentage of gross revenue comes from accommodation for different property size. The smallest properties are most likely to be more reliant on accommodation revenues (as evidenced by the percentage for the B&B property), because they may not have large areas or stocks for game viewing or hunting. The profitability of properties when accommodation revenue makes up a large percentage of total gross revenue will most likely be more sensitive to fluctuations in tourist demand. This relates also to the sources of revenue for different-size properties, as laid out in table 8.13. For the KZN Wildlife category, almost half of revenue comes from live game sales, and thus is unrelated to occupancy rates and direct tourism demand. Larger properties may be able to diversify their revenue streams beyond a strong reliance on accommodation revenue. Thus, for properties where accommodation demand is important to profitability, there will likely be greater focus on management activities that are seen as contributing to meeting tourist requirements for satisfactory game ranch experiences. (See the previous section "Business Orientation and Management Strategies.")

Income

Falkena (2000) estimates gross farm income per hectare in a similar ecological region as the study area to be R535 on a small game reserve, R1,443 on a medium-size reserve, and R1,751 on a large reserve. This implies that, in terms of revenue generated, larger farms are expected to have a greater turnover per hectare than smaller farms. Income trends

Table 8.16 Average Gross Income (rand)

Property Size (N)	Gross Income	Gross Income per Hectare
Bed and breakfast (1)	1,666,700	13,889
Small (6)	524,312	718
Medium-size (8)	859,610	528
Large (4)	10,393,716	826
KZN Wildlife (3)	23,035,831	386

Source: Producer Survey.

on the properties studied, reported in table 8.16, show that smaller reserves generated more revenue per hectare than medium-size and KZN Wildlife reserves. The trend is otherwise consistent with Falkena's findings for income generated per hectare, although values are less than half the magnitude of those found by Falkena.

The low figure for medium-size reserves in comparison with the smaller properties may simply reflect a combination of bed densities, pricing structures, and actual occupancy rates of those properties for which data were available. However, it is also possible that this trend reflects the reliance of smaller operations in Zululand on state-owned game reserves for providing game viewing experiences.

As part of their trip, the private operator often takes visitors on day trips to the public reserves. This adds to the operator's gross turnover without a corresponding investment in land. This observation is supported by the figures presented in table 8.13 that show medium-size properties as the ones that seem to least exploit the game viewing market, with game viewing contributing only 21 percent to total farm revenue. In other words, reliance on hunting and live game sales as evidenced by the medium-size properties produce lower turnover than the alternative strategy of relying on public assets for game viewing.

In the case of the public KZN Wildlife Reserves, the low returns are likely to reflect the low bed densities (as shown in table 8.2) and the low accommodation prices (average prices at KZN reserves are similar to those at the medium-size properties). The high income figures for the B&B category highlight the income-intensive use it makes of its land. The B&B is likely to be even more—if not completely—reliant on the public reserves for providing game viewing attractions.

Cost Structure

As part of the survey, private game reserve managers were asked to provide data about the full gamut of annual expenditures. These included labor and other variable annual costs such as yearly licenses, fees, and services; physical inputs to the business; marketing; utilities; and other overhead costs. Depreciation costs are excluded from the analysis because the quality of these figures varied considerably (see also the observation above regarding difficulties with the figures for fixed investment in physical infrastructure). For the private game reserves, then, the analysis centers on the variable cost component of total expenditures, which is separated into labor and nonlabor costs.

In the case of the KZN Wildlife properties, the direct expenditures attributable to tourism operations on the reserves were obtained. However, in order to arrive at total expenditures attributable to the existence and functioning of the state reserves—the on-reserve costs—information on other inputs rendered directly to the reserves, such as land management and infrastructure maintenance, was also required.

In addition, a portion of line-item headquarters (off-reserve) costs, such as management, administration, and reservations, is attributable to each reserve in the system. The on-reserve but non-tourism-related expenditures were identified from the overall enterprise accounts with the assistance of KZN Wildlife. To estimate the off-reserve cost component, the total on-reserve costs from the three state reserves in the sample were used to calculate their individual share of total on-reserve costs for the whole KZN system. This percentage for each of the three reserves was applied to the total off-reserve or headquarters costs for the park system to obtain the estimated amount of off-reserve costs.

As would be expected, average total costs are higher for the substantially larger properties, but when looked at in per-hectare terms the costs are inversely related to property size (table 8.17). In part, this can be related to the fact that, as property size increases, the number of employees per hectare declines. (See table 8.3 for the trend in average number of employees per hectare on private game reserves.) Even on larger properties where the product on offer is a higher priced luxury wildlife experience, and so would be likely to have more employees per bed, the sheer size of the properties could "drown out" this effect.

Table 8.17 Annual Variable Expenditures, According to Property Size

Property Size (N)	Average Total Variable Expenditures		Average Labor Costs	
	(rand)	(rand per hectare)	(rand)	(rand per hectare)
Bed and breakfast (1)	1,668,600	13,905	450,600	3,755
Small (5)	555,006	725	224,403	294
Medium-size (7)	680,897	408	257,982	164
Large (1)	970,871	179	489,200	90
KZN Wildlife (3)	25,555,457	461	4,301,604	83

Source: Producer Survey.

The average number of beds per hectare (see table 8.2) also follows the same inverse relationship.

As was shown in the previous section, the income generated on a game reserve can usually be categorized according to a specific product. Yet many inputs to a game reserve may be used concurrently for hunting and nonconsumptive wildlife viewing; for example, drivers and trackers may be employed to assist photo safari tourists and later in the week to assist a trophy hunter. The attempt to attribute expenditures to purposes was therefore much less reliable than for revenues.

However, cost structures for different types of operations as a whole can be compared to identify trends. This is depicted in figure 8.7. For both single-purpose game viewing and mixed-purpose private reserves, the tendency is still clearly for per-hectare costs to decline with property size. No discernable difference in the pattern of this tendency could be noted between the two different types of game operation.

The price of accommodation is one characteristic of a game reserve product and can reveal some indication of potential labor input, and hence economic benefit for the local community through wages. Bed density (beds per hectare) is another characteristic of game reserve product that can potentially reveal some indication of management's emphasis on biodiversity conservation. The cost structures for farms with different bed densities may reflect a different emphasis placed on the type of wildlife experience that is intended. For example, a property that has a high bed density may be fostering more of a "B&B" experience as opposed to a property with a low bed density that aims for a "wilderness experience."

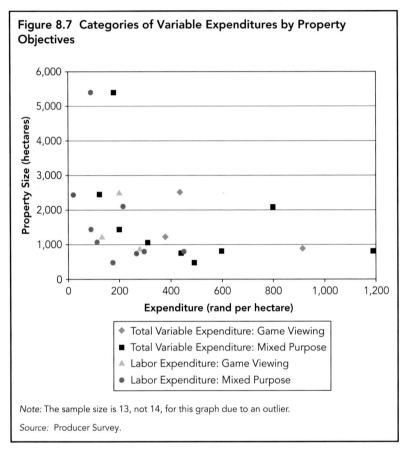

Figure 8.7 Categories of Variable Expenditures by Property Objectives

Note: The sample size is 13, not 14, for this graph due to an outlier.

Source: Producer Survey.

Where there is more emphasis on the wilderness experience in the product, there is likely a higher emphasis on land and game management. This would be reflected in rather disaggregated cost data, where the expenditures per hectare for land and game management would be higher on low-density properties relative to high-density ones of a similar size.

Figure 8.8 shows that for similar bed densities, it is possible to have a range of cost structures. The total and labor cost per hectare points for properties of both low and medium bed density are spread along the horizontal axis. A larger sample size would allow for comparing bed densities within each category of property size (B&B, small, medium-size, and large). Otherwise, property size can mask whether a variation in the per-hectare cost structure is due to sheer size or due to increased expenditures on costs related to land and game management.

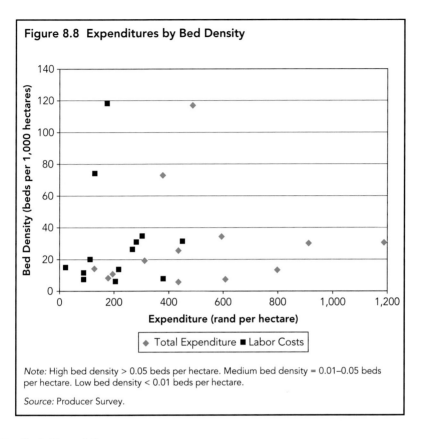

Figure 8.8 Expenditures by Bed Density

Note: High bed density > 0.05 beds per hectare. Medium bed density = 0.01–0.05 beds per hectare. Low bed density < 0.01 beds per hectare.

Source: Producer Survey.

Profitability of Reserves

Behr and Groenewald (1990a) predicted that game farming would probably not be a major South African agricultural enterprise in the future. Other studies have shown that game ranching is a relatively low-profit enterprise (Bond 1993; Barnes and Kalikawe 1994; Barnes and De Jager 1996). The low apparent profitability of game ranching can be attributed largely to the necessity of relatively high capital investment and poor market development (Barnes and De Jager 1996). Barnes and De Jager (1996) showed that in terms of financial profit, game ranches in Namibia only realized a net profit of N$9 per hectare in 1996. However, Behr and Groenewald (1990b) found that in 1985–86, certain South African game reserves on which predominantly trophy hunting took place earned a net farm income of as much as R8.6 per R100 capital invested in comparison with cattle farms in Natal, which earned R4.5 per R100 capital invested.

Net farm income, however, does not provide a complete measure of profitability, because it excludes debt-service expenses (interest payable plus principal debt repayments) and other foreign factor costs. Low cash return on capital is, therefore, a legitimate cause for concern (Behr and Groenewald 1990b). Eloff (cited in Nel 1991) showed, although not conclusively, that game ranches in South Africa earn as much as R53 per hectare annually, and return on capital invested was 3.6 percent a year.

It is noted that returns on game farming calculated in these studies considered only cash returns and omitted capital appreciation. Consequently, these predications of poor profitability make the game farming option seem unattractive to new investors. Strong growth in the area under conservation during the past decade suggests that, at least in the short term, higher returns on capital can be expected.

Net operating income is not an ideal measure of profitability because it excludes explicit consideration of investment costs of capital, but it does provide a given means of comparison between the properties studied. When rendered in per-hectare terms, the resulting profitability measure can then be compared with land acquisition costs or operating profit from competing activities as a preliminary indication of the current health and strength of the game reserve business.

The data in table 8.18 describe the profitability trends observed on the study properties. Smaller operations in the sample area are still in the red before consideration of investment costs. This may not be surprising, given that several of the properties are relatively newly converted (from cattle) and are still trying to market themselves and fill their beds (personal communication with landowners in Hluhluwe, South Africa, 2000). This result also corroborates Barnes and De Jager's (1996) findings that large-scale properties can be more efficient both financially and economically. Only the large properties in the above sample generated a positive annual operating income.

For the landed private game reserves included in the sample, net returns before investment increase with property size. Per hectare, the smaller reserves are in negative territory, at a shortfall of R100, whereas the medium-size properties show a small surplus of R18 and the large property a sizable profit of R471. Given the small sample size, these results should be taken as indicative rather than conclusive of the broader population.

Table 8.18 Profitability of Private Game Reserves and Public Protected Areas

Measure	Privately Owned Reserves (number of properties)				State-Owned Reserves (number of properties = 3)
	Bed and Breakfast (1)	Small (5)	Medium-Size (5)	Large (1)	
Per-reserve averages (millions of rand)					
Annual gross income	1.66	0.48	0.60	3.52	23.04
Annual variable expenditures	1.66	0.56	0.68	0.97	25.56
Annual net operating income	-0.002	-0.07	-0.009	2.55	-2.52
Per-reserve averages (rand per hectare)					
Annual gross income	13,889	624	379	651	386
Annual variable expenditures	13,905	725	362	179	461
Annual net operating income	-16	-100	18	471	-75
Game and land value (rand per hectare)	14,000	7,900	4,800	5,000[a]	8,600[b]

[a]Includes land value only.
[b]Figures are for Hluhluwe-Umfolozi Park only.

Source: Producer Survey.

The game and land values as shown are significant. If they are assumed to represent 60 percent to 70 percent of total fixed costs, they would be between R7,000 and R13,000 per hectare for the landed properties, or between US$1,000 to US$2,000 in 2000 prices. Clearly, the sample suggests that most properties are far from providing a sufficient return on capital invested, with the exception of the single large property that appears to be near to breaking even.

Net returns per hectare are larger for the large private game reserve (and the medium-size reserves) than for the state-owned game reserves, which record an average shortfall per hectare of R75. Differences in annual expenses account for this discrepancy. Annual costs per hectare on the large privately owned game reserve amount to R179, whereas state-owned reserves have expenditures of R461.

At first glance, this suggests that KZN Wildlife may be overspending and stands to increase profits greatly if its cost structures are reviewed. However, this may also be due to conflation of regulatory and reserve costs in the overall KZN Wildlife system. Other factors that may affect this comparison are lower wage rates in the private sector and the potential for underspending on conservation activities in private reserves.

In sum, this assessment of the profitability of Zululand private game reserves corroborates studies that have shown that game ranching is a low-profit, low-cash-return activity (Behr and Groenewald 1990a, 1990b; Bond 1993; Barnes and Kalikawe 1994). In the case of the KZN Wildlife reserves, it is clear that revenues from tourism and game sales come respectably close to covering the full costs of conservation.

CONCLUSIONS

Perhaps the most important finding of the survey is to demonstrate regional differences in the game ranching industry in Northeastern KZN relative to other regions of South Africa. Game reserves within the region differ widely with respect to management focus, products offered, and sources and magnitude of income, costs, and profitability. This variation is related to game reserve size and product orientation.

Per hectare, larger privately owned game reserves tend to have fewer beds, fewer employees, and lower investment in game. Land values, though, are not too different across the medium-size and large properties. However, they have lower costs and earn relatively larger return on capital invested than smaller privately owned reserves. These larger properties will, of course, tend to have higher bed densities than smaller reserves, but a larger sample would be required to tease out how much the bed density is related to a property's emphasis on biodiversity management.

Privately owned game reserves in the sample are more likely to overstock game on their properties than state-owned reserves, indicating a greater focus on profitability relative to conservation effectiveness. An analysis of the costs of private reserves compared with state-owned ones suggests that either state-owned reserves could considerably reduce costs, or alternatively that private ones could be spending too little on conservation activities.

For the sample studied, it is clear that the private game reserves have not yet achieved a reasonable level of operating profit and therefore remain in a start-up, investment phase. The relative success of the public game reserves and of one of the larger properties, and the high occupancies they achieved, does hold out the prospect of future business success. However, it remains unclear if these success stories are predicated on the sheer extent of the properties and the diversity of species and attractions they can therefore offer.

Two factors are likely to provide time for the game and nature tourism industry to mature. First, the traditional alternative of raising livestock, principally cattle, remains unattractive in economic terms. Though it might be argued that it would provide higher operating profits in the short run, it clearly does not have the potential upside that comes with nature tourism, particularly game viewing.

Second, the current policy of providing government the opportunity of first right of refusal to purchase properties put on the market to satisfy the land claims by citizens who previously were disadvantaged may be creating inertia in the land market. Given that most of the private game reserves are located on a contiguous swathe of prime land bordering the N2 highway and with good access to the surrounding private reserves, there may be a tendency for landowners to stick with game and nature tourism longer than otherwise would be likely. This is the case because putting the land up for sale might result in it being subdivided and effectively taken off the market as such. This may explain in part—alongside the stated conservation objective—the degree to which a significant number of landowners suggest that their focus is not solely on profitability and a pure business orientation.

REFERENCES

Barnes, J. I., and J. L. V. De Jager. 1996. "Economic and Financial Incentives for Wildlife Use on Private Land in Namibia and the Implications for Policy." *South African Journal of Wildlife Research* 26(2):37–46.

Barnes, J. I., and M. C. Kalikawe. 1994. "Game Ranching in Botswana: Constraints and Prospects." *Proceedings 3rd International Wildlife Ranching Symposium: Wildlife Ranching: a Celebration of Biodiversity*. Pretoria, South Africa, October 27–30, 1992.

Behr, J., and J. A. Groenewald. 1990a. "Commercial Game Utilisation on South African Farms." *Agrekon* 29(1):55–58.

———. 1990b. "Profit Potentials in Game Ranching." *Agrekon* 29(1):59–65.

Bond, I. 1993. *The Economics of Wildlife and Land Use in Zimbabwe: An Examination of Current Knowledge and Issues*. Project Paper 36. Harare: WWF Multispecies Animal Production Systems Project.

Creemers, G., B. James, and S. R. D. Ferrer. 2000. "Links between Public and Private Tourism-Conservation Businesses in NE KZN." Paper presented at the KZN-Wildlife Scientific Services Symposium, September, Pietermaritzburg, South Africa.

Du P. Bothma, J. 1996. *Game Ranch Management*. Pretoria: Van Schaik.

Eloff, T. 1999. "Quick Facts: Hunting and Conservation in South Africa." Unpublished Report. University of Potchefstroom, Potchefstroom, South Africa.

Falkena, H. B. 2000. "Bulls, Bears and Lions: Game Ranch Profitability in Southern Africa." The South African Financial Sector Forum, Rivonia, South Africa.

James, B. M., and Creemers, G. 2000. "Technical Report on Accommodation Database." Report to the World Bank Research Project on Nature Tourism and Conservation. Cascades, KwaZulu Natal: Brousse-James & Associates and KZN Wildlife.

James, B. M., and P. S. Goodman. 2000. "Ecological Study." Report to the World Bank Research Project on Nature Tourism and Conservation. Cascades, KwaZulu Natal: Brousse-James & Associates and KZN Wildlife.

Nel, C. 1991. "Gun Talk: Game Ranches Need Hunters." *Farmers' Weekly*. November 1991.

Standard Bank AgriReview. 2000. *AgriReview: A Quarterly Agricultural Review*. May. Johannesburg, South Africa.

World Bank. 2001. *The Little Green Data Book 2001*. Washington, D.C.

———. 2002. *World Development Indicators 2001*. Washington, D.C.

PART IV

TOWARD A NATURE TOURISM ECONOMY: ASSESSING THE ALTERNATIVES

CHAPTER 9

TOURISM EXPENDITURES AND REGIONAL ECONOMIC DEVELOPMENT IN KWAZULU-NATAL

A Social Accounting Matrix

David Mullins and Lindi Mulder

Nature tourism links not only with the economy in a direct way, but also has multiple forward and backward linkages. To fully explain the economic and socioeconomic effects of nature tourism, it is important to have a detailed knowledge of nature tourism's economic environment. For this purpose, economists have traditionally used input–output models. However, a straightforward focus on inputs and outputs leaves aside many socioeconomic questions of interest to policymakers. To provide a better explanation of the socioeconomic environment alongside the economic environment, economists have turned to social accounting matrices (SAMs).

SAMs use a matrix presentation to represent the flow of funds and the linkages of demand, production, and income within a national or regional economy. SAMs can be designed with a special emphasis on social rather than economic entities (for example, low-income households), and thereby also provide information about equity and distributional concerns (while taking into account the interdependence of a large number of economic variables). There are few—but growing—applications of SAMs to tourism (Grant Thornton Kessel Feinstein 2000).

In the case of the Northeastern KwaZulu-Natal region (NE KZN) of South Africa, little detailed analysis of this nature exists. The opportunity to build a SAM, provided a way of answering important questions regarding the interaction of policy, institutional, and managerial variables associated with the development of nature tourism (see chapter 10). This chapter presents the results of an initial effort to build a SAM for the study area that explicitly includes nature tourism accounts. This SAM is then used to estimate the impact of nature tourism in general—as well as the impact of the changes in nature tourism expenditures induced by policies—on production and income distribution in the study area.

The chapter begins by laying out the methodology and framework of the SAM as compiled for the region and continues on to an analysis of the nature and magnitude of the economic impact of nature tourism in the study area. The discussion then turns to the economic efficiency of nature tourism, employing multiplier analysis to elaborate on the potential effects of key socioeconomic and economic variables. A short set of conclusions wraps up the chapter. Additional details on the SAM framework, structure, and components are provided in appendix 9-A below.

METHODOLOGY

Study Area

The project area partially overlaps two areas known as Zululand and Maputoland, and is among the poorest regions in KwaZulu-Natal as well as in the rest of South Africa. The major industrial centers of Richard Bay and Empangeni are excluded so that the rest of the urban centers are small villages acting as service centers to the surrounding rural areas. Five magisterial districts are included in the project area: Enseleni, Ingwavuma, Hlabisa, Ngotshe, and Ubombu. For purposes of the SAM, a Region 1 (study area) and Region 2 (rest of Natal) are identified. Map 1.3 (chapter 1) depicts the study area (in red) as well as the rest of the province.

Land use is divided between commercial and communal farmers, with public reserves contributing a sizable percentage (see chapter 1). Because of the many climatic zones in the area, a number of agricultural and animal products are produced—sugarcane, forest plantations, livestock, and fruit and vegetables. Manufacturing is on a very small scale, except for the sugar mills and sawmills.

In recent years many of the cattle farmers have been changing to game farming, which is contributing to the fast growth of the hunting and game-viewing industry. Included in the area are some of the most well-known nature assets of the province and the country: the Great Saint Lucia Wetland Complex and five game parks—Hluhluwe-Umfolozi (HUP), Ithala, Mkhuze, Ndumo, and Tembo. Added to this, the warm climate and scenic coastline all contribute to providing the study area with significant nature tourism potential.

The Social Accounting Matrix

The social accounting matrix is a relatively recent development in the field of national accounting. In layperson's terms, a SAM is a matrix depicting the linkages that exist among all the different role players in the relevant national or regional economy (such as business sectors, households, and government). It is similar to an input–output table in that it reflects all the intersectoral linkages present in an economy.

Further, the development of the SAM is significant because it provides a framework within the context of the national accounts in which the activities of households are accentuated and prominently distinguished. The household is indeed the basic unit in which significant decisions are made on such important economic variables as expenditures and saving. By combining households into meaningful groups, the SAM makes it possible to distinguish clearly among, and to study, the effects, interaction, and economic welfare of each group.

Accordingly, the SAM serves a dual purpose in the national accounts of a country or a region. First, it is a reflection of the magnitude and linkages of the stakeholders in an economy. Second, once a SAM has been developed, it becomes a powerful econometric tool to conduct various economic analyses.

The first step in developing a SAM is to determine all possible interactions and transactions (flows) among the various sectors and economic role players in the designated area. These flows must also take into account the different regions specified for purposes of this study and the fact that interregional flows will be the order of the day. Seven economic entities are identified in the SAM:

- Activities

- Commodities

- Factor payments (that is, gross operating surplus and labor)

- Enterprises

- Households

- Government

- Capital (investment and savings)

Each of these entities exists within the two principal regions identified in the SAM:

- Northeastern KwaZulu-Natal (Region 1)

- The rest of KwaZulu-Natal (Region 2)

The relationships within the SAM are modeled for these two regions. To complete the model, reference is also made to the rest of South Africa and the rest of the world. In spatial terms, then, the SAM examines a set of four concentric circles, each representing a different "economy." In appendix 9-A the full structure of the SAM is presented, along with a glossary of terms and components to aid the reader in understanding the framework.

Building the SAM: Data

The main sources of data are the KwaZulu-Natal Tourism Authority and Tourism South Africa (SATOUR). The SATOUR data were based on surveys conducted in 1998. In addition, data were obtained from the World Bank, of which this study is one component, as well as standard sources of data on economic activity in the province. Because the tourism data are all survey related, the SAM is dependent on data collected from tourists with regard to their expenses. Thus all the data used in the SAM come from the spending side and not from actual field surveys.

Because the objective of this study is to estimate the impact of nature tourism, the ideal definition of a tourist would in this case be a person visiting the study area solely for the sake of nature tourism. This would automatically exclude visitors coming to the area for business reasons. Yet because the surveys, though comprehensive, concentrated only on actual money spent by tourists and other visitors, no attempt was made to differentiate among the different groups of visitors, and the statistical information was accepted on face value (in other words, the number of visitors and money spent).

A survey of foreign and resident tourists conducted in the study area as part of the World Bank On-Site Survey (see chapter 3) provides information on the extent and pattern of tourist itineraries and expenditures in the study area. Foreign visitors typically spend two weeks or more in the country, of which 3.5 nights on average are spent in NE KZN. Day visitors typically take one-day trips to Hluhluwe-Umfolozi Park, whereas overnight visitors typically spend 2 nights in the park.

As far as residents are concerned, itineraries in NE KZN are fairly similar, with the exception that day visitors spend less time in the study area as a whole. Residents typically visit the study area as a destination, as is reflected by the negligible amount of time on their itineraries outside the study area (table 9.1).

Table 9.1 Visitor Numbers, Length of Stay, and Expenditure Figures by Type of Visitor to Hluhluwe-Umfolozi Park

| | Length of Stay | | | Expenditures | |
| | | | | In NE Zululand | In Rest of South Africa |
Visitors to HUP	At HUP (days or nights)	Inside NE Zululand (nights)	Outside NE Zululand (nights)	(rand per capita per night)	(rand per capita per night)
Foreigners					
Day visitors	1.0	3.4	13.8	432	606
Overnight visitors	2.0	3.5	12.4	467	682
Residents					
Day visitors	1.0	1.7	0.4	208	551
Overnight visitors	2.0	3.2	0.7	206	629
Total	6.0	11.8	27.3	1,313	2,468

HUP = Hluhluwe-Umfolozi Park.

Source: KwaZulu-Natal Nature Conservation Service (various years).

Within NE KZN, the principal difference between foreigners and residents is that foreigners spend more than twice as much per night (R450) on average as do residents (R200). This difference is moderated when expenditures in the rest of the country are considered, however, for the difference is largely an artifact of the sample and the brief travel time outside the study area (so that those in the sample who do stay overnight skew the per capita expenditures per night upward).

In comparison, in a study of the KwaZulu-Natal domestic tourism market, Seymour (1998) found that the average spent in KZN (including travel to KZN) per overnight visitor ranged from R383 (September) to R728 (January). The results from the study area for this SAM are limited to NE KZN and exclude travel expenditures to KZN, but they are still roughly consistent with Seymour's. The distribution of expenditures differs somewhat across the studies, with shopping expenditures making up between 20 percent and 37 percent of total costs in Seymour's study (travel costs to KZN excluded), and only 4 percent in the present survey. In comparison with other costs, shopping expenditures seem unreasonably high in the Seymour study. For example, in the January survey shopping expenditures were twice as high as those on accommodation.

The figures can also be compared with other international visitor surveys. SATOUR (1998) reported average expenditures of R17,500 for foreign visitors to South Africa. This is about R7,500 more than the figures from the current study. However, SATOUR's numbers included all prepaid expenditures (including airfares), and no correction was made for that portion of air and package expenditures retained in source market countries, nor for travel to multiple countries. Comparing expenditures while in South Africa, the two surveys produce fairly similar results. SATOUR reported average expenditures of R5,900 while inside South Africa, whereas the present survey indicates R5,000 and R5,100 for day visitors and overnight visitors, respectively.

The data obtained for the SAM from the KwaZulu-Natal Tourism Authority (KZN Domestic Tourism Decision Surveys International) focused mainly on the tourist situation in KZN. From these data, spending patterns as well as the total number of visitors to Northeastern KwaZulu-Natal emerged. Conversely, data obtained from SATOUR were used as a control measure with regard to foreign and actual tourists' spending patterns in KwaZulu Natal. By combining these two sets of

Table 9.2 Total Tourist Spending in Region 1 and Region 2, According to Origin of Tourists (millions of 1998 rand)

Region of Spending	Region of Origin				
	Region 1	Region 2	Rest of South Africa	Rest of World	Total
Region 1	19	63	115	380	577
Region 2	38	1,116	2,483	1,627	5,264
Total	57	1,179	2,598	2,007	5,841

Sources: KZN Domestic Tourism, *Decision Survey International;* SATOUR (1998).

data and adjusting tourist numbers and amounts to 1998 figures, table 9.2 was constructed using the World Bank expenditure surveys. This table shows the total spending of tourists to the study region and KwaZulu Natal.

It must be noted that the evaluation of these figures should be considered against the background of the discussion on the relevant definitions of a tourist and tourism in the study area. A full explanation of the data sets employed and the construction of the individual component matrices of the SAM can be found in Conningarth Consultants (2002).

Solving the Model

To analyze the impact of nature tourism activities on both Regions 1 and 2, it was necessary to develop two distinct matrices that reflect the exogenous stimuli of nature tourism on the economies of both regions. These matrices are referred to as final demand matrices because the builder of the SAM model usually views final demand as exogenous to the model:

- Final Demand Matrix 1: A matrix relating to the nature tourism spending in Region 1 of tourists residing in Region 1, Region 2, and the rest of the world. In the discussions below, this matrix is referred to as FD1.

- Final Demand Matrix 2: A matrix that depicts tourist spending in Region 2 by tourists from Region 1, Region 2, and the rest of the world. This matrix is referred to as FD2.

Each of the above-mentioned final demand matrices was developed to explicitly reflect each aspect of nature tourism spending. The resulting final demand matrices show clearly the extent to which each sector will be affected as a result of nature tourism spending. By using these matrices to stimulate the SAM model exogenously, information can be obtained on the economic and socioeconomic effects of nature tourism. Since FD1 and FD2 are matrices relating to nature tourism spending in Region 1 and 2, respectively, per definition they are already part of the SAM and do not have to be calculated separately.

The so-called SAM Model $(I–A)^{-1}$ is developed by first dividing the SAM into endogenous and exogenous portions. Second, one has to develop a coefficient matrix (A) of the endogenous portion, which is then subtracted from a unity matrix (I). The model is then the inverted matrix $(I–A)^{-1}$.

By multiplying the inverse matrix $(I–A)^{-1}$ with each of the final demand matrices described above, the economic impact of nature tourism is determined. These formulas provide a brief explanation of this process:

- Impact on Region 1 due to nature tourism spending in Region 1 by tourists from Region 1, Region 2, and the rest of the world: $(I–A)^{-1} \times FD1$.

- Impact on Region 2 due to nature tourism spending by tourists from Region 1, Region 2, and the rest of the world: $(I–A)^{-1} \times FD2$.

THE ECONOMIC IMPACT OF NATURE TOURISM

This section provides an overview of the impact of nature tourism on the economy of NE KZN and also highlights important aspects. Attention will also be given to the linkage effect of nature tourism spending in Region 1 on the rest of the KZN Province (that is, Region 2). Furthermore, the impact of total spending on nature tourism in the province will be analyzed. The discussion will be conducted under the headings of activities, factor payments, enterprises, household income, and employment creation. It should be noted that the relevant SAM is a formidable source of information. Consequently, the analysis presented here is merely a fraction of the totality of information that could be obtained.

The first two columns of table 9.3 (the following observations also apply to most of the tables below) depict the impact of the nature tourism sector; the first shows the impact in terms of millions of rand at 1998 prices, whereas the second shows the percentage structure. The third and fourth columns present the 1998 situation of the economy of the relevant region. The fifth column shows the impact of nature tourism as a percentage of the economy of the relevant region.

The results given represent in most instances the total impact of nature tourism. As has been discussed, this impact is based on input–output analysis (SAM). In elementary terms, it means that all downstream effects have been accounted for. For instance, the nature tourism impact is not only on those businesses that supply goods and services directly to tourists, but also on the businesses that supply inputs such as food, beverages, and fuel.

Even the ripple effects are measured further downstream, taking into account the sectors that supply intermediate products (such as fuel and foodstuffs). The analysis also takes into account the household expenditures that will flow from an increase in spending of the additional employment (both direct and indirect) resulting from nature tourism.

At this stage, it is important to state that the total gross geographical product (GGP) at 1998 prices of the study area is R415 million. The impact of nature tourism in GGP terms as a proportion is 20.7 percent (see table 9.7 below).

Impact of Nature Tourist Spending in Region 1 on the Economy of Region 1

Activities (Production Values in the Economic Sectors)

The main objective when activities were identified for purposes of analysis was to select those activities that exemplified the most prominent features of Region 1. A list of these activities is provided in appendix 9-A. The most prominent of these were the activities pertaining to nature tourism businesses.

Table 9.3 shows the impact of nature tourism on Region 1 of spending in Region 1. In terms of production values, the nature tourism industry

Table 9.3 Nature Tourism Impact on Region 1 of Spending in Region 1, by Main Sector

Sector	Nature Tourism Impact		Total Region 1 (NE KZN) Spending		Magnitude of Impact (percent)
	Value (millions of rand)	Percent	Value (millions of rand)	Percent	
Regional economy, excluding nature tourism	66	10.4	2,141	78.9	3.1
1. Primary sector	7	1.1	883	32.5	0.8
2. Secondary sector	11	1.7	664	24.4	1.7
3. Tertiary sector	38	6.0	451	16.6	8.5
4. Community services	10	1.6	144	5.3	6.9
Nature tourism–related sectors	574	89.6	574	21.1	100.0
5. Trade	43	6.7	43	1.6	100.0
6. Transport	115	18.0	115	4.2	100.0
7. Accommodation	207	32.4	207	7.6	100.0
8. Food and drink	141	22.0	141	5.2	100.0
9. Hunting	38	6.0	38	1.4	100.0
10. Viewing	7	1.0	7	0.2	100.0
11. Conservation and other	24	3.8	24	0.9	100.0
Total	641	100.0	2,715	100.0	23.6

NE KZN = Northeastern KwaZulu-Natal.
Note: Measured in terms of production units at 1998 prices.

Source: Conningarth Consultants (2002); database.

is responsible for 23.6 percent of the total economy of Region 1. The revenue for nature tourism is R574 million. This amount represents 21 percent of the total production value in Region 1 if measured against the total revenue. The impact of nature tourism on the unrelated tourism sectors is about 66 million (2.4 percent) of the total production value in Region 1. However, the impact of nature tourism on the unrelated sectors themselves is about 3.1 percent. The main reason for this small percentage is the low linkage between the nontourism sectors and nature tourism. This is due to the relatively small secondary sectors in Region 1.

Table 9.4 shows the impact of nature tourism divided among public, private, and informal sectors. Of the total impact of R643 million, R71 million (11 percent) is generated by the public sector, R567 million (88 percent) by the private sector, and R4 million (less than 1 percent) by the informal sector. The public sector is strongly involved through the role of KZN Wildlife in administering public reserves, accommodation, and related services. The informal sector's share is mainly represented by trade.

Table 9.5 summarizes the impact of the tourists from the four places of origin: Region 1 (study area), Region 2 (rest of KZN), the rest of South Africa, and the rest of the world. It can be seen that tourists from outside KZN have a share of more than 82 percent of the total tourism impact on Region 1 and that the tourism industry is therefore very dependent on tourists from outside KZN. In table 9.6, the nature tourism impact is analyzed in terms of the origin of tourists and their impact on the full set of related activities.

Gross Geographical Product

In table 9.7, the impact of nature tourism spending in Region 1 by main sector is given as a result of such spending in Region 1. The difference between this subsection and the previous subsection is that the impact is measured in terms of GGP, whereas previously it was measured in terms of production values.

Factor Payments

Table 9.8 presents the impact of nature tourism on factor payments (labor and capital). The labor analysis is given in terms of skilled, semiskilled,

Table 9.4 Nature Tourism Impact on Region 1 of Spending in Region 1, According to Public, Private, and Informal Activities

Sector	Public-Sector Impact		Private-Sector Impact		Informal-Sector Impact		Total Impact	
	Value (millions of rand)	Percent	Value (millions of rand)	Percent	Value (millions of rand)	Percent	Value (millions of rand)	Percent
Regional economy, excluding nature tourism			66	11.7			66	10.3
1. Primary sector			7	1.3			7	1.1
2. Secondary sector			11	1.9			11	1.7
3. Tertiary sector			38	6.7			38	5.9
4. Community services			10	1.8			10	1.6
Nature tourism–related sectors	71	100.0	501	88.3	4	100.0	576	89.7
5. Trade	12	17.0	27	4.7	4	100.0	43	6.7
6. Transport			115	20.3			115	17.9
7. Accommodation	33	46.7	175	30.8			208	32.3
8. Food and drink	6	8.0	135	23.9			141	21.9
9. Hunting	4	5.4	35	6.1			38	6.0
10. Viewing	4	5.4	3	0.5			7	1.0
11. Conservation and other	12	17.5	12	2.1			25	3.8
Total	71	100.0	567	100.0	4	100.0	643	100.0
Percentage distribution	11.1		88.3		0.67		100.0	

Notes: Measured in terms of production units at 1998 prices. Due to the rounded-off basis, the total impact value of 643 differs slightly from the total of 641 in table 9.3. Blank cells indicate negligible percentages.

Source: Conningarth Consultants (2002); database.

Table 9.5 Nature Tourism Impact, According to Origin of Tourists

	Impact	
Origin of Tourists	Value (millions of rand)	Percent
Region 1	24	3.7
Region 2	88	13.7
Rest of South Africa	166	25.8
Rest of world	365	56.8
Total	643	100.0

Source: Conningarth Consultants (2002); database.

and unskilled categories. From this table, it can be deduced that nature tourism's impact in NE KZN favors the semiskilled and unskilled labor categories—a situation that is relatively better than that for the total region. In the case of capital (that is, gross operating surplus), the biggest impact of nature tourism is on large commercial enterprises (27.8 percent). However, in the case of the total Region 1, the main stakeholders are also the large commercial enterprises (66 percent).

Enterprises

Table 9.9 shows the impact of nature tourism on enterprises. According to the SAM, small commercial enterprises are benefiting the most from nature tourism spending in Region 1. It is surprising that the tour operators of Region 1 are not benefiting that much. Most of the tour groups visiting Region 1 are organized by tour operators outside Region 1.

Households

Households form one of the most important entities identified for purposes of this project. Six types of households were investigated: rural (high income, medium income, and low income) and urban (high income, medium income, and low income).

Table 9.10 shows the impact of nature tourism on households in Region 1. Rural households appear to be the main beneficiaries, receiving 79 percent (R224 million) of the value generated by nature tourism. It is therefore not surprising to note that a high portion of the total income is being received by low-income households, R113 million or 40 percent of the total.

Table 9.6 Nature Tourism Impact on Region 1 of Spending in Region 1, According to Origin of Tourists

Sector	Region 1 Tourists		Region 2 Tourists		Rest of South African Tourists		Rest of World Tourists		Total Tourists	
	Value (millions of rand)	Percent	Value (millions of rand)	Percent	Value (millions of rand)	Percent	Value (millions of rand)	Percent	Value (millions of rand)	Percent
Regional economy, excluding nature tourism	2	10.1	9	10.1	17	10.2	38	10.3	66	10.3
1. Primary sector	0	1.2	1	1.2	2	1.2	4	1.1	7	1.1
2. Secondary sector	0	1.9	2	1.8	3	1.7	6	1.6	11	1.7
3. Tertiary sector	1	5.5	5	5.5	10	5.8	22	6.0	38	5.9
4. Community services	0	1.5	1	1.5	2	1.5	6	1.6	10	1.6
Nature tourism–related	21	89.9	79	89.9	149	89.8	327	89.7	576	89.7
sectors										
5. Trade	0.5	19.1	2	2.0	11	15.7	30	8.2	43	6.7
6. Transport	3	7.2	7	8.0	21	9.6	85	23.2	115	17.9
7. Accommodation	11	27.5	40	45.7	53	30.2	103	28.2	208	32.3
8. Food and drink	4	29.7	18	20.6	43	24.3	75	20.7	141	21.9
9. Hunting	2	3.9	10	10.8	9	3.6	18	4.9	38	6.0
10. Viewing	0	0.3	0	0.4	4	1.9	3	0.7	7	1.0
11. Conservation and other	0	2.2	2	2.5	8	4.4	14	3.9	25	3.8
Total	24	100.0	88	100.0	166	100.0	365	100.0	643	100.0
Percentage distribution	3.7		13.7		25.9		56.8		100.0	

Note: Measured in terms of production units at 1998 prices.

Source: Conningarth Consultants (2002); database.

Table 9.7 Nature Tourism Impact on Region 1 of Spending in Region 1

Sector	Nature Tourism Impact Value (millions of rand)	Percent	Total Region 1 (NE KZN) Spending Value (millions of rand)	Percent	Magnitude of Nature Tourism Impact (percent)
Regional economy, excluding nature tourism	36	8.7	1,623	81.1	2.2
1. Primary sector	4	0.9	524	26.2	0.7
2. Secondary sector	4	0.9	175	8.7	2.1
3. Tertiary sector	24	5.9	275	13.7	8.9
4. Community services	4	1.0	649	32.4	0.6
Nature tourism–related sectors	379	91.3	379	18.9	100.0
5. Trade	35	8.9	35	1.8	100.0
6. Transport	62	15.8	62	3.1	100.0
7. Accommodation	157	39.4	157	7.8	100.0
8. Food and drink	70	17.5	70	3.5	100.0
9. Hunting	30	7.6	30	1.5	100.0
10. Viewing	5	1.3	5	0.3	100.0
11. Conservation and other	20	5.1	20	1.0	100.0
Total	415	100.0	2002	100.0	20.7

NE KZN = Northeastern KwaZulu-Natal.

Note: Measured in terms of gross geographical product at market prices.

Source: Conningarth Consultants (2002); database.

Table 9.8 Nature Tourism Impact on Region 1 of Spending in Region 1, in Terms of Labor and Capital Factor Payments

Factor Payment	Nature Tourism Impact		Total Region 1 (NE KZN) Spending		Magnitude of Nature Tourism Impact (percent)
	Value (millions of rand)	Percent	Value (millions of rand)	Percent	
Labor					
Skilled	53	30.4	603	53.4	8.9
Semiskilled	2	24.1	167	14.8	25.3
Unskilled	80	45.5	360	31.8	22.2
Total	176	100.0	1,130	100.0	15.5
Capital (gross operating surplus)					
Public game reserves	29	12.3	29	3.4	100.3
Private game reserves	51	21.2	51	5.8	100.2
Large commercial	67	27.8	575	66.0	11.6
Small commercial	59	24.5	127	14.6	46.2
Tour operators	3	1.5	2	0.5	82.1
Local communities	30	12.7	85	9.7	36.0
Total	240	100.0	872	100.0	27.5

Note: Totals may exceed 100 percent because of rounding.

Source: Deduced from Social Accounting Matrix for Northeastern KwaZulu-Natal, Conningarth Consultants (2002).

Table 9.9 Nature Tourism Impact on Region 1 of Spending in Region 1, in Terms of Enterprises

Type of Enterprise	Nature Tourism Impact Value (millions of rand)	Percent	Total Region 1 (NE KZN) Spending Value (millions of rand)	Percent	Magnitude of Nature Tourism Impact (percent)
1. Public game reserves	29	13.4	91	9.8	32.5
2. Private game reserves owners	46	20.7	74	13.8	61.9
3. Large commercial	54	24.7	479	51.3	11.4
4. Small commercial	58	26.3	126	14.3	46.1
5. Tour operators	2	1.1	6	0.4	41.6
6. Local communities	30	13.8	89	10.5	34.0
Total	221	100.0	922	100.0	25.5

Source: Conningarth Consultants (2002); database.

Table 9.10 Nature Tourism Impact on Region 1 of Spending in Region 1, in Terms of Households

Type of Household	Nature Tourism Impact Value (millions of rand)	Percent	Total Region 1 (NE KZN) Spending Value (millions of rand)	Percent	Magnitude of Nature Tourism Impact (percent)
Rural	224	78.8	2,179	73.6	10.3
High-income	70	24.7	696	23.5	10.1
Medium-income	49	17.3	401	13.5	12.2
Low-income	105	36.8	1,082	36.6	9.7
Urban	60	21.2	780	26.4	7.7
High-income	29	10.2	388	13.1	7.5
Medium-income	23	8.0	283	9.6	8.0
Low-income	9	3.0	109	3.7	7.8
Total	284	100.0	2,959	100.0	9.6
High-income	99	35.0	1,084	36.7	36.7
Medium-income	72	25.2	684	23.1	23.1
Low-income	113	39.8	1,191	40.2	40.2

Source: Conningarth Consultants 2002. Database.

Table 9.11 Nature Tourism Impact on Region 1 of Spending in Region 1, in Terms of Employment

Sector	Nature Tourism Impact		Total Region 1 (NE KZN) Spending		Magnitude of Nature Tourism Impact (percent)
	Value (millions of rand)	Percent	Value (millions of rand)	Percent	
Regional economy, excluding nature tourism	549	7.8	17,176	72.6	3.2
1. Primary sector	117	1.7	8,590	36.3	1.4
2. Secondary sector	57	0.8	3,693	15.6	1.5
3. Tertiary sector	347	4.9	4,489	19.0	7.7
4. Community services	28	0.4	404	1.7	6.9
Nature tourism–related sectors	6,487	92.2	6,487	27.4	100.0
5. Trade	262	3.7	262	1.1	100.0
6. Transport	789	11.2	789	3.3	100.0
7. Accommodation	4,346	62.2	4,346	18.4	100.0
8. Food and drink	653	9.3	653	2.8	100.0
9. Hunting	256	3.7	256	1.1	100.0
10. Viewing	66	0.9	66	0.3	100.0
11. Conservation and other	115	1.6	115	0.5	100.0
Total	7,036	100.0	23,664	100.0	29.7

Source: Deduced from Social Accounting Matrix for Northeastern KwaZulu-Natal, Conningarth Consultants (2002).

Employment

Table 9.11 shows the employment impact supported by nature tourism spending in Region 1. Nature tourism spending is responsible for 7,036 jobs, of which more than 92 percent are in nature tourism–related sectors. Directly and indirectly, nature tourism spending contributes nearly 30 percent to total employment in Region 1.

Impact on Region 2 due to Spending in Region 1

The impact on GGP of Region 2 as a result of nature tourism spending in Region 1 is reflected in table 9.12. As expected, the impact of nature tourism is mostly on Region 1 (76 percent). It is important to note

Table 9.12 Nature Tourism Impact on Region 1 and Region 2 of Spending in Region 1, in Terms of Gross Geographical Product at Factor Cost

| Region of Impact | Nature Tourism Impact | | Total Region 1 (NE KZN) Spending | | Magnitude of Nature Tourism Impact (percent) |
	Value (millions of rand)	Percent	Value (millions of rand)	Percent	
Region 1	415	76.3	2,002	2.2	20.8
Region 2	129	23.7	90,329	97.8	0.1
Total impact	545	100.0	92,331	100.0	0.6

Source: Deduced from Social Accounting Matrix for Northeastern KwaZulu-Natal, Conningarth Consultants (2002).

Table 9.13 Nature Tourism Impact on Region 1 and Region 2 of Spending in Region 1, in Terms of Employment

| Region of Impact | Nature Tourism Impact | | Total Region 1 (NE KZN) Spending | | Magnitude of Nature Tourism Impact (percent) |
	Value (millions of rand)	Percent	Value (millions of rand)	Percent	
Region 1	7,071	73.9	23,664	1.6	29.9
Region 2	2,500	26.1	1,474,177	98.4	0.2
Total impact	9,571	100.0	1,497,841	100.0	0.6

Source: Deduced from Social Accounting Matrix for Northeastern KwaZulu-Natal, Conningarth Consultants (2002).

that the impact of nature tourism spending in Region 1 represents nearly 1 percent of the total GDP of KZN Province (0.6 percent).

In table 9.13, the impact on employment in Region 2 as a result of nature tourism spending in Region 1 is shown. The jobs created in KZN Province due to nature tourism spending in Region 1 total 9,571.

Impact on KwaZulu-Natal of Nature Tourism Spending in Regions 1 and 2

In this subsection, the full impact on KZN Province (Regions 1 and 2) of nature tourism spending in Regions 1 and 2 is discussed. This is done in terms of GGP and employment.

Table 9.14 Nature Tourism Impact on Region 1 and Region 2 of Spending in Region 1 and Region 2, in Terms of Gross Geographical Product at Factor Cost

Region of Impact	Spending in Region 1		Spending in Region 2		Total KZN Spending	
	Value (millions of rand)	Percent	Value (millions of rand)	Percent	Value (millions of rand)	Percent
Region 1	415	76.3	26	0.5	442	8.2
Region 2	129	23.7	4,790	99.5	4,919	91.8
Total KZN Province	545	100.0	4,816	100.0	5,470	100.0

Source: Deduced from Social Accounting Matrix for Northeastern KwaZulu-Natal, Conningarth Consultants (2002).

Table 9.15 Nature Tourism Impact on Region 1 and Region 2 of Spending in Region 1 and Region 2, in Terms of Employment

Region of Impact	Spending in Region 1		Spending in Region 2		Total KZN Spending	
	Value (millions of rand)	Percent	Value (millions of rand)	Percent	Value (millions of rand)	Percent
Region 1	7,071	73.9	473	0.7	7,544	9.5
Region 2	2,500	26.1	69,497	99.3	71,997	90.5
Total KZN Province	9,571	100.0	69,970	100.0	79,541	100.0

Source: Deduced from Social Accounting Matrix for Northeastern KwaZulu-Natal, Conningarth Consultants (2002).

The total impact on GGP in KZN Province due to nature tourism is R5.4 billion (table 9.14). Although this figure is significant, it is still much lower with regard to similar impact figures quoted elsewhere for the province. This is mostly due to the definition of a tourist that is used in this study, which is much narrower. The impact of nature tourism accounts for about 6 percent of the total GGP of KZN Province.

In table 9.15, the employment impact on Regions 1 and 2 as a result of nature tourism spending in Regions 1 and 2 is shown. Approximately 80,000 jobs (directly and indirectly) are sustained by nature tourism in KZN Province. Of this amount, about 9.5 percent is due to nature tourism–related activities in Region 1 and 90.5 percent in Region 2.

ECONOMIC MULTIPLIERS: IMPACT EFFICIENCY ANALYSIS

The objective of this chapter is to give an indication of the efficiency of nature tourism spending in Region 1 with regard to the economic variables in Region 1. The efficiency will be viewed from two angles. First, the efficiency of the various nature tourism spending categories in terms of tourists will be analyzed. Second, the nature tourism–related sectors will be examined. The comparisons will be done using multipliers, which means that the impact on various economic variables of spending R1 million on nature tourism will be measured.

Three macroeconomic variables will be analyzed and reported on:

- Gross domestic product (GDP)

- Employment

- Household income (the impact on low-income household income, as well as the impact on the income of all households including low-income households, is provided).

For example, an increase in spending by foreign tourists of R1 million will have an impact on employment creation, which can be measured via multiplier analysis.

The multipliers for both Region 1 and Region 2 are provided. The multipliers for Region 2 should be interpreted as the impact on a specific macroeconomic variable in Region 2 due to nature tourism spending that takes place in Region 1. This is also referred to as the linkage impact on Region 2.

Nature Tourism Spending

Table 9.16 provides the multipliers for the tourists according to their origin. Three aspects are of importance:

- The multipliers among the various types of tourists (tourists from Region 1, tourists from the rest of the world, and so on) do not differ extensively.

- The linkage between Region 1 and Region 2 is evident. Spending in Region 1 will lead to a significant impact on Region 2.

Table 9.16 Multipliers for Tourists According to Origin (effect in 1998 rand of spending R1.00)

Measure	Tourists from Region 1	Tourists from Region 2	Tourists from the Rest of South Africa	Tourists from the Rest of the World
Gross domestic product				
Region 1	1.97	2.18	2.11	2.12
Region 2	0.58	0.65	0.65	0.69
Total	2.55	2.83	2.76	2.81
Employment (jobs per millions of rand)				
Region 1	45	47	38	35
Region 2	11	12	13	13
Total	56	59	51	48
Income of low-income households				
Region 1	0.63	0.68	0.63	0.55
Region 2	0.20	0.21	0.19	0.18
Total	0.83	0.89	0.82	0.73
Total household income				
Region 1	1.36	1.51	1.46	1.44
Region 2	0.78	0.87	0.85	0.90
Total	2.14	2.37	2.31	2.34
Low-income households as a percentage of total household income	38.90	37.70	35.30	31.40

Note: Multiplier analysis for nature tourism spending in Region 1.

Source: Deduced from Social Accounting Matrix for Northeastern KwaZulu-Natal, Conningarth Consultants (2002).

- The low-income households gain significantly from nature tourism spending. Low-income as a percentage of total income is approximately 39 percent.

Table 9.17 provides the multipliers for tourists according to their income categories. The remarks pertaining to table 9.17 are valid for table 9.18 as well.

Nature Tourism–Related Sectors

The full set of multipliers for the different nature tourism–related sectors is provided in Conningarth Consultants (2002). These multipliers are

Table 9.17 Multipliers for Tourists According to Income Categories (effect in 1998 rand of spending R1.00)

Measure	High-Income Households	Medium-Income Households	Low-Income Households
Gross domestic product			
Region 1	2.85	2.86	2.68
Region 2	0.85	0.85	0.86
Total	3.70	3.71	3.54
Employment			
(jobs per million rand)			
Region 1	53	58	54
Region 2	16	16	16
Total	69	75	70
Income of low-income households			
Region 1	0.82	0.88	0.79
Region 2	0.26	0.28	0.26
Total	1.08	1.15	1.04
Total household income			
Region 1	1.97	1.97	1.83
Region 2	1.13	1.14	1.13
Total	3.10	3.11	2.96
Low-income households as a percentage of total household income	34.90	37.10	35.20

Note: Multiplier analysis for nature tourism spending in Region 1.

Source: Deduced from Social Accounting Matrix for Northeastern KwaZulu-Natal, Conningarth Consultants (2002).

important for analysis purposes and projections if a specific subsector is examined. In most cases, they will be used only as part of a modeling system.

In table 9.18, the nature tourism sector multipliers are depicted according to ownership. The first important effect is as a result of the relatively high multipliers of Region 2 in relation to Region 1. This is an indication of the strong backward linkages that Region 2 has with Region 1. Many of the commodities consumed in Region 1 are supplied by Region 2.

For the multipliers according to ownership in general, it is also important to note that the multipliers for the informal sectors of Region 1 are much higher than those of the public and private sectors. For instance,

Table 9.18 Multipliers for Nature Tourism Sectors According to Ownership (effect in 1998 rand of spending R1.00)

Measure	Public Tourist Activities	Private Tourist Activities	Informal Tourist Activities
Gross domestic product (at factor cost)			
Region 1	0.70	0.73	0.85
Region 2	0.27	0.21	0.18
Total	0.96	0.94	1.03
Employment (jobs per million rand)			
Region 1	9	14	26
Region 2	5	4	3
Total	14	18	30
Income of low-income households			
Region 1	0.18	0.20	0.41
Region 2	0.07	0.06	0.06
Total	0.25	0.26	0.47
Total household income			
Region 1	0.46	0.51	0.64
Region 2	0.34	0.28	0.24
Total	0.80	0.79	0.88
Low-income households as a percentage of total household income	31.00	33.50	53.50

Note: Multiplier analysis for nature tourism spending in Region 1.

Source: Deduced from Social Accounting Matrix for Northeastern KwaZulu-Natal, Conningarth Consultants (2002).

in the case of low-income households, for R1 million in nature tourism spending, the impact is nearly double for the informal sector relative to the public and private sectors. This is understandable if it is taken into account that the informal sector is mainly represented by low-income households.

Table 9.19 presents the multipliers for the average of the related and unrelated nature tourism sectors. The results suggest that the impact of nature tourism is on a par with the rest of the economic sectors and in most cases is larger on the various macroeconomic variables than unrelated nature tourism activities. In table 9.20, the multipliers are given for the main categories of the nature tourism–related sectors.

Table 9.19 Multipliers for Related and Unrelated Nature Tourism Sectors
(effect in 1998 rand of spending R1.00)

Measure	Average for Unrelated Nature Tourism Activities	Nature Tourism Subsectors
Gross domestic product (at factor cost)		
Region 1	0.63	0.72
Region 2	0.27	0.22
Total	0.89	0.95
Employment (jobs per million rand)		
Region 1	11	12
Region 2	5	4
Total	16	17
Income of low-income households		
Region 1	0.14	0.20
Region 2	0.06	0.06
Total	0.21	0.26
Total household income		
Region 1	0.40	0.49
Region 2	0.34	0.30
Total	0.74	0.79
Low-income households as a percentage of total household income	28.00	32.90

Note: Multiplier analysis for nature tourism spending in Region 1.

Source: Deduced from Social Accounting Matrix for Northeastern KwaZulu-Natal, Conningarth Consultants (2002).

CONCLUSIONS

The social accounting matrix compiled for this study provides an appropriate framework for analyzing the impact of nature tourism in NE KZN. Specifically, the two-region SAM approach was very helpful in identifying the linkages that exist between Region 1 and Region 2 of KZN Province. The surveys for Region 1 that form part of the broader World Bank research project were incorporated into the SAM. The data for Region 2 were then calculated by subtracting the data for Region 1 from that of KZN Province.

Although the figures obtained from the KZN Conservation Authority (KwaZulu-Natal Nature Conservation Service, various years) are probably

Table 9.20 Multipliers for Nature Tourism-Related Sectors (effect in 1998 rand of spending R1.00)

Measure	Tourist Trade Activities	Tourist Transport Activities	Tourist Accommodation Activities	Tourist Food and Beverages	Tourist Recreational Activities	Tourist Conservation Activities	Tour Operators
Gross domestic product (at factor cost)							
Region 1	0.88	0.62	0.81	0.56	0.89	0.88	0.78
Region 2	0.19	0.31	0.20	0.21	0.20	0.20	0.21
Total	1.07	0.93	1.02	0.76	1.09	1.09	0.99
Employment (jobs per million rand)							
Region 1	7	8	22	6	7	10	6
Region 2	4	6	4	4	4	4	4
Total	11	14	26	10	11	14	10
Income of low-income households							
Region 1	0.23	0.12	0.28	0.13	0.22	0.15	0.12
Region 2	0.04	0.06	0.09	0.04	0.05	0.06	0.04
Total	0.28	0.18	0.37	0.17	0.27	0.21	0.16
Total household income							
Region 1	0.63	0.39	0.55	0.39	0.66	0.54	0.56
Region 2	0.27	0.37	0.31	0.24	0.25	0.35	0.26
Total	0.90	0.76	0.86	0.63	0.91	0.89	0.82
Low-income households as a percentage of total household income	30.90	24.00	42.70	26.40	29.40	23.70	20.00

Note: Multiplier analysis for nature tourism spending in Region 1.

Source: Deduced from Social Accounting Matrix for Northeastern KwaZulu-Natal, Conningarth Consultants (2002).

reliable enough to form the control totals of the SAM, detailed survey data would have considerably improved the detailed coefficients as far as production and spending patterns are concerned. The SAM research project has, however, contributed significantly in theory and practice to explaining the linkage effects of nature tourism.

As far as the findings are concerned regarding the impact of nature tourism, the following are of importance:

- Nature tourism plays a major role in the economy of NE KZN. It creates a GGP of R415 million at 1998 market prices and employment of 7,036, which, respectively, account for 20.7 percent and 29.7 percent of GGP and employment of the total economy of the study area.

- The study also proves that significant linkages exist between nature tourism spending in Region 1 and the impact in Region 2.

- In absolute values, and in terms of efficiency, nature tourism has a very positive effect on relieving poverty and unemployment.

- The research has also exposed the importance of nature tourism for KZN Province as a whole.

- The importance of foreign tourists, in the study area in particular, also emerges from this study.

To improve the efficiency of the study, it is important to update the SAM currently developed for this study with information from ongoing surveys. It is also important that the SAM be used to undertake specific policy analyses regarding nature tourism.

APPENDIX 9-A. THE SOCIAL ACCOUNTING MATRIX FRAMEWORK

Structure

The structure of the components of the SAM is outlined below, first for Region 1 and then Region 2. The SAM table containing these components appears as table 9-A.1.

Table 9-A.1 Social Accounting Matrices Framework for KwaZulu-Natal

SAM 1		R1 Northeastern KwaZulu-Natal — Activit 1	Com 2	Factors 3	Enterp 4	Househ 5	Govern 6	Capital 7	R2 Rest of KwaZulu-Natal — Activit 1	Com 2	Factors 3	Enterp 4	Househ 5	Govern 6	Capital 7	R3 Rest of the World	Total
R1 1 Activities		—	P^{11}	—	—	—	—	—	—	P^{12}	—	—	E^{12}	—	—	E^{13}	g^1
2 Commodities		X^{11}	—	—	—	C^{11}	G^{11}	I^{11}	—	—	—	—	—	—	—	—	q^1
3 Factor payments		Wa^{11}	—	—	—	—	Wg^{11}	—	—	—	—	—	—	—	—	—	e^1
4 Enterprises		—	—	Q^{11}	Qv^{11}	—	Trg_E^{11}	—	—	—	Q^{12}	Qv^{12}	—	Trg_E^{12}	—	—	Z_U^1
5 Households		—	—	L^{11}	Tu^{11}	Trh_H^{11}	Trg_H^{11}	—	—	—	L^{12}	—	Trh_H^{12}	Trg_H^{12}	—	Trh_H^{13}	Z_H^1
6 Government		Ti^{11}	Ta^{11}	Tf^{11}	—	Td^{11}	—	—	—	Ta^{12}	Tf^{12}	—	Td^{12}	—	—	—	Z_G^1
7 Capital		—	—	—	Quv^{11}	Sh^{11}	—	—	—	—	—	—	Sh^{12}	—	Sa^{12}	—	Z_C^1
R2 1 Activities		—	P^{21}	—	—	—	—	—	—	P^{22}	—	—	—	—	—	E^{23}	g^2
2 Commodities		—	—	—	—	—	—	—	X^{22}	—	—	—	C^{22}	G^{22}	I^{22}	—	q^2
3 Factor payments		—	—	—	—	—	—	—	Wa^{22}	—	—	—	—	Wg^{22}	—	—	e^2
4 Enterprises		—	—	Q^{21}	Qv^{21}	—	Trg_E^{21}	—	—	—	Q^{22}	Qv^{22}	—	Trg_E^{22}	—	—	Z_U^2
5 Households		—	—	L^{21}	—	Trh_H^{21}	Trg_H^{21}	—	—	—	L^{22}	Tu^{22}	Trh_H^{22}	Trg_H^{22}	—	Trh_H^{23}	Z_H^2
6 Government		—	—	—	—	—	—	—	Ti^{22}	Ta^{22}	Tf^{22}	—	Td^{22}	—	—	—	Z_G^2
7 Capital		—	—	—	—	Sh^{21}	—	Sa^{21}	—	—	—	Quv^{22}	Sh^{22}	—	—	—	Z_C^2
R3 Rest of the world		—	M^{31}	W^{31}	—	Trh_H^{31}	Trg_H^{31}	Sa^{31}	—	M^{32}	W^{32}	—	Trh_H^{32}	Trg_H^{32}	Sa^{32}	—	Z_A
TOTAL		g^1	q^1	e^1	Z_U^1	Z_H^1	Z_G^1	Z_C^1	g^2	q^2	e^2	Z_U^2	Z_H^2	Z_G^2	Z_C^2	Z_A	

— = zero.

Source: Robinson (1989); specifically, chapter 8, "Multisectoral Models."

Region 1: Northeastern KwaZulu-Natal (R1; R2 is Region 2)

Column 1: Activities

X^{11}:   Intermediate consumption; Commodities required by Activities in R1 as inputs

Wa^{11}:   Remuneration of Labor and Capital in R1

Ti^{11}:   Indirect Taxes raised on Activities

Column 2: Commodities

P^{11}:   Production of Commodities by each activity in R1 and sold in R1

Ta^{11}:   Indirect taxes on products in R1 (value-added tax, or VAT)

P^{21}:   Imports to R1 from R2

Ta^{21}:   Indirect taxes on products in R2 (VAT)

M^{31}:   Imports from the (a) rest of South Africa and (b) rest of the world

Column 3: Factors

Q^{11}:   Dividends and interests to R1

L^{11}:   Salaries and wages to Households in R1

Tf^{11} Indirect taxes (tax on Capital and Labor) to Government in R1

Q^{21}:   Dividends and interest to R2

L^{21}:   Salaries and wages to Households in R2

Tf^{21}:   Indirect taxes (tax on Capital and Labor) to government in R2 from R1

W^{31}:   Salaries and wages to Households in the (a) rest of South Africa and (b) rest of the world

Column 4: Enterprises

Qv^{11}:   Profits distributed to Households in R1

Tu^{11}:   Enterprise taxes

Quv^{11}:   Undistributed Profits

Qv^{21}:   Profits from R1 distributed to Households in R2

Column 5: Households

E^{21}:   Private consumption expenditures by Households in R1 on Tourism Activities in R2

C^{11}:   Private consumption expenditures by Households in R1

$Trh_H{}^{11}$:   Transfers from Households in R1 to Households in R1

Td^{11}:   Direct taxes and transfers paid to the Government in R1

Sh^{11}:   Household savings in R1

$Trh_H{}^{21}$:   Transfers from Households in R1 to Households in R2

Td^{21}:   Direct taxes and transfers paid to the Government in R2

Sh^{21}:   Household savings in R2

$Trh_H{}^{31}$:   Transfers from Households in R1 to Households in the (a) rest of South Africa and (b) rest of the world

Column 6: Government

G^{11}:   Government consumption expenditures

Wg^{11}:   Remuneration of government employees

$TRg_E{}^{11}$: Transfers to Enterprises in R1

$TRg_H{}^{11}$: Transfers to Households in R1

$TRg_E{}^{21}$: Transfers to Enterprises in R2

$TRg_H{}^{21}$: Transfers to Households in R2

Column 7: Capital

I^{11}:   Gross investment in R1

Sa^{21}:   Capital flow from R1 to R2

Sa^{31}:   Capital flow from R1 to (a) rest of South Africa and (b) rest of the world

Region 2: Rest of KwaZulu-Natal

Column 1: Activities

X^{22}:   Intermediate consumption; Commodities required by Activities as inputs in R2

Wa^{22}:   Remuneration of Labor and Capital in R2

Ti^{22}:   Indirect Taxes raised on Activities

Column 2: Commodities

P^{22}:   Production of Commodities by each activity in R2 and sold in R2

Ta^{22}:   Indirect taxes on commodities in R2 (VAT)

P^{12}:   Imports of R2 from R1

Ta^{12}:   Indirect taxes on commodities in R1 (VAT)

M^{32}:   Imports from the (a) rest of South Africa and (b) rest of the world

Column 3: Factors

Q^{22}:   Dividends and interests to R2

L^{22}:   Salaries and wages to Households in R2

Tf^{22} Indirect taxes (tax on Capital and Labor) to Government in R2

Q^{12}:   Dividends and interest to R1

L^{12}:   Salaries and wages to Households in R1

Tf^{12}:   Indirect taxes (tax on Capital and Labor) to government in R1

W^{32}:   Salaries and wages to Households in (a) rest of South Africa and (b) rest of the world

Column 4: Enterprises

Qv^{22}:   Profits distributed to Households in R2 from enterprises

Tu^{22}:   Enterprise taxes

Quv^{22}:   Undistributed Profits

Qv^{12}:   Profits from R2 distributed to Households in R2

Column 5: Households

E^{12} Private consumption expenditures by Households in R2 on Tourism Activities in R1

C^{22}:   Private consumption expenditures by Households in R2

$Trh_H{}^{22}$:   Transfers from Households in R2 to Households in R2

Td^{22}:   Direct taxes and transfers paid to the Government in R2

Sh^{22}:   Household savings in R2

$Trh_H{}^{12}$:   Transfers from Households in R2 to Households in R1

Td^{12}:   Direct taxes and transfers paid to the Government in R1

Sh^{12}:   Household savings in R1

$Trh_H{}^{32}$:   Transfers from Households in R2 to Households in (a) rest of South Africa and (b) rest of the world

Column 6: Government

G^{22}:   Government consumption expenditures

Wg^{22}:   Remuneration of government employees

$TRg_E{}^{22}$:   Transfers to Enterprises in R2

$TRg_H{}^{22}$:   Transfers to Households in R2

Sg^{22}:   Government savings

$TRg_E{}^{12}$:   Transfers to Enterprises in R1

$TRg_H{}^{12}$:   Transfers to Households in R1

Column 7: Capital

I^{22}:   Gross investment in R2

Sa^{12}: Capital flow from R2 to R1

Sa^{32}: Capital flow from R2 to (a) rest of South Africa and (b) rest of the world

Detailed Entities

The entities mentioned above were all subdivided into different components. Each entity has its own set of components. For instance, when reference is made to the activities, it is a collective referral to the 58 different activities (production sectors) identified for purposes of constructing the SAM.

Tables 9-A.2 and 9-A.3 contain a list of the constituent components of each entity. However, a brief overview in this regard will be helpful. The following is an inventory of the number of constituent components of each entity:

(i)   Activities: 58 components (Region 1); 26 components (Region 2)

(ii) Commodities: 58 components (Region 1); 26 components (Region 2)

(iii) Factor payments—labor: 3 components

(iv) Factor payments—capital: 6 components (Region 1); 5 components (Region 2)

(v)   Enterprise: 6 components (Region 1); 5 components (Region 2)

(vi) Households: 10 components (Region 1); 7 components (Region 2)

(vii) Government: 5 components (expenditure side); 5 components (income side)

(viii) Capital: 2 components

This implies that each of the entries in the SAM framework (cells) may be either matrices or vectors or, in certain instances, a single figure.

The matrices depicted in the SAM framework formed the basic building blocks in the construction of the regional SAM. The construction of these matrices is explained in the annex to the book.

Table 9-A.2 List of Entities for Region 1: Northeastern KwaZulu-Natal

Activities

1	R1	Activity	Sugarcane farming
2	R1	Activity	Fruit and vegetable farming
3	R1	Activity	Livestock commercial farming
4	R1	Activity	Other commercial farming
5	R1	Activity	Subsistence farming
6	R1	Activity	Forestry
7	R1	Activity	Mining
8	R1	Activity	Sugar mills
9	R1	Activity	Food and beverages
10	R1	Activity	Clothing and textiles furniture
11	R1	Activity	Wood products (including paper mills) furniture
12	R1	Activity	Other commercial manufacturing
13	R1	Activity	Handcrafts
14	R1	Activity	Water and electricity
15	R1	Activity	Construction
16	R1	Activity	Trade commercial
17	R1	Activity	Trade informal
18	R1	Activity	Transport commercial
19	R1	Activity	Transport informal—(combi-taxi)
20	R1	Activity	Financial and business services
21	R1	Activity	Community and social services
22	R1	Activity	Tourist trade—public: souvenirs/curios
23	R1	Activity	Tourist trade—private: souvenirs/curios
24	R1	Activity	Tourist trade—informal: food and firewood
25	R1	Activity	Tourist trade—informal: curios
26	R1	Activity	Tourist trade—informal: culture and entertainment
27	R1	Activity	Tourist transport—air international
28	R1	Activity	Tourist transport—air domestic scheduled
29	R1	Activity	Tourist transport—air domestic unscheduled
30	R1	Activity	Tourist transport—touring buses
31	R1	Activity	Tourist transport—car rentals
32	R1	Activity	Tourist transport—own
33	R1	Activity	Tourist accommodation, public: huts and chalets
34	R1	Activity	Tourist accommodation, public: bush lodges and camps
35	R1	Activity	Tourist accommodation, private: hotel
36	R1	Activity	Tourist accommodation, private: guest houses, holiday farms
37	R1	Activity	Tourist accommodation, private: bed and breakfast
38	R1	Activity	Tourist accommodation, private: huts and chalets
39	R1	Activity	Tourist accommodation, private: bush lodges and camps
40	R1	Activity	Tourist accommodation, private: holiday flats
41	R1	Activity	Tourist food and drinks, public: takeout

(continued)

Table 9-A.2 (*Continued*)

Activities

42	R1	Activity	Tourist food and drinks, public: sit down
43	R1	Activity	Tourist food and drinks, private: takeout
44	R1	Activity	Tourist food and drinks, private: sit down
45	R1	Activity	Tourist entertainment/recreational, hunting: private—meat
46	R1	Activity	Tourist entertainment/recreational, hunting: private—trophy
47	R1	Activity	Tourist entertainment/recreational, hunting: public—meat
48	R1	Activity	Tourist entertainment/recreational, hunting: public—trophy
49	R1	Activity	Tourist entertainment/recreational, viewing: private guided tours
50	R1	Activity	Tourist entertainment/recreational, viewing: private walks
51	R1	Activity	Tourist entertainment/recreational, viewing: public guided tours
52	R1	Activity	Tourist entertainment/recreational, viewing: public guided walks
53	R1	Activity	Tourist entertainment/recreational, viewing: public entrance fees
54	R1	Activity	Tourist entertainment/recreational, other: private
55	R1	Activity	Tourist entertainment/recreational, other: public
56	R1	Activity	Tourist conservation services: private
57	R1	Activity	Tourist conservation services: public—biodiversity (research)
58	R1	Activity	Tourist: tour operator services (travel agencies)

Commodities

59	R1	Commodities	Sugarcane
60	R1	Commodities	Fruit and vegetables
61	R1	Commodities	Livestock—commercial
62	R1	Commodities	Other commercial farming products
63	R1	Commodities	Subsistence farming products
64	R1	Commodities	Forestry products
65	R1	Commodities	Mining products
66	R1	Commodities	Sugar
67	R1	Commodities	Food and beverages
68	R1	Commodities	Clothing and textiles
69	R1	Commodities	Wood products and paper products, furniture
70	R1	Commodities	Other commercial manufacturing products
71	R1	Commodities	Handcrafts
72	R1	Commodities	Water and electricity
73	R1	Commodities	Construction
74	R1	Commodities	Trade commercial

(*continued*)

Table 9-A.2 (Continued)

Commodities

75	R1	Commodities	Trade informal
76	R1	Commodities	Transport commercial
77	R1	Commodities	Transport informal—(combi-taxi)
78	R1	Commodities	Financial and business services
79	R1	Commodities	Community and social services
80	R1	Commodities	Tourist trade—public: souvenirs/curios
81	R1	Commodities	Tourist trade—private: souvenirs/curios
82	R1	Commodities	Tourist trade—informal: food and firewood
83	R1	Commodities	Tourist trade—informal: curios
84	R1	Commodities	Tourist trade—informal: culture and entertainment
85	R1	Commodities	Tourist transport—air international
86	R1	Commodities	Tourist transport—air domestic scheduled
87	R1	Commodities	Tourist transport—air domestic unscheduled
88	R1	Commodities	Tourist transport—touring buses
89	R1	Commodities	Tourist transport—car rentals
90	R1	Commodities	Tourist transport—own
91	R1	Commodities	Tourist accommodation, public: huts and chalets
92	R1	Commodities	Tourist accommodation, public: bush lodges and camps
93	R1	Commodities	Tourist accommodation, private: hotel
94	R1	Commodities	Tourist accommodation, private: guest houses, holiday farms
95	R1	Commodities	Tourist accommodation, private: bed and breakfast
96	R1	Commodities	Tourist accommodation, private: huts and chalets
97	R1	Commodities	Tourist accommodation, private: bush lodges and camps
98	R1	Commodities	Tourist accommodation, private: holiday flats
99	R1	Commodities	Tourist food and drinks, public: takeout
100	R1	Commodities	Tourist food and drinks, public: sit down
101	R1	Commodities	Tourist food and drinks, private: takeout
102	R1	Commodities	Tourist food and drinks, private: sit down
103	R1	Commodities	Tourist entertainment/recreational, hunting: private—meat
104	R1	Commodities	Tourist entertainment/recreational, hunting: private—trophy
105	R1	Commodities	Tourist entertainment/recreational, hunting: public—meat
106	R1	Commodities	Tourist entertainment/recreational, hunting: public—trophy
107	R1	Commodities	Tourist entertainment/recreational, viewing: private guided tours
108	R1	Commodities	Tourist entertainment/recreational, viewing: private walks

(continued)

Table 9-A.2 (Continued)

Commodities

109	R1	Commodities	Tourist entertainment/recreational, viewing: public guided tours
110	R1	Commodities	Tourist entertainment/recreational, viewing: public guided walks
111	R1	Commodities	Tourist entertainment/recreational, viewing: public entrance fees
112	R1	Commodities	Tourist entertainment/recreational, other: private
113	R1	Commodities	Tourist entertainment/recreational, other: public
114	R1	Commodities	Tourist conservation services: private
115	R1	Commodities	Tourist conservation services: public—biodiversity
116	R1	Commodities	Tourist: tour operator services

Factor Payments—Labor

117	R1	Factors	Labor, skilled
118	R1	Factors	Labor, semiskilled
119	R1	Factors	Labor, unskilled

Factor Payments—Capital (gross operating surplus)

120	R1	Factors	Capital, public game reserves
121	R1	Factors	Capital, private game reserves owners
122	R1	Factors	Capital, large commercial
123	R1	Factors	Capital, small commercial
124	R1	Factors	Capital, tour operators
125	R1	Factors	Capital, local communities

Enterprises

126	R1	Enterprises	Public game reserves
127	R1	Enterprises	Private game reserves owners
128	R1	Enterprises	Large commercial
129	R1	Enterprises	Small commercial
130	R1	Enterprises	Tour operators
131	R1	Enterprises	Local communities

Households

132	R1	Households	Normal spending rural—high-income
133	R1	Households	Normal spending rural—medium-income
134	R1	Households	Normal spending rural—low-income
135	R1	Households	Normal spending urban—high-income
136	R1	Households	Normal spending urban—medium-income
137	R1	Households	Normal spending urban—low-income
138	R1	Households	Tourist—high-income
139	R1	Households	Tourist—medium-income
140	R1	Households	Tourist—low-income
141	R1	Households	Tourist—marine

(continued)

Table 9-A.2 (*Continued*)

Government

142	R1	Government	Government—national
143	R1	Government	Government—provincial—education
144	R1	Government	Government—provincial—health
145	R1	Government	Government—provincial—other
146	R1	Government	Government—local

Capital

147	R1	Capital	Capital—corporate sector and household
148	R1	Capital	Capital—government

Table 9-A.3 List of Entities for Region 2: Rest of KwaZulu-Natal

Activities

1	R2	Activities	Agriculture
2	R2	Activities	Mining
3	R2	Activities	Food, beverages, and tobacco
4	R2	Activities	Clothing, textiles, and footwear
5	R2	Activities	Wood, furniture, paper, and printing
6	R2	Activities	Chemicals
7	R2	Activities	Nonmetallic mineral products
8	R2	Activities	Metal and machinery, transport equipment
9	R2	Activities	Other manufacturing
10	R2	Activities	Water
11	R2	Activities	Electricity
12	R2	Activities	Construction
13	R2	Activities	Trade
14	R2	Activities	Accommodation and catering
15	R2	Activities	Transport and communication
16	R2	Activities	Business services
17	R2	Activities	Community services
18	R2	Activities	Tourist trade: public, private, and informal
19	R2	Activities	Transport: tourist—air
20	R2	Activities	Transport: tourist—buses and car rentals
21	R2	Activities	Transport: tourist—own car
22	R2	Activities	Tourist: accommodation—public and private
23	R2	Activities	Tourist: food and drink—public and private
24	R2	Activities	Tourist: entertainment/recreational—public and private
25	R2	Activities	Tourist: conservation services—public and private
26	R2	Activities	Tourist: tour operator services

(continued)

Table 9-A.3(*Continued*)

Commodities

27	R2	Commodities	Agriculture
28	R2	Commodities	Mining
29	R2	Commodities	Food, beverages, and tobacco
30	R2	Commodities	Clothing, textiles, and footwear
31	R2	Commodities	Wood, furniture, paper, and printing
32	R2	Commodities	Chemicals
33	R2	Commodities	Nonmetallic mineral products
34	R2	Commodities	Metal and machinery, transport equipment
35	R2	Commodities	Other manufacturing
36	R2	Commodities	Water
37	R2	Commodities	Electricity
38	R2	Commodities	Construction
39	R2	Commodities	Trade
40	R2	Commodities	Accommodation and catering
41	R2	Commodities	Transport and communication
42	R2	Commodities	Business services
43	R2	Commodities	Community services
44	R2	Commodities	Tourist trade: public, private, and informal
45	R2	Commodities	Transport: tourist—air
46	R2	Commodities	Transport: tourist—buses and car rentals
47	R2	Commodities	Transport: tourist—own car
48	R2	Commodities	Tourist: accommodation—public and private
49	R2	Commodities	Tourist: food and drink—public and private
50	R2	Commodities	Tourist: entertainment/recreational—public and private
51	R2	Commodities	Tourist: conservation services—public and private
52	R2	Commodities	Tourist: tour operator services

Factor Payments—Labor

53	R2	Factors	Labor, skilled
54	R2	Factors	Labor, semiskilled
55	R2	Factors	Labor, unskilled

Factor Payments—Capital (gross operating surplus)

56	R2	Factors	Capital, public game reserves
57	R2	Factors	Capital, private game reserves owners
58	R2	Factors	Capital, commercial
59	R2	Factors	Capital, tour operators
60	R2	Factors	Capital, local communities

(*continued*)

Table 9-A.3(*Continued*)

Enterprises

61	R2	Enterprises	Public game reserves
62	R2	Enterprises	Private game reserves
63	R2	Enterprises	Commercial
64	R2	Enterprises	Tour operators
65	R2	Enterprises	Local communities

Households

66	R2	Households	Normal spending—high-income
67	R2	Households	Normal spending—medium-income
68	R2	Households	Normal spending—low-income
69	R2	Households	Tourist—high-income
70	R2	Households	Tourist—medium-income
71	R2	Households	Tourist—low-income
72	R2	Households	Tourist—marine

Government

73	R2	Government	Government—national
74	R2	Government	Government—provincial—education
75	R2	Government	Government—provincial—health
76	R2	Government	Government—provincial—other
77	R2	Government	Government—local

Capital

78	R2	Capital	Capital—corporate sector and household
79	R2	Capital	Capital—government

Imports

1	R3	Imports	Rest of South Africa
2	R4	Imports	Rest of world

EXPORTS: Rest of South Africa

3	R3	Exports	Tourist—high-income
4	R3	Exports	Tourist—medium-income
5	R3	Exports	Tourist—low-income
6	R3	Exports	Tourist—marine

EXPORTS: Rest of World

7	R4	Exports	Tourist—high-income
8	R4	Exports	Tourist—medium-income
9	R4	Exports	Tourist—low-income
10	R4	Exports	Tourist—special 1
11	R4	Exports	Tourist—special 2

EXPORTS: Goods and Services

REFERENCES

Conningarth Consultants. 2002. *Social Accounting Matrix for North Eastern KwaZulu-Natal (RSA)*. A Report to the World Bank Project on Nature Tourism and Conservation. Pretoria.

Grant Thornton Kessel Feinstein, 2000. *Simulated National Satellite Account for South African Travel and Tourism*. A Study for Tourism South Africa, September 2000.

Kwa-Zulu-Natal Nature Conservation Service. Various years. Unpublished estimates provided to World Bank research project.

Robinson, Sherman. 1989. *Handbook of Development Economics*. Berkeley: University of California.

SATOUR (Tourism South Africa). 1998. *A Survey of South Africa's Foreign Visitor Market*. January and August.

Seymour, J. 1998. *KwaZulu-Natal's Domestic Tourism Market: June '98–September '98*. Durban: KwaZulu-Natal Tourism Authority.

CHAPTER 10

CREATING A NATURE TOURISM ECONOMY

A Multicriteria Analysis of Options for Policy, Institutions, and Management

Bruce Aylward

Efforts to examine conservation finance and tourism have typically relied on the use of economic valuation techniques to demonstrate that visitors are willing to pay to engage in ecotourism or nature tourism activities (Wells 1997). Inherent in such a simplistic approach is a lack of applied economic analysis of the supply and demand relationships in nature tourism markets, the relationships among different sites, and the backward and forward linkages to more generic tourism goods and services. Proposals to increase conservation finance by raising charges on the basis of such studies are likely to miss important economic trade-offs; moreover, they are unlikely to provide any information on the potential social and environmental effects of conservation finance proposals.

To better explain economic and environmental linkages involved in nature tourism, the Nature Tourism and Conservation Project developed a general, sectoral, multimarket analytic framework that clarifies the principal direct and indirect links among the various economic, environmental, social, and policy variables (see annex A to the book). Although the multimarket model is largely a heuristic device, the studies undertaken as part of this project all represent efforts to examine—in quantitative terms where possible—aspects of this model in a practical, empirical fashion.

This chapter aims to bring together the information and insights generated by these components in one overarching analysis and thereby to respond to four key issues related to nature tourism and conservation finance: (1) the sustainability of resource use, (2) the relative benefits to and interactions among multiple users, (3) the roles of the public and private sectors in nature tourism activities, and (4) the impact of these activities on social equity. Because of the mix between quantitative and qualitative information and the wide range of indicators, a multicriteria analysis is used to examine the options for moving toward a nature tourism economy in the study area.

The options explored include a number of familiar methods of increasing revenues from tourism through fees and charges. However, a larger set of policy, managerial, and institutional choices faced by relevant actors is also examined, including possible investments and conservation activities by the public and private sectors. In addition, the potential effects of changes in a few important exogenous variables (variables controlled at higher political levels or not controlled by human action) are included, though when possible these are presented as policy options to mitigate or improve exogenous negative situations. Thus the chapter examines the benefits of curtailing crime rather than the effects of existing levels of crime.

Policy or other changes in the study area will affect the following ingredients of sustainable development (whether or not they are the intended objective):

- Economic development (at the national, provincial, and study area levels)

- Social equity within the country and the study area

- Biodiversity conservation in the province and the study area.

By examining the response of indicators for these criteria to specific options, explicit recommendations are derived from the analysis regarding how to use conservation finance options and other variables to improve economic development, social equity, and environmental sustainability in the study area. Broader lessons for nature tourism–related policies are also advanced.

Because political, institutional, and managerial contexts are fundamental to the trade-offs in nature tourism, they will determine the choice of policy or control variables that may be reasonably manipulated. Collaboration is thus necessary with state agencies, the private sector, nongovernmental organizations, and civil society groups in order to understand local limitations on the realm of the possible.

Indeed, the results presented below were presented to and commented on by a multisectoral group of tourism experts in a workshop hosted by the Development Bank of South Africa in May 2002. The analysis thus reflects an initial ground-truthing. The results of the workshop suggest that many of the ideas, concepts, and actions examined in this chapter are already rapidly being incorporated into policy in the South African context. Nevertheless, as an effort in applied economic and policy research, the project continues to question the remaining local limitations, and attempts to portray the full range of options open to the relevant actors in this area.

CONCEPTUAL AND ANALYTICAL FRAMEWORK FOR AN INTEGRATED MULTIMARKET MODEL

Figure 10.1 provides a simple indication of the flow of the policy analysis that is developed in this chapter. The modeling simulates choices available to policymakers, property owners, and others and assesses how they affect the nature tourism market. Depending on the policy,

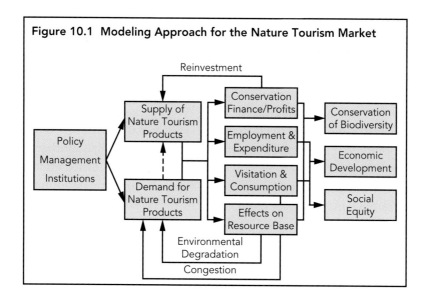

Figure 10.1 Modeling Approach for the Nature Tourism Market

management, or institutional choices being assessed, supply or demand in the nature tourism market is altered, which in turn affects consumption and production in the nature tourism market and subsequently affects conservation finance, employment and expenditures, visitation, and the resource base.

These effects serve as a series of indicators for the desired outcomes of development, equity, and conservation. By comparing results under the status quo with those obtained following simulation of a change in policy, an understanding of the direction, magnitude, and relative importance of the induced change in outcomes can be obtained.

The feedback effect of three of these indicators—conservation finance, the environmental impact of tourism on the resource base, and visitation—can also be incorporated into the assessment process by developing a feedback loop that includes environmental degradation, congestion, and reinvestment in conservation. Each of these will play back into the demand for and supply of nature tourism. Such a feedback loop permits a more farsighted perspective on outcomes, given that many of the effects on biodiversity conservation will occur over a longer time frame than the immediate economic or equity effects.

Changes in social, economic, and environmental conditions that are derived largely outside the nature tourism market—such as changes in crime, malaria, and income—also affect the demand for and supply of nature tourism. The framework can thus be used to look at the effects on nature tourism and related outcomes of either allowing an existing trend to persist or of investing in a reversal of the trend. For example, the potential benefits to nature tourism of policies and programs to address malaria can be estimated by assessing a scenario in which the incidence of malaria is reduced.

Clearly, a policy designed to maximize one of the three outcomes of development, equity, and conservation may not maximize another and, indeed, may even lead to negative direct or indirect feedback effects. A policy to stimulate demand for tourism to spur economic development, for example, may increase usage of the resource base to the point where natural capital is degraded, leading to a reduction in the natural asset or its quality in subsequent rounds. Similarly, a policy with a narrow objective related to conservation finance may have positive or negative effects on any or all of the three outcomes. Raising entrance fees may dampen demand and reduce pressure on the resource base, and at the same time provide additional funds for land management, positively influencing biodiversity conservation through two channels. However, such a policy may shift consumption from local to foreign tourists, thus affecting social equity in a negative fashion. These are the sorts of questions and trade-offs to which the policy analysis framework is designed to respond, although the answers in this analysis will be fairly specific to the type of nature tourism asset and the characteristics of the producers and consumers in the nature tourism market under review.

A simple left-to-right modeling framework does not convey adequately the front-to-back relationships that actually exist between different markets and sites involved in the nature tourism market within a given region, country, or locality. This dynamic is portrayed in figure 10.2, which attempts to demonstrate the back-and-forth linkages that may exist in the case of this study. Market linkages may exist between different public protected areas (both inside and outside the study area) and between the public areas and the private game reserves. Similarly, other providers of tourism services (transport, tours, accommodation, air

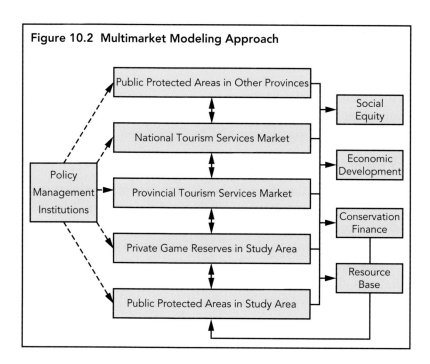

Figure 10.2 Multimarket Modeling Approach

travel, and so forth) at the local, provincial, and national levels may be affected by changes in demand for and supply of the nature tourism sites. Alternatively, changes in policy that affect these broader markets (such as a tax on hotels or airport usage) may lead to spillover effects for the nature tourism site markets themselves.

Thus it would be ideal not only to conduct an integrated analysis of the effects of different control variables (the right-to-left flow and feedback loops) but also to link the different markets to track how changes cascade through the various markets and conservation areas. Such an analysis is called a multimarket approach because it employs quantitative data on the economic relationship between different markets and sites—be they substitutes or complements. Annex A provides the outline of an analytical multimarket framework adapted to the case of nature tourism. The extent to which the policy analysis below can realize such an analysis in quantitative terms is necessarily limited. Application of the full framework is subject to the sites selected, the true nature of the multimarket relationships (substitutes or complements), and the resources and information available. Nonetheless, the analysis below attempts to combine a range of different data, studies, and models as a first step in this direction.

METHODOLOGY

The methodology employed in the policy analysis is explained by presenting the policy options that will be explored, the indicators that will be assessed, and the parameters and data employed.

Policy Options: Instruments and Variables

The analysis assesses the effects of a series of current proposals—economic policy instruments, institutional approaches, and management alternatives—aimed at improving the overall sustainability of nature tourism in the study area. The options that are analyzed are shown in table 10.1, which also indicates each option's entry point into the analysis and the scale at which the decision to choose the option is taken and at which level it affects consumers of nature tourism. Figures 10.3 and 10.4 illustrate how the instruments and outcome measures vary from public to private areas.

Table 10.1 Instruments and Variables Affecting the Sustainability of Nature Tourism

Instrument or Variable	Entry Point	Scale of Decision (D) and Impact on Nature Tourism Consumer (I)			
		Local	Province	National	International
1. Economic policy instruments					
(a) Raising entrance fees at public protected areas (PPAs)	Demand for visits to PPAs and private game ranches and reserves (PGRs)	I	D (KZN) and I	D (KNP) and I	I
(b) Raising community levies at PPAs	Demand for visits to PPAs and PGRs	I	D (KZN) and I	Yes	I
(c) Differentiating entrance fees at PPAs	Demand for visits to PPAs and PGRs	I	D (KZN) and I	D (KNP) and I	I
(d) Levying an airport tax or ticket fee	Demand for travel to the rest of South Africa	—	—	D	I
(e) Incentives for PGRs	Profitability of PGRs	I	D and I	D and I	I
2. Institutional and managerial options					
(f) Expansion of beds in PPAs	Demand for visits to PPAs	I	D and I	D and I	I
(g) Private concessions for tourism services in PPAs	Conservation finance	D and I	D and I	I	I
(h) Integrating land management (dropping fences)	Supply of nature tourism asset	D and I	D and I	I	I
(i) Ecological management on PGRs	Resilience	D	I	I	I
3. Other influencing or exogenous variables					
(j) Household income growth	Demand for nature tourism	I	I	I	I
(k) Reducing crime	Demand for travel to the rest of South Africa	D	D	D	I
(l) Reducing incidence of disease (malaria and HIV/AIDS)	Demand for travel to the rest of South Africa and KZN	D	D	D and I	I
(m) Increasing expenditures on marketing	Demand for travel to the rest of South Africa	—	D	D and I	I

KZN = KwaZulu-Natal; KNP = Kruger National Park.

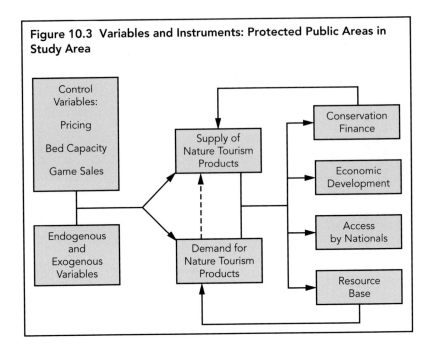

Figure 10.3 Variables and Instruments: Protected Public Areas in Study Area

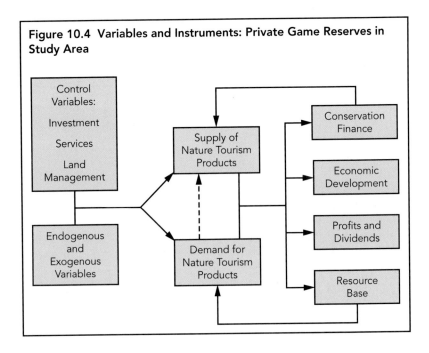

Figure 10.4 Variables and Instruments: Private Game Reserves in Study Area

Given competing demands for public funds in the South African context, the proposals reflect in large part the need to improve the financial balance of the public protected areas in the study area. Raising conservation finance or achieving cost-efficient conservation and tourism service provision are therefore the explicit goals of many of the instruments and variables. Many of the proposed economic policy instruments (such as raising entrance fees and airport taxes) refer to opportunities to increase the financial return on the management of public protected areas. Meanwhile, a number of managerial and institutional options influence the roles of the public and private sectors in tourism services and land and game management and, therefore, have a bearing on the efficiency of provision of these activities. Several additional instruments and variables included arise out of the substudies, including the role of land and ecological management in the conservation of biodiversity on private lands, and enhancing the tourism experience by improving attractiveness and limiting congestion (hence, with spillover effects for conservation finance).

In addition, a series of general influences or exogenous variables may affect nature tourism in the study area. These consist of factors that are viewed in the current context as negatives for tourism demand. For example, high crime levels, the persistence of malaria, the spread of HIV/AIDS, and low expenditures on promotion in foreign markets all tend to have negative and largely uncontrollable effects on the nature tourism market in the study area. At the same time, the analysis of these effects can be taken as evidence of the potential benefits that would accrue in the form of increased demand when efforts are undertaken to resolve these problems.

Indicators for Assessing Sustainable Development in the Nature Tourism Sector

Each of the policy options will be assessed against a set of indicators for conservation finance, economic development, social equity, and biodiversity conservation (table 10.2). With a few additions and subtractions, the list in the table reflects the quantitative indicators presented in the discussion of the contribution of nature tourism in the study area provided in chapter 1 of this volume. However, a number of important relationships

Table 10.2 Indicators of Sustainability for Nature Tourism

Indicator	Type of Indicator	Source of Indicator
Conservation finance		
• Visitation	Quantitative	Demand studies
• Entrance fee revenues	Quantitative	Demand studies
• Accommodation revenues	Quantitative	Demand studies
• Revenues from earmarked airport tax and ticket fees	Quantitative	Demand studies
• Game sales receipts	Qualitative	Game sales study
• Hunting revenues	Qualitative	Producer Survey
• Increased cost-efficiency in operation of public protected areas	Qualitative	Producer Survey
Economic development		
• Tourist expenditure	Quantitative	Demand studies
• Gross geographical product (output)	Quantitative	Social Accounting Matrix (SAM)
• Employment	Quantitative	SAM
• Household income	Quantitative	SAM
Social equity		
• Distribution of change in employment	Quantitative	SAM
• Distribution of change in household income	Quantitative	SAM
• South African nationals' access to parks and reserves	Quantitative	Demand studies
Conservation of the resource base and biodiversity		
• Extent of environmental footprint	Quantitative	Ecological Survey[a]
• Extent of tourism impact	Qualitative	Ecological Survey
• Congestion impact	Qualitative	Ecological Survey and demand studies
• Reinvestment in biodiversity conservation in private game reserves (landscape, vegetation, species, genetic vigor, and connectivity)	Qualitative/ Quantitative	Ecological Survey[a] and Producer Survey
• Reinvestment in protected area management (KwaZulu-Natal Wildlife)	Qualitative	Ecological Survey

[a] Refers to the section of the ecological survey in which a series of hypothetical questions explores how landowners would respond to changes in tourist demand.

are either not quantifiable or there is no basis in the study for their quantification. Thus, the form in which the indicator appears, either "quantitative" or "qualitative," is also given in the table. Finally, the source of the parameter or qualitative judgment on how the indicator responds to changes in the system is indicated, referencing the sub-study component from which this information is derived.

Analysis of the impact of a particular policy instrument or scenario yields a series of estimates for the assessment indicators. To choose preferred alternatives or to rank options, it is necessary to summarize the pros and cons of each policy for each indicator and to compare the results. To keep such a multicriteria analysis simple, each of the outcomes is assigned a score on the basis of a holistic but subjective assessment of the overall impact of the series of indicators. The scores used are:

- –2 (substantially worse)
- –1 (a little worse)
- 0 (no change)
- 1 (a little better)
- 2 (much better)

A primary objective of the project is to identify options for generating conservation finance without adversely affecting the other indicators. Thus, the instruments are assessed in terms of their potential to contribute to conservation finance while minimizing any trade-offs across the other indicators. Further, these estimates can be assessed without giving priority to the conservation finance objective. In other words, multicriteria scores can be calculated as a way of ranking options and can be plotted on a multicriteria graph to provide a visual interpretation of the results. These disaggregated results can then be employed to better explain and compare specific options.

Response Parameters and Feedback Relationships

The information employed to assess the changes in the indicators under each of the policy options and scenarios comes primarily from the sub-components of the project. A number of the responses between the instruments, intervening variables, indicators, and feedback loops are summarized below. Responses and parameters that are shared between many of the policy options or that can be expressed only in generic qualitative terms are covered here in the interest of efficiency. Those that are specific to a given option or instrument are covered in the analysis of individual options. In general, the order in which the analysis is undertaken consists first of evaluating effects on demand, which in turn affect expenditures and conservation revenues, which in turn lead to changes in the economic impact of nature tourism. Changes in visitation also have environmental and tourism feedback loops. Both sets of responses are covered below, starting with demand, moving on to the economic impact, and then addressing the feedback loops.

Response of Demand to Price Changes: Price Elasticities

As was indicated above, many of the policy options involve altering pricing policies to obtain an increase in conservation revenues. Because these economic instruments alter the prices of the components of the tourist package, it is necessary to know how a given price change alters the demand for the component or the package as a whole. Economists refer to this measure of responsiveness—that is, how behavior with regard to the demand for a good changes in response to a change in its price—as the price elasticity of demand.

Price elasticities of demand are the ratio of the percentage change in quantity demanded to the percentage change in price. Thus, by knowing, for example, the percentage increase in projected entrance fees, the original quantity demanded, and the elasticity, it is possible to solve the equation to obtain the new quantity that will be demanded at the new price level. Because each of the different instruments involves a different elasticity measure with its own analysis in the demand studies done for this project, the elasticities are not presented here but rather are discussed under the appropriate section for each instrument.

It is worth stressing, however, that the overall conclusion of the three demand studies (on-site, household, and origin country) was that demand is inelastic with respect to price. That is, a small change in price has little effect on tourist demand, and only at significantly higher prices are tourists likely to opt for other destinations or change their itineraries. This result held for both residents and foreigners. The implication—explored further below—is that conservation revenues can be greatly increased without large losses in visitor numbers. The net effect of a large increase in price and a small drop in visitor numbers will be relatively large increases in revenues.

Response of Demand to Changes in Other Variables

In addition to changes in price, changes in other exogenous variables can affect tourist demand. As with price elasticities, a number of these were investigated in quantitative assessments in the demand studies and are discussed below.

Response of the Economy to Changes in Demand: Expenditure Multipliers

Changes in demand for tourism in South Africa and nature tourism in Northeastern (NE) Zululand will affect the number of visitors who come to NE Zululand, where they visit on their trip, and how long they stay. All of these changes will affect the level of tourist expenditures in the regional economy. The Social Accounting Matrix (SAM) provides the multipliers that can be used to understand how these changes in final demand will affect the NE Zululand economy and the rest of the KwaZulu-Natal (KZN) economy. The multipliers are shown in table 10.3. Most of the quantitative scenarios involve a change in the number of visitors to the KZN reserves; the effects of these changes are analyzed by the type of tourist (from which region) and by the type of ownership for the activities that see a change in demand. The average multipliers for the non-tourist-related sectors and the nature tourism subsectors are also provided for comparison purposes.

Linking demand models to the SAM is complicated by incomplete knowledge of how shifts in demand play out spatially. The demand surveys and models do not always predict where a tourist will go when a changed variable precipitates a shift of demand away from the study area. Likewise, there will be limits on what the demand surveys and models reveal about the geographic origins of additional tourists who might visit the study area in the future (under specific scenarios).

The SAM contains four regions: NE Zululand, the rest of KZN, the rest of South Africa, and the rest of the world. The multipliers generated from SAM models and other such regional economic models often lead to the belief that net gains are occurring to the economy, whereas it is

Table 10.3 Multiplier Analysis for Nature Tourism Spending in Northeastern Zululand (effect in rand of spending R1.00 at 1998 prices)

Measure	Multipliers for Tourists According to Origin				Multipliers for Nature Tourism-Related Sectors According to Ownership			Multipliers for Related and Non-Nature-Tourism-Related Sectors	
	Tourists from NE Zululand	Tourists from the Rest of KZN	Tourists from the Rest of South Africa	Tourists from the Rest of the World	Public-Sector Tourist Activities	Private-Sector Tourist Activities	Informal-Sector Tourist Activities	Average for Non-Tourism-Related Sectors	Nature Tourism Subsectors
1. Gross domestic product—total	2.55	2.83	2.76	2.81	0.96	0.94	1.03	0.89	0.95
In NE Zululand	1.97	2.18	2.11	2.12	0.70	0.73	0.85	0.63	0.72
Unskilled labor	0.54	0.56	0.43	0.38					
Skilled labor	0.21	0.24	0.26	0.28					
In rest of KZN	0.58	0.65	0.65	0.69	0.27	0.21	0.18	0.27	0.22
2. Employment—total (full-time equivalent jobs per R1 milllion in spending)	56	59	51	48	14	18	30	16	17
In NE Zululand	45	47	38	35	9	14	26	11	12
In rest of KZN	11	12	13	13	5	4	3	5	4
3. Household income—total	2.14	2.37	2.31	2.34	0.80	0.79	0.88	0.74	0.79
In NE Zululand	1.36	1.51	1.46	1.44	0.46	0.51	0.64	0.40	0.49
In rest of KZN	0.78	0.87	0.85	0.90	0.34	0.28	0.24	0.34	0.30
Low-income groups—total	0.83	0.89	0.82	0.73	0.25	0.26	0.47	0.21	0.26
In NE Zululand	0.63	0.68	0.63	0.55	0.18	0.20	0.41	0.14	0.20
In rest of KZN	0.20	0.21	0.19	0.18	0.07	0.06	0.06	0.06	0.06
Low-income as a percentage of total	38.9	37.7	35.3	31.4	31.0	33.5	53.5	28.0	32.9

KZN = KwaZulu-Natal.

Source: SAM produced by Conningarth Consultants (2002).

rather a matter of which regions in the economy gain and which lose. In recognition of this, the use of multipliers in this study is constrained to examining effects of expenditures in NE Zululand on output, income, and employment within NE Zululand. If a tourist spends one less day in NE Zululand, then the decrease in output in the rest of KZN that occurs due to a decrease in spending in NE Zululand cannot be taken as a "loss" in output if there exists the possibility that the tourist will simply spend one more day in, for example, Durban. In that case, the rest of KZN actually will see an increase in output after the change in demand and expenditures. Thus, in the analysis of economic development, the focus is primarily on the region of NE Zululand and how its economy fares, regardless of how the other regions fare.

The multipliers for nature tourism sectors according to ownership enable a comparison of how an expenditure of R1 in the public sector compares with the same expenditure in the private sector. In terms of multiplier effects on gross domestic product (GDP), household income, and that share of household income going to low-income groups, the private sector has a small, almost indistinct edge on the public sector. The numbers on employment effects are more definitive. Each R1 million in expenditure in the private sector creates 14 jobs, compared with 9 jobs in the public sector. This provides additional evidence for the hypotheses presented in chapter 1 that private game ranches and reserves (PGRs) are more labor intensive than their public-sector counterparts. The final column in table 10.3 presents the multipliers for non-tourism-related sectors and for nature tourism sectors. Nature tourism subsectors do better than nonrelated tourism sectors in terms of GDP, employment, and income received by low-income households.

Reinvestment Feedback Loop: Indirect Effect of Increases in Visitation Rates and Conservation Revenues on Biodiversity Conservation

As was alluded to above, the amount of land under conservation by the private sector in the study area has increased dramatically in the past decade. As shown by the Producer Survey, the profitability of these enterprises is far from assured. But at the same time, it is clear that the bottom line is not the only motive driving entrepreneurs.

To obtain preliminary information on how changes in demand might affect the behavior of private game reserve owners, the Ecological Survey included a series of questions regarding the actions that owners would take in response to some fairly severe increases and decreases in occupancy rates. Due to the hypothetical nature of the questions, the large increment in demand posited, and the variability in responses obtained, it is not useful to try to characterize their responses in quantitative terms. However, the general tenor and direction of responses are useful in gauging how a change in demand for the services of private game reserve would reflect on the owners' investment in and commitment to biodiversity conservation.

Because these are general directional statements, they apply equally across a number of options and scenarios and, therefore, they are summarized in table 10.4. Along with the relatively small sample group of private game reserve owners, the questions were also asked of KZN Wildlife for the three reserves in the core study areas included in the Ecological Survey.

The overall results suggest that for private game reserves a large increase in demand would spur significant reinvestment, not just in facilities but also in land and game. Though the adequacy of management on private game reserves in terms of water hole density, invasive species management, overstocking, out of range species, and so on remains in question, there appears to be little doubt that increased conservation revenues will lead to increased reinvestment in conservation. A complete failure in demand indicates that there is a limit past which all but the most committed owners cannot go, and at which point most properties would be returned to their preceding use—cattle raising. However, the addition of venison as an additional product from the range, as specified in some responses, means that abandonment of private game reserve involvement would not imply a complete return to former production methods (that is, purely cattle ranching).

Degradation Feedback Loop: Direct Effect on Resource Base of Increases in Visitation Rates

There is a common perception that rapid growth in demand in nature tourism or ecotourism can lead to the destruction of the resource base on which the tourism depends. No doubt this perception is fed by a number of high-profile cases, such as beach hotels in Indonesia depleting

Table 10.4 Tourism and Land Management under Demand Scenarios

Scenario	Result and Impact on Biodiversity Conservation in Private Game Ranches and Reserves and Public Protected Areas
1. No tourism demand	Most PGR respondents indicated that the land would be put into production of cattle and venison, or that the land would not have been purchased. The impact on biodiversity conservation would therefore be negative. Because most of the properties originally were purely cattle farms, the move to game ranching (the addition of venison) would imply a small improvement over the situation where the demand was never expected and farms were not converted into game reserves.
2. A "doubling in tourism demand"	It is a measure of the low occupancy rates at present that only 2 of 27 PGR respondents to this open-ended question suggested that they would buy more land; most indicated that they would fill existing beds.
…and how demand would be catered to?	The vast majority of PGR respondents indicated that they would meet the higher demand by filling existing beds; 11 respondents indicated that they would be able to expand facilities and accommodation on this basis. There was no direct impact on biodiversity, although the opportunity would exist to improve management with the extra revenue, as well as the changes in land, game, and infrastructure covered below. The PPAs indicated the increase in demand would facilitate development of neighboring communal land.
…and expansion of road network?	No significant change in the road network was indicated by PGR respondents. It is interesting that all three PPAs indicated that they would increase the network and would consider allowing off-road driving in clearly defined areas.
…and expansion of infrastructure?	Expansion of facilities in the PGRs would lead to small increases in the infrastructure footprint. A marginal negative for biodiversity.
…and additional land purchase?	Asked a closed-ended question about whether they would purchase additional land in order to meet higher demand, 11 of the PGR respondents suggested that they would. A total of at least 23,000 hectares were mentioned, that is, specific adjacent properties. Others felt they had enough land for their purposes. A significant positive for biodiversity conservation.

(continued)

Table 10.4 *(Continued)*

Scenario	Result and Impact on Biodiversity Conservation in Private Game Ranches and Reserves and Public Protected Areas
...and additional game purchase?	Practically all PGRs indicated they would add specific numbers of stock. The most often-mentioned species were buffalo, rhino, and giraffe. A significant positive for biodiversity conservation, although concern for overstocking remains an issue. The PPAs indicated that they would introduce additional game only for biological reasons, not in response to changes in tourist demand.

PGR = private game reserves; PPA = public protected areas.

Sources: Answers to Ecological Survey questions; James and Goodman (2001).

all the sand to build hotels, or coral lagoons being killed off by clumsy, sunscreen-lathered tourists, or—to give a more apropos example—the degradation of the Amboseli National Park range in Kenya due to uncontrolled off-road driving. Some of these cases may be exceptions, whereas some may be more pervasive.

Still, it is also likely that potential degradation is linked to the type of ecosystem at hand and its susceptibility and sensitivity to human visits. Thus, the fact that the more tourists who swim and clamber around a coral reef, the more damage will occur, has very little consequence with regard to the effect of driving vehicles around reserves in Southern Africa on dirt or tarred roads, or even off-road.

The Ecological Survey generally found veld (vegetation) conditions on the private game reserves to be acceptable, although certainly not ideal. It is perhaps not surprising that the reserves performed best on the "animal condition" score, with the large majority of reserves rating the highest score in this category. Clearly, the average tourist has difficulty identifying poor or "unnatural" vegetation, but most would be able to tell the difference between a well-fed antelope or an emaciated one. However, the KZN Wildlife reserves were not systematically assessed on the same scoring system for veld condition (due to their size, this was not practical). Thus, it is not possible to draw conclusions as to how far the management of these private game reserves is from not just "ideal," but also "practically ideal."

Most of the properties prohibit off-road driving, and many do not let guests drive their vehicles around the property, requiring instead that guests be guided by staff. Also, the one reserve that allows off-road driving did not score any worse in the veld condition assessment. Thus, it is hard to sustain the conclusion that increases in demand in the Zululand area will have significant negative or catastrophic effects on the resource base or on biodiversity. Indeed, the reverse is true; as was suggested above, increases in demand are likely to play out in increased investment in land, infrastructure, and game with a net positive for biodiversity. More effective land management is needed on these reserves, but it most likely is not achievable on a shoestring budget.

Congestion Feedback Loop: Response of Tourists to Increases in Visitation

The other consequence of increased demand for nature tourism in the study area would be an increase in the density of tourists. As suggested above, the KZN Wildlife reserves indicated that they would consider expanding the road network with a doubling of demand. It was reported that occupancy rates are 92 percent at Hilltop Camp in Hluhluwe-Umfolozi Park (HUP), contrasting sharply with the low occupancy rates at private game reserves. However, the perception of tourists is perhaps the best way to judge whether congestion is becoming a problem and, if so, to what extent. To assess this factor, a number of scenarios were posed to tourists interviewed in HUP, Ithala Game Reserve, and Kruger National Park as part of the Visitor Survey (chapter 3).

Day visitors were asked to assess whether they felt a doubling of visitors would have reduced the quality of their experience. Some 42 percent of foreigners and 49 percent of residents indicated that it would. They were then asked about their willingness to pay to avoid congested areas. Due to small sample sizes, the results need to be treated with caution. For South African residents, more than 70 percent indicated that they would be willing to pay an extra fee (from R10 to R60) to avoid the congested area and go to an area with the current level of crowding. Only 8 percent of residents were willing to go to the congested area. Other respondents chose to spend time elsewhere on their vacation. Though the sample is small, it does suggest that residents will be sensitive to crowding as tourism increases at these sites.

Foreign day visitors showed a similar level of willingness to pay a fee (from US$3 to US$45) to avoid the doubling of visitation scenario, although a larger overall proportion (17 percent) indicated a willingness to pay the current fee and go to the congested area. Although a small sample size limits the conclusions, the foreign day visitor sample did not show a marked decrease in willingness to pay the extra fee until it exceeded US$20. In the case of resident day visitors, even at the higher fee levels a similar drop-off in those willing to pay the fee was not noticed.

The congestion or "crowding effect" variable was also included in the assessment of factors influencing decisions of overnight tourists (residents and foreigners) regarding their itineraries. With the larger, overnight visitor sample sizes and current congestion levels, this variable did not emerge as a significant factor in how tourists allocated the days in their itineraries.

However, comparing HUP and Kruger, it appears that those overnight tourists concerned about crowding are more likely to spend more days at HUP and fewer days at Kruger, relative to other tourists. This result seems logical, given that Kruger is a much more popular, mainstream destination with a significantly larger number of visitors, more extensive facilities, and even tarred roads. Thus, there is likely to be significant congestion at entrances and exits and near the main camps and service centers, which annoys visitors in search of a more private wildlife experience. Meanwhile at HUP, the roads are relatively uncongested even at peak times, such as Christmas.

The overall message is that at current levels congestion is not a significant factor. But at much higher levels of visitation, it is likely that tourists would be willing to pay a significant fee to have a congestion-free game viewing experience.

ANALYSIS OF OPTIONS

In the following sections and subsections, the analysis of the policy options is presented. The options (outlined earlier in this chapter in table 10.1) are grouped according to four objectives:

1. Raising conservation finance for public protected areas by profiting from inelastic demand for nature tourism, including (a) raising

entrance fees, (b) differentiating entrance fees, and (c) introducing or increasing departure and airport charges

2. Achieving development with equity by reallocating public and private roles, including (a) expanding KZN Wildlife accommodations in HUP, (b) offering private concessions for tourism services in public protected areas (PPAs), and (c) raising the community levy

3. Enhancing biodiversity conservation in private game reserves, including (a) enhancing incentives for PGRs, (b) integrating land management by dropping fences, and (c) improving ecological management on PGRs, and

4. General policy responses that can promote demand for nature tourism, including (a) reducing crime, (b) reducing the incidence of malaria and HIV/AIDS, and (c) increasing expenditures on promotion and marketing.

The baseline conditions in the core study area were discussed at length in chapter 1. To simplify the analysis, quantitative modeling is undertaken for HUP only. Pending receipt of data for recent years on visitors to HUP and their composition, the figures employed in the simulations are based on available characterizations of visitors to HUP from revenue data and past visitation data.

Expenditure patterns in NE Zululand and in the rest of South Africa, as well as the length of stay in the country (broken down by "within NE Zululand" and "rest of the country"), are derived from the expenditure data in the On-Site Survey presented above. These data are summarized in table 10.5.

Pricing for entrance fees, the community levy, and accommodation reflect KZN Wildlife tariff charts effective as of November 1, 2001. It is worth noting that these fee structures differ significantly from those in effect when this project was designed and fieldwork initiated.

A number of assumptions regarding how the new tariff system works are necessary and are made pending verification of actual KZN Wildlife policies. Current entrance fees are R30 per person and are paid at the gate by day visitors and as part of the cost of accommodation by overnight visitors. For the purposes of the analysis, it is assumed that overnight visitors thus pay the entrance fee on a nightly basis (in other

Table 10.5 Visitor Numbers, Length of Stay, and Expenditure Figures by Type of Visitor to Hluhluwe-Umfolozi Park

Visitors to HUP	Number of Visitors	At HUP (days and nights)	Length of Stay Inside NE Zululand (nights)	Outside NE Zululand (nights)	Expenditures (rand per capita per night) In NE Zululand	In Rest of South Africa
Foreigners	63,125					
Day visitors	31,875	1.0	3.4	13.8	432	606
Overnight visitors	31,250	2.0	3.5	12.4	467	682
Residents	126,875					
Day visitors	95,625	1.0	1.7	0.4	208	551
Overnight visitors	31,250	2.0	3.2	0.7	206	629
Totals	190,000					

HUP = Hluhluwe-Umfolozi Park.

Note: The expenditures per capita for residents in the rest of South Africa are unusually high because the sample includes many whose length of stay (that is, travel time to HUP) is less than one day.

Sources: The number of visitors based on revenue data from 2000 and 2001 and James and Goodman (2001); the length of stay and expenditure data are from the On-Site Survey (as reported in chapter 1).

words, again and again) because the accommodation charge does not vary by the number of nights spent in the park.

The amount of the community levy is not made explicit on the current tariff charts; it is assumed, however, that the previous policy of a levy of R10 per night on overnight visitors as part of the accommodation charge continues. The earlier practice of charging day visitors a community levy of R1 is no longer in force. The per-bed weighted-average accommodation charge for facilities at HUP is calculated to be R250 a night based on bed and price information in the current tariff sheet. The net revenue from accommodation per night is thus R210. The accommodation includes a 14 percent value added tax (VAT), so the actual revenues garnered by KZN are R175 if the VAT is applied to the full accommodation price.

Given recent fluctuations in the rand, for the most part downward, any exchange rate chosen is likely to be incorrect at any given moment. For the sake of convenience, a figure of R12 per US$1.00 is used for expressing rand figures in dollars. All of the calculations are, however, carried out in rand, and the results are expressed in rand. A few of the significant figures are converted to dollar figures for ease of understanding by those unfamiliar with the rand. So, for example, the average overnight guest to HUP pays an entrance fee of US$2.50 (R30), a community levy of US$0.83 (R10) to the community development fund, and US$3.00 (R35) to the government in VAT. This leaves accommodation revenues of US$14.50 (R175) per guest for KZN Wildlife.

The quantitative results are presented in detail in appendix 10-A. The policy options are identified by their respective number and letter. The analyses of the two options most amenable to quantitative analysis—raising and differentiating entrance fees—include a number of pricing scenarios that are also included in appendix 10-A.

Many of the indicators are assessed qualitatively. For the sake of convenience, these are scored, albeit in a subjective manner, using the same 5-point scale that is used in the multicriteria analysis. A summary of the quantitative and qualitative results by indicator and for each option (and scenario) is provided in table 10.6. The discussion of each of the options covers variables and parameters particular to the option and provides a brief textual summary of the results by the four indicator areas: conservation finance, economic development, social equity, and biodiversity conservation.

Table 10.6 Summary of Results by Option and Indicator, Including Multicriteria Scores

Column groups: **Raising Conservation Finance for Public Protected Areas** = Raising Entrance Fees (1a a–c, 1c d), Differentiating Entrance Fees (1c e–f), Airport Tax (1d g–h); **Achieving Development with Faculty** = Expansion of Accommodation (2a), Concessions in PPAs (2b); **Enhancing Biodiversity Conservation from PGRs** = Raising Levies (1b), Incentives for PGRs (3a), Dropping Fences (3b), Ecological Management (3c); **General Policy Responses That Can Promote Demand for Nature Tourism** = Reducing Crime (4a), Reducing Malaria (4b), Reducing HIV/AIDS, Increasing Promotion (4c).

Results	Quantitative scenario	Raising Entrance Fees 1a (a)	1a (b)	1a (c)	1c (d)	Differentiating Entrance Fees 1c (e)	1c (f)	Airport Tax 1d (g)	1d (h)	Expansion of Accommodation 2a (na)	Concessions in PPAs 2b (na)	Raising Levies 1b (na)	Incentives for PGRs 3a (na)	Dropping Fences 3b (na)	Ecological Management 3c (na)	Increase in Demand (i)	Reducing Crime 4a (na)	Reducing Malaria 4b (na)	Reducing HIV/AIDS (na)	Increasing Promotion 4c (na)
General results (changes in …)																				
Day visitors to HUP																				
Foreigners	Days	(797)	(3,453)	(4,250)	(3,186)	(13,813)	(15,805)	0	(3,188)							1.594				
Residents	Days	(11,475)	(49,725)	(61,200)	0	0	0	0	0							4,781				
Overnights at HUP																				
Foreigners	Nights	(1,563)	(6,771)	(8,333)	(6,250)	(27,083)	(30,990)	0	(6,250)	+1	+1	0	0	0	0	3,125				
Residents	Nights	(7,600)	(32,500)	(40,000)	0	0	0	0	0	+2	+1	0	0	0	0	3,126				
Tourist expenditure in South Africa	Million R	0	0	0	0	0	0	0	(53.0)	0	0	0	0	0	0	26.5				
Tourist expenditure in NE KZN																				
Foreigners	Million R	(0.73)	(3.16)	(3.89)	(2.92)	(12.66)	(14.47)	0.00	(9.76)	+1	+2	0	0	0	0	4.88				
Residents	Million R	(1.55)	(6.70)	(8.24)	0.00	0.00	0.00	0.00	0.00	+1	+1	0	0	0	0	1.20				
Conservation finance																				
(changes in …)	Score	1	2	2	1	2	2	1	2	1	2	0	1	1	0	1	1	0	1	1
Entrance fees at HUP	Million R	6.3	18.0	18.8	9.9	26.6	26.9	0.0	(0.3)	+1	0	0	0	+1	0	0.4	+1	0	+1	+1
Departure tax revenue	Million R							7.58	17.04	0	0	0	0	0	0					
Accommodation revenues at HUP	Million R	(1.6)	(5.9)	(8.5)	(1.1)	(4.7)	(5.4)	0.0	(1.1)	+1	0	0	0	0	0	1.1	+1	0	+1	+1
Net conservation revenues at HUP	Million R	4.7	11.2	10.3	8.8	21.8	21.5	0.0	(1.4)	+1	+2	0	0	+1	0	1.5	+1	0	+1	+1
PGR net revenues	Qualitative	+1	+1	+1	+1	+1	+1	0	−1	−1	−1	0	+1	+1	0	+1	+1	0	+1	+1
Game sales receipts	Qualitative	0	0	0	0	0	0	0	0	0	0	0	+1	+1	0	+1	+1	0	+1	+1
Hunting revenues	Qualitative	0	0	0	0	0	0	0	0	0	0	0	0	−1	0	+1	+1	0	+1	+1
Economic development																				
(Changes in …)	Score	−1	−2	−2	−1	−2	−2	0	−2	0	1	0	1	1	0	1	1	1	2	1
GDP in NE KZN	Million R	(4.9)	(21.1)	(26.9)	(6.2)	(26.8)	(30.7)	0.0	(20.7)	0	+1	0	+1	+1	0	12.9	+1	+1	+2	+1

Indicator	Unit	C1	C2	C3	C4	C5	C6	C7	C8	C9	C10	C11	C12	C13	C14	C15	C16	C17	C18	C19	C20	C21
Employment in NE KZN	Jobs	(91)	(395)	(486)	(102)	(443)	(507)	0	(342)	0	+1	0	0	+1	0	+1	222	+1	+1	+1	+2	+1
Household income in NE KZN	Million R	(3.3)	(14.5)	(17.8)	(4.2)	(18.2)	(20.8)	0.0	(14.1)	0	+1	0	0	+1	0	+1	8.8	+1	+1	+1	+2	+1
Social equity (changes in …)		-1	-2	-2	-1	-1	-1	0	-1	1	1	1	1	1	0	1	1	1	1	2	1	1
Unskilled/skilled labour receipts	Rand	-176%	-176%	-176%	-136%	-136%	-136%	0%	-136%	0%	+1%	+1%	+1%	+1%	0%	+1%	147%	+1%	+1%	+1%	+2%	+1%
Low income/total %	Rand	-42%	-42%	-42%	-38%	-38%	-38%	0%	-38%	0%	+1%	+1%	+1%	+1%	0%	+1%	39%	+1%	+1%	+1%	+2%	+1%
Household receipts	Rand	-42%	-42%	-42%	-38%	-38%	-38%	0%	-38%	0%	+1%	+1%	+1%	+1%	0%	+1%	39%	+1%	+1%	+1%	+2%	+1%
Community levy collected	Million R	(0.09)	(0.39)	(0.48)	(0.06)	(0.27)	(0.31)	0.00	(0.06)	+1	+1	0	+1	+1	0	+1	0.06	+1	0	0	+1	+1
Access of residents	Days	(18,975)	(82,225)	(101,200)	+1	+2	+2	0	+1	-1	0	+1	+1	+1	0	+1	7,906	+1	+1	+1	-	+1
Biodiversity conservation (changes in …)		1	2	2	1	2	2	1	2	1	1	1	2	1	1	2	1	1	0	1	1	1
Environmental footprint	Qualitative	-1	0	0	0	0	0	0	-1	-1	0	+1	+1	+1	0	+1	0	-1	0	0	0	0
Tourism impact	Qualitative	+1	+1	+1	+1	+1	+1	0	+1	0	0	0	0	-1	0	0	-1	-1	0	0	0	-1
Congestion	Qualitative	+1	+1	+1	+1	+1	0	0	-1	0	0	+1	0	0	0	-1	-1	0	0	-1	-1	-1
Reinvestment by PGRs	Qualitative	+1	+1	+1	+1	+1	+1	0	-1	0	0	+1	+1	+2	+1	+1	+1	+1	0	+1	+2	+1
Reinvestment by KZN Wildlife	Qualitative	+1	+2	+2	+1	+2	+2	+1	+2	+2	0	+1	0	+1	0	+1	+1	+1	0	+2	+2	+1

HUP = Hluhluwe-Umfolozi Park; PGR = private game reserve; PPA = public protected area.

Source: Multimarket model calculations.

Raising Conservation Finance for Public Protected Areas: Profiting from Inelastic Demand for Nature Tourism

The demand studies (see chapters 2 through 5) assessed the response of a number of actual or potential visitor groups to increases in entrance fees, departure taxes, and ticket charges, and found that in general tourist demand is unresponsive (or inelastic) with respect to increased charges. Foreign tourists, in particular, are not likely to change their behavior until these charges become substantial. In other words, existing or new fees may be used to raise substantial amounts of conservation finance before demand drops off significantly. The potential effects of a number of these alternatives are explored below. First, however, we give a brief summary of the parameters and methods employed.

The Contingent Behavior Models in the On-Site Survey (see chapter 4) examined the responsiveness of visitors at HUP, Ithala, and Kruger to changes in prices. The effect of changing prices at the parks the tourists were visiting and the other parks (that is, at Kruger if interviewed in a NE Zululand reserve and vice versa) were explored. Own- and cross-price demand elasticities were thus tested. The results suggested that the effects between regions (the cross-price effects) were not significant. This suggests that the two areas (Kruger and NE Zululand) are not substitutes, as was initially expected, but rather that they may be weak complements, with Kruger being the prime attraction.

Significant responses where observed for resident and foreign overnight tourists at HUP and Kruger. The coefficients and elasticities are shown in table 10.7. Although policy simulations for Kruger are not carried out

Table 10.7 Overnight Visitor Responsiveness to Entrance Fees, Hluhluwe-Umfolozi Park and Kruger National Park

Park and Entrance Fee	Resident Overnight		Foreign Overnight	
	Coefficient	Elasticity	Coefficient	Elasticity
HUP (R30 and $2.50)	−0.004	−0.120	−0.010	−0.025
Sensitivity—high		−0.180		−0.038
Sensitivity—low		−0.060		−0.0125
KNP (R30 and $2.50)	−0.004	−0.120	−0.006	−0.015

HUP = Hluhluwe-Umfolozi Park; KNP = Kruger National Park.
Note: Due to the models used in the entrance fees analysis, the elasticities are equal to the coefficient multiplied by the current price. The current price applied in the simulations is indicated in parentheses.
Source: Chapter 3, this volume.

in this analysis, the figures are included for the purpose of comparison. At the current HUP entrance fee of R30, resident overnight visitors are considerably more responsive to additional price rises (elasticity of –0.12) when compared with foreign overnight visitors (elasticity of –0.025). The elasticities refer to the degree to which the number of nights spent at HUP would change. Thus, they can be used to calculate changes in overnight stays at HUP in response to changes in the entrance fee.

As noted above, the entrance fee is no longer charged at the gate but as part of the accommodation. Though the manner in which a fee is charged can be an important factor in responsiveness, for the purposes of this analysis it is assumed that the response is dictated by the overall cost of the visit. Comparable elasticities were not obtained for day visitors to HUP. The overnight elasticities are used, therefore, to assess the likelihood that increases in the entrance fee paid by day visitors at the gate would lead them to change their itinerary and choose another attraction. A sensitivity analysis for the elasticities is included below, using a wide margin around the elasticities derived from the demand studies.

With respect to changes in expenditures, the On-Site Survey suggests that overnight visitors that change the length of their stay at HUP will restructure their itinerary to shorten the portion of their trip spent in NE Zululand. The figure for daily expenditures in NE Zululand for each type of tourist is multiplied by the change in trip length to obtain the change in expenditures by tourists in NE Zululand. For day visitors, this is less likely to be the case, and, as a result, no change in expenditures in NE Zululand is expected to occur when pricing diverts day visitors from HUP to other NE Zululand attractions. The changes in expenditures stimulate further changes in the economic development and social equity indicators based on the multipliers covered above.

Raising Entrance Fees at Hluhluwe-Umfolozi Park

The policy option of raising entrance fees involves raising fees uniformly for all visitors to HUP. Overnight and day visitors—foreign and resident—will all pay the same entrance fee. Given current entrance fees of R30 and the expected low level of responsiveness to these fees, significant changes in fee levels will be necessary to see substantial changes in demand. However, as the entrance fee is increased to much higher levels, the number of day visitors and overnight visitors will fall. At some point, an entrance feel level will be reached that will maximize entrance fee revenue—when the effects on revenue of an increase in price is outweighed by the loss of visitors.

In addition, the increase in entrance fees will lead to a drop in community levy and accommodation revenue as the number of overnight visitors to HUP is reduced. An iterative process is thus used to find the fee level at which entrance fees and the change in conservation revenues are maximized. Given the configuration of the model and the assumptions made, the level of entrance fee that maximizes entrance fee revenue is approximately R190 (US$16). The level of fee that maximizes conservation revenues is R160 (US$13).

These fees are markedly higher than those deemed appropriate (on average) by residents (R20–26) and foreigners (R77–86) interviewed in the On-Site Survey and higher, indeed, than the average fee that respondents to the survey report having paid in other countries. Still, these fees are on a par with the entrance fees paid by foreigners for similar attractions in other nearby countries (for example, the game parks of Kenya and Tanzania).

Because the R160 fee maximizes conservation revenues, it is used for the sake of argument in the multicriteria analysis. For comparison, results are also compiled for a more modest across-the-board hike in entrance fees to R60 and for the maximum R190 fee (see appendix 10-A for the full quantitative model results). These scenarios are labeled in appendix 10-A as scenarios (1) R60, (2) R160, and (3) R190. A summary of the quantitative and qualitative results and the scores awarded to each criterion is provided below for the R160 scenario:

General results

- Decrease in visitation by residents: approximately a 50 percent drop in day visits and overnights

- Decrease in visitation by foreigners: approximately 10 percent for both day visits and overnights

- Decreases in expenditures in NE Zululand by foreigners of R3 million and residents of R6 million

Conservation finance (score +2)

- Increase in entrance fees collected at HUP of R18 million, a 250 percent increase

- Decrease in accommodation revenue at HUP of R6 million, a 25 percent drop

- Increase in net conservation revenue of R11 million, an increase of about 33 percent

- Increase in net conservation revenue at PGRs and other KZN Wildlife reserves as tourists, particularly day visitors, shift to these reserves

Economic development (score –2)

- Decrease of output (GDP) in NE Zululand of R21 million

- Loss in employment of 395 jobs in NE Zululand

- Fall in household income of R15 million

Social equity (score –2)

- Drop in receipts by unskilled labor in NE Zululand of R5 million, representing a 76 percent larger drop than for skilled labor

- Loss in income received by low-income households in NE Zululand of R6 million, representing 42 percent of total lost household income in NE Zululand

- Drop in the community levy collected of R400,000, or one-third of total

- Major decrease in access for South Africans to HUP

Biodiversity conservation (score +2)

- A minor increase in the environmental footprint in PGRs can be expected as a result of the shift in demand from PPAs to PGRs

- Decrease in any tourism impact and congestion at HUP, as total visits decline

- A reinvestment of revenue in biodiversity conservation by PGRs leads to increases in landscape, vegetation, and species conservation and marginal improvements in connectivity; little change in the maintenance of genetic vigor is expected

- A large reinvestment of conservation revenues by KZN Wildlife improves protected area management.

As intended, this alternative maximizes conservation finance with the potential to lead to large improvements in biodiversity conservation. However, side effects of raising entrance fees across the board are large losses to the local economy and significant negative effects on the less-well-off South Africans, whether unskilled workers or low-income households, and on South Africans who want to enjoy their natural patrimony.

A sensitivity analysis of the results examined the effects of a significant under- or overestimate in the elasticities. The changes had substantial effects on key indicators such as net conservation revenues, change in GDP, and change in income to low-income households. At the new elasticities, the fee levels that maximized conservation revenues no longer applied. If demand were 50 percent more inelastic than expected, the optimizing fee level drops to R100 (from R160); and if demand is half as elastic as expected, the optimizing fee level shoots up to R330.

Perhaps the best and most conservative measure of sensitivity in this case is to note that if visitation is 50 percent more elastic than expected, the maximum conservation revenue that can be generated (at R100) is more than halved, falling from the R11 million cited above to R5 million. The loss in GDP is reduced from R21 million to R17 million, and the loss in income to low-income household drops from R6 million to R5 million. In other words, the sensitivity of the results to higher elasticities is felt proportionately more in terms of net conservation revenue than in terms of the impact on development or equity.

Differentiating Entrance Fees at Hluhluwe-Umfolozi Park

An alternative to raising entrance fees across the board is to differentiate among various classes of tourist, charging different amounts to different groups for the same site. Though this might be done in many different ways (on age, job status, or nationality, for example), by far the most common point of differentiation in pricing of nature tourism is the distinction between residents and foreign tourists. In this option, a similar exercise is carried out to the first option above, using the same parameters and variables, but leaving the fee charged to residents at current levels and raising those charged to foreigners. Again, iteration is used to find the fee level that maximizes entrance fee revenue as well as overall conservation revenue.

Given that foreigners are less responsive than residents to price changes, these fee levels are much higher—three times higher, in fact—than previously. The fee that maximizes entrance fees is R625 (US$52), and the fee that maximizes overall conservation revenues is R550 (US$46). For the sake of comparison, the effect of a more moderate increase to R150 (US$13) is also simulated. This represents a US$10 increase in the cost to a foreign tourist, and thus will be compared with the effect of a US$10 departure tax under the final policy option in this category.

A US$50 entrance fee is indeed quite high. There are other natural attractions that charge this much—such as the fees for viewing mountain gorillas in Rwanda—although they tend to be far more unusual natural assets. Still, the history of HUP and the large herd of rhinoceroses, as one example, do argue for it being a "jewel in the crown"—in this case, of the KZN Wildlife set of natural assets. If this fee seems high, it should also be set against the fee levels charged at the more upmarket PGRs that have substantial assets. The daily charge at such locales can run from US$100 to US$400. Of course, the amenities and services that come with such a price tag make up a large part of the pricing structure, but the attractiveness of the ecosystem and game quality are also factors.

HUP is unique in the area in its combination of game diversity and reserve size. Given that the accommodation and other costs would add only an additional US$17 to the total, the overseas guest would be paying approximately US$65 for sensible and convenient lodging and access to the biodiversity offered by HUP. Comparatively speaking, this is not a bad deal, when the average American or European tourist can barely expect to obtain a tiny room with no view for the same price in their home cities.

In any event, for the purpose of drawing out the distinctions among the options, this aggressive pricing scenario is pursued for the multi-criteria analysis. The summary of results is as follows:

General results

- No change in visitation by residents

- Decrease in visitation by foreigners: approximately 44 percent for day visits and overnights

- Decreases in expenditures in NE Zululand by foreigners of R13 million

Conservation finance (score +2)

- Increase in entrance fees collected at HUP of R27 million, a 360 percent increase
- Decrease in accommodation revenue at HUP of R5 million, a 25 percent drop
- Increase in net conservation revenue of R22 million, an increase of about 80 percent
- Increase in net conservation revenue at PGRs and other KZN Wildlife reserves as foreign tourists, particularly day visitors, shift to these reserves

Economic development (score −2)

- Decrease of output (GDP) in NE Zululand of R27 million
- Loss in employment of over 440 jobs in NE Zululand
- Fall in household income of R18 million

Social equity (score −1)

- Fall in receipts by unskilled labor in NE Zululand of R5 million, representing a 36 percent larger drop than for skilled labor
- Loss in income received by low-income households in NE Zululand of R7 million, representing 38 percent of total lost household income in NE Zululand
- Drop in community levy collected of R270,000, one-third of the total
- Large increase in access for South Africans to HUP, as current guests at PGRs and current nonvisitors take advantage of empty beds left by foreigners

Biodiversity conservation (score +2)

- A minor increase in the environmental footprint in PGRs can be expected as a result of the shift in demand from PPAs to PGRs
- Decrease in any tourism impact and congestion at HUP, as total visits decline
- A reinvestment of revenues in biodiversity conservation by PGRs leads to increases in landscape, vegetation, and species conservation

and marginal improvements in connectivity; little change in maintenance of genetic vigor is expected

- A large reinvestment of conservation revenues by KZN Wildlife improves protected area management.

Again, aggressive pricing can be summarized as providing the potential for large increases in conservation finance but with a negative impact on the local economy and the less well off. In comparison with an across-the-board fee hike, a differentiation of fees raises more conservation revenues, causes more economic losses, and is less regressive (not as prejudicial to equity). Whether this option will lead to more conservation will depend heavily on how the additional revenue is used.

A similar sensitivity analysis to that conducted for the previous option provides an indication of the susceptibility of these results to relatively large changes in expected elasticities. With the higher elasticities, the optimizing fee level drops to R360; and with the lower elasticity, it rises to R1,160. Again, a conservative approach is to focus on the higher elasticity situation. In this case, the sensitivity analysis shows a less than 50 percent drop in potential net conservation revenue gains at the R360 price level (from R22 million to R13 million). Due to the higher spending levels of foreign tourists, the effects at this price level on the loss of GDP and household income are minor.

The responsiveness of these indicators is, thus, more muted than in the case of the across-the-board entrance fee increase, although there is the same pattern in terms of a higher sensitivity on the part of conservation revenues (as opposed to development or equity measures) to the risk of higher-than-expected elasticities. Still, on balance, the fee differentiation alternative maintains a proportionately larger amount of net conservation revenues at the higher elasticities (R13 million of the expected R22 million with differentiation, as opposed to R5 million of the expected R11 million without differentiation). The differentiation option thus appears slightly more robust in the face of any uncertainty over elasticities.

Departure Taxes and Ticket Fees

The On-Site Survey evaluated the responsiveness of overnight foreign tourists to the institution of a departure tax or a ticket fee. Implicitly, the intention is that a portion of the proceeds of such a tax or fee would be dedicated to conservation activities, given that many foreigners come to South Africa for the purpose of nature tourism. Respondents did not seem to distinguish significantly between the two vehicles (the tax or the fee), and, again, a very high tax or fee was necessary for a significant number of foreign tourists to change their plans to visit South Africa. The intention in this analysis is to examine the effect of extracting conservation revenue at another point in the tourist experience, and to compare the results with those obtained with the differentiated entrance fees above.

Two scenarios were evaluated. In the first, a US$10 tax or fee is put in place. The results of the contingent valuation exercise suggest that such a fee increase would not induce existing tourists to alter plans to visit the country. In the second scenario, a US$25 tax is put in place. From the valuation exercise, it is expected that this would persuade 10 percent of existing visitors to HUP to drop their plans to visit South Africa. It is assumed in the scenarios that foreign day visitors would behave likewise.

In contrast to the entrance fee scenarios, a decision to go to another country or not to travel at all leads to a complete loss of all expenditures by that tourist in NE Zululand, the rest of KZN, and the rest of South Africa. Though the change in expenditures reflects losses to NE Zululand and the rest of the country, the indicators for development and equity focus only on the effects felt in the NE Zululand economy. Many countries use either departure taxes or ticket charges to generate resources from the tourist trade. Figures of from US$10 to US$20 are not uncommon. At present, South Africa does not have either type of charging system. Again, to make the comparisons vivid, the more aggressive pricing scenario is scored for the multicriteria analysis, although both are presented in the results tables and appendix A. A summary of the results follows:

General results

- No change in visitation by residents

- Decrease in visitation by foreigners of 6,000, or 10 percent each for day and overnight visitors

- Decreases in expenditures in NE Zululand by foreigners of R10 million and an even larger decrease of R53 million in expenditures in the rest of South Africa

Conservation finance (score +2)

- Tax revenues (potential conservation finance) of R17 million are collected from those foreign tourists who enter the country and visit HUP

- Loss at HUP in entrance fee and accommodation revenue of R1.4 million occurs due to the tourists who cancel their trip to South Africa

Economic development (score –2)

- Decrease of output (GDP) in NE Zululand of R21 million

- Loss in employment of more than 342 jobs in NE Zululand

- Fall in household income of R14 million

Social equity (score –1)

- Fall in receipts by unskilled labor in NE Zululand of R4m, representing a 36 percent larger drop than for skilled labor

- Loss in income received by low-income households in NE Zululand of R5 million, representing 38 percent of total lost household income in NE Zululand

- Drop in community levy collected of R60,000

- Small increase in access for South Africans to HUP, as current guests at PGRs or current nonvisitors take empty beds left by foreigners

Biodiversity conservation (score +2)

- No change in the environmental footprint in PGRs

- Minor decrease in any tourism impact and congestion at HUP, as total visits decline

- No change in reinvestment of revenues in biodiversity conservation by PGRs

- Providing tax receipts are dedicated, at least in part to nature tourism, a large reinvestment of conservation revenues by KZN Wildlife improves protected area management.

As with the other two options for raising conservation finance from inelastic tourist demand, this option performs well in raising conservation finance. Given that institutional barriers would need to be overcome to ensure that the proceeds were devoted to conservation, this approach would be risky if conservation finance were the objective.

Conversely, the negative effects are more muted than in the case of entrance fee differentiation. In fact, if the US$10 scenario is examined, it is clear that it performs well, for it generates finance without any real effect on the economy or on equity. It generates the same amount of revenue as does the similar increase (R150) under the differentiation scenario, although, because many foreign tourists visit a number of reserves and parks, the resources would in theory need to be "shared" across a number of sites. Whether nature tourism could "claim" the proceeds at the smaller tax level—particularly where there were no "pains" incurred to realize the "gain"—is even more questionable.

On balance, then, differentiating entrance fees appears to be the best choice for raising conservation finance, combined if feasible with a "conservation" departure tax. In all likelihood, the level of entrance fee would need to be increased gradually over time to allow foreign tourists to adjust gradually to the impact on their pocketbook. Of course, it would also be possible to raise entrance fees to residents at the same time or to differentiate among residents. A further alternative would be to raise or differentiate the community levy, as is discussed further below. In effect, the different quality levels of lodging and the discounts for children accomplish this in a fashion already. The next two options provide alternatives for differentiating among residents.

Achieving Development with Equity: Reallocating Public and Private Roles

Achieving development with equity revolves around questions of the institutional base for developing and benefiting from the nature tourism market in the study area. To this end, alternatives for managing HUP are presented that focus on the role of KZN Wildlife, of the private sector, or of local communities.

The supply of lodging at HUP has remained constant for a number of years. The Ecological Survey reports that occupancy rates are currently 92 percent. Comparison of revenue figures with prices and bed numbers in 2000–2001 confirms that occupancy rates are very high, to the point that undoubtedly many visitors cannot stay in the reserve when they would prefer to do so. As was noted above, PGRs in the study area have much lower occupancy rates.

This divergence probably reflects three factors: the convenient and reasonable accommodation at HUP, the environmental amenities, and the low price of lodging. In other words, the high occupancy rates at HUP indicate that tourists are getting a better deal for the money spent. The previous set of options explored one way for effectively ramping back on demand—raising the price of staying at HUP. The alternative is to expand supply.

There are many questions as to how this might happen. KZN Wildlife could build more accommodation in HUP—as it has in the past—or concessions for suitable sites within the reserve could be auctioned off. Another alternative would be to work with adjacent communities to develop their capacity to provide lodging for tourists. Such an option would require funding; one way to generate funds in the tight HUP accommodation market would be to increase the community levy and channel the incremental resources to efforts to develop lodging on neighboring communal lands. The triumvirate of options discussed below is undertaken on a purely qualitative basis, drawing from information collected for this project, much of which is summarized earlier in this chapter and in the other chapters above.

Expansion of Accommodation in HUP by KZN Wildlife

Under the option of expansion of accommodation, KZN would seek financing to build and operate new lodges, chalets, camps, and the like in HUP. Implicit in the analysis is that much the same types of accommodation would be built as already exist. Thus, to the extent that high occupancies in HUP lead visitors to stay in PGRs outside the park or to forgo a visit to the region, the increase in accommodation, other things being equal, will lead to an increase in visitation and revenues at HUP. Without data on this unmet demand, the magnitude of the effect is hard to predict. It is assumed here—given concerns regarding "over-building" in the reserve and KZN Wildlife's long hiatus in building new accommodation facilities—that the amount of additional lodging would be relatively restrained.

Similarly, given the low occupancies observed in the PGRs around HUP, it is unlikely that the increment in supply would attract large new numbers of tourists to the region. Therefore, it is assumed that visitors shifting from PGRs in the study area would largely consume the expansion in the supply of beds in HUP. The potential effects are summarized below, along with the multicriteria scores:

General results

- Actual or prospective overnight visitors (now at PGRs) would benefit as additional spaces opened up in HUP, leading to more overnights

- Day visitors to HUP would benefit in a minor fashion in terms of downward pressure on prices outside of HUP if the expansion in accommodation is significant and HUP overnight accommodations continue to be priced competitively

- A small increase in expenditures would occur as tourists currently unable to find lodging at HUP are accommodated

Conservation finance (score +1)

- Small increase in entrance fees, accommodation revenue, and net conservation revenue to HUP as more tourists are accommodated

- A minor decrease in net conservation revenue at PGRs and other KZN Wildlife reserves can be expected as tourists, particularly day visitors to HUP, shift to spending nights at HUP

Economic development (score 0)

- A minor and relatively insignificant increase in output (GDP), employment, and household income in NE Zululand will result from the additional visits to the region

Social equity (score +1)

- Minor but insignificant improvements in receipts by unskilled labor and income received by low-income households in NE Zululand

- Small increase in the community levy

- A small increase in access for South Africans to HUP can be expected with the increase in supply and relaxation of the need to book early to beat out foreigners for spaces

Biodiversity conservation (score –1)

- A small increase in the environmental footprint in PGRs can be expected as a result of the installation of new facilities in HUP

- Small increase in any tourism impact and congestion at HUP, as total number of overnight accommodations and visitors increases

- A decrease in net revenues to PGRS leads to a small decline in reinvestment of revenues in biodiversity conservation by PGRs

- The small increase in reinvestment of conservation revenues by KZN Wildlife improves protected area management.

Private Concessions for Tourism Services in HUP

There are many alternatives to public construction, ownership, and operation of infrastructure. An alternative currently being explored in the case of public protected areas in South Africa is that of private concessions. The South African National Parks Board (SANPB) is moving ahead with an aggressive program of this nature in Kruger National Park, and KZN Wildlife is developing guidelines for a similar program.

In this option, it is assumed that the concession carries with it a limited zone of exclusive transiting rights, the idea being to permit the development of more upmarket facilities and avoid congestion issues for the private entrepreneur. Evaluation of this alternative is difficult, given the lack of experience with such initiatives in the study area. Instead, lessons derived from the Producer Survey on the operational and structural differences between private and public reserves are employed in evaluating this option. The expected results and scores are as follows:

General results

- The impact on total visitation would be small, with some of the visitors coming from the existing population of visitors to upmarket properties in the study areas, and others being additional visitors attracted to the new facilities

- A small increase in expenditures would occur as new high-spending tourists would come to NE Zululand, particularly the upmarket foreign tourist

Conservation finance (score +2)

- Depending on how the deal is structured, the potential exists for a large increase in net conservation revenue as the sites are auctioned off

- A minor decrease in net conservation revenue at HUP, PGRs, and other KZN Wildlife reserves can be expected as some tourists shift to spending nights at the new sites in HUP

Economic development (score +1)

- A small increase in output (GDP), employment and household income in NE Zululand will result from the additional visits to the region to experience the new attraction

Social equity (score +1)

- Small improvements in receipts by unskilled labor and income received by low-income households in NE Zululand

- Small increase in the community levy

- Small decrease in access for South Africans to HUP due to the exclusive use agreements

Biodiversity conservation (score +1)

- A small increase in the environmental footprint in PGRs can be expected as a result of the installation of new facilities in HUP

- No change in any tourism impact and congestion at HUP, because the new concessions are high value, low volume

- The large increase in reinvestment of conservation revenues by KZN Wildlife improves protected area management.

Comparing the two alternatives for putting more accommodation in HUP, the concessions alternative is better across the board on three out of four of the multicriteria scores. Clearly, this alternative carries with it more transaction costs for KZN Wildlife because it would represent a new business endeavor. However, if the conservation revenues can be realized—and the preliminary experience of the SANPB suggests that they can be—the alternative looks promising.

Raising Community Levies at HUP

The sensitivity of tourists to community levies was not explicitly assessed in the demand studies. However, it is likely that up to some reasonable extent, tourist preferences for conservation and community development are likely to be consistent. It may even be the case that foreign tourists would be more inclined to contribute to the development of rural communities than to the conservation of biodiversity. Thus, the average tourist to South Africa may perceive that more progress has been made on the latter than on the former.

It is hypothesized, therefore, that an increase in the community levy could generate additional revenue without greatly affecting demand, perhaps even more so than in the case of entrance fees. The principal difference would be that the benefits of such a program would be felt directly in a positive impact on equity, rather than in increased funding for land management in the KZN Wildlife reserves.

This option is examined below under the assumption that capital generated from increased community levies could be effectively used to assist communities to develop alternative lodging options. Marrying the equity and conservation objectives through hikes in the community levy may mitigate some of the potential negative effects of the "pure" conservation finance options explored above. Clearly, success in implementation would underpin the continued interest by tourists in supporting higher levies. The expected results and scores are as follows:

General results

- The impact on visitation and expenditures would be negligible because the objective would be to extract what tourists are willing to pay for community development—and not to impose a large mandatory fee

Conservation finance (score 0)

- No change

Economic development (score 0)

- A minor but relatively insignificant increase is expected in output (GDP), employment, and household income in the adjacent communities from the usage of the funds

Social equity (score +1)

- The initiative is progressive because the majority of the funds would go to low-income communities and community organizations near the park

- Small increase in the community levy

- Minor but relatively insignificant increase in access for South Africans to HUP, provided that residents would be attracted to the community lodging

Biodiversity conservation (score +1)

- The program represents a small reinvestment by KZN Wildlife in the communities with consequent positive implications for the long-run sustainability of HUP as a protected area.

Although this alternative would face a number of challenges, it might provide an attractive complement to a policy of creating concessions for sites within HUP.

Enhancing Biodiversity Conservation from Private Game Reserves

A number of alternatives exist for increasing the private sector's contribution to biodiversity conservation through the establishment and management of PGRs. These are explored only briefly, because the data on the potential effects of these options on conservation in PGRs is limited.

Incentives for PGRs

In theory, if privately held areas are providing a public good, that is, bio-diversity conservation, then there is justification for payment by society to these entities for the environmental services provided. This new concept—under experimentation in different parts of the world—replaces the idea of incentives as subsidies. In the simplest case, such an incentive might be a direct payment to areas that participate in an active way in conservation activities, as agreed on by the relevant body, in this case probably KZN Wildlife. The expected effects and scores are as follows:

General results

- Little to no impact on visitation or expenditures is expected because this option's focus is as an additional revenue stream for PGRs

Conservation finance (score +1)

- These incentives would function as a small increase in net conservation revenue at HUP and PGRs

- Because the incentives would promote the practice of converting land from other uses to game, this would increase the demand for and revenues from game sales

Economic development (score +1)

- A small increase in output (GDP), employment, and household income in NE Zululand will result from the additional expenditures on conservation

Social equity (score +1)

- Small improvements in receipts by unskilled labor, income received by low-income households in NE Zululand

- Small increase in access for South Africans due to the expansion of PGRs

Biodiversity conservation (score +1)

- A small decrease in the environmental footprint in PGRs can be expected as a result of the cleaning up of old agricultural installations on land newly converted to game

- A small improvement in tourism impact and congestion in PGRs can be expected as the area under conservation is increased, spreading these effects over a larger area

- A small increase in reinvestment of the incentives in biodiversity conservation by PGRs leads to increases in landscape, vegetation, and species conservation and marginal improvements in connectivity; little change in the maintenance of genetic vigor is expected.

Integrating Land Management: Dropping Fences

The alternative of integrating land management envisions that the large, segmented areas under private control would be opened up to one large connected area where wildlife could move freely (if fences between properties were dropped). In addition, fences around public protected areas might also be dropped and communal lands brought into the fold (as has already happened in arrangements between PGRs and between PGRs and PPAs). Viewed from the air, much of the study area is already under conservation; however, the full benefits in conservation and nature tourism are not realized due to the fragmented nature of the terrestrial landscape. The effects and scores are summarized as follows:

General results

- Little or no effect on visitation or expenditures is expected, because this option focuses on the spatial character of the landscape and the overall attractiveness of the landscape and nature tourism product in the study area

Conservation finance (score +1)

- Small increase in entrance fees and net conservation revenue at HUP from the possibility of charging for transiting rights within HUP

- Small increase in net conservation revenues to PGRs as a result of having a more diverse attraction for visitors

- Dropping fences would increase game sales by enabling groups of owners to acquire species that previously could not be held on smaller properties either due to expense or range constraints

- Hunting revenues might decline as hunting yielded to game viewing over time

Economic development (score +1)

- A small increase in output (GDP), employment, and household income in NE Zululand will result from the additional expenditures on conservation and price rises among PGRs

Social equity (score +1)

- Small improvements in receipts by unskilled labor and income received by low-income households in NE Zululand

- Small increase in access for South Africans due to the improved connectivity and species representation on PGRs

Biodiversity conservation (score +2)

- A small decrease in the environmental footprint can be expected as fences are dropped

- Major improvement in biodiversity conservation in PGRs due to greatly improved connectivity and genetic vigor of the system.

As with a number of the options explored here, dropping fences carries with it significant barriers in the transaction costs of developing agreements. These may be just as important as the potential benefits; however, the spatial landscape argues for a more integrated approach to land and game management.

Ecological Management on PGRs

The Ecological Survey examines the full range of land, water, and game management practices of PGRs and provides a series of recommendations. Although this is not a topic for an economics chapter, it suffices to say that there are many areas for improvement in the day-to-day management of the PGRs, actions that if taken would improve biodiversity conservation and its sustainability. Thus, additional conservation revenues received by PGRs could usefully be aimed at ecological improvements on existing lands. Given that this is a purely ecological measure, the multicriteria scores are all zero, except for biodiversity conservation, which receives a +1.

General Policy Responses that Can Promote Demand for Nature Tourism

The intent of this policy analysis is to provide specific advice on how to improve the sustainability of tourism in the study area, rather than to speculate on the horrors that might befall the region in a worst-case scenario. Clearly, for example, a drastic increase in the crime rate would decrease the attraction of South Africa for foreign tourists and depress tourism in Zululand.

Rather than dwell on the negatives, an effort is made here to assess how to achieve the desired outcomes, and to provide analysis and argument for making the changes that are necessary to promote sustainability. Thus the analysis of general policy responses that can affect, or promote, demand focuses on what the benefits of reducing negative influences would be and what investments can be made to stimulate demand.

Because the outcome of all these efforts would be in the first instance an increase in demand, the first step in the analysis, then, is to develop a default scenario in which demand grows over time. As is generally known and as was shown in the demand studies, income is positively related to the demand for nature tourism. Other things being equal, it is likely that income growth in South Africa and origin countries (for tourism) will continue.

Rising Demand over Time—Income Effect

A number of the options considered above have examined the effect of changing the price of the nature tourism experience. However, changes in (effective) income may also play a role in determining participation in nature tourism. Efforts to assess tourists' willingness to pay to visit natural sites have typically found that income is a significant and important predictor (Lindberg 1998; Wells 1997). As a result, a rise in income over time can be expected to increase tourists' willingness to pay.

In a number of the models developed earlier in this volume as part of the demand studies, income did not emerge as a significant variable. However, as indicated above, demand was generally found to be inelastic and, thus, it is not surprising that income did not emerge as a significant variable—if the price being charged had little effect on behavior, then it stands to reason that having more income would not be terribly important. In addition, the analyses of entrance fees and airport taxes showed them to be relatively small components of the overall trip cost. In the site selection models, trip cost was, however, a significant predictor of tourists' choice of destination.

More to the point is the effect of a general rise in incomes on the decision to participate in nature tourism. In the Household Survey, the three most frequently cited reasons by people who had been to a reserve in the past but indicated it was unlikely they would go again were:

• Financial constraints, 35 percent

• Time constraint, 19 percent

• Parks too expensive and geared for foreigners, 11 percent.

Respondents who had never been to a reserve and did not plan on going also cited financial constraints and the expense of going to parks as the major reasons for deciding against such a trip or simply never even considering a trip. Those who thought it likely they would visit a reserve in the future, even though they had not made such a trip in the past three years, cited an improvement in financial constraints as the major factor that had changed their outlook. Presumably, then, increases in incomes would help to overcome these principal objections and limitations to residents venturing forth to see reserves and parks.

In the study of the Netherlands market for nature tourism (see chapter 3), income was not modeled directly as a predictor of visitation. However, in the choice-modeling exercise, the cost of the air ticket and local costs were highly significant and had a very strong negative effect on the choice of country destination. Compared with other countries, lowering the local costs by 150 Dutch guilders and flight costs by 1,000 guilders would increase South Africa's market share from 35 percent to 74 percent, a huge increase. Thus, rising incomes in origin countries are also—as expected—likely to affect visits to the country and provide "new" foreign tourists to the market.

To provide a rough indication of the potential impact over time of income growth, a scenario is constructed in which a 5 percent increase in demand by both foreigners and South African residents occurs. The analysis assumes that prices for the nature tourism experience remain constant. The quantitative results and scores are summarized below:

General results

- Increase in day visitors and overnight stays of 5 percent (in HUP and elsewhere)

- Increase in expenditures in South Africa (outside of NE Zululand) of R26 million

- Increase in expenditures within NE Zululand of R6 million

Conservation finance (score +1)

- Increase in entrance fees collected at HUP of R400,000, a 5 percent increase

- Increase in accommodation revenue at HUP of R1.1 million, a 5 percent increase

- Increase in net conservation revenue of R1.5 million, an increase of about 5 percent

- Increase in net conservation revenue at PGRs and other KZN Wildlife reserves as demand increases for their services as well

Economic development (score +1)

- Increase in output (GDP) in NE Zululand of R13 million

- Gain in employment of over 220 jobs in NE Zululand

- Increase in household income of R9 million

Social equity (score +1)

- Increase in receipts by unskilled labor in NE Zululand of R2.5 million, representing 47 percent more than is received by skilled labor

- Increase in income received by low-income households in NE Zululand of R3.5 million, representing 39 percent of the total increase in household income in NE Zululand

- Increase in the community levy of R60,000

- A small increase in access for South Africans to HUP, although there will be limits on overnights due to high occupancies

Biodiversity conservation (score +1)

- No change in the environmental footprint in HUP or PGRs

- A small increase in tourism impact and congestion at HUP, as the total number of overnights and visitors increases

- An increase in net revenues to HUP and PGRs leads to reinvestment of revenues and improvement in biodiversity conservation by both HUP and PGRs.

The increased demand scenario, as expected, provides moderate positive effects across all the criteria.

Reducing Crime

The demand studies found that, in general, crime appeared to be a significant concern for foreign tourists and the main negative factor for prospective visitors to the game parks and South Africa. For this reason, it may be expected that actions taken to reduce crime would lead to a significant increase in demand, as was portrayed above. The multicriteria scores for reducing crime are thus the same as the 5 percent demand increase scenario.

Reducing the Incidence of Disease: Malaria and HIV/AIDS

The demand studies found that the risk of malaria was not an important factor in trip decisions for foreigners. Respondents in the Netherlands case study ranked South Africa higher than average for countries in the region on this attribute; visitors interviewed in KZN Wildlife reserves rated malaria as important but less so than most other variables and malaria was not a significant predictor of country choice in the site selection model (see chapters 3 and 4).

For foreigners, crime was much more of a generalized concern. Residents rated malaria as an important factor in trip decisionmaking in the Household Survey (see chapter 2), and malaria was a significant and negative explanatory variable for resident visitors to Northern

Kruger National Park in the On-Site Survey (chapter 4). The difference between foreigners and residents may be explained as follows.

A large proportion of foreigners visiting Zululand also visit Kruger, which is itself a malarial area. So just as for the Dutch visitors contemplating a trip to other African countries, KZN is relatively low risk. Further, the availability of prophylactic medications may serve to reduce the concern evinced by foreigners. Locals that engage repeatedly in nature tourism, however, are more knowledgeable about malaria as well as about alternative malaria-free destinations and—unlike the foreign tourist making their trip of a lifetime to see big game in Kruger or Zululand—will be more concerned and selective in this regard.

As a result, it is not expected that efforts to reduce malaria would greatly benefit the nature tourism industry in the study area by generating a positive increment in demand, although combating malaria would improve the marketability of Zululand as a nature tourism destination, particularly to residents. Clearly, however, reducing the incidence of malaria in Zululand would greatly benefit the inhabitants of the region, with positive spillover benefits for the economy. Thus, reducing the incidence of malaria scores a 2 on equity and a 1 on economic development, but a zero on conservation finance and conservation of biodiversity.

In the On-Site Survey, foreigners indicated that the presence of HIV/AIDS was the least important of 15 factors in determining their choice of destination. A similar question was not asked of residents, given that their exposure varies little with their decision to engage in nature tourism in Zululand. Thus, it is unlikely that an improvement in the situation in South Africa with respect to the incidence of HIV/AIDS will have an impact on demand in the same manner as with crime or malaria. The potential effect of HIV/AIDS is more pervasive.

Nature tourism is just one sector of the economy, an economy that is facing a major challenge and readjustment in the face of rising morbidity and mortality rates due to AIDS. This will affect demand—in the total number of active, middle-income consumers of nature tourism, and supply—in the continued supply of skilled and semiskilled labor to operate game reserves and tourism facilities. Even further, the prospects of recruiting "new" nature tourists from previously disadvantaged segments of the population may evaporate as these upwardly mobile groups are equally affected by AIDS. Thus, reducing the incidence of AIDS scores a 1 on equity, a 2 on economic development, and a 1 on conservation finance and conservation of biodiversity.

Increasing Expenditures on Marketing

The project did not explicitly examine the effect of current marketing and promotion activities. During the course of the project, a number of such programs directed toward overseas markets were developed. Instead, the participation study explores the potential to increase demand from hitherto unreached groups, particularly resident Asians and Africans. Under the assumption that such programs do increase demand, the marketing alternative is scored as per the 5 percent increase in demand recounted above.

EXAMINING THE TRADE-OFFS AND POTENTIAL SYNERGIES: MULTICRITERIA ANALYSIS OF POLICY OPTIONS

The scores presented for each of the options are summarized in figure 10.5. The conservation finance options appear to yield the lowest overall sustainability score, as reflected in the summation of the outcome scores for development, equity, and conservation. This is in large part an artifact of the modeling effort, but it does highlight important issues to consider before embarking on drastic efforts to raise conservation finance. The static nature of the analysis penalizes the conservation finance options because the monies generated are generated but not expended.

Clearly, depending on how and where they are spent, some of the development and equity effects would be greatly reduced. Second, in a number of the other options, important costs—whether transaction or implementation costs—are left out of the analysis. In part, this has to do with the narrow focus of the analysis on the effects as felt in NE Zululand. Costs and benefits outside this framework do not appear.

Indeed, the tough decisions regarding how to finance development (for example, tourism promotion campaigns), conservation (for example, the KZN Wildlife subsidy from the government), and health and social programs (for example, crime and HIV/AIDS programs) are all

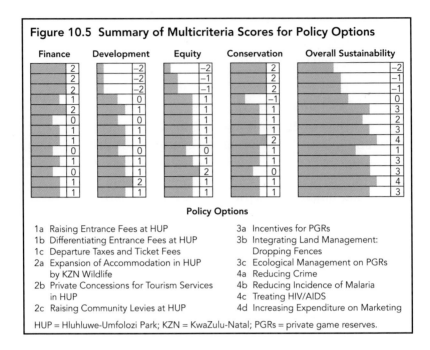

Figure 10.5 Summary of Multicriteria Scores for Policy Options

Policy Options

1a Raising Entrance Fees at HUP
1b Differentiating Entrance Fees at HUP
1c Departure Taxes and Ticket Fees
2a Expansion of Accommodation in HUP
    by KZN Wildlife
2b Private Concessions for Tourism Services
    in HUP
2c Raising Community Levies at HUP

3a Incentives for PGRs
3b Integrating Land Management:
    Dropping Fences
3c Ecological Management on PGRs
4a Reducing Crime
4b Reducing Incidence of Malaria
4c Treating HIV/AIDS
4d Increasing Expenditure on Marketing

HUP = Hluhluwe-Umfolozi Park; KZN = KwaZulu-Natal; PGRs = private game reserves.

made far away from the region. The model does not attempt to incorporate a share of these costs into the analysis.

Thus, any direct comparison of the multicriteria scores across categories needs to be qualified by these concerns. Rather, the comparison is best made within categories—such as between the conservation finance options—particularly when the options are likely to be mutually exclusive alternatives. Another use of the scores is in examining potential combinations of options—of options that complement each other—that could contribute as an integrated response to the issue of creating a viable nature tourism economy.

A concern raised by stakeholders and reviewers relates to the weighting used in aggregating scores under the overall sustainability heading. As presented in figure 10.5, each of the three criteria that determine sustainability is weighted equally. As a brief sensitivity analysis of these results to the weighting employed, figure 10.6 presents the same set of scores with social equity weighted twice as heavily as development and conservation. This reflects the concerns of stakeholders that equity is the overriding concern of policymakers in the South African context.

Figure 10.6 Sensitivity of Multicriteria Scores to a Twice-as-Heavy Weighting for Social Equity

Finance	Development	Equity	Conservation	Overall Sustainability
2	-2	-4	2	-4
2	-2	-2	2	-2
2	-2	-2	2	-2
1	0	2	-1	1
2	1	2	1	4
0	0	2	1	3
1	1	2	1	4
1	1	2	2	5
0	0	0	1	1
1	1	2	1	4
0	1	4	0	5
1	2	2	1	5
1	1	2	1	4

Policy Options

1a Raising Entrance Fees at HUP	3a Incentives for PGRs
1b Differentiating Entrance Fees at HUP	3b Integrating Land Management:
1c Departure Taxes and Ticket Fees	Dropping Fences
2a Expansion of Accommodation in HUP	3c Ecological Management on PGRs
by KZN Wildlife	4a Reducing Crime
2b Private Concessions for Tourism Services	4b Reducing Incidence of Malaria
in HUP	4c Treating HIV/AIDS
2c Raising Community Levies at HUP	4d Increasing Expenditure on Marketing

HUP = Hluhluwe-Umfolozi Park; KZN = KwaZulu-Natal; PGRs = private game reserves.

The main result of doubling the weighting for social equity is to "stretch" out the sustainability scores and exaggerate the differences between those options that score worse on equity and those that score better. In a minor fashion, there is a reorganization of the strict ranking of options among those options with high scores, but this merely demonstrates that the weighting favors those that have a 2 score for equity. For the sensitivity analysis of weighting to have more of an impact, it would be preferable to gather together different stakeholders to discuss and agree on an appropriate weighting scheme. In a similar fashion, many of the multicriteria scores, particularly those based on qualitative assessment, would best be determined by such a group—as a means of enriching and validating the multicriteria analysis, as well as increasing its policy relevance.

There are trade-offs and complementarities among the options. One of the advantages of multicriteria analysis is the ability to compare different types of criteria without necessarily having to aggregate them. With three or more criteria, this is more difficult, and hence the rough

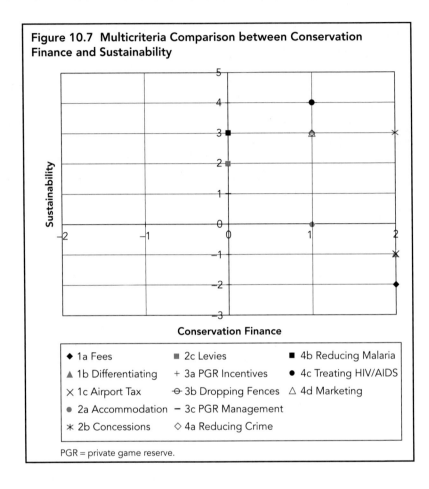

Figure 10.7 Multicriteria Comparison between Conservation Finance and Sustainability

attempt at a sustainability score above. Nevertheless, to facilitate an analysis of trade-offs and complementarities across the options, the three outcome criteria and the conservation finance criteria are mapped against each other in the figures that follow.

To begin the analysis, the conservation finance criteria are mapped against the overall sustainability score (figure 10.7). The first observation that can be made is that none of the options has a negative impact on conservation finance. This may simply reflect the degree of emphasis placed in this project on examining the alternatives to improve conservation finance. The tendency that can be noted is for an upward and leftward (negative) sloping relationship to the right of the *y* axis. In other words, there seems to be a trade-off between sustainability defined here and conservation finance as such—although none of the options examined has a negative influence on conservation finance. Were the direct costs of some of the options—such as funding for marketing—included, these options might be shown to ultimately have a negative effect on conservation finance. Assuming a fixed national budget, increases in social expenditures to fight HIV/AIDS might well have a negative impact on public flows to KZN Wildlife and conservation finance. Indeed, lower annual budget appropriations for KZN Wildlife may be attributable to such changes in government priorities.

Turning to the comparison of economic development and biodiversity conservation outcomes, the spread of results is considerable (see figure 10.8). Again, the vast majority of the options were positive with respect to biodiversity conservation; however, the conservation finance options display a very strong trade-off between these two outcomes— providing the strongest positive impact on conservation, but also a very negative impact on economic development. The majority of the other options lie in a tight arc in the first quadrant.

Two observations are thus possible. First, to achieve ever higher levels of biodiversity conservation, there ultimately may be a trade-off with economic development—particularly when such efforts rely on extreme efforts to generate conservation finance. Second, combining options with strong positive effects on conservation finance with those that have a positive economic impact may lead to more satisfactory outcomes with respect to these criteria.

The mapping of results for economic development and social equity displays an almost linear relationship of positive slope (figure 10.9). In other words, these two outcomes are highly correlated. The finding that emerged from the SAM in chapter 9 that nature tourism, for the most part, is a progressive industry—that is, when it succeeds, low-income groups and unskilled workers benefit disproportionately—presaged this relationship.

Obviously, as seen in the case of the conservation finance options, the converse applies equally—reductions in output in the nature tourism market are going to affect poor people disproportionately. This will be an important consideration in assessing a policy that affects the nature tourism sector and, again, argues for the importance of ensuring that

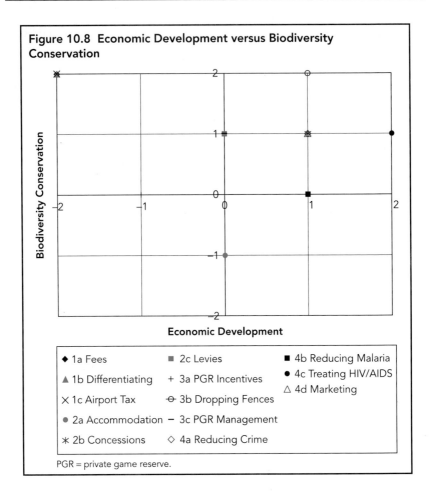

Figure 10.8 Economic Development versus Biodiversity Conservation

conservation finance revenues are reinvested in ways that are neutral or positive with respect to equity.

Finally, the comparison of social equity and biodiversity conservation again shows a relatively linear relationship of negative slope, indicating that there are trade-offs between realizing equity and conservation (figure 10.10). Again, only one option (expanding accommodations) actually has a negative impact on conservation, but the figure indicates that as efforts are made to raise the level of biodiversity conservation, the degree of equity achieved will lessen. This is somewhat disheartening, but again reflects largely the influence of the conservation finance alternatives that fall in the second quadrant.

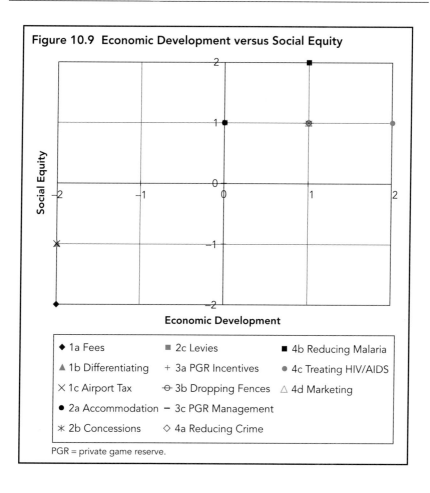

Figure 10.9 Economic Development versus Social Equity

Symbol	Label	Symbol	Label	Symbol	Label
◆	1a Fees	■	2c Levies	■	4b Reducing Malaria
▲	1b Differentiating	+	3a PGR Incentives	●	4c Treating HIV/AIDS
✕	1c Airport Tax	⊖	3b Dropping Fences	△	4d Marketing
●	2a Accommodation	−	3c PGR Management		
✳	2b Concessions	◇	4a Reducing Crime		

PGR = private game reserve.

However, given that many of the approaches considered are market-oriented or private-sector approaches to conservation, it may well confirm fears that market-oriented approaches are inequitable. This is currently a topic of considerable debate, given the emphasis on "pro-poor" development strategies by donor agencies, and the upsurge of interest in market-oriented approaches to the provision of environmental services. Some have pointed out that these difficulties can be overcome if they are made explicit in the design of market-oriented approaches (Landell-Mills and Porras 2002). As has already been stated, this requires formulating integrated packages of options that build on the synergies between them.

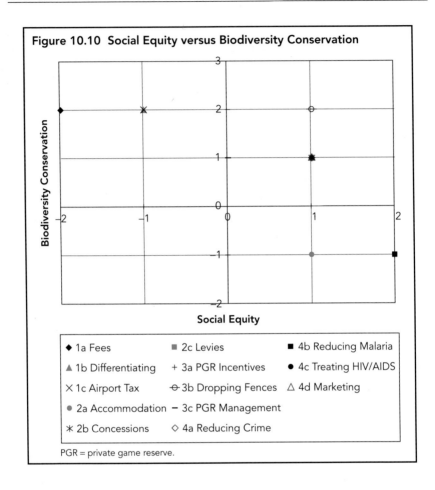

Figure 10.10 Social Equity versus Biodiversity Conservation

Legend:
◆ 1a Fees   ■ 2c Levies   ■ 4b Reducing Malaria
▲ 1b Differentiating   + 3a PGR Incentives   ● 4c Treating HIV/AIDS
✕ 1c Airport Tax   ⊖ 3b Dropping Fences   △ 4d Marketing
● 2a Accommodation   − 3c PGR Management
✳ 2b Concessions   ◇ 4a Reducing Crime

PGR = private game reserve.

CONCLUSIONS AND RECOMMENDATIONS

This chapter has examined a series of policy, institutional, and managerial options for improving and expanding nature tourism's role in development, equity, and conservation in the study area. NE Zululand has a rich history of experience and success in the wildlife industry—by both public and private organizations. The question asked in this book is whether these achievements can be furthered by building a nature tourism economy that can take conservation activities in the region to a new level while still making headway toward the social and economic development of the previously disadvantaged. With respect to the respective categories of options explored, three key findings emerge from the analysis.

First, demand for game viewing, particularly that of foreigners, is unresponsive to price. Thus, significant gains in conservation revenues are easily achieved through price differentiation between foreigners and residents. Although the across-the-board increase in KZN Wildlife entrance fees effective in November 2001 moves in this direction, the merging of the fee into the accommodation price is unlikely to facilitate the differentiation necessary to generate substantial new revenue. Instead, differentiation of fees with annual incremental increases in fees paid by foreigners is recommended. Initially, a doubling each year of the fees paid by foreigners is recommended, with quarterly monitoring of the response at the end of each year and a full evaluation at the end of the second year (when entrance fees are US$10). In addition, the feasibility of increasing the community levy for foreigners should also be assessed.

Second, achieving development with equity, while generating conservation finance, will require renewed efforts to involve the private sector in the tourism business in public protected areas through the establishment of concessions. If uncertainty surrounds such concessions, they could be made for limited periods. For accommodation, this would preclude fixed installations, at least initially. But the decision on how to best make innovative use of the opportunity should be discussed directly with the private sector.

Third, efforts to improve biodiversity conservation in the study area need to focus on the opportunity presented by the growth in private game reserves to improve on the current haphazard approach and uneven management, and to fully capitalize on the opportunity to go beyond a "wildlife industry" toward a "nature tourism economy" in the core part of the study area. At the same time, areas for improvement in the management of the public reserves—such as alien species management—do exist and should be tackled as conservation revenues are increased.

These three recommendations are of course fairly specific to the KZN Wildlife reserves and to Hluhluwe-Umfolozi Park because they were the center of attention in the options analysis. A larger set of recommendations concerns the massaging of the set of options considered into a package that best achieves development, equity, and conservation in the study area. Although it would be difficult to be precise in scoring a complete package, it is possible to select a number of the most promising options in each of the first three categories. The larger issues associated with crime, disease, and marketing are left aside for this purpose. The five options that seem to form an effective package are

- Differentiating entrance fees at HUP
- Private concessions for tourism services in HUP
- Raising community levies at HUP
- Integrating land management: dropping fences
- Ecological management on PGRs.

Differentiation of entrance fees, private concessions, and raising community levies hold out the most promise for raising conservation finance. They also provide a means to ensure that revenue flows to each of the three principal participants in nature tourism: KZN Wildlife, the private sector, and the local communities. Each of these groups has a contribution to make to conservation, and ensuring that local communities benefit is part of satisfying both conservation and equity objectives.

An additional component of moving forward on equity is ensuring that opportunities exist for communities to invest in nature tourism and other economic activities. Activating and fully capitalizing the Community Fund with increased levies and entrance fees, therefore, is part and parcel of the recommended approach. At the same time, a concerted investment by KZN Wildlife in assisting PGRs to manage their ecological assets and in collaborating with PGRs to drop fences, as well as improving management on KZN reserves, are important means of reinvesting the increase in conservation revenues and of ensuring that the PGRs are connected to the larger conservation picture in the region.

By reinvesting revenues in on-the-ground work in the reserves and in the community, the potential downside of revenue generation is avoided and the lost revenue and tourist expenditures are effectively replaced by the increased revenue from the reduced number of foreign tourists. Establishing an integrated package of actions along these lines points the way toward a nature tourism economy in Zululand.

Appendix 10-A. Scenario Results

Scenario-Specific Parameters	Unit	Base Original Amounts	Raising Conservation Finance								Exogenous Increase in Demand
			Raising Entrance Fees			Differentiating Entrance Fees			Departure Tax		
			1a	1a	1a	1b	1b	1b	1c	1c	3
			(i)	(ii)	(iii)	(i)	(ii)	(iii)	(i)	(ii)	(i)
Parameters and Variables											
DEMAND DRIVERS—RAND PRICES & INCREASES IN DEMAND											
HUP—Entrance Fees											
Foreigners											
Day	Rand	30	60	160	190	150	550	625	30	30	30
Overnight	Rand	30	60	160	190	150	550	625	30	30	30
Residents											
Day	Rand	30	60	160	190	30	30	30	30	30	30
Overnight	Rand	30	60	160	190	30	30	30	30	30	30
HUP—Other Charges											
Com. Levy on Accommodation	Rand	10	10	10	10	10	10	10	10	10	10
Accommodation	Rand	175	175	175	175	175	175	175	175	175	175
Increase in Number of Visitors											
Foreigners											
Day		0%									5%
Overnight		0%									5%
Residents											
Day		0%									5%
Overnight		0%									5%

(continued)

Appendix 10-A. (Continued)

Raising Conservation Finance spans the Raising Entrance Fees, Differentiating Entrance Fees, and Departure Tax column groups.

Scenario-Specific Parameters	Unit	Base Original Amounts	Raising Entrance Fees 1a (i)	1a (ii)	1a (iii)	Differentiating Entrance Fees 1b (i)	1b (ii)	1b (iii)	Departure Tax 1c (i)	1c (ii)	Exogenous Increase in Demand 3 (i)
DEMAND DRIVERS—DOLLAR PRICES											
HUP—Entrance Fees											
Foreigners											
Day	US$	2.50	5.00	13.33	15.83	12.50	45.83	52.08	2.50	2.50	2.50
Overnight	US$	2.50	5.00	13.33	15.83	12.50	45.83	52.08	2.50	2.50	2.50
Residents											
Day	US$	2.50	5.00	13.33	15.83	2.50	2.50	2.50	2.50	2.50	2.50
Overnight	US$	2.50	5.00	13.33	15.83	2.50	2.50	2.50	2.50	2.50	2.50
HUP—Other Charges											
Community Levy	US$	0.83	0.83	0.83	0.83	0.83	0.83	0.83	0.83	0.83	0.83
Accommodation	US$	14.58	14.58	14.58	14.58	14.58	14.58	14.58	14.58	14.58	14.58
Departure Tax	US$								10.00	25.00	
ELASTICITIES/PERCENTAGE CHANGES											
Foreigners (coefficient for US$ fee)											
Day			(0.025)	(0.025)	(0.025)	(0.025)	(0.025)	(0.025)	100%	90%	100%
Overnight			(0.025)	(0.025)	(0.025)	(0.025)	(0.025)	(0.025)	100%	90%	100%
Residents (coefficient for rand fee)											
Day			(0.120)	(0.120)	(0.120)	(0.120)	(0.120)	(0.120)	100%	100%	100%
Overnight			(0.120)	(0.120)	(0.120)	(0.120)	(0.120)	(0.120)	100%	100%	100%

(continued)

General Results

	Unit										
Length of stay in NE KZN											
Foreigners											
Day	Days	3.40							3.40	3.06	3.40
Overnight	Days	3.50							3.50	3.15	3.50
Residents											
Day	Days	1.70							1.70	1.70	1.70
Overnight	Days	3.20							3.20	3.20	3.20
Length of stay in HUP											
Foreigners	Nights	2.00	1.95	1.78	1.73	1.80	1.13	1.01	2.00	1.80	2.00
Residents	Nights	2.00	1.76	0.96	0.72	2.00	2.00	2.00	2.00	2.00	2.00
Number of HUP Visits		190,000							190,000	183,688	199,500
Foreigners		63,125							63,125	56,813	66,281
Day		31,875	31,078	28,422	27,625	28,688	18,063	16,070	31,875	28,688	33,469
Overnight		31,250							31,250	28,125	32,813
Residents		126,875							126,875	126,875	133,219
Day		95,625	84,150	45,900	34,425	95,625	95,625	95,625	95,625	95,625	100,406
Overnight		31,250							31,250	31,250	32,813
Number of Overnights at HUP	Nights	125,000	115,938	85,729	76,667	118,750	97,917	94,010	125,000	118,750	131,250
Foreigners—Overnight	Nights	62,500	60,938	55,729	54,167	56,250	35,417	31,510	62,500	56,250	65,625
Residents—Overnight	Nights	62,500	55,000	30,000	22,500	62,500	62,500	62,500	62,500	62,500	65,625
Entrance Fees	Million R	7.6	13.9	25.6	26.4	17.5	34.2	34.5	7.6	7.3	8.0
Foreigners	Million R	2.8	5.5	13.5	15.5	12.7	29.4	29.7	2.8	2.5	3.0
Day	Million R	1.0	1.9	4.5	5.2	4.3	9.9	10.0	1.0	0.9	1.0
Overnight	Million R	1.9	3.7	8.9	10.3	8.4	19.5	19.7	1.9	1.7	2.0

(continued)

Appendix 10-A. (Continued)

432

Scenario-Specific Parameters	Unit	Base Original Amounts	Raising Conservation Finance								Exogenous Increase in Demand
			Raising Entrance Fees			Differentiating Entrance Fees			Departure Tax		
			1a	1a	1a	1b	1b	1b	1c	1c	3
			(i)	(ii)	(iii)	(i)	(ii)	(iii)	(i)	(ii)	(i)
General Results (continued)											
Residents	Million R	4.7	8.3	12.1	10.8	4.7	4.7	4.7	4.7	4.7	5.0
Day	Million R	2.9	5.0	7.3	6.5	2.9	2.9	2.9	2.9	2.9	3.0
Overnight	Million R	1.9	3.3	4.8	4.3	1.9	1.9	1.9	1.9	1.9	2.0
Community Levy (Overnights only)	Million R	1.3	1.2	0.9	0.8	1.2	1.0	0.9	1.3	1.2	1.3
Foreigners	Million R	0.6	0.6	0.6	0.5	0.6	0.4	0.3	0.6	0.6	0.7
Residents	Million R	0.6	0.6	0.3	0.2	0.6	0.6	0.6	0.6	0.6	0.7
Accommodation Revenues	Million R	21.9	20.3	15.0	13.4	20.8	17.1	16.5	21.9	20.8	23.0
Foreigners	Million R	10.9	10.7	9.8	9.5	9.8	6.2	5.5	10.9	9.8	11.5
Residents	Million R	10.9	9.6	5.3	3.9	10.9	10.9	10.9	10.9	10.9	11.5

REFERENCES

de la Harpe, R., and W. Charlton-Perkins. 1995. *Hluhluwe-Umfolozi Park: Great Game Parks of Africa*. Cape Town: Struik.

Dennis, N., R. de la Harpe, and B. J. Barker. 1999. *The National Parks and Other Wild Places of Southern Africa*. London: New Holland.

Hughes, G. R. 2001. "The Natal Parks Board experience in Southern Africa." In T. L. Anderson and A. James, eds., *The Politics and Economics of Park Management*. Lanham, Md.: Rowman & Littlefield.

James, B. M., and P. S. Goodman. 2001. *Ecological Study*. Report to the World Bank Research Project on Nature Tourism and Conservation. Cascades, KwaZulu Natal: Brousse-James & Associates and KZN Wildlife.

Landell-Mills, N., and I. Porras. 2002. *Silver Bullet or Fools' Gold: Developing Markets for Forest Environmental Services and the Poor*. London: International Institute for Environment and Development.

Lindberg, K. 1998. "Annex 1: Demand and Supply Functions in Nature Tourism." Nature Tourism and Conservation project proposal to the World Bank Research Committee. Washington, D.C.: World Bank.

Wells, M. 1997. *Economic Perspectives on Nature Tourism, Conservation, and Development*. World Bank Environment Department Paper 55. Washington, D.C.

ANNEX: A MULTIMARKET MODEL FOR NATURE TOURISM

Bruce Aylward

OBJECTIVES AND APPROACH

This annex presents an analytical approach—in this case a multimarket model—that provides useful insight on the policy, managerial and institutional choices associated with nature tourism. To simplify the presentation, the framework is pared down to the bare minimum; however, the general concepts embodied here can be used to examine specific aspects of the real-world relationship among nature tourism and conservation finance, environmental sustainability, and local economic development.

The basic objective of the model is to assess the extent to which nature tourism offers potentially valuable opportunities for generation of revenues, not just for economic development associated with the formal tourism sector but also for nature conservation and the development of local communities. The emphasis is thus on the contribution that nature tourism can make to conservation finance and local economies, as well as to the economy as a whole. A secondary objective concerns the extent to which nature tourism is environmentally sustainable.

Before turning to the development of the analytical framework, it is worth summarizing the general state of the knowledge in this field, as revealed by literature reviews undertaken as part of the Nature Tourism and Conservation Project. As was stated above, much of the work in this field has consisted of the measurement of the willingness-to-pay for nature tourism sites, particularly through the use of the contingent valuation and travel cost methods (Wells 1997). The general aim of this research appears to be the derivation of values for nature tourism sites as a means of demonstrating the importance of their conservation. There is, however, a lack of applied economic analysis of the supply and demand relationships in these nature tourism markets, as well as their relationships. For example, research into price elasticities of demand for nature tourism is still at a formative stage and there is no research examining supply issues (see Lindberg 1998a). As a consequence, it is not surprising that there is no quantitative policy analysis found in the literature.

This situation suggests that the priority need is to develop a micro- or sectoral level framework for analyzing these problems. Further, it will be vital to verify that such a framework is applicable given information constraints, and that the framework has the ability to capture relevant information and respond to the information needs of decisionmakers in the private and public sectors. Given the absence of this type of analysis, it is reasonable to assume that the necessary database, particularly with regard to directly observable behavior in developing countries with poor statistical databases, will be weak if not nonexistent. In the first instance, then, the data required to motivate such a framework will need to be gathered directly through surveys of market participants. Demonstration of the utility of such a framework, however, may then motivate a more systematic approach to collection of relevant data.

ANALYTICAL FRAMEWORK

A traditional utilitarian approach to the problem under which the sole objective is to maximize national income would clearly be inadequate for the purpose of this study. A better definition would be a stable or a (generally) increasing level of national income from nature tourism. To address conservation, a physical sustainability criterion may be added, stating that this level of income is subject to the nondeterioration or depreciation of the nature tourism asset base. It would also be ideal if the social effects of this tourism are also nonnegative or, at a minimum, balanced by gains in economic development. In other words, the objective of nature tourism should be to maximize national income over time, subject to an environmental constraint and an equity constraint.

At the level of individual sites or operations, a narrow focus on revenue maximization and reinvestment in facilities and conservation might be a logical strategy with regard to the need for conservation finance. However, viewed more broadly—from a regional or national perspective—nature tourism has a multimarket dimension.

Choices regarding products and prices offered at one site affect the equilibrium between supply and demand at other sites and in related markets. For example, in a regional context, the issue of how high fees for foreigners may be raised at a particular park may need to be balanced by consideration of the potential effects on the local economy if tourists divert to other destinations. To the extent that both the public and private sectors are involved in service provision in nature tourism, this may call for balancing the needs and objectives of both sectors.

At the same time, the effects of policy and managerial decisions, such as pricing decisions, will have an impact on asset preservation, whether through direct physical effects or the availability of funding for maintenance. The consequences of these decisions are also felt in local communities because, for example, higher fees may lead to lower local employment (because of fewer tourists), while lower fees may enable communities offering services or handicrafts to garner a larger share of tourist expenditures. Pricing decisions may also affect the level of access by nationals and locals to a given site by effectively altering its level of exclusivity. A single policy decision may therefore affect all three criteria: economic, environmental, and equity.

From an economic perspective, the determination of the effects of different nature tourism policies may be approached by means of a multimarket model. In such a model, each of the markets is specified and the relationships among these markets, whether they are complements or substitutes, are developed.

As part of this process, policy variables, such as pricing, taxes, and subsidies, are built into the model so that it can subsequently be used to simulate how changes in policies play out in terms of national and international demand, as well as national supply and ultimately national income. In the case of nature tourism, establishing a feedback loop between visitation demand and environmental degradation enables the issue of nature tourism preservation to be explicitly included in the multimarket framework. Finally, to detail the economic effects of changes in market demand, a social accounting matrix (SAM) may be used to determine leakages and multipliers at different societal levels, thus shedding light on important indicators of social well-being (such as employment).

The Multimarket Model

The following discussion adapts a fairly standard multimarket model to a generic case of nature tourism. The objective is to derive a model that demonstrates how the principal nature tourism markets will reach equilibrium in response to changes in supply and demand conditions—with the addition of a feedback loop that includes an ecological damage function relating visitation (demand) to the quality (or quantity) of the nature tourism asset.

The advantage of the multimarket approach is that adjustments to price variables may be made in the model to explore the partial equilibrium effects of such changes on quantities supplied and demanded in the various markets. Once the equilibrium effects on demand are determined, a SAM or input–output model may then be used to determine how supply factors will adjust to meet the new level of demand. The SAM will thus provide detail on a range of important economic effects at the local, regional, and national levels, including the effects of multipliers and leakages.

Many formulations for such a model may be envisioned. Central to the policy aims of the model is that it distinguish between the market for the nature tourism site experience (as reflected in entrance and other use fees), the market for tourism services in the community surrounding the site (LS), and the market for tourism services outside this community (NS).

However, it is also clear that at one level or another (perhaps local; perhaps national, regional, or international), there exists the potential for substitution or complementarity between different nature tourism sites. To provide for the interaction between different sites the model therefore includes two nature tourism sites, S1 and S2. In the formulation presented below, it is assumed that the two sites are adjacent to the same community (see figure A-1) and are substitutes. As a result, they both result in the consumption of locally available tourism sites.

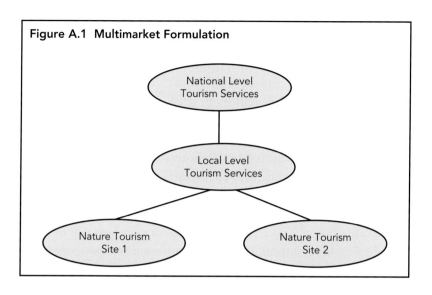

Figure A.1 Multimarket Formulation

A number of alternative formulations of a two-site model may be envisioned:

- When the two sites are public protected areas (and substitutes or complements) in different provinces, leading to the differentiation between the geographic location of the local services consumed (LS1 and LS2)

- When the two sites are substitutes and are located in different countries, leading to a differentiation between both the national and local services consumed

- When the two sites are public-sector and private-sector complements, with the public site serving as the primary attraction.

To more accurately portray reality, the model may subsequently be adapted to account for a number of different sites and attractions, as well as additional markets. For example, a number of different accommodation markets may be identified, each with its own particular relationship to sites with different characteristics. To the extent that the relationships of substitution and complementarity can be modeled, the complexity of the model may be increased while still providing the opportunity to analyze the effects of changes in policy control variables.

It is also likely that where international and domestic demand for sites exists, it will be necessary to distinguish between the two visitor populations. This is of particular importance given the often-mentioned strategy of capturing international consumer surplus by instituting raises in entrance fees for foreign visitors to sites.

The supply and demand relationships (structural equations) for the four markets are presented below. In accordance with theory, own- and cross-price variables (denoted by P) motivate the quantity demanded, Q^D, in each of the markets. Site characteristics or attractiveness, A, is another key variable in the demand equations. Income, I, and other socioeconomic variables, SE, may also explain demand.

In the case of supply, own price and the price of inputs will determine supply. To simplify notation, P is used to represent relevant input prices, with subscripts of K for capital, W for labor, and L for land. The price of land, reflecting the opportunity cost of land under other uses, is assumed to enter into the supply function only in the case of the two sites. Site characteristics may also serve as explanatory variables in the case of the two sites. Subscripts refer to the relevant market, and superscripts are used to denote supply and demand. The expected nature of the explanatory relationship is denoted by superscripts as well.

The structural equations are as follows:

$$Q_{NS}^S = f(P_{NS}^{(+)}, P_K^{(-)}, P_W^{(-)}) \tag{1}$$

$$Q_{NS}^D = f(P_{NS}^{(-)}, P_{LS}^{(-)}, P_{S1}^{(-)}, P_{S2}^{(-)} A_{S1}^{(+)}, A_{S2}^{(+)}, I^{(+)}, SE^{(+)}) \tag{2}$$

$$Q_{LS}^S = f(P_{LS}^{(+)}, P_K^{(-)}, P_W^{(-)}) \tag{3}$$

$$Q_{LS}^D = f(P_{LS}^{(-)}, P_{NS}^{(-)}, P_{S1}^{(-)}, P_{S2}^{(-)}, A_{S1}^{(+)}, A_{S2}^{(+)}, I^{(+)}, SE^{(+)}) \tag{4}$$

$$Q_{S1}^S = f(P_{S1}^{(+)}, P_K^{(-)}, P_W^{(-)}, P_L^{(-)}) \tag{5}$$

$$Q_{S1}^D = f(P_{S1}^{(-)}, P_{NS}^{(-)}, P_{LS}^{(-)}, P_{S2}^{(+)}, A_{S1}^{(+)}, A_{S2}^{(-)}, I^{(+)}, SE^{(+)}) \tag{6}$$

$$Q_{S2}^S = f(P_{S2}^{(+)}, P_K^{(-)}, P_W^{(-)}, P_L^{(-)}) \tag{7}$$

$$Q_{S2}^D = f(P_{S2}^{(-)}, P_{NS}^{(-)}, P_{LS}^{(-)}, P_{S1}^{(+)}, A_{S1}^{(-)}, A_{S2}^{(+)}, I^{(+)}, SE^{(+)}) \tag{8}$$

The basic identities equating supply and demand are as follows:

$$Q^S_{NS} = Q^D_{NS}, Q^S_{LS} = Q^D_{LS}, Q^S_{S1} = Q^D_{S1} \text{ and } Q^S_{S2} = Q^D_{S2} \qquad (9, 10, 11, 12)$$

Provision for policy variables that affect pricing in the NS and LS sectors may be made, for example, by defining the demand price, P^D, in these two markets as derived from the supply price and the wedge inserted by a value tax, TX, such as a percentage sales tax:[1]

$$P^D_{NS} = P^S_{NS}(1 + TX_{NS}) \qquad (13)$$

$$P^D_{LS} = P^S_{LS}(1 + TX_{LS}) \qquad (14)$$

These taxes may include tourist taxes on accommodation and food, as well as less specific value-added or sales taxes. At the national level, the existence of a departure or airport tax may also be included as a tax paid by foreign visitors. If desired, a similar formulation of an efficiency price plus tax may be used to specify the effective user price of the nature tourism sites. In general, however, site fees are set artificially and not determined by the market, so that such a formulation is of little practical utility. Instead, as the project intends to evaluate the impact of changes in price levels, it is just as simple to take P_{S1} and P_{S2} as policy control variables in and of themselves.

The attractiveness of a site will depend on its environmental characteristics, EC, the level of environmental damage, D, the sum of congestion effects, CG, the level of conflict between different site uses, CF, and the type of facilities provided at the site, F. The latter are constituted by those facilities to which access is included along with the payment of the entrance fee. Associated products requiring extra payments are included directly in the demand equation. The attractiveness of a given site can therefore be represented as follows:

$$A_{S1} = A_{S1}(D_{S1}, EC_{S1}, CG_{S1}, CF_{S1}, F_{S1}) \qquad (15)$$

$$A_{S2} = A_{S2}(D_{S2}, EC_{S2}, CG_{S2}, CF_{S2}, F_{S2}) \qquad (16)$$

The damage function is itself a function of both visitation and the area that is transformed to accommodate this usage. The latter may be termed the environmental footprint, EF, of the site. The damage function thus has both fixed and variable components related to nature tourism. The degree of damage will vary according to a number of site conditions. These include the resilience, R^U, and resistance, RT^U, and of the ecosystem to usage by tourists. As suggested by Lindberg (1998b), resistance is the ability to withstand tourism and resilience is the ability to recover from tourism.

Other factors that may affect damage include site characteristics, such as topography, the timing and location of damaging events, and the type of activity causing the damage. These are simply denoted by O. Actual observed environmental damage may be mitigated by the site manager. Thus, it is important to include damage mitigation effort, E^{DM}, as explanatory variables in the damage functions, ϕ and ψ for sites 1 and 2 respectively:

$$D_{S1} = \phi(Q_{S1}^D, EF_{S1}, RT_{S1}^U, R_{S1}^U, O_{S1}, E_{S1}^{DM}) \tag{17}$$

$$D_{S2} = \psi(Q_{S2}^D, EF_{S2}, RT_{S2}^U, R_{S2}^U, O_{S2}, E_{S2}^{DM}) \tag{18}$$

It is envisioned that visitation and subsequent environmental damage will have a lagged feedback effect on visitation in a subsequent period, channeled through the attractiveness function. In some cases, the effect of damage in a given period may not lead to a decay immediately; rather, it may decay over time.

The other determinants of site attractiveness may be divided into those that are a function of visitation (*CG, CF*), those that are essentially unrelated to the intensity of site demand (*EC, F*), and other miscellaneous factors.[2] For congestion and conflict effects, equations similar to (17) and (18) could be specified because these effects will depend on the level of use, the expenditure of effort on mitigation, and the (fixed) characteristics of natural and human-made facilities at the site. Thus, depending on the case, these variables may be specified as determined by a lagged relationship with demand as well as a managerial control variable.

In the case of environmental characteristics, these may simply be the natural characteristics of the site attractions. However, in many cases, these characteristics will not be "natural" but will instead be modified as site operators expend effort to manipulate site attractiveness. These characteristics may then be a product of managerial effort. The tourist facilities available at the site are simply taken as an exogenous variable, although they may be altered through capital investment. For the time being, however, the emphasis on the damage function feedback loop precludes the need to specify all of these equations, and thus these variables are assumed to be exogenous. In the specification of the model for application in the case study, these variables are more precisely defined.

To arrive at these welfare changes, it is only necessary to set out the revenues as gained under the initial system. These are simply the price of the product multiplied by the quantity demanded. Total revenues are as follows:

$$R = Q_{NS}^D P_{NS} + Q_{LS}^D P_{LS} + Q_{S1}^D P_{S1} + Q_{S2}^D P_{S2} \qquad (19)$$

If a tax on tourist services is present, this may be distinguished as follows:

$$R = Q_{NS}^D P_{NS}^S + Q_{NS}^D TX_{NS} + Q_{LS}^D P_{LS}^S + Q_{LS}^D TX_{LS} + Q_{S1}^D P_{S1} + Q_{S2}^D P_{S2} \qquad (20)$$

Using subscripts to denote the labor, capital, and land used in the four markets, the total costs of nature tourism are as follows:[3]

$$C = (K_{NS} + K_{LS} + K_{S1} + K_{S2})P_K + (W_{NS} + W_{LS} + W_{S1} + W_{S2})P_W$$
$$+ (L_{S1} + L_{S2})P_L \qquad (21)$$

The profits earned for the economy by tourism are simply revenues minus costs:

$$\pi = R - C \qquad (22)$$

The distribution of these profits across different sectors can then be specified. The profits earned by private-sector national and local tourism services are, respectively:

$$\pi_{NS} = Q_{NS}^D P_{NS}^S - K_{NS} P_K - W_{NS} P_W \qquad (23)$$

$$\pi_{LS} = Q_{LS}^D P_{LS}^S - K_{LS} P_K - W_{LS} P_W \qquad (24)$$

The revenues that are in theory available for conservation finance are the entrance fees garnered at sites 1 and 2:

$$R_{CF} = Q_{S1}^D P_{S1} + Q_{S2}^D P_{S2} \qquad (25)$$

The net revenues to the government sector are as follows:

$$R_G = Q_{NS}^D TX_{NS} + Q_{LS}^D TX_{LS} \qquad (26)$$

The total costs of conservation at sites 1 and 2 are

$$C_C = (K_{S1} + K_{S2})P_K + (W_{S1} + W_{S2})P_W + (L_{S1} + L_{S2})P_L \qquad (27)$$

Assuming public ownership of sites 1 and 2, the latter three equations can be summed to yield government profit (net cost). They are specified individually because an objective of the research is to assess the impact of policy measures on conservation finance. If, however, both sites are operated by a single public-sector agency and nature tourism is the only source of monetary receipts for the sites, then the net financial "profitability" of conservation at these two sites may be summarized as

$$\pi_C = Q_{S1}^D P_{S1} + Q_{S2}^D P_{S2}$$
$$- \left\{ (K_{S1} + K_{S2})P_K + (W_{S1} + W_{S2})P_W + (L_{S1} + L_{S2})P_L \right\} \qquad (28)$$

Because protected areas provide other benefits to society besides simply nature tourism, it is not assumed there that the objective of policy measures is to ensure that $R_{CF} > C_C$. The objective is instead to assess how change in the policy control variables affects both conservation finance and net profits to the economy, taking into account the effects on the environment. As per the above discussion, a number of potential objectives that may be pursued in altering the policy control variables:

1. Maximize net profit to the economy

2. Maximize conservation finance, R_{CF} subject to a nondecreasing net profit to the economy, π.

3. Carry out either 1 or 2 above without increasing environmental degradation, D_{S1} or D_{S2}.

4. An additional objective might be to further constrain the options above by providing for an equity constraint that ensures a given level of access by residents to public protected areas.

Discussion

Summarizing the multimarket model, up through equation 14, there are 23 variables, divided as follows:

Exogenous (7): I, SE, P_K, P_W, P_L, A_{S1}, A_{S2}

Policy and managerial (4): P_{S1}, P_{S2}, TX_{NS}, TX_{LS}

Other predetermined (2): P_{NS}^D, P_{LS}^D

Endogenous (10): $Q_{NS}^S, Q_{NS}^D, Q_{LS}^S, Q_{LS}^D, Q_{S1}^S, Q_{S1}^D, Q_{S2}^S, Q_{S2}^D, P_{NS}^S, P_{LS}^S$

As a simultaneous system of equations, the system contains 14 equations and has 10 endogenous variables. There are 13 predetermined variables composed of 7 exogenous variables, 4 policy and managerial variables, and 2 other predetermined variables. All the equations are overidentified, because the maximum number of slope coefficients is 8 in equations 2, 4, 6, and 8. The addition of the damage function feedback loop would not change this situation.

As was suggested above, the multimarket model is a very simple representation of nature tourism. In most cases, the number of sites, markets, and visitor populations would be considerably larger, generating an even larger system of equations. The feasibility of actually estimating such systems in an actual case study is likely to be limited. In all likelihood, such a multimarket model would be constructed piecewise, employing parameters derived from separate econometric analyses.

The more immediate relevance of the model is as a means of explaining linkages among different sites and markets in a conceptual and empirical manner, particularly as regards the absolute and relative changes in quantity demanded. For example, in the simple model presented above, an increase in the price of access to site 1 will shift demand to site 2. Whether total demand will remain unchanged is unclear; however, the model does clarify that the relative site attractiveness of the two sites may be an important factor here. If the two sites are relatively similar, then total demand may not change greatly, and the extent of consumption of local and national services may remain constant.

Conversely, if site 1 offers a different type of experience than site 2, the latter may be relatively unresponsive to price changes at site 1.

By implication, total demand (and revenue) for the two sites and for associated services at the local level will fall. If tourists' itineraries are diverted to other national sites, then the revenue earned from national services may not be affected. If tourists are, in effect, shunted to another country, than there is also a loss of revenue from national tourism services. Government revenues from tax collection can also be expected to fall as long as total demand by international tourists falls.

The net effect of the price change on conservation finance will be felt through the effect on demand and revenues at sites 1 and 2. If demand at site 1 is relatively unresponsive (inelastic) to price changes and the change is moderate, revenues at site 1 will likely increase. Revenues at site 2 can be expected to increase if the site is a substitute (to some degree) for site 1.

The model may also be employed to simulate the damage function over time and to assess the economic effects of this feedback loop. For instance, assume that site 2 is a reasonable substitute for site 1, but that it is also more susceptible to environmental damage than site 1. The effects of the above-mentioned change in the price of access to site 1 may then be expanded to incorporate the negative effects of increased demand on the quality of site 2.

It was suggested above that the revenue effects on site 2 would be non-negative and likely of a positive nature. This assumption may need to be revised, however, if the diversion of tourists to site 2 increases the rate at which the site is degraded. The model suggests that the net effect would be either to lower the attractiveness of the site and/or to cause an increase in expenditures on damage mitigation. The former would lower future demand for the site, thus causing the expected increase in future revenues to be dampened. The latter would raise costs.

As long as the environmental effect is marginal, the net effect of the price increase at site 1 will still be to increase the profitability of site 2, though to a lesser degree than in the case when environmental effects are not considered. However, should the change in demand be substantial or should an environmental threshold be crossed, there is always the possibility that profitability may actually be lowered at site 2.[4] The point is that if these environmental feedback effects are significant, then their omission may lead a purely economic multimarket model to produce misleading results.

Although the model provides conceptual guidance in simulating the effects of such a policy change, the net effect on national income will be difficult to determine a priori. Certainly, it is clear that to the extent that the price raises cause tourists to be diverted to other countries, the gain in conservation finance will need to be traded off against losses in the tourism services sector and tax receipts. Again, as such a model is expanded in scope, the more it becomes possible to employ it for conceptual purposes. However, as the model and its relationships grow, the more it becomes necessary to quantify these relationships to keep track of the net effect of a given policy change on the key indicators.

NOTES

1. Corresponding changes to equations 1 through 8 would be to substitute, as appropriate, the supply prices into equations 1 and 2 and the demand prices into equations 2, 4, 6, and 8.
2. This assumes a short-run perspective in which the capital required to build new facilities is not mobile. In the long run, F will be a function of the quantity demand, because increases in demand will, other things being equal, lead to an increase in facilities made available to tourists.
3. This exposition employs a single variable to represent quantities of inputs (and outputs) and their prices, and thus it represents a simplification of the real world, in which vectors of inputs and prices would often be required.
4. In such a case, it would need to be considered whether displaced tourist demand from site 2 would return to site 1, would be diverted to another substitute site, or would stay home.

REFERENCES

Lindberg, K. 1998a. "Annex 1: Demand and Supply Functions in Nature Tourism." Nature Tourism and Conservation project proposal to the World Bank Research Committee. Washington, D.C.: World Bank.

Lindberg, K. 1998b. "Annex 2: Environmental Damage Functions in Nature Tourism." Nature Tourism and Conservation project proposal to the World Bank Research Committee. Washington, D.C.: World Bank.

Wells, M. 1997. *Economic Perspectives on Nature Tourism, Conservation and Development.* World Bank Environment Department Paper 55. Washington, D.C.

MAPS

Map 1.1

Map 1.2

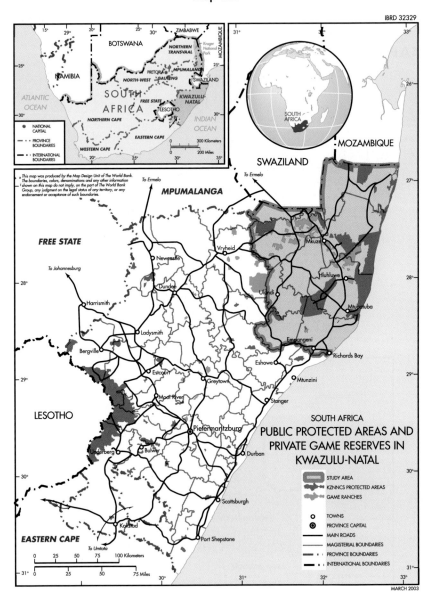

BOTSWANA

ZIMBABWE

NAMIBIA

NORTHERN
TRANSVAAL

Kruger
National
Park

PRETORIA

MPUMALANGA

GAUTENG

SWAZILAND

SOUTH
AFRICA

NORTH-WEST

FREE STATE

KWAZULU-
NATAL

ATLANTIC
OCEAN

NORTHERN CAPE

LESOTHO

INDIAN
OCEAN

EASTERN CAPE

WESTERN CAPE

NATIONAL
CAPITAL

PROVINCE
BOUNDARIES

INTERNATIONAL
BOUNDARIES

300 Kilometers

200 Miles

SOUTH
AFRICA

MOZAMBIQUE

SWAZILAND

This map was produced by the Map Design Unit of The World Bank.
The boundaries, colors, denominations and any other information
shown on this map do not imply, on the part of The World Bank
Group, any judgment on the legal status of any territory, or any
endorsement or acceptance of such boundaries.

To Ermelo

To Ermelo

MPUMALANGA

FREE STATE

To Johannesburg

Vryheid

Mkuze

Newcastle

Hluhluwe

Dundee

Ulundi

Harrismith

Mtubatuba

Ladysmith

Empangeni

Bergville

Eshowe

Richards Bay

Estcourt

Greytown

Mtunzini

Moot River

Stanger

LESOTHO

Pietermaritzburg

SOUTH AFRICA

PUBLIC PROTECTED AREAS AND
PRIVATE GAME RESERVES IN
KWAZULU-NATAL

Underberg

Bulwer

Durban

STUDY AREA

KZNNCS PROTECTED AREAS

GAME RANCHES

Scottsburgh

TOWNS

PROVINCE CAPITAL

EASTERN CAPE

Kokstad

MAIN ROADS

MAGISTERIAL BOUNDARIES

PROVINCE BOUNDARIES

INTERNATIONAL BOUNDARIES

To Umtata

Port Shepstone

0   25   50   75   100 Kilometers

0   25   50   75 Miles

MARCH 2003

Map 1.3

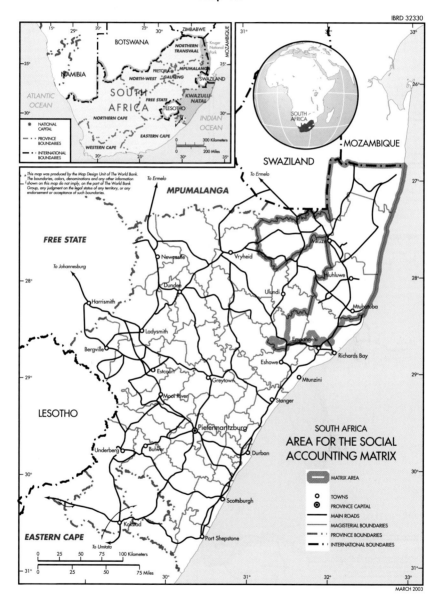

ZIMBABWE

BOTSWANA

NORTHERN
TRANSVAAL

Kruger
National
Park

MOZAMBIQUE

NAMIBIA

PRETORIA
NORTH-WEST
GAUTENG
MPUMALANGA
SWAZILAND

ATLANTIC
OCEAN

SOUTH
AFRICA

FREE STATE
KWAZULU-
NATAL

NORTHERN CAPE
LESOTHO

INDIAN
OCEAN

NATIONAL
CAPITAL

PROVINCE
BOUNDARIES

INTERNATIONAL
BOUNDARIES

EASTERN CAPE

WESTERN CAPE

0   300 Kilometers

0   200 Miles

SOUTH
AFRICA

MOZAMBIQUE

SWAZILAND

This map was produced by the Map Design Unit of The World Bank.
The boundaries, colors, denominations and any other information
shown on this map do not imply, on the part of The World Bank
Group, any judgment on the legal status of any territory, or any
endorsement or acceptance of such boundaries.

To Ermelo

To Ermelo

MPUMALANGA

FREE STATE

Newcastle

Vryheid

Mkuze

To Johannesburg

Dundee

Hluhluwe

Harrismith

Ulundi

Mtubatuba

Ladysmith

Bergville

Empangeni

Richards Bay

Estcourt

Eshowe

Greytown

Mtunzini

Mooi River

Stanger

LESOTHO

Pietermaritzburg

SOUTH AFRICA
AREA FOR THE SOCIAL
ACCOUNTING MATRIX

Underberg

Bulwer

Durban

MATRIX AREA

TOWNS

PROVINCE CAPITAL

MAIN ROADS

MAGISTERIAL BOUNDARIES

PROVINCE BOUNDARIES

INTERNATIONAL BOUNDARIES

Scottsburgh

Kokstad

EASTERN CAPE

Port Shepstone

To Umtata

0   25   50   75   100 Kilometers

0   25   50   75 Miles

Map 1.4

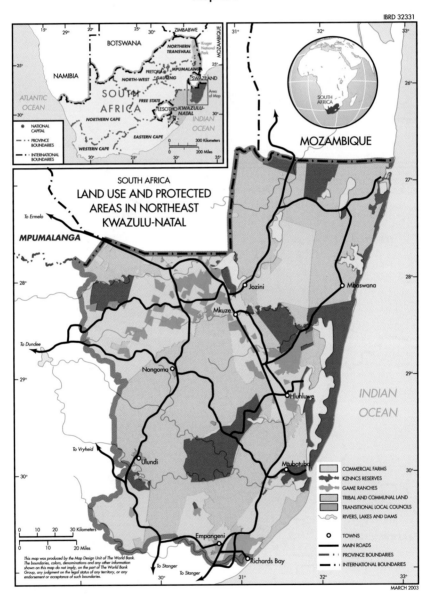

ZIMBABWE
BOTSWANA
NORTHERN TRANSVAAL
Kruger National Park
NAMIBIA
PRETORIA
MPUMALANGA
GAUTENG
NORTH-WEST
SWAZILAND
ATLANTIC OCEAN
SOUTH AFRICA
FREE STATE
LESOTHO
KWAZULU-NATAL
Area of Map
NORTHERN CAPE
INDIAN OCEAN
EASTERN CAPE
WESTERN CAPE

⊙ NATIONAL CAPITAL
–·– PROVINCE BOUNDARIES
–··– INTERNATIONAL BOUNDARIES

300 Kilometers
200 Miles

MOZAMBIQUE

SOUTH AFRICA
SOUTH AFRICA
LAND USE AND PROTECTED AREAS IN NORTHEAST KWAZULU-NATAL

To Ermelo

MPUMALANGA

Jozini
Mbaswana
Mkuze

To Dundee

Nongoma
Hluhluwe

INDIAN OCEAN

To Vryheid
Ulundi
Mtubatuba

COMMERCIAL FARMS
KZNNCS RESERVES
GAME RANCHES
TRIBAL AND COMMUNAL LAND
TRANSITIONAL LOCAL COUNCILS
RIVERS, LAKES AND DAMS
⊙ TOWNS
— MAIN ROADS
–·– PROVINCE BOUNDARIES
–··– INTERNATIONAL BOUNDARIES

0 10 20 30 Kilometers
0 10 20 Miles

Empangeni

To Stanger
To Stanger
Richards Bay

This map was produced by the Map Design Unit of The World Bank.
The boundaries, colors, denominations and any other information
shown on this map do not imply, on the part of The World Bank
Group, any judgment on the legal status of any territory, or any
endorsement or acceptance of such boundaries.

MARCH 2003

Map 1.5

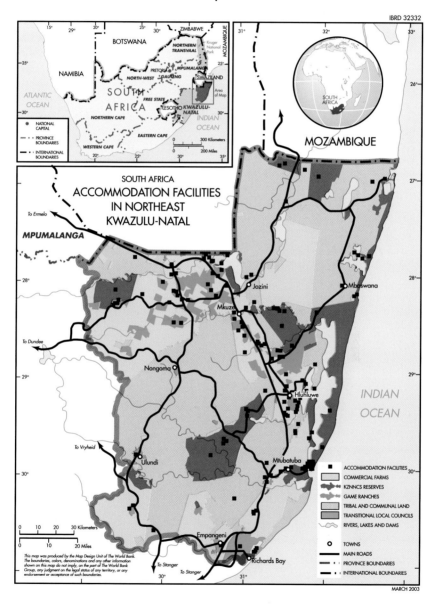

SOUTH AFRICA
ACCOMMODATION FACILITIES
IN NORTHEAST
KWAZULU-NATAL

MOZAMBIQUE

MPUMALANGA

To Ermelo

To Dundee

To Vryheid

Jozini

Mbaswana

Mkuze

Nongoma

Hluhluwe

INDIAN OCEAN

Ulundi

Mtubatuba

Empangeni

Richards Bay

To Stanger

To Stanger

ACCOMMODATION FACILITIES
COMMERCIAL FARMS
KZNNCS RESERVES
GAME RANCHES
TRIBAL AND COMMUNAL LAND
TRANSITIONAL LOCAL COUNCILS
RIVERS, LAKES AND DAMS
TOWNS
MAIN ROADS
PROVINCE BOUNDARIES
INTERNATIONAL BOUNDARIES

0   10   20   30 Kilometers
0   10   20 Miles

This map was produced by the Map Design Unit of The World Bank.
The boundaries, colors, denominations and any other information
shown on this map do not imply, on the part of The World Bank
Group, any judgment on the legal status of any territory, or any
endorsement or acceptance of such boundaries.

ZIMBABWE
BOTSWANA
NORTHERN TRANSVAAL
Kruger National Park
NAMIBIA
PRETORIA
MPUMALANGA
NORTH-WEST
GAUTENG
SWAZILAND
SOUTH AFRICA
Area of Map
ATLANTIC OCEAN
FREE STATE
LESOTHO
KWAZULU-NATAL
NORTHERN CAPE
INDIAN OCEAN
EASTERN CAPE
WESTERN CAPE

NATIONAL CAPITAL
PROVINCE BOUNDARIES
INTERNATIONAL BOUNDARIES

0   300 Kilometers
0   200 Miles

SOUTH AFRICA

MARCH 2003

INDEX

policy analysis (*cont.*)
  public protected areas (PPAs)
    conservation finance, 394–404
    degradation feedback loop, 385–86
    instruments and variables, 376
    multiplier analysis for nature tourism
      spending, 383
    private concessions at, 407–9, 428
    social equity and economic
      development, 404–10
  qualitative modeling, 391–93
  quantitative modeling, 389–91
  response parameters, 379–88
  results and recommendations, 426–32
  scenario results, 429–32
  sustainable development, 377–79
political support for conservation efforts,
  tourism engendering, 205
Pongola Nature Reserve, 69, 76, 215
Pongolapoort Dam, 8, 9, 215, 223
pooled models, 110
Porter, Sarah, vi, 287–324
PPAs, *see* public protected areas (PPAs)
pratincole, redwinged, 231
predators, conservation and nature tourism,
  216, 226–27
prices and pricing, *see* economics of reserves;
  fees and costs; sales of live game
priority landscapes, conservation and nature
  tourism, 214, 220–21, 237
private concessions at public protected areas
  (PPAs), 407–9, 428
private game ranches and reserves (PGRs), 9,
  287, 289
  accommodations, 11–12, 14, 295–96, 404–7
  acreage classified as, amount of, 287,
    293–95
  acreage/size of, 287, 293–95
  bed numbers, 295–96
  biodiversity conservation, 26–28, 207–13,
    225–26, 229–40, 410–13, 427
  business and management strategies, *see*
    business and management strategies
  conservation finance, 29
  cost structure, 316–19
  differences compared to public reserves,
    322–23

ecological management, 413, 428
economic development, 16–17, 18
employment/job creation, 298, 299, 300
fees, charges, and pricing policies, 36–39,
  316–19
"game farmers' day," 240
hunting, 33, 38, 262
land values, 308
live capture, species commonly for, 262
mail surveys, 208
Natal Game Ranchers Association, 31–32,
  211, 233, 250, 262–63, 275, 277
nonmanagement employment on PGRs,
  bed price as determinant of, 23
personal and farm goals, 300–304
policy analysis, *see* policy analysis
profitability, 18, 288–89, 319–22
public reserves, tours of, 36, 315
risk, main sources of, 307
sales of live game, 31–32, 262, 264, 265
social equity, 21–24
viewing of game, 38–39
private tourist accommodations, 11–14
privately owned land, 8
Producer Survey, 5, 14, 29, 32, 39, 287–324,
  see also characteristics of reserves
product moment correlation coefficients,
  228
profitability of reserves, 18, 288–89, 319–22
protection of wildlife, *see* conservation and
  nature tourism
public protected areas (PPAs), 8–10, 287, 289
  accommodations, 11–14, 35–37, 296,
    404–7
  acreage classified as, 287, 293–95
  acreage/size, 287, 293–95
  bed numbers, 295
  biodiversity conservation, 26, 27, 204–5,
    209–11, 213, 225–26, 229–32
  conservation finance, 29, 394–404
  cost structure, 316–19
  differences compared to private reserves,
    322–23
  economic development, 16–17, 18
  employment/job creation, 300
  fees, charges, and pricing policies, 35–37
  hunting, 32–33, 262